CW01151797

Logic, Argumentation & Reasoning

Interdisciplinary Perspectives from the Humanities and Social Sciences

Volume 32

Series Editor
Shahid Rahman, University of Lille, CNRS-UMR 8163: STL, France

Managing Editor
Juan Redmond, Instituto de Filosofia, University of Valparaíso, Valparaíso, Chile

Editorial Board Members
Frans H. van Eemeren, Amsterdam, Noord-Holland, The Netherlands
Zoe McConaughey, Lille, UMR 8163, Lille, France
Tony Street, Faculty of Divinity, Cambridge, UK
John Woods, Dept of Philosophy, Buchanan Bldg, University of British Columbia, Vancouver, BC, Canada
Gabriel Galvez-Behar, Lille, UMR 8529, Lille, France
Leone Gazziero, Lille, France
André Laks, Princeton/Panamericana, Paris, France
Ruth Webb, University of Lille, CNRS-UMR 8163: STL, France
Jacques Dubucs, Paris Cedex 05, France
Karine Chemla, CNRS, Lab Sphere UMR 7219, Case 7093, Université Paris Diderot, Paris Cedex 13, France
Sven Ove Hansson, Division of Philosophy, Royal Institute of Technology (KTH), Stockholm, Stockholms Län, Sweden
Yann Coello, Lille, France
Eric Gregoire, Lille, France
Henry Prakken, Dept of Information & Computing Sci, Utrecht University, Utrecht, Utrecht, The Netherlands
François Recanati, Institut Jean-Nicord, Ecole Normale Superieur, Paris, France
Gerhard Heinzmann, Laboratoire de Philosophie et d'Histoire, Universite de Lorraine, Nancy Cedex, France
Sonja Smets, ILLC, Amsterdam, The Netherlands
Göran Sundholm, 'S-Gravenhage, Zuid-Holland, The Netherlands
Michel Crubellier, University of Lille, CNRS-UMR 8163: STL, France
Dov Gabbay, Dept. of Informatics, King's College London, London, UK
Tero Tulenheimo, Turku, Finland
Jean-Gabriel Contamin, Lille, France
Franck Fischer, Newark, USA
Josh Ober, Dept of Pol Sci, West Encina Hall 100, Stanford University, Stanford, CA, USA
Marc Pichard, Lille, France

Logic, Argumentation & Reasoning (LAR) explores links between the Humanities and Social Sciences, with theories (including decision and action theory) drawn from the cognitive sciences, economics, sociology, law, logic, and the philosophy of science.

Its main ambitions are to develop a theoretical framework that will encourage and enable interaction between disciplines, and to integrate the Humanities and Social Sciences around their main contributions to public life, using informed debate, lucid decision-making, and action based on reflection.

- Argumentation models and studies
- Communication, language and techniques of argumentation
- Reception of arguments, persuasion and the impact of power
- Diachronic transformations of argumentative practices

LAR is developed in partnership with the Maison Européenne des Sciences de l'Homme et de la Société (MESHS) at Nord - Pas de Calais and the UMR-STL: 8163 (CNRS).

This book series is indexed in SCOPUS.

Proposals should include:

- A short synopsis of the work, or the introduction chapter
- The proposed Table of Contents
- The CV of the lead author(s)
- If available: one sample chapter

We aim to make a first decision within 1 month of submission. In case of a positive first decision, the work will be provisionally contracted—the final decision about publication will depend upon the result of an anonymous peer review of the complete manuscript.

The complete work is usually peer-reviewed within 3 months of submission.

LAR discourages the submission of manuscripts containing reprints of previously published material, and/or manuscripts that are less than 150 pages / 85,000 words.

For inquiries and proposal submissions, authors may contact the editor-in-chief, Shahid Rahman at: shahid.rahman@univ-lille.fr, or the managing editor, Juan Redmond, at: juan.redmond@uv.cl

Acknowledgments

The book presented here owes so much to so many people and institutions, and I want to apologize if I forgot anyone, knowing full well that the forgotten are more numerous than I would like to admit. First and foremost, I want to thank Patrice Canivez. His support and generosity have been unflagging throughout this whole process. His initial enthusiasm for the project encouraged me along, and his continual critique, correction, and conversation have made this a deeply formative experience. I would also like to thank Bob Brandom, both for his interest in the project and for his careful critique and correction when I got things wrong about his views. Shahid Rahman, Giuseppina Strummiello, and Isabelle Thomas-Fogiel must all also be thanked. Each of them read the first version of this text and gave me valuable critical feedback. Additionally, thank you as well to Shelby Hinte and Neil Burkey. They generously and carefully read through the manuscript in order to help clean up my language and style. All of these people have helped make this text clearer and sharper.

This book was born out of my doctoral dissertation. A great deal of the research was thus made possible by two generous grants, one from the Institut Éric Weil and another from the Conseil Régional Nord-Pas de Calais. Without these grants, I don't know if I would have set out on this project, and even if I had, it would have been under much harsher conditions. Additionally, the reworking of this material was made possible by the Université de Lille and the University of Pittsburgh. I thank the Université de Lille for allowing me to go work with Bob Brandom in Pittsburgh, and the University of Pittsburgh for welcoming me as a visiting scholar during the Fall 2021 semester. I also want to thank the École doctorale Sciences de l'Homme et de la Société, and Laboratoire Savoirs, Textes, Langage.

Additionally, I would like to thank Thomas Bénatouïl, Luis Manuel Bernardo, Christian Berner, Corneliu Bilba, Judikael Castelo Branco, Hauke Brunkhorst, Pierre Chauveau-Thoumelin, Evanildo Costeski, Ophélie Desmons, Bertille De Vlieger, José-Manuel Durón García, Marco Filoni, Arnaud François, Betty Gabriels, Ulysse Gadiou, Fatiha Iznasni, Gilbert Kirscher, Benoît Leclercq, Alain Lernould, Clément Lion, Claire Louguet, Claudio Majolino, Armel Mazéron, Zoé McConaughey, Édouard Mehl, Marcelo Perine, Jean Quillien, David Rasmussen,

Gérard Raulet, Laurence Romain, Clémence Sadaillan, Ondrej Svec, Caroline Taillez, Francisco Valderio, and Andrea Vestrucci, who all provided different kinds of help and discussion through the process of writing this work.

Finally, I would like to end on a personal note. I have had the chance to live a full meaningful life so far and it is in large part thanks to the people I have had in it. Thank you to my mother and my sisters, and to the rest of the family. To my many friends, you are far more numerous than the space here will allow, thus I will merely say thank you. I must also say to Emma, all my love. Thank you all for the agreement and the conflict, for creating the situations that have pushed me to think and to think reasonably. I certainly owe you all more than I myself will ever know.

Contents

1	**Introduction**..	1
	References..	10
2	**Discourse and Violence in Eric Weil's *Logic of Philosophy***.........	13
	2.1 Discourse and Violence.....................................	13
	2.2 Weil's Characterization of Violence.........................	16
	2.3 The Logic of Violence and the Violence in Logic.............	23
	2.4 Attitudes and Categories....................................	30
	2.5 Hegel and the Categories of Philosophy......................	35
	2.6 Reprises..	38
	2.7 Systematicity and Openness..................................	40
	References..	45
3	**Logic as the Organization of Forms of Coherence**....................	47
	3.1 Introduction..	47
	3.2 Organizational Strategies of the *Logic of Philosophy*.......	50
	3.3 The Background of Discourse.................................	57
	3.4 The Genesis of and Development of Coherent Discourse........	66
	3.5 Immanence Versus Dissatisfaction............................	73
	3.6 The Individual's Relationship to Discourse..................	85
	3.7 Conclusion – The Beginning Is at the End....................	95
	References..	96
4	**Pragmatism, Inferentialism, and Expressivism**.......................	99
	4.1 Introduction – Orders of Explanation........................	99
	4.2 Pragmatism's Narrative......................................	105
	4.3 Semantic Pragmatism...	113
	4.4 Inferentialism..	117
	4.5 The Two Sources of Contemporary Expressivism................	124
	4.6 The Taxonomy of Expressivism................................	131
	4.7 Conclusion – Pragmatism and Eric Weil.......................	139
	References..	140

5	**Pragmatism, Expressivism, and Inferentialism in the *Logic of Philosophy***	143
	5.1 Introduction	143
	5.2 The Role of Error in the *Logic of Philosophy*	145
	5.3 The Paradox of Certainty	153
	5.4 Weil's Expressivism and the Placement Problem	161
	5.5 The Necessity in Discourse and Narrow Expressivism	168
	5.6 A Case for Inferentialism	173
	5.6.1 Weil's Critique of Reference	173
	5.6.2 The Development of Inferential Concepts in the Initial Categories	178
	5.7 Conclusion	183
	References	184
6	**The Language of Conflict and Violence**	187
	6.1 Introduction	187
	6.2 Sentience and Sapience	189
	6.3 *De Dicto* and *De Re* Ascription in a Platonic Space	203
	6.4 Discursive Commitments and Conflict	209
	6.5 The Use of Violence	219
	6.6 Violence and Spaces of Reasons	224
	6.7 Conclusion	228
	References	230
7	**The *Logic of Philosophy* as a Theory of Argumentation**	233
	7.1 Introduction	233
	7.2 Serious Conversation, Dialogue, and Discussion	236
	7.3 Orientation, Satisfaction, Contentment, and Action	245
	7.4 The Conceptual Analysis of the Reprise of *God*	253
	7.5 Argumentative Strategy in the *Logic of Philosophy*	267
	7.6 Conclusion	275
	References	275
8	**Justification and Pluralism in the *Logic of Philosophy***	279
	8.1 Introduction	279
	8.2 Eric Weil's Three-Tier Notion of Justification	281
	8.2.1 Foundations, Coherence, and Contexts	281
	8.2.2 Epistemic Authority	285
	8.2.3 Naïve Authority and What Goes Without Saying	289
	8.2.4 Justificatory Strategies and the Evolution of Authority	293
	8.3 Relativism and Pluralism as Discursive Commitments	300
	8.3.1 The Shape of the Problem	300
	8.3.2 Monism and Relativism	302
	8.3.3 The Insufficiency of Relativism	310
	8.3.4 Horizontal and Vertical Pluralism	313
	8.4 The Choice of Reason	318
	References	320

9	**Conclusion**	323
	References	327

Bibliography 329

Index 337

Abbreviations[1]

LP	*Logique de la philosophie* (1950)
PP	*Philosophie politique* (1956)
PM	*Philosophie morale* (1961)
PK	*Problèmes kantiens* (1970)
EC.I	*Essais et conférences : tome I* (1970)
EC.II	*Essais et conférences : tome II* (1971)
ENHP	*Essais sur la nature, l'histoire et la politique* (1999)
PR.I	*Philosophie et réalité : tome I* (2003)
PR.II	*Philosophie et réalité : tome II* (2003)

---

[1] In order to avoid making the reading of this text too cumbersome, I have limited the number of works that are abbreviated. I only use abbreviations for Eric Weil's major publications, and only in citations. So page one of the *Logique de la philosophie* is cited as (LP, 1) for example. For the collections of essays, I cite the name, the volume, and then the page number. For page one of the first volume of *Essais et conférences*, I cite as follows (EC.I.1). All of Eric Weil's essays that were originally published in English, I cite the direct publication and not the French translations, and thus do not use abbreviations.

Chapter 1
Introduction

The *Logic of Philosophy* is a curious book, both in its composition and its reception.[1] The author, Eric Weil, does his reader few favors. It's difficult to read. The sentences are long: clause after subordinate clause is set one inside the other and stacked one atop another. It is dense. The ideas unfold slowly and there are lots of them to keep track of. Its density is a consequence of its style of composition, which can be best described as arid. Few people are cited directly, and few names are used. Almost every reference is oblique, present in the sentence construction or in the use of a term that almost, but never quite, refers. These references are therefore present to the most searching eye, but shadowy and obscure for those whose culture is not up to snuff when compared to that of Weil's. And Weil was a man of broad and deep culture.

The book is both humble and ambitious. It is humble in that it is the result of one person consciously wrestling with the problem of understanding, who wanted to understand what it means to understand, and the limits of that understanding. It is also incredibly ambitious because Eric Weil claims to resolve the problem, that of the act of understanding, and thus to close a chapter of the history of philosophy.

Eric Weil was subject to exaggerated and wildly divergent reactions and opinions of him varied widely. Alexandre Koyré was, according to Alexandre Kojève, completely "gaga" for him,[2] Raymond Aron called Weil one of the few superior minds that he knew in his life,[3] and said that he "he had an exceptional, almost flawless,

---

[1] All translation from the *Logic of Philosophy* are from the current draft version that is under contract with University of Chicago Press, Eric Weil, *Logic of Philosophy*, trans. Sequoya Yiaueki (Chicago: University of Chicago Press, Forthcoming). The page numbers refer to the French edition of the *Logique de la philosophie*. Unless otherwise noted, all translations in this work are my own.
[2] Strauss (1997), 276.
[3] Aron (1983), 94.

culture."[4] Pierre Bourdieu notes that, for him, Weil was one of the few thinkers to represent rigorous philosophy and also notes how profoundly Weil influenced him in his student years.[5] Leo Strauss on the other hand said "he has rarely met a man as empty,"[6] and Hannah Arendt, who harbored a great dislike for Weil, thought he was a "stupid monster."[7] People were charmed by him and formed a deep attachment to him or they found him intolerable.

Similarly, the book was hailed as a masterpiece or ignored.

Initially written as a doctoral dissertation, Jean Wahl referred to it as "the Phenomenology of Spirit 1950" during the defense. This turn of phrase was taken up as the subtitle to the article about the defense that appeared in the newspaper *Le Monde*. In addition to Wahl, the defense committee included the likes of Jean Hyppolite and Maurice Merleau-Ponty. Kojève wrote about the importance of the book to Strauss and admits that he regrets not having written it himself.[8] Paul Ricœur came back to the book again and again during his long career, and even took on the mantle of a post-Hegelian Kantian, a term that he claims was a description Weil had used for himself.[9]

While we cannot say that the book fell stillborn from the presses (it was reviewed in numerous scholarly journals and it has never been out of print in French), it seems legitimate to wonder, from a specifically English-speaking perspective seventy years on, whether it is not flirting with the dustbin of history. It seems legitimate because Weil himself is not widely known, a reference here or there to his book, *Hegel and the State*,[10] or a mention to one of his articles in passing, but not much more. This viewpoint however is a bit hasty. It says more about the English-speaking world's access to Weil's philosophy than about the interest of the philosophy itself. It is only limitedly available in English, despite being translated into numerous languages and being the subject of full studies in those same languages.[11] This book seeks to at least partially correct this. It presents original research that seeks to enrich contemporary Weil studies by proposing an inferentialist reading of the *Logic of Philosophy*. This reading allows highlighting the interest of Weil's approach in relation to certain debates in contemporary philosophy that doubles as a critical examination of Weil's work aimed at the English-speaking public.

---

[4] Aron (1983), 731.
[5] Bourdieu (1987), 13–14.
[6] Strauss (1997), 281.
[7] Astrup (1999), 185.
[8] Strauss (1997), 277.
[9] Ricœur (2013), 541–542. For an analysis of the role that this expression plays in Ricœur's philosophy, see Piercey (2007).
[10] Weil (1998).
[11] Besides *Hegel and the State*, which was translated into English by Mark A. Cohen, and a collection of Weil's essays originally published in English, *Valuing the Humanities* (1989), edited by William Kluback, one must dive into long out of print collections and journals in order to access Weil's work in English.

1 Introduction

Eric Weil's main philosophical questions turn around the relationships between violence and reasonableness, between violence and philosophical discourse, between violence and language, and thus also the role that language and discourse play in reasonableness. In order to investigate these relationships, Weil insists on the kinds of stances we take in discourse, the types of responsibility that we take on because of these stances, and what these responsibilities commit us to. This develops a mutual feedback. Eric Weil thinks that concrete reasonableness is a consequence of taking a stance, taking on responsibilities, and shouldering the consequences of these responsibilities, because it is only when we take a stance, take on responsibility, shoulder consequences that we can have a concept of reasonableness. In order to develop this thought, Weil deploys three guiding concepts, *attitudes*, *categories*, and *reprises*. In Weil's specific technical sense, the attitude is the initial implicit grasp of meaning as it is lived in an individual's life. It does not seek to justify itself, does not seek coherence, does not seek to *ground* one's knowledge of the world, because the attitude grasps this meaning as already present in a meaningful world. However, once this immediate presence is disrupted, once the possibility of other reasonable positions must be considered, in other words, once it becomes a question of justification, of coherence, and of grounding, this implicit grasp of meaning must be made explicit. It must be transformed into a *category*, into a coherent grasp of meaning that makes claims of universality and coherence. Eric Weil thus presents the *Logic of Philosophy* as a suite of categories, as a suite of the coherent grasps of meaning that have been elaborated in history, as a suite of the different discursive shapes. Thus, Weil's use of the concept of a category is different from the classic categories of substance and form, of cause and effect, etc. This creates a division between what Weil calls *philosophical* categories and *metaphysical* categories, between framework concepts and ground-level ones. Philosophical categories are the discursive grasp of a pure (that is, coherent and autonomous) attitude. Metaphysical categories are the categories that a philosophical category uses to grasp the world, they are thus in this sense *meta-scientific*. Because each philosophical category has used the metaphysical categories differently, the shape of metaphysical and ontological objects in each coherent grasp of meaning differs. This difference brings out the importance of the *reprise*. The reprise is the explanation of the conceptual content of one philosophical category under the language of another. It allows for evaluation and justification. It allows for a theory of argumentation that turns around both the communication and the reception of discourse.

There is a striking analogy to be made between what Weil calls philosophical categories and what Wilfrid Sellars calls the "space of reasons."[12] For Sellars, the space of reasons is the logic space of "of justifying and being able to justify what one says."[13] The concept of the space of reasons is the uniting factor of a certain philosophical orientation that could be qualified as "post-Sellarsian." This orientation has been richly developed in the work of Robert Brandom and other philosophers

---

[12] Sellars (1997), §36.
[13] Sellars (1997), §36.

of a similar ilk.[14] The philosophical question that guides this book asks whether a cross-reading of the *Logic of Philosophy* and Brandom's specific position can be mutually fruitful. The idea of reading the *Logic of Philosophy* in relation to other authors is not new. There have already been studies that read the *Logic* in relation to Martin Heidegger and Max Weber,[15] in relation to Alfred Whitehead,[16] in relation to Jürgen Habermas,[17] to Michel Foucault,[18] in relation to the phenomenological tradition,[19] and to authors of the hermeneutical tradition such as Hans-Georg Gadamer,[20] and Paul Ricœur.[21] Thus, the novelty of this book is not in reading Weil in relation to another tradition, but rather in reading the *Logic of Philosophy* in relation to a tradition that has hitherto been absent from Weil studies, namely contemporary pragmatism. However, this work does not focus merely on a comparison between Weil's work and the pragmatist tradition. Rather it makes the claim that this reading is mutually beneficial to both Weil studies and to the pragmatist tradition. What is notable about the post-Sellarsian tradition in pragmatism is that it, like Weil, insists on the notion of discursive commitment. This is the main insight of Brandom's development of his logical expressivism and of his inferentialism.[22]

Brandom claims that language and meaning are best understood, not according to the dominant representationalist tradition, which seeks to create (or find) a correspondence between language and a non-discursive world, but rather should be understood according to the notion of expression, that is, of saying something meaningful. According to this form of expressivism, the tools needed for saying something meaningful are conceptually more primitive than those used for representing something in the world. Additionally, in his development of inferentialism, Brandom claims that conceptual content is best understood pragmatically according to the commitments that one takes on in discourse. These commitments create symmetrical *entitlements*, *obligations*, and *incompatibilities*, or to say the same thing differently, other commitments that one can take on, must take on, or are prohibited from taking on depending on their initial commitment. Brandom's major insight is that what matters in understanding constellations of commitments, entitlements, obligations, and incompatibilities is the way they are *inferentially* articulated. According to this claim, the goal of logic, and of discursive argumentative practices in general, is to make explicit in language what was implicit in practice.

Starting from the similarity in the importance that both theories give to the discursive commitments that seek to make explicit in a philosophical discourse what is

---

[14] Brandom (1994, 2001, 2015); McDowell (1996, 2013); Kukla and Lance (2008); Peregrin (2014).
[15] Ganty (1997).
[16] Breuvart (2013).
[17] Deligne (1998); Ganty (1997); Bizeul (2006); Bobongaud (2011).
[18] Marcelo (2013); Strummiello (2013)
[19] Gaitsch (2014).
[20] Breuvart (1987); Buée (1987).
[21] Roman (1988); Marcelo (2013); Valdério (2014).
[22] Brandom (1994, 2001).

implicit in practices, *Action, Meaning, and Argument* argues that the *Logic of Philosophy* and post-Sellarsian pragmatism should be read together because each fills specific lacunae in the other. From the side of Weil studies, there has been an effort to read the *Logic of Philosophy* as the development of the different discursive resources that each category adds to reasonable argumentative discourse.[23] This work falls in line with that effort, but in order to facilitate the dialogue between Weil's main philosophical insights and recent developments in contemporary philosophy, it claims that Weil studies should be enriched by the conceptual apparatus of inferentialism. This book argues that Weil can and should be read according to the basic conceptual commitments of a certain strain of pragmatism, notably Robert Brandom's post-Sellarsian inferential expressive pragmatism. This strain of pragmatism tries to articulate conceptual content in relation to pragmatic considerations, namely the types of commitments that one takes on in discourse as well as the practices of inference and judgment. However, because this book also aims at showing the way that inferentialism can be enriched by the key insights of the *Logic of Philosophy*, it develops those insights in a Weilian direction, namely by focusing on the difference that Weil makes between language (the creation of meaning) and discourse (the coherent grasp of meaning), and the place of violence in our discursive practices. Weil claims that philosophy is based on the choice to be reasonable, that is, to understand coherently and universally. Because he theorizes this as a free choice, it is opposed to another free choice, that of choosing violence. In other words, the individual is always faced with a choice between universality and particularity (both mediated and unmediated). But because the individual is seen as always already conditioned, Weil articulates the choice as one between whether to make oneself into unmediated particularity by becoming violent, or by remaining violent in the face of arguments, or by aiming to destroy coherence and discourse from within. The central argument is that this choice is at the heart of the question of understanding, and that, in order for philosophy to understand itself philosophically, it must take this possibility into account. Violence is not just important because it allows us to characterize the refusal of all discourse. It is important because, within discourse, it is also found in the refusal of certain types of discourse, the refusal to be convinced by specific types of arguments. The problem that this refusal poses for the possibility of argumentation thus becomes the confrontation between different forms of argumentative logics. *Action, Meaning, and Argument* claims that inferentialism is not only uniquely situated to absorb this insight because it already interprets meaning, as Weil does, according to discursive commitments, but also that this tradition must respond to the problem Weil poses because of the conceptual apparatus of commitments, entitlements, obligations, and incompatibilities that inferentialism uses.

Action, Meaning, and Argument presents both Weil's theory and inferentialism in their own terms before progressing to a cross-reading of these two positions. With these considerations in mind, the chapter, "Discourse and Violence in Eric Weil's

---

[23] Quillien (1982); Kirscher (1989); Canivez (1999); Bernardo (2003); Guibal (2011, 2012).

Logic of Philosophy," presents the guiding concepts of the *Logic of Philosophy*. It presents the general orientation of Weil's project as well as his characterization of violence. Starting from that characterization, it presents the specificity of Weil's use of the concepts of attitudes and categories. Weil presents four types of categories in the *Logic of Philosophy*: philosophical categories, metaphysical categories, the categories *of* philosophy, and the formal categories. The philosophical categories are the shapes of different coherent discourses and, in this way, are seen as structural. The metaphysical categories are the meta-scientific ground-level categories that are developed to be used in the particular sciences. Within the philosophical categories, there are the categories *of* philosophy and the formal categories. The categories *of* philosophy characterize the individual's relationship to discourse. With this in mind, they can be thought of, to use Brandom's term,[24] as pragmatic metavocabularies. This is because they develop the individual's relationship to the semantic content of the philosophical categories. Finally, there are the "transcendental" formal categories that serve as a recapitulation of the other categories. For Weil, they also characterize the possibility of discourse and of life lived as a meaningful unity. For Weil, Hegelian philosophy represents the first category of philosophy (the first pragmatic metavocabulary). Because Weil was an important commentator of Hegel and because he sees the *Logic of Philosophy* as a radical transformation of Hegel's project, this chapter also presents how Weil's work should be situated in relation to Hegel's. Afterwards, this chapter presents the importance of the notion of the reprise and Weil's concept of open systematicity.

The next chapter, "Logic as the Organization of Forms of Coherence" continues the development of Weil's conceptual distinctions and gives a general presentation of the categories. For Weil, a logic of philosophy is nothing other than the articulated totality of the philosophical categories and the possibility of their intercommunication.[25] Thus, this chapter presents some of the different organizational problems present in the *Logic of Philosophy* as well as an argument about how these problems should be resolved. The organization of the *Logic of Philosophy* can be articulated in numerous ways, according to Reason and Freedom, according to Antiquity and Modernity, according to different fundamental contradictions present in different kinds of logics. In fact, because of the difference between metaphysical categories and philosophical categories that Weil makes, it is argued that this multiplicity of organizational concepts is normal. Each category deploys metaphysical concepts differently and some metaphysical concepts appear, disappear, reappear—taking on more or less importance. With this in mind, this chapter presents and defends the possibility of reading the *Logic of Philosophy* as a development of the resources of reasonable argumentative discourse. It also highlights the importance of orders of explanation to Weil's project. This allows insisting on certain key organizational articulations that will be necessary for the rest of the book.

---

[24] Brandom (2015).

[25] Throughout this work I will use the typological convention of capitalizing and italicizing *Logic of Philosophy* the book to separate it from the logic of philosophy the system, which will be in lower case.

1 Introduction

In Chap. 4, the reading of pragmatism that will guide the rest of the work is presented. Robert Brandom insists, much like Eric Weil, on the philosophical importance of orders of explanation in philosophy. Brandom's particular order of explanation is pragmatist. Because of this, Chap. 4 looks to show how we should situate Brandom as both a practitioner and theorist of pragmatism. Just what pragmatism is exactly is a matter of some contention, and this chapter tries to show that, *pace* the idea that pragmatism disappeared for the better part of the twentieth century, pragmatism has remained a vital force within philosophy. After situating Brandom in the pragmatist tradition, this chapter will look at Brandom's semantic pragmatism. This position defends that language use should be understood starting from specific practices. These practices center around the act of committing to conceptual content with the goal of making explicit what is implicit within that commitment. In order to do this, Brandom develops multiple notions, including endorsements, obligations, and entitlements. It is endorsements, obligations, and entitlements that allow us to track both what different individuals are committed to, as well as what we commit to when we enter into discursive practices with them. This will be essential to understanding the social articulation of Brandom's "game of giving and asking for reasons." At the level of content, Brandom develops a sophisticated alternative to classical representationalism. In order to do so, he looks at concepts role-functionally. Concepts are seen as being determined by the roles that inferences and incompatibilities play. Together, incompatibilities and inferences help determine the scope and limits of concepts. Inferring from central commitments and their incompatibilities to their consequences is thus seen as a central practice. This gives credence to the philosophical position of expressivism, which seeks to explain meaning starting from the individual's expression of it and not from some immutable meaning that preexists the individual in a non-discursive external world. Expressivism however is not a single homogenous position. Multiple expressivisms exist. In order to see which expressivism best fits with the pragmatist program, the chapter investigates the motivations of two different types of expressivism, which can be loosely called meta-ethical or Humean expressivism and German expressivism. Some of the tools and solutions of these two species of expressivism match up. Modern expressivism even seems to be converging towards a single point.[26] Nonetheless, the initial motivating factors of these two expressivisms were radically different. Meta-ethical expressivism was trying to make sense of value judgments in a causally determined impersonal nature.[27] This is different from the German expressivist model, which claims from the start that all language use, and not just a certain species of moral or esthetic claims, is expressive. Brandom's logical expressivism is a spiritual descendant of German expressivism, but it remains significantly different. In order to show why this is the case, the chapter ends by showing the tension at the heart of Herder's founding statement of expressivism.[28]

---

[26] Blackburn (1984); Price (2013).
[27] Stevenson (1944); Ayer (1949); Hare (1952).
[28] Herder (2008).

This will allow us to better see how expressivism fits in with some of the key intuitions of pragmatism, namely, the rejection of representationalism and the valorization of practices. This will also put us in a better position to understand the specific strain of pragmatism to which Eric Weil's work will be compared.

The next two chapters, "Pragmatism, Expressivism, and Inferentialism in the *Logic of Philosophy*" and "The Language of Conflict and Violence," both have the same goal of showing that a cross-reading of inferentialism and the *Logic of Philosophy* can be productively fecund. Chapter 5 mobilizes the concepts presented in Chap. 4 in order to show how to read Weil along pragmatist, expressivist, and inferentialist lines. This chapter underlines the importance of the role of error in the progression of the *Logic of Philosophy* and why Eric Weil's own philosophical position should also be considered as developing a pragmatic metavocabulary that aims at explaining the structure and development of concrete determined content. Because Weil's own mature position (developed in the last three categories, *Action, Meaning,* and *Wisdom*) insists on the importance of openness to novelty, change, and other reasonable positions, the development of semantic content will also be seen as open-ended. These observations are used to claim that Weil's development of discursive resources in the *Logic of Philosophy* can be restated in inferentialist terms without loss, and in fact to great benefit. Following the enrichment of the *Logic of Philosophy* in the direction of inferentialism, Chap. 6 proceeds to develop the way in which reading inferentialism in terms of Weil's central insights presents inferentialism with a problem that it must answer.

If inferentialism defends a model of language-use based on commitments, entitlements, obligations, and incompatibilities, then it must recognize that individuals can freely take on a commitment to ignore the entitlements of others, to ignore their own obligations and to ignore the incompatibilities in their own discourse. In other words, inferentialism, more than any other philosophical position, shows just how deeply Weil's critique touches the philosophical tradition that sees the human individual as a rational being. Inferentialism situates itself in relation to the Kantian and Hegelian model of rationality, which Brandom terms sapience. This rationality depends on an individual's ability to act according to laws that they give themselves. Weil's critique shows that this rationality is something that individuals can abandon by refusing to universalize themselves and their discourse. In other words, Weil posits that the individual can leave discourse in order to *feel* as though they are in a position of unmediated particularity. This unmediated particularity does not grasp itself in discourse (which it refuses) because that would bring it back into the game of universality. Instead, it presents itself in action. Weil claims that precisely because it *can* be grasped in discourse as the refusal of all discourse, it can be understood coherently. Because this refusal presents itself in action, it is not something that discourse can overcome. But, because it can be grasped by discourse as irreducible, it provides a form of coherence. The question thus asks what role discourse plays faced with this possibility.

In order to answer this question, Chap. 7, "The *Logic of Philosophy* as a Theory of Argumentation," presents the *Logic of Philosophy* in terms of an argumentative philosophical practice that faces the possibility of violence head-on. Weil postulates that violence is irreducible to discourse, that it can irrupt at any moment, because individuals can always choose it. Thus, the question of what philosophy should do in the face of this possibility becomes essential. This chapter argues that because Weil sees the choice between reason and violence as the most fundamental choice an individual can make, choosing reason must be seen as a meta-commitment to settle differences non-violently (that is, through argumentative means) in the face of violence. Philosophy depends on this meta-commitment because philosophizing, for Weil, is the paradigmatic form of reasonable behavior. Thus, this chapter moves from a pragmatist reading of Weil towards the defense of a Weilian practice of philosophizing, which is a normative practice of deploying reasonable arguments in the face of the possibility of violence. In Chap. 8, "Justification and Pluralism in the *Logic of Philosophy*," this philosophical practice is tested against the contemporary questions of epistemic authority, justification, and pluralism. This chapter argues that using the *Logic of Philosophy* as the basis of a theory of argumentation allows us to see foundationalism, coherentism, and contextualism not as different mutually exclusive justificatory options but as different points of views and moments in argumentative justificatory practices in general. These justificatory mechanisms correspond to the problems of monism, relativism, and pluralism, respectively; they are functions of local, global, and "polycentric" justificatory practices. Because foundationalism and monism both seek to have a unique point of view, they correspond to local justificatory practices. They respond to individual claims and they attempt to judge these individual claims against the background of our other discursive commitments. When local justificatory practices fail because of a lack of sufficient overlap between interlocutors, or when certain core commitments are seen as being contradictory, individuals must reflexively analyze the coherence of their own position. Coherentism and relativism are thus both seen to correspond to this reflexive justificatory moment whereby multiple reasonable positions are considered as self-standing wholes. By judging different positions in their (approximative) globality, interlocutors try to discern whether there are good reasons to hold one position over another. When there is no clear reason to hold one coherent position over another, individuals must seek to find points of contact that allow dialogue to continue and that allow differences to be minimized, and compromises to be found *without* recourse to violence. Should individuals participate in such practices, they admit that there is at least, for the moment, a non-decidability between these discursive positions, but they also refuse to see this undecidability as vicious or insurmountable. In other words, they maintain their meta-commitment to reasonable (that is, non-violent) argumentative practices. Polycentric, pluralist justificatory practices are thus seen as being sensitive to the different contexts between diverse discursive positions with distinct contents that are actually held by different concrete individuals. This is why the *Logic of Philosophy* is seen as grounding the possibility of an interactive and dynamic philosophical practice. *Action, Meaning, and Argument* takes monism, relativism, and pluralism to be real discursive positions that people can hold, just as local, global, and polycentric justification practices are real practices that people can employ. However, taking philosophy to be a type of argumentative practice, *Action, Meaning, and Argument* advocates that the task philosophizing can and should give to itself is that of moving individuals from monism and relativism towards pluralism. Philosophy should thus work to get people to see the value of understanding the functional role of foundationalist and coherentist claims as *moments* of concrete justificatory practices, but also as insufficient to maintain the meta-commitment to reasonable discourse. This book understands philosophy, the philosophical practice itself, as a plastic and adaptable activity that considers the diversity of concrete human contexts where individuals create meaning and find meaning in their lives.

References

Aron, R. 1983. *Mémoires*. Paris: Julliard.
Astrup, A.-S. 1999. *Hannah Arendt—Heinrich Blucher, correspondance, 1936–1968*. Paris: Calmann-Lévy.
Ayer, A.J. 1949. *Language, truth and logic*. 2nd ed. London: Victor Gollancz.
Bernardo, L.M. 2003. *Linguagem e discurso: Uma hipótese hermenêutica sobre a filosofia de Eric Weil*. Lisbon: Imrensa Nacional – Casa da Moeda.
Bizeul, Y. 2006. Moral und Politik bei Eric Weil. In *Gewalt, Moral und Politik Bei Eric Weil*, 131–157. Hamburg: Lit Verlag.
Blackburn, S. 1984. *Spreading the word*. Oxford: Oxford University Press.
Bobongaud, S.G. 2011. *La dimension politique du langage*. Rome: Gregorian & Biblical Press.
Bourdieu, P. 1987. *Choses dites*. Paris: Les Éditions de Minuit.
Brandom, R. 1994. *Making it explicit – Reasoning, representing & discursive commitment*. Harvard University Press.
———. 2001. *Articulating reasons – An introduction to inferentialism*. Harvard University Press.
———. 2015. *From empiricism to expressivism*. Harvard University Press.
Breuvart, J.-M. 1987. Tradition, effectivité et théorie chez E. Weil et H.G. Gadamer. In *Cahiers Éric Weil tome I*, ed. J. Quillien. Villeneuve-d'Ascq: Presses Universitaires du Septentrion.
———. 2013. *Le questionnement métaphysique d'A.N. Whitehead*. Louvain-la-Neuve: Les Éditions Chomatika.
Buée, J.-M. 1987. La Logique de la philosophie et l'herméneutique de Gadamer. In *Cahier Éric Weil tome I*, ed. J. Quillien. Lille: Presses Universitaires du Septentrion.
Canivez, P. 1999. *Weil*. Paris: Les Belles Lettres.
Deligne, A. 1998. *Éric Weil: Ein zeitgenössischer Philosoph*. Bonn: Romanistischer Verlag.
Gaitsch, P. 2014. *Eric Weils Logik der Philosophie: Eine phänomenologische Relektüre*. Freiburg: Verlag Karl Alber.
Ganty, É. 1997. *Penser la modernité*. Namur: Presses Universitaires de Namur.
Guibal, F. 2011. *Le sens de la réalité: Logique et existence selon Éric Weil*. Paris: Éditions du Félin.
———. 2012. Langage, discours, réalité: Le sens de la philosophie selon Éric Weil. *Laval Théologique et Philosophique 68* (3): 593–617.
Hare, R.M. 1952. *The language of morals*. Oxford: Oxford University Press.
Herder, J.G. 2008. *Herder: Philosophical writings*. Trans. M. N. Forster. Cambridge, UK: Cambridge University Press.
Kirscher, G. 1989. *La philosophie d'Éric Weil*. Paris: Presses Universitaires de France.
Kukla, R., and M. Lance. 2008. *"Yo" and "lo": The pragmatic topography of the space of reasons*. Cambridge, MA: Harvard University Press.
Marcelo, G. 2013. Paul Ricœur et Eric Weil. Histoire, vérité et conflit des interprétations. *Cultura. Revista de História e Teoria das Ideias 31*: 247–266. https://doi.org/10.4000/cultura.1881.
McDowell, J. 1996. *Mind and world*. 2nd ed. Cambridge, MA: Harvard University Press.

References

———. 2013. *Having the world in view – Essays on Kant, Hegel, and Sellars (reprint)*. Cambridge, MA: Harvard University Press.
Peregrin, J. 2014. *Inferentialism: Why rules matter*. New York: Palgrave Macmillan.
Piercey, R. 2007. What is a post-Hegelian Kantian? The case of Paul Ricœur. *Philosophy Today 51* (1): 26–38.
Price, H. 2013. *Expressivism, pragmatism and representationalism*. Cambridge, UK: Cambridge University Press.
Quillien, J. 1982. La cohérence et la négation: Essai d'interprétation des premières catégories de la *Logique de la Philosophie*. In *Sept études sur Éric Weil*, ed. G. Kirscher and J. Quillien, 145–185. Villeneuve-d'Ascq: Presses Universitaires de Lille.
Ricœur, P. 2013. *Le conflit des interprétations: Essais d'herméneutique*. Paris: Éditions du Seuil.
Roman, J. 1988. Entre Hannah Arendt et Éric Weil. *Esprit (1940–) 140/141* (7/8): 38–49.
Sellars, W. 1997. *Empiricism & the philosophy of mind*. Cambridge MA: Harvard University Press.
Stevenson, C.L. 1944. *Ethics and language*. New Haven: Yale University Press.
Strauss, L. 1997. *De la tyrannie. Correspondance avec Alexandre Kojève, 1932–1965*. Paris: Gallimard.
Strummiello, G. 2013. Ripresa, a priori storico, sistemi de pensiero. *Cultura: Revista de História e Teoria Das Ideias 31*: 195–212.
Valdério, F. 2014. Linguagem, violência e sentido: A propósito de um debate entre Éric Weil e Paul Ricœur. *Argumentos: Revista de Filosofia 6* (11): 159–171.
Weil, E. 1956. *Philosophie politique*. Paris: Librairie Philosophique Vrin.
———. 1989. In *Valuing the humanities*, ed. W. Kluback. Chico: Historians Press.
———. 1998. *Hegel and the state*. Trans. M. A. Cohen. Baltimore, MA: Johns Hopkins Press.
———. Forthcoming. *Logic of philosophy*. Trans. S. Yiaueki. University of Chicago Press.

Chapter 2
Discourse and Violence in Eric Weil's *Logic of Philosophy*

2.1 Discourse and Violence

Eric Weil's *Logic of Philosophy* is a book about philosophical discourse, about meaning and action, but in being a book about these things, Weil does something surprising. He reformulates them in relation to violence. Discourse, according to the philosophical tradition, is supposed to be what brings people to agreement, what settles disputes, what establishes the Good, the Just, the Beautiful. It is supposed to be what reveals what is real and decides what is true. Weil accepts that characterization of discourse, but, by framing it in relation to violence, Weil uncovers something radical. Discourse cannot itself be separated from violence. If it could, violence would be overcome thanks to discourse, but Weil shows how discourse on its own does not overcome or eliminate violence. Weil asks however what to do when faced with someone who not only refuses agreement, but refuses all discussion. Not because of ignorance, or because of a misunderstanding, but precisely because they understand what discourse and agreement implies. By framing it this way, Weil articulates something that everyone knows but that philosophy forgets: individuals can refuse discourse, not because of a problem with discourse, but because they understand what it entails. This is why Weil frames discourse in relation to violence. The reason that Weil's formulation is surprising is because he does not present it as solely being a practical problem. It is also a conceptual problem. In other words, it is not merely a moral or political question. It is also a question about the role that violence plays in our understanding.

It is a problem that was born in a historical context. As a secular German Jew who had escaped Germany on the eve of the Second World War, Weil wrote this book in its dusky shadow. He could not turn away from individuals' capacity of choosing violence. This led Weil to believe that the choice between violence and discourse is a-reasonable. That is, it cannot be deduced, precisely because this radical form of violence is one that refuses all justification and all argumentation, every

© The Author(s), under exclusive license to Springer Nature Switzerland AG 2023
S. Yiaueki, *Action, Meaning, and Argument in Eric Weil's Logic of Philosophy*, Logic, Argumentation & Reasoning 32,
https://doi.org/10.1007/978-3-031-24082-9_2

premise and conclusion. If individuals are able to choose violence, are able to choose to participate in inhumane acts *and* if they are raised in a community (which means, structured by discourse) then violence is not foreign to reasonable discourse. Indeed, for Weil, the philosophical understanding of violence is only possible once reasonable discourse has been brought to its most radical conclusion. This conclusion is, for Weil, to be found in the Hegelian philosophical project and can be understood as an absolutely coherent discourse that thinks the whole of reality and itself.[1] These conclusions show us that discourse makes claims on us that *we* are bound to acknowledge because of their rectitude. By framing violence the way he does, Weil shows that we can refuse to be bound by well-founded coherent discourse and that this refusal is not meaningless or empty. It also shows how Weil goes further than Hegel does. Because this refusal is not meaningless, it shows how, for Weil "the absolute is not on its own all of meaning, but only a determined meaning which does not understand itself as such, which does not see meaning precisely because it confuses it with the absolute, with the developed truth of being."[2] In other words, "by recognizing that freedom is irreducible to reason, Weil recognizes at the same time that freedom takes shape in diverse attitudes, themselves irreducible to one another by the very fact that they are shapes of freedom."[3]

This is the historical lesson that Weil learned in the Germany of his time, and it is the human possibility that Weil seeks to understand. In order to do so, he frames the relationship between discourse and violence in terms of human freedom. Discourse can only be refused knowingly if the individual knows what discourse and argument imply.[4] Premises can only be refused knowingly because the individual acknowledges that premises lead to conclusions. Justification can only be refused knowingly because the individual knows that justification submits them to the constraints of argument. The individual who refuses discourse also refuses it knowingly and leaves argumentation because they no longer want to be subject to its norms. In this way, the individual makes a choice and that choice can be to abandon reasonableness. The problem that this poses, according to Weil, is that this possibility exists in all discourse. Weil understands radical violence as the possibility of knowingly refusing all discourse, of abandoning discourse by choosing violence. This possibility for Weil only exists because violence is already found *in* discourse.

---

[1] The relationship between Weil's philosophy and that of Hegel has been much written about. For commentators that specifically tackle the way that Weil's philosophical project should be understood as integrating and surpassing Hegel's see Kirscher (1970), (1992); Juszezak (1977); Livet (1984); Ricœur (1984); Rockmore (1984); Roth (1988); Burgio (1990); Jarczyk and Labarrière (1996); Guibal (2003).

[2] Kirscher (1970), 378.

[3] Kirscher (1992), 252–253.

[4] The adverb in English "knowingly" here systematically translates the French adverbial locution *en connaissance de cause*. Which could also be rendered as "deliberately" or as "with full knowledge of the fact." Knowingly seems the best translation because in English it covers both the deliberate dimension and the dimension of being fully informed.

2.1 Discourse and Violence

It is found in discourse as *a form of coherence* that refuses all other forms of coherence.

The individual can coherently retain their commitment to violence. They can take a stance and refuse reasonable arguments, refuse premises and their conclusions. They can refuse any inferential move that *ought* to be recognized. This is the refusal of the individual who leaves discourse in order to not be held responsible to it. However, *inside of* discourse, this refusal is always against another determined form of coherence. For Weil, the radical refusal is present in every dispute that can take a turn for the worst, in every stubborn interaction where people respond out of spite, every dismissive interaction where people refuse out of hand to listen to their interlocutor or to take them seriously *because* they represent a different point of view. It exists every time somebody says, *I know you're right*, or *I understand*, and then adds *but I don't care*. It exists as a positive project whereby individuals organize their lives around violence and through the use of violence, whereby individuals are ready to use violence to silence all discourse. What Weil proposes in the *Logic of Philosophy* is a way to diagnose this problem and a way to face this problem through argumentation.

Indeed, argumentation is central to Weil's work. According to Weil, believing, taking for true, acting, all these things imply a certain notion of commitment. We take a stance and we hold to it. We are required to if we want our thought to be determined. And the more finely elaborated our thought is, the more commitments we explicitly take on. But taking on a commitment for something also indelibly means taking on a commitment against something. When somebody commits to the position that modern experimental science explains reality, it means that they cannot appeal to God in order to explain that same reality. When somebody commits to the position that homosexuality is a moral failing, it means that they cannot accept that homosexuals can be good people. This highlights the normative element of commitments, when we take them on, we accept being governed by them and by all that they imply. These are not the only norms that govern discourse though. Yes, the logical implications of commitments are important, but what Weil's formulation of the question shows is that the pragmatic norms that govern discourse are just as important as the logical ones. These pragmatic norms start from the individual's own willingness to submit themselves to the logical norms in the first place. For argumentation and discourse to get underway, individuals must submit themselves to the constraints of discourse, they must see reasons as valid, they must see justification as having real force, they must see the normative weight of better reasons as being the last word. By framing violence as a problem of discourse, Weil shows that as long as people hem close to what is essential in their position, without modification, without the recognition that some critique is legitimate, they are at an impasse that holds the potential for violence.

2.2 Weil's Characterization of Violence

Eric Weil speaks abundantly of violence.[5] But as Gilbert Kirscher has noted,[6] Weil uses violence as a *generic* term to designate philosophy's *other* without giving a truly precise definition. Violence is the feeling of absurdity, or arbitrariness, of what happens to the individual but doesn't depend on them (LP, 21). It is what is forbidden inside of a community (LP, 25). It is the exterior danger that the world and that others inflict on the individual and the interior dangers that the individual inflicts on themself (LP, 26). It is the incoherent (LP, 82). It is what can destroy what the human community has built (LP, 27). It is what cannot be overcome, either physically or intellectually (LP, 29). It is the *given* (LP, 48), which is only given because it is violent and only violent because it is given and thus demands a reconceptualization in order to be grasped as making up part of our *conceptual* landscape. It is the "nature that surrounds the reasonable" (LP, 334). It is the "reign of sentiment" (LP, 352). What I will posit here, even though it will only be justified in what follows, is that violence is the name that Weil gives to particularity, philosophy (or reason) the name that he gives to universality. But violence is more than just a name for particularity, it is the formal concept of concrete particularity recognized and grasped in its particularity.

Weil characterizes violence in multiple ways, but he also provides two descriptions of violence that allow us to understand what exactly is meant when we call it the formal concept of concrete particularity recognized and grasped in its particularity. These descriptions are found in *Philosophie politique* and in the *Logic of Philosophy*. The story he tells in both is more or less the same, however the way that he approaches the story is not. In *Philosophie politique*, Weil presents the development of the historical content of the *sentiment* of violence in order to understand violence as a practical and political problem, that is, as a problem of organized human action. In the *Logic of Philosophy*, he presents violence as a logical problem, as a presentation of the way that the philosophical tradition has reduced violence in order to bring it into discourse by subsuming it under the logical role of contradiction. Both of these aspects are important to understanding why Weil characterizes violence the way he does and why he sees violence as being the central

---

[5] The question of violence has been tackled in the secondary literature from numerous points of view. In fact during a workshop at the Université de Lille in 2017 Jean Quillien said "Qui dit Weil, dit violence, langage et systematicité" or "one cannot speak about Weil without speaking about violence, language, and systematicity." With this in mind, much written on Weil deals with how he characterizes violence in some way or another, therefore it will be sufficient here to merely direct the reader to those works that deal directly with violence or that see Weil's characterization of violence as central to their theses as opposed to those that deal with other aspects of his work through the prism of violence. The main collections of articles that deal with these question are Canivez and Labarrière (1990) and Bizeul (2006). There have also been several full studies that give special attention to the role of violence in Weil's work, notably Perine (1982), Kirscher (1992), and those for whom Weil's conceptualization of violence is central such as Strummiello (2001). See also, Roy (1975); Morresi (1979); Perine (1987).

[6] Kirscher (1999), 12.

philosophical problem.[7] Thus, while following the main lines of the argument of each presentation separately, we will nonetheless use the resources from both to present Weil's full characterization of violence.

Both presentations share the same major points: there is an evolution of the concept of violence. There is the violence of nature, social violence, individual violence, historical violence, and there is the determined violence that lives at the heart of discourse itself. However each type of violence only becomes visible in history. Each type therefore only becomes graspable in discourse thanks to the evolution of discourse itself as it elaborates itself through that history. Social violence is only visible because natural violence has been partially understood and sufficiently reduced. Individual violence is only grasped after social and political violence is, etc. Thus, these different forms of violence are all interlocked. The violence of nature became visible because communities organized themselves together in order to overcome it. However, by organizing communities to protect themselves against a hostile nature, the fight with the violence of nature reveals social and political violence. The individual violence against others and against oneself is only grasped because it is seen as an outgrowth of social and political violence. Weil develops the differences between these diverse forms of violence by starting with an analysis of the violence of nature in *Philosophie politique*.

For Weil, the violence of nature is "the initial violence, and every other conception of violence (passion, natural temptation, human violence against the human being, etc.) is grounded in it" (PP, 62). The violence of nature is what humanity is subjected to by being natural things. It is the violence of our competition with other species, the violence that we face by being the fragile bodies we are, subject to the violence of disease, of injury, of death. It is the violence of the world in its movement—of floods and droughts, earthquakes and volcanoes. This violence is insurmountable for the single individual. Individuals must unite as an "organized group" to overcome it, and "society *is* this organization" (PP, 62). It is the organization of the struggle with nature as "social labor" (PP, 63). Because individuals have organized themselves into groups united by social labor, they have a discourse that transforms the natural world in order to make room for human goals and activities. This discourse aims at humanity's technical grasp of nature, because without this grasp, humanity is subject to all the changes in the weather and the climate, to droughts and floods, to the sudden irruption of natural phenomena, to the variety of beasts that could prey on us. We organize ourselves together to protect ourselves from these things, but in developing a discourse, we also subject ourselves to them *as* violent. Disasters are only disastrous because they disrupt *our* lives. The failure of crops that lead to famine are only failures because these crops are supposed to provide a stable food source for *us*. Volcanoes and earthquakes are only dangerous because *we* have built our lives in their shadow or along their fault lines. But if we can predict these things, we feel we can shelter ourselves from them. This is the goal

---

[7] This overlap leads many interpreters to fuse the two presentations, focusing on the logical presentation and enriching it with the analyses that are present in *Philosophie politique*. See Kirscher (1992); Canivez (1993); Ganty (1997); Savadogo (2003); Guibal (2009).

of the community's technical discourse, but because conditions change, this discourse changes as well.

Weil notes that "[e]very human society essentially struggles with external nature" (PP, 62), because again, it is not as individuals that we initially transform our activity in order to transform nature, but as a "organized group." It is thus "impossible to define natural violence without historical reference (to the history of human societies)" (PP, 64). Violence is disclosed as violence in discourse and it is modified thanks to discourse. By presenting the struggle with nature as an initial form of violence that grounds all other forms, and insisting on its essentially historical character, Weil is in some sense providing a genealogy of violence. He is presenting the historical and logical conditions that were needed to recognize violence and to give a complete characterization of violence. Logically and historically (because, for Weil these two orders do not line up *necessarily*), the organization of individuals into communities is the condition for grasping violence. For Weil, "the individual is [...] the product of society, in their individuality as in their existence" (PP, 63). The struggle against this initial violence is what changed out activity into work, into a meaningful activity that aims at transforming nature and its own procedures. It is "in and through work [that the human being] can transform their manner of working" (PP, 64). However, individuals being organized into a group that struggles against nature is also what makes them subject to social and political violence.

In humanity's initial struggle with initial violence, the community, not the individual, is the subject (LP, 25). This is because it is the community's tradition that houses the discourse that has allowed for its own survival. In this way, those inside the community, those that share the same tradition and same discourse, are seen as working to preserve this community against external violence. Because each organized group is particular, external violence is not, in this genealogy, merely the violence of nature, it is also the violence of other organized groups. The group in which the individual finds themself provides the meaning that the individual finds in the world. Within this group, violence is prohibited. Those that are in the group, that have ruled out violence in their relations with other group members consider themselves to be "genuine human beings" (LP, 25), precisely because they have ruled out violence.[8] These genuine human beings are those that share the same goals and that agree on the same means of achieving them. They share the same unconscious awareness of what matters to the group, the same ways of behaving. In other words,

---

[8] It must be noted that Weil is merely using the term "genuine human" as a descriptive term. He starts his analysis of violence from the way that the Greek tradition grasped violence and so he is merely *describing* the normative characterization that the Greeks give to themselves in relation to non-Greeks. This characterization is present throughout Greek writings, and so one example will suffice. Aristophanes' play the *Wasps* explicitly sets up this opposition (1996), 1075–80. William Shepherd provides a useful analysis of the formation of Greek identity as a consequence of the Greco-Persian War, and his translation of these lines is particularly striking. He translates them as "We alone are true sons of this soil, the true men of Attica./ We are the manliest of all races./ We gave our greatest service fighting for our country./ When the Barbarians came, they blew smoke over our city/ And set it ablaze, desperate to seize our nests." In Shepherd (2019), 147.

2.2 Weil's Characterization of Violence

they share the same "sacred."[9] It is the community however that holds this sacred, and its sacred character is precisely what makes it go unseen. It is the unwritten law that acts upon all individuals. To protect this sacred, the community must protect itself from external violence, and this includes the external violence of other groups that do not share in this sacred.

From inside a determined community, inhabited by those who have ruled out violence, the members of other groups are not seen as genuinely human beings, because "such beings may be human beings on the outside, but they are not fully entitled to this term because they do not recognize what defines the human being." (LP, 25). Despite their outer similarities to members of a determined community, they don't recognize what really matters. For any determined community that faces such simulacra of humanity, this other "sacred" is incomprehensible. This is the pre-philosophical grasp of the community and its traditions. To those inside of a determined community, these foreigners, these outsiders, "have not yet lifted themselves out of nature; they may have human features, but we neither understand them nor what they do and what they say: they babble *bar-bar*, they twitter like birds, they ignore the sacred, they live with neither shame nor honor" (LP, 25). Thus, in the pre-philosophical grasp of meaning and of life within a community, different communities present a threat and a menace. The community must be protected from them. In other words, "[v]iolence is the only way of establishing any contact with them—which is why they are not human beings" (LP, 25).

The violent contact between different groups has subjected one group under another. It has absorbed failed communities and brought into a single community different traditional and historical sacreds, without actually eliminating those sacreds, while nonetheless subordinating them to the sacred of the dominant community. This is the starting point of social and political violence. It separates the community into different social strata, into masters and slaves, into the rich and the poor, into different people with different roles who live together in uneasy harmony. This remains pre-philosophical and pre-modern, but it is also the starting point of philosophy. Weil notes that the "self-aware individuality can only establish itself once the initial struggle no longer occupies all of the community's strength: before even the most rudimentary thought can be born, society must have reserves at its disposal and no longer need to dedicate all of the time of all its members to the struggle for life" (PP, 63). It must move from a rudimentary organization of social

---

[9] The sacred plays a key role in Weil's account of normativity. Weil does not treat normativity as a block, but rather divides it into different interlocking aspects which include the *tradition*, the *sacred* (or *essential*), *what goes without saying*, and a specific idea of *natural law*. I will treat most of these aspects separately throughout this work, with the exception of Weil's conception of natural law, which falls more properly under the moral and political aspects of his systematic philosophy. Nonetheless we can say a word on Weil's conception of natural law. For Weil, natural law is not some metaphysically autonomous predetermined fixed state. Rather, it is born in moral reflection. It is what deploys the norms that are present in the ethical (*sittlich*) life of a concrete historical community in order to ground its critique of the community's positive, explicit, laws. It is thus always formally present as what grounds all moral critique. For Weil's treatment of natural law, see (PP, § 11–14, PR.II.111–124), and for a reading of Weil's theory, see Canivez (2002).

labor where "maximum effort, thus more or less equal for everyone, is required from men, from women, from children and where the harvest must suffice to cover the needs close to the physiological minimum" all the way to "contemporary societies, in which an extremely complex organization allows according members a freedom of movement inconceivable in other forms of work" (PP, 63). In essence, there is a rationalization of forms of work. It is the progressive rationalization of social labor that allows individuality to develop, that allows different forms of reflection. But this, for Weil, is a fundamentally ambivalent process.

In its pre-modern form, social labor is understood as defensive. It strives to protect the community from the unchained force of the natural world. Because the progressive rationalization of social labor has transformed work itself, in its modern form, social labor is understood as offensive. It comes up with strategies and tools to overcome nature and to make the world a truly human one, one in which individuals can find true satisfaction. Thus the rationalization of work surpasses and suppresses traditional forms of social labor, while neither surpassing nor suppressing traditional beliefs and social structures. Technical effectiveness is, for Weil, the principle of the modern organization of social labor, but this effectiveness leads to the depreciation or abandonment of everything that had previously given meaning to the individual, what had previously been essential to their lives, to their values, and to their sacred. Technical effectiveness is not interested in which class is more honorable, or whether the woman's place is in the home, whether the home is a sacred space which must not be disturbed, whether a person's sexual orientation makes them moral or immoral, etc. Within a rationalized organization of social labor, it is the capacities of the individual to add to the rationalization and production of this social labor itself that is of the greatest importance. Weil notes that "for society, it makes no difference if A rather than B is gifted, strong, rich, intelligent: there will always be the privileged and the unprivileged, the only thing that matters to society is seeing these places suitably filled" (PP, 78). In this way, it is only as individuals fill social roles that they are recognized before the law. However, because these roles need to be suitably filled, no one is essentially attached to the role they fill.

No individual is essentially a baker or a blacksmith, and as long as anyone can learn to do that role just as well or better, each person is replaceable in their role, because "the best yield will be attained there where each place is occupied by the individual the most apt to fill it" (PP, 86). Within the modern organization of social labor, each individual becomes no more than the material that is used to fill the roles that are recognized by society and that are recognized before the law. But as Weil also notes, this process is essential to the development of the individual,[10] because "*thingification* in modern society is the price of *personification*" (PP, 80). Grasping oneself as an individual is only possible when one wants to grasp who and what they are when all of the contingent factors are taken away, and this is only possible when

---

[10] For a different development of the historical understanding of modern individuality, see Taylor (1989).

the individual is seen as endlessly replaceable in all their roles. This can lead the individual to grasp what is universal about themselves, their "transcendental self," their existence as a moral subject, or it can lead them to reinforce what is particular about themself, their violence, their attachment to traditional roles that have either disappeared or that are in the process of disappearing. For the moral individual, "the universal must overcome and *inform* the particular" (PP, 27) however there is nothing that requires this to happen. Because of this tension, Weil considers that the condition of the modern individual is principally one of dissatisfaction. The individual becomes a "private" individual (PP, 98) whose values and whose feelings are in conflict with the rationalization of social labor, and with society at large. Initially, this private character is particular, is what the tradition has left over. Therefore no society is completely rational, and it only will be when there is a global organization of social labor that assigns places to individuals based on their skills, qualities, and talents. In other words, "the perfect rational organization would be the perfect human victory over external nature" (PP, 94), but this remains an un-accomplishable dream, or a terrible defeat, when the growing mastery of nature threatens to destroy that nature itself, and thus, threatens to destroy all possibility of a truly human life.

Because nature is only known from the past, the future remains uncertain, because traditional values are in conflict with the modern rationalization of social labor, society itself is conflictual. This conflict expresses itself by the way society is broken into different social strata which, by their very existence, prevent the complete rationalization of social labor. And this conflict does not go unnoticed. Rather, it gives rise to the individual's feeling of injustice. This injustice is found for Weil in the individual who:

> has the feeling of not having access to all the functions for which they believe themself apt, of being deprived of certain chances, of suffering from the fact that others, installed in the advantageous places thanks to the conditions of their historical position, exclude the individual from such places in order to keep them for themselves without any rational justification (PP, 86).

This feeling of injustice is the main symptom of social and political violence. However, even if it can be diagnosed and reduced, this social violence cannot be completely weeded out. This is because there is a tension between society and the individual who has the feeling of injustice. For Weil, "society, by virtue of its principle, requires that the individual's individuality disappears. Yet, society is requiring this of individuality and can only hope to obtain this from individuality" (PP, 95). Society demands that individuality universalize itself and demands that it surpass and suppress what is particular, what is violent, what is passionate, what it irrational within individuality itself. This pressure is a "pressure on an individual who lives in their historical individuality, and it is this individual that submits themself to the rule of society (or who revolts against it), not through what is *socialized* in them, but through what they retain as *personal*" (PP, 95). This is, for Weil, the heart of the problem described in the genealogy of the feeling of violence.

Society, social labor, philosophy, reasonable discourse, rationality, all these things universalize the individual, however, they only do so by asking the individual to give up what is particular about them. To do so, they cannot appeal to the universal, but must appeal to the particular. Thus the individual must universalize themselves *from* the particular. Society allows the individual to grasp themselves as individual, without however overcoming individuality, and this individuality, which must constantly make an a-rational choice (that is, unjustified and unjustifiable except after the fact) to become reasonable, can also always choose their particularity. It can do so unconsciously, by being a slave to their passions, by letting their anger or jealousy overtake them, by drowning in a feeling of meaninglessness and absurdity within their own lives, by lashing out. But, and this is more dangerous, they can do so consciously. They can create self-serving ideologies, they can lie, they can be cruel, for no other reason than that *they* wanted to.

Weil radicalizes the problem of violence by characterizing it as the formal concept of particularity recognized as particular because in doing so, he breaks from the entire philosophical tradition. Weil's critique of the philosophical tradition is that it has misunderstood violence. Taking just Socrates' claim that no one is unjust knowingly in the *Gorgias*,[11] or Kant's presentation of the weakness of will in *Religion within the Boundaries of Mere Reason*,[12] we can see that the philosophical tradition, by grasping violence as error or weakness, sees it as a problem in reason. Weil on the other hand presents violence as reason's *other*. Thus violence cannot be reduced to reason and cannot be overcome by clearing out error or by fortifying the will. This does not mean however that Weil thinks that violence cannot be understood. In fact, what is important is the way that Weil's solution allows us to understand interdiscursive violence. For Weil, different individuals have different goals and different lives, thus they have different discourses. Philosophy has long sought to bring all these discourses together under a single unified absolutely coherent discourse, however, the possibility of the irruption of particularity presenting itself as particular means that any discourse can be refused. Anyone can rebel against any content. This is *the* problem of the unity of discourse. There is no discourse that forces adhesion in and of itself. In fact, trying to force adhesion would be to turn to violence in the name of reason, and thus an abandonment of reason itself. The violence that is found in discourse, the natural violence, the social violence, the individual violence, conditions discourse. Violence is structurally linked to discourse, without being the same as discourse. The violence that exists inside of the individual's discourse (as the historical articulation of these forms of violence that the individual does not grasp) is what gives the individual their feeling of injustice, and it is this feeling that leads individuals to reject specific determined discourses.

It is unjust that a disease takes someone *we* love and not somebody else; it is unjust that some people have the time and the means to organize their life as they see fit when *we* don't; it is unjust that *my* desire goes unrecognized and unsated. However, when the individual struggles to understand this injustice they transform it, either by accepting it as part of the human condition or by changing the

---

[11] Plato (1997a), 509 d–e.
[12] Kant (1998), 6.29–6.32.

conditions that led to the injustice. People cure disease, they find ways to accomplish their goals and then work to help others who find themselves in similar situations of disadvantage accomplish their own. But the problem, again, is that nothing *forces* the individual to understand their feeling, to understand their particularity. This gives rise to interdiscursive violence. Everyone has a more *or* less coherent discourse, a more *or* less comprehensive way of understanding themself and the world. But these discourses, for as coherent as they may be, are contradictory between them. If the individual does not sacrifice their particularity on the altar of universality, this discourse will remain contradictory. Thus, the problem of violence that Weil highlights is not that individuals can overcome dissatisfaction or injustice with the help of discourse—the entire philosophical tradition has said as much—it is that individuals can choose not to. They can refuse to recognize arguments, they can refuse to recognize what is valid from another point of view, and they can do so in order to hold on to their concrete particularity. They can choose to enclose themselves in their feeling instead of raising themselves up to discourse, and thus arguments and reason can have no hold on them. The importance of this fact, that we recognize when we are faced with someone who propagates hate speech, who produces acts of terrorism, who does not want to recognize another discourse but rather wants to destroy it, is at the center of Weil's logical characterization of violence.

2.3 The Logic of Violence and the Violence in Logic

The genealogy of the problem as it is articulated in *Philosophie politique* aims at understanding violence as a practical and political problem. It develops the tension that concrete particularity is in with universality by showing how the individual feeling of particularity developed and how it can come to be grasped, but also how it can always reject universality. This tension is at the heart of Weil's logical articulation of the problem (LP, 22–53), where he develops different forms of logic into what Gilbert Kirscher calls the different "shapes of violence."[13] The logical forms present the different shapes of violence as they appear in discourse, as different types of contradiction. In other words, for Weil, there are different fundamental contradictions that allow coherent discourse to develop. It is this development that allows us, from our point of view, to grasp violence as the formal concept of concrete particularity recognized as particular. However, it is also because these are different developments of that possibility that they were unable to grasp violence as such. Weil thus presents the way in which the philosophical tradition has grasped violence by illustrating four different types of fundamental contradictions, and thus four different types of logic that define the shapes of violence. It will only be after Weil reformulates his problem, as it has been grasped in the tradition, that he will propose his fifth logical moment, a fifth shape of violence, which for him, allows a

---

[13] Kirscher (1992), 113–168.

full grasp of the problem of violence. The four traditional moments are (1) the formal (but not formalized) logic of the dialogical practices in a political community; (2) the logic of classic ontology conceived as the science of being; (3) transcendental logic with its opposition between freedom and nature; and (4) the logic of the absolutely coherent discourse that develops and grasps itself and contradiction as the development of the Concept.

The first moment grasps violence merely as formal contradiction. This is the Socratic practice of public debate in the Greek city-state. This contradiction is formal because it has no content, but remains at the surface level of language. Nonetheless, it is an essential step because it makes a fundamental discovery about the possible contradiction between different contents. The violence that it aims at overcoming is the violence that disrupts the political unity and stability of the city-state. Individuals confront each other publicly and must convince the audience that their interlocutor is saying something contradictory. It seeks the agreement of reason with itself. This is what Socrates means by saying that no one is unjust willingly: when individuals grasp reason, they see what justice is.[14] Public debate clears out all the contradiction in discourse. If it succeeds people will know what to do and how to act, they will reestablish the values of the community, and find the lost stability that the traditional community had. However, this formal reduction of violence can lead people to admit absurd conclusions. Weil notes how this formal contradiction allows one to "to demonstrate that an opponent has horns, since they admit that they still have whatever they have not lost and that they have not lost any horns" (LP, 139).

The second form of logic aims at giving content to discourse and to do so it conceives of the fundamental contradiction as that between reason and nature, between Being and becoming. Reason is what is true and eternal, nature is what is fleeting and thus holds error. The violence that we undergo is the violence of this fleeting, changing becoming. When what is reason within us, what is true and eternal, agrees with the eternal reason of Being, violence is supposed to disappear. In order to bring this about, an ontological science of Being must be elaborated and must be given discursive form. Only then will the calm contemplation of reason give satisfaction to the individual. Violence will be understood as what it is, the contradiction with reason. The development of this form of logic, based on the grasp of violence as the fundamental contradiction of Being and becoming, of reason and nature, allows multiple coherent discourses. It is, for Weil, this contradiction that is at the heart of the objective science of Plato and Aristotle, as well as the contradiction that guides the Stoic and Epicurean responses to this science. It is the contradiction that allows the initial development of modern empirical science, but that discourse also creates a new problem, one that Kant was the first to see fully. It creates a contradiction between facts and values.

---

[14] Plato's articulation of the problem of weakness of will, *akrasia*, is most fully characterized in the dialogue *Protagoras*, see Plato (1997b), 352 c.

2.3 The Logic of Violence and the Violence in Logic

In order to overcome the contradiction of facts and values, transcendental logic presents a different contradiction, that between freedom and nature. Nature is the realm of facts, transcendental logic accepts this; however, these facts depend on the values of the knowing subject, and it is only the knowing subject in themselves that can assign values. This is the problem of "reconciling human *freedom* with scientific determinations, of reconciling the concept of the human being as a speaking, questioning, choosing, acting being with that of a reasonably determined world that determines the human being" (LP, 44). This contradiction, between nature and freedom, is formulated for transcendental logic as the difference between knowledge and thought. The world is known scientifically, but freedom cannot be known this way, however it can be grasped and understood, because it can be thought. This opposition brings all contradiction into discourse. In Socratic dialogical logic, contradiction was at the surface of language. In the logic of classic ontology, it was between discourse and the world. Here, it is at the heart of discourse itself. The same individual is determined by discourse and determines discourse itself, but the one thing this discourse can't grasp is the freedom that allows discourse to be grasped.

Discourse must find a content for this freedom. In order to have a content, contradiction must become the motor of thought. The opposition is no longer between reason and nature, nor freedom and nature: the opposition is within discourse as the different concrete contents in which the finite (as a thinking subject) thinks the infinite (as the comprehensive totality of discourse). In other words, Hegel discovers that the contradiction between different contents is an essential moment of the develop of any content. Nature—Being—is thus reconciled with freedom. Here discourse becomes "the grasp of Being by itself and for itself" (LP, 50) and Hegel provides the paradigmatic model of such a discourse. All opposition is understood as necessary steps by which Reason understands itself as "Being, which is nothing other than Reason determining itself in its Freedom" (LP, 50). Thus, according to this reason, contradiction does not disappear, it is not overcome, it is given its rightful place in the development of reason and at the interior of this reasonable discourse, the individual understands themselves as they are, as the discourse that grasps itself and the world. Thus, everything is in its place and everything is completed. This, for Weil, is the accomplishing of the philosophical tradition, a total grasp of the totality of nature and of the individual in discourse. Nonetheless, he notes that a problem remains, and that the absolutely coherent discourse glosses over this problem. What is it? It is the problem of the individual's real satisfaction. For Weil, the contradiction that this logic is unable to resolve is the contradiction between the abstract universal idea of satisfaction in discourse and the possibility of the concrete particular individual that remains unsatisfied facing discourse. In other words, Hegel discovered the possibility of a coherent discourse concerning freedom, but was unable to grasp the radicality of the freedom that he had discovered.

This leads Weil to propose a fifth logical moment, a fifth shape of violence. Here the opposition is between truth and freedom. It is an opposition not in discourse but in action. Discourse is the domain of truth, life is the domain of freedom, and nothing can force the free individual to reflect on truth, to decide to understand themselves coherently, to shoulder the effort of discourse itself. The final scandal of reason is that any individual can refuse (though not refute) the absolutely coherent discourse. Discourse depends on shared principles, and once those shared principles are decided, discourse, if carried out long enough, should lead to agreement, to truth, to understanding. But any principle can be refused at any point. By characterizing this refusal, Weil discovers that the most basic contradiction is not between content, but between grasping content because of the goodness of the content and refusing to grasp content *despite* its goodness.

Philosophy has always felt the need to prove its own necessity; it has always shown that *if* one wants to think coherently and universally, *then* they must follow the rules that discourse gives to itself. This final opposition shows that there is no necessity in this conditional reasoning itself. People can refuse to think coherently, to understand, and not because they have made a mistake, or because they are weak-willed, but because they don't want to understand reasonably. And here, they don't want to think coherently precisely because they understand what thinking coherently implies. It implies giving up on their particularity. What Weil will try to show is that unless philosophy understands this concrete freedom, it will be unable to interpret itself as the realization of freedom in the world. Thus, for Weil, philosophy is grounded on freedom in the search for truth, but this means that this freedom can also always make another choice. It can choose violence. This, for Weil, is the final contradiction of philosophy, but it is only a contradiction for the person who thinks that philosophy needs to be justified. And Weil thinks that it does not, but he also thinks that only the completion of philosophical discourse will show this. Philosophy creates itself in its refusal of violence, in the act of philosophizing. It is free (unjustified and unjustifiable), and it is only once the individual has chosen philosophy, has chosen to understand comprehensively, that any question of justification enters into the picture. Weil's goal then in the *Logic of Philosophy* is to understand and to make explicit this free choice, and for him the only way to do so is to place violence at the center of philosophical discourse.

This philosophical reflection presents the different types of philosophical logics that have allowed different readings of the relationship between discourse and violence. For Weil, this development has been exemplified by different thinkers, Socrates, Plato and Aristotle, Kant, Hegel, who have developed these logics and who have allowed violence to be understood discursively. Patrice Canivez notes that "for Weil, every form of philosophical logic corresponds to a certain manner of determining the violence that is the object of discourse."[15] This object of discourse, this particularity that discourse grasps, is determined and understood thanks to the notion of contradiction. Particularity is the stuff that reasonable discourse seeks to universalize, and in order to do so, each form of logic defines a fundamental contradiction that must be grasped. Each form of logic operates a double reduction of violence: violence is reduced to what is contradictory within reasonable discourse, and then discourse uses this contradiction to purify itself by defining everything in

---

[15] Canivez (1993), 11.

2.3 The Logic of Violence and the Violence in Logic

contradiction as being incoherent and thus inessential, and thus reduces the concrete violence in the world.

By subsuming violence under the logical role of contradiction, violence is what is in contradiction with reasonable discourse. It is the formal concept of the particular recognized in its particularity. Canivez notes that:

> In these traditional shapes of philosophical rationality, violence is apprehended, characterized, formalized under the form of *contradiction*. Each determined form of contradiction thus corresponds to a determined form of philosophical logic: the contradiction of interests to the formal (but not formalized) logic of coherence that is the essential principle of Socratic dialogue; the contradiction between this formally coherent discourse and multiform reality of the sensible world to the logic of the classic ontology that reconciles discourse and phenomena by reducing them down to the unity of Being; the contradiction between nature and freedom to the transcendental logic of Kantian criticism; the contradiction as the principle of historical becoming of reason to the absolute coherence of Hegelian discourse.[16]

Each of these different logical forms allow the different shapes of violence to be made explicit. This is precisely the way in which Weil's work must be understood as a *logic*; he articulates different types of contradictions and then provides the organization for grasping these forms of contradiction. The philosophical tradition that sees the human being as an animal gifted with rational language has assumed that violence and particularity could be absorbed into discourse, and it is just a matter of elaborating the correct discourse which does so. Weil however presents a new shape of violence, one that is "irreducible to the logical form of contradiction."[17] This new shape of violence finds its source in human freedom. There is no contradiction between the exercise of human freedom and violence, just as there is no contradiction in the idea that human freedom can be exercised violently, but there is an opposition between freedom and truth. This is what distinguishes Weil's logic from Socratic dialogue, from Plato's contemplative science, from Kant's categorical imperative, and from the Hegelian dialectical movement of thought.

Weil's seeks to show that violence cannot just be seen as epiphenomenal. In other words, violence (and language) is what is at the core of freedom itself. He helps us to understand how the radical form of violence is violence towards discourse itself, refusing any coherent, comprehensive, universal organization of meaning. It thus not only refuses all of the logical norms of a specific discourse, it refuses all the pragmatic norms as well. It refuses validity, justification, the normative weight of better reasons. It ignores every premise and every contradiction. It refuses all the constraints of argumentation. However, even though Weil characterizes the radical refusal of all normative constraints and of all discourse according to violence, he also highlights that pure violence is not the form that this radical refusal *must* always take. In fact, the way we most often encounter the radical refusal is in its banal deployment in everyday discursive practices, in the indifference that an individual can show towards discourse, in the quickly elaborated *ad hominem* attack, in the

---

[16] Canivez (1993), 11–12.
[17] Canivez (1999), 63.

mocking dismissal of premises that are presented, in the indifference to the discourse of others. By refusing discourse and all of its norms, these banal forms of refusal are still radical.

Reasonable discourse seeks agreement, and within the unity of reasonable discourse radical refusal is supposed to be impossible. For Plato, the Good is objective. It is to be pursued by everyone and as soon as people no longer mistake *a* good for the pursuit of *the Good*, this unity will be reached. For Kant, the categorical imperative governs all rational agents and it is thanks to this that the possibility of a kingdom of ends, where all agents are free from fear and doubt and are thus free to act morally, can be seen as an ideal that we must strive to realize. Both philosophers frame the radical refusal as being an impossibility as soon as people recognize the necessity of the concepts that unify discourse. Weil's formulation of the problem differs precisely in that he claims that reasonable discourse is shot through with this radical refusal. It is violent *because* it is born in human freedom. It is a human choice to submit oneself to the pragmatic and logical norms of discourse, but for this choice to be free, it has to be a possibility and not a necessity. It is a choice because it is free, and violent because it is arbitrary and made in the face of violence. It is free and violent because at any time, anybody can make another choice: they can refuse discourse and choose violence.

According to the tradition, the unity of discourse is supposed to be what resolves violence. But Weil's formulation of the problem forces us to ask whether there is indeed such a unity. Can these innumerable commitments be reduced down to a single thing that rules over all others? If reasonable action in discourse is a choice, it is because discourse reveals choices as choices by showing the range of possibility. One of those possibilities is that people can always choose to live outside of discourse. They can always refuse coherence. They can thus always make the free choice to shatter any unity that is created. Because these two possibilities exist side by side, discourse cannot be reduced to a concrete unity, but Weil also asks whether all concrete commitments can be understood in discourse and thanks to discourse. In other words, he asks whether discourse has a formal unity. The goal of the *Logic of Philosophy* is to show that all concrete commitments, even those that seek to undermine and destroy discourse from the inside, even those that refuse all discourse, can indeed be understood under the formal unity of meaning, which characterizes all efforts to create an identity between concrete human situations and the concrete discourses that grasp those situations.

These different concrete discourses are built out of the manifold commitments that individuals take on. They are built around something that is so important to these individuals that they cannot give it up. They are born out of the expression of human freedom that can resist any proposed unity for reasons. Weil shows that unity is a possibility but not a necessity. It can be posited in order to understand the diversity of concrete discourses and is present each time conflict is overcome. But because it is only a possibility, some positions *are* irreducible to others. In other words, people can live full meaningful lives according to multiple discourses. Weil accepts this. He asks however whether that irreducibility is infinite, or whether some commitments can be reduced down to a manageable plurality. The formal

2.3 The Logic of Violence and the Violence in Logic

possibility of unity and the concrete reality of understanding show that this irreducibility is not infinite. Most commitments can be reduced down to several fundamental positions that can be compared and judged. This also shows that Weil's radical discovery of the possibility of refusing all discourse is not the most habitual form of refusal. Rather, the habitual form is a specific refusal based on specific commitments.

In every debate, everyone is pro-something and yet debates are mired in opposition. In the debate around abortion—to give a non-Weilian example—some are pro-life and some are pro-choice. However the oppositions are *between* discourses and are thus not the purview of internal contradiction. If somebody decides that life starts at conception and that life is the thing of greatest value, this value will coherently take precedence over the conditions in which the life will be raised, the pregnant person's life goals or desire and willingness to have a child. Someone arguing from this side will accept that even if the life was conceived by rape, by violence, this life matters more than the violence that the pregnant person underwent or that the child may undergo after birth. If somebody decides personhood is what matters in *human* life, then during the early stages of pregnancy, when the developing fetus is more a part of the pregnant person than a separate thing, the pregnant person's choice is what is essential to the debate. In this case, someone arguing from this side can build a coherent argument from that premise. The question thus focuses more on the pregnant person's capacity to raise the child, the situation in which the child is born, the age of the pregnant person, or simply, whether or not they want a child. However, when there are opposed and radically different conceptions of things, arguments don't even seem to get off the ground. This, again, is the problem Weil faces head on.

At the heart of the problem lies the fact that having a discourse means taking a stance. Weil says that:

> [The individual's] action (as well as their discourse, to the extent that this discourse forms an integral part of their action) reveals, to the observer, what they pursue *deep down*, reveals the center they use to orient themself in their world. But this center does not appear to be the center in their own eyes, it does not even appear, just like the spot under their feet does not appear to the human being standing there. They are speaking about it constantly (for the interpreter) without ever formulating it: as soon as it were formulated, this principle could be doubted and would already be off-center in a world whose center would have changed by this discovery's very fact, in the same way that the ground that I see is not the ground that holds me up (LP, 82).

What this means (and this will become central as I work to bring out what Weil's work shares with pragmatism, expressivism, and inferentialism) is that Weil presents a radical conception of commitment. This radical conception takes the initial commitment to be a completely free self-determination. Once that commitment is made it means accepting that there are things to which one is also committed, as well as things that are incompatible with one's stance. In order to do so, the individual must draw out what they "pursue deep down," they must make the implicit commitments in their pragmatic stance towards discourse explicit in that discourse. As we will see, this relationship between implicit practice and explicit discourse appears in Weil's *Logic of Philosophy* as the relationship between the *attitude* and the *category*. This however does not mean that the same things are incompatible in every discourse. The different shapes that freedom determines for itself give rise to different commitments and different discourses. Indeed, there are multiple discourses than can be built around opposing stances.

The person that holds this or that position may not be aware of what grounds it. This is normal, they aren't aware of it because they live in it. It is what is essential to their life. For them, it may be an intuition, a feeling, a hunch. Whatever it is, it is meaningful and it is the source of the meaning that they see their life as having. This essential governs their other commitments and thus gives shape to the specific things they refuse. It is only when individuals turn back to their action, to their choices, to their positions to understand them, that the contours of this meaning become clear. When this happens, this meaning can be reduced down and organized, the essential can be grasped as essential. This changes the essential however. It is no longer the silent center of their life: it is an overt claim. Thus, there is meaning as it is lived and meaning as it is grasped in discourse. However, it is because the meaning that is lived can be grasped in discourse that it can be understood. This distinction defines the two driving concepts just mentioned, *attitudes* and *categories*.[18]

2.4 Attitudes and Categories

An attitude is the feeling of meaning that is lived in each person's life. When this meaning is grasped in discourse according to its central organizing concept, it is a category. If a discourse can grasp an attitude, and present it as a coherent position that is irreducible to any other grasp of meaning, it is what Weil calls a *pure* attitude. Pure attitudes allow for meaning to be grasped as coherent discourse. Because Weil

---

[18] Multiple in-depth studies have been done focusing on the *categories* in the *Logic of Philosophy*. William Kluback, for instance, insists on the way the progression of categories situates Weil as a neo-Kantian interpreter of the philosophical tradition, in Kluback (1987). Gilbert Kirscher reads the categories in relationship to what he calls the *"aporia* of the beginning" which analyses the place the opening philosophical gesture itself has in a system that sees philosophical discourse as a free self-determining act, in Kirscher (1989). Patrice Canivez offers an analysis that focuses on the individual's relationship to discourse and how this results in a specific type of philosophical practice, in Canivez (1999). Both Mahamadé Savadogo (2003) and Francis Guibal (2011) for their part insist on the way the categories enact a shift from ontological discourses on being and reality towards an anthropological understanding of discourse itself, with Savadogo emphasizing the political consequences and Guibal, the individual's act of constituting meaning. Because, for Weil, it is the categories that have a discursive form, most attention has been placed on their role in discourse. There have nonetheless also been important studies that focus on the relationship between attitudes and categories such as the classic article by Roland Caillois (1953) or the introductory presentation of Weil's work by Patrice Canivez (1998). There is also Peter Gaitsch's recent phenomenological reading of the *Logic of Philosophy*, which places specific importance on the role of attitudes, in Gaitsch (2014).

2.4 Attitudes and Categories

reframes discourse in terms of violence, a coherent discourse can be understood as a discourse that holds together in the face of violence while still allowing violence to be grasped and reduced thanks to the discourse itself. This is a discourse that recognizes violence's place in it, but in doing so makes violence discursive. It subsumes violence under the rules of language as contradiction. This logical role allows discourse to separate the essential from what must be refused, ruled out, or put at arm's length. From within an attitude, this violence is contradictory because it is lived as unacceptable, as false, as immoral. From the category's point of view, this violence is contradictory because it is understood as what limits discourse's coherence. This implies that different attitudes have different levels of comprehensiveness, both in terms of understanding or being understandable, and in terms of being inclusive.

The more comprehensive a discourse, the less is ruled out. The less is ruled out, the more universal the discourse. Discourses have greater levels of comprehensiveness when they take in and explain a greater swath of human experience in the world. Building on the criterion of comprehensiveness, Weil thus adds the criterion of universality in order to understand the different pure attitudes. Different levels of comprehensiveness are organized as different levels of universality. These two criteria, comprehensiveness and universality, allows Weil to organize the different discursive centers that structure attitudes, and to understand how different grasps of meaning are themselves to be understood. The logic of philosophy is this organization. It presents the different attitudes that can be grasped according to their comprehensiveness and universality.

Weil's presentation of the relationship between discourse and violence has another surprising consequence; the philosophical attitude, the attitude of understanding, becomes one among many, and thus philosophy itself is seen as a possibility and not a necessity. In discovering that it is not a necessity, the philosophical attitude discovers something that every non-philosopher already knew. What the non-philosopher misses though is that every time they seek to understand the world around them as a coherent whole, every time they seek to understand their life as a unity, they themselves enter into the philosophical attitude. And here they come face to face with the historical role that philosophers have played in articulating the coherence that allows them to grasp the meaning they seek.

Concrete human attitudes are historically and phenomenologically articulated. In this way, they are different from pure attitudes. Pure attitudes are governed not by historical or by phenomenological criteria but by the logical criterion of non-contradiction, where the logical role of contradiction is to grasp the violence that has been reduced. Because their organizing criterion is logical, pure attitudes are ideal-types. In other words, they don't correspond to real concrete attitudes, which are mixed and which must always face concrete violence. Pure attitudes are thus able to be grasped coherently because they show how violence is to be ruled out. This grasp in coherent discourse allows concrete attitudes to be understood according to the violence they refuse and the contradictions they rule out. When a pure attitude is grasped in coherent discourse, it is considered a *philosophical category*.

Weil makes three major distinctions in the *Logic of Philosophy* between philosophical categories, metaphysical categories, and the categories of philosophy.[19] The logic of philosophy is built around the notion of philosophical categories. These categories are understood as "the translation of *a* determined attitude in *an* elaborated discourse" (LP, 147) and they "determine the ways in which thought thinks itself and constitutes itself for itself" (LP, 341). In making this claim, Weil highlights that thinking is a free activity, but he also highlights the fact that when we engage in it, we delimit and determine. We take stances about what is essential and what is not. We commit ourselves to things. In our concrete attitudes this deed is something we are only partially aware of—when we are aware of it at all—because our attitudes are initially grounded in our historical and cultural situation. The philosophical categories are the conceptual structures that explain how attitudes grasp the world and themselves. Their role is structural because they explicate the frameworks within which different kinds of thinking happens. Philosophical categories translate the essential of an attitude into a coherent stance towards the real, the world, experience, etc. This is different from metaphysical categories.

For Weil, metaphysical categories, such as Aristotelean categories and Kantian categories, are metaphysical, or more properly, meta-scientific. They are ground-level categories. This is because they "belong to science, not to philosophy, to metaphysics, which has always quite rightly been interpreted as the first science, and not to the logic of philosophy" (LP, 147). They are the concepts that allow reality to be understood scientifically, to be "grasped as an object" (LP, 147). Weil's claim is that grasping the world as an object always implies a certain notion of orientation. Metaphysical categories such as "[c]ause and effect, substance and accident, *the one and the other*, the idea, the communion of great kinds or of number-ideas, form and matter, potentiality and actuality, time, space" (LP, 147) do not provide any such orientation. In fact, they only make sense because thought is already oriented. Every attitude uses metaphysical categories, but they do not use the same ones in the same ways. This is because the use of the metaphysical categories is determined by the orientation that the attitude itself provides. By making a distinction between metaphysical categories and philosophical categories, Weil allows us to understand the historical and social aspect of the development of thought: if different metaphysical categories are used by different philosophical categories then they are not eternal structures of the world but are instead determined by other discursive commitments.[20] He argues this by showing how different philosophers justify their usage of metaphysical concepts:

---

[19] A fourth distinction, between concrete categories and formal categories, is made at the interior of the philosophical categories, but I will come to this point later.

[20] In this way, Weil's categories share certain traits with both Michel Foucault's notion of *épistémè* and with Thomas Kuhn's notion of paradigms. For two different treatments of the relationship between Weil's categories and these other concepts, see Marcelo (2013); Strummiello (2013). Robert Brandom's recent reading of Hegel makes a very similar distinction (using other terms) between ground-level concepts that are used to grasp specific determined concepts and framework-

2.4 Attitudes and Categories

> To ground his ontology, Aristotle does not use the concepts of essence, of attribute, of place, etc. He uses the principle that says that reasoning cannot go on infinitely—a principle that is not grounded on ontology and its categories, but that allows the conception of a first science. Kant does not build his transcendental ontology with the help of his table of categories but the help of the "ideas" of freedom and eternity, of the transcendental *ideal*, of the kingdom of ends. Hegel himself recognizes the difference between the *Logic of Being* (the one of metaphysical categories), the one *of Essence*, and the one *of Reality*, the last of which must, among other things, make it possible to understand the meaning of the first part of the entire logic, that is, of the metaphysical categories. [...] [The logic of philosophy] is only interested in *metaphysical* categories to the extent that they reveal the *philosophical* categories, these discursive centers from which an attitude expresses itself in a coherent fashion (or that, in the case of attitudes that refuse all discourse, can be grasped by philosophical discourse) (LP, 146, n. 1).

For Weil, metaphysical categories do not govern thought, but their usage can help to show what does. When shared concepts are used differently, individuals can unearth underlying commitments. Concrete attitudes are mixed, so individuals express their essential without necessarily being aware of it. It is lived as the substratum that holds reality together. It becomes an object of thought when someone takes on the philosophical attitude and seeks to eliminate the contradiction that exists in this essential. When individuals make the free choice to understand, they seek to grasp as a concept the reality of what is essential to them. Metaphysical categories can help to uncover philosophical categories precisely because people's different uses of these concepts show that some uses are contradictory to others. This contradiction attests to different commitments. These different commitments can thus help to bring out the structure of different pure attitudes.

Here, the relationship of the logic of philosophy to the history of philosophy is important. For Weil, pure attitudes are revealed by the philosophers who do the logical work of elaborating them into coherent discourse, but all pure attitudes are present throughout all of human history in the mixed form of concrete attitudes. This means that the philosophers who have elaborated such discourses did so to answer a specific question. It also means that pure attitudes, in the form of different categories, help us to understand something that goes beyond the historical discourse where it was grasped fully for the first time. Pure attitudes thus appear as categories at historically determined moments. This does not mean however that the historical order corresponds to the logical one. Their logical organization does not depend on their historical appearance, rather it depends on the level of coherence and universality they provide. It depends on how comprehensive they are.

Within history, Augustine formulated a discourse that grasps the attitude of the faithful believer coherently and in doing so discovered a pure attitude (*God*), but this attitude is not limited to Augustine's work. It can be used to understand all the great monotheistic religions. Michel de Montaigne and Pierre Bayle both elaborated discourses that grasped the irreducibility of the interpretative effort necessary for understanding the variety of human interests, and in doing so, discovered the pure

---

explicating concepts that are used to make the normative structure of discursiveness explicit, in Brandom (2019).

attitude of the intellectual curiosity that refuses to reduce any of those interests to any other (*Intelligence*). This focus on different human interests also allows structurally understanding relativism more generally. Immanuel Kant opened the path to understanding the moral individual thanks to the synthetic unity of apperception that unites the knowing subject and the moral subject. It is the same subject-for-itself that "exists and [...] *knows* itself immediately in the consciousness of its search for a world and for a meaningful existence, in the consciousness of a rule of the duty and of the ought that surpasses and negates every given and that, hence, constitutes the human being and reveals them to himself as what they truly are" (PK, 54). But Weil nonetheless sees Johann Gottlieb Fichte as the one that hewed this unity down to its most essential characteristics by elaborating the pure attitude of moral consciousness in the Absolute *I* (*Consciousness*). This attitude has a farther-ranging application, because it can also be used to understand the different dilemma of moral philosophy and the domain of moral action. Hegel elaborated a discourse that grasped the idea of totality as being central to human understanding and grasped the philosophical attitude in absolute knowing (*The Absolute*). But this idea can be used to grasp the idea of philosophical understanding in general. Auguste Comte's philosophical discourse is based on the notion of progress and on science; thus it was able to grasp the attitude of scientific positivism (*Condition*), but this same discourse is also used both to understand the goals of modern experimental science and different forms of scientism. Friedrich Nietzsche grasped the attitude of the individual who sees themself as the source of all values in their self-creation and in doing so he discovered the pure attitude of the creative personality (*Personality*). This attitude shows itself useful to understand numerous historical artistic figures and the act of creation in general.

Once these discourses have been elaborated, they show how the different irreducible stances taken in discourse are to be understood. This allows us to understand both the conditions of their historical emergence *and* the logic of actual stances that are taken in the concrete discourses we face. Despite that, the logic of philosophy only derivatively cares about the historical order of their appearance. This is why it is a logic of philosophy and not a history of philosophy. Weil's logical order is a progression, but a progression built on how comprehensive these discourses are. The progression follows the development of what these discourses allow us to grasp. It is defined by the universality and coherence that each category's central explanatory concept provides. This is why *Consciousness* precedes *Intelligence*. The unity of consciousness provides a conceptual ground for Bayle and Montaigne's positions even though Kant and Fichte were writing in their wake. The unity of conscious is more logically primitive because any interest must always also be considered someone's interest. The *Personality* precedes *The Absolute* because it acts as a conceptual ground for this later concept. The creative personality takes a stance in their creation and thus creates values. This is a pure attitude. By showing that these values also depend on the recognition of others, *The Absolute* provides a more coherent position. Nietzsche's notion of the creative personality thus provides a conceptual ground for the totality found in Hegel's thought even though Hegel developed his discourse before Nietzsche developed his own.

2.5 Hegel and the Categories of Philosophy

The movement between the categories brings out Weil's relationship to Hegel. It is this relationship that will help us to understand *the categories of philosophy*. By organizing the different grasps of meaning that philosophy presents, Weil's project bears strong resemblance to the Hegelian project in *The Phenomenology of Spirit*. This is not surprising. Weil thinks that Hegel uncovered and grasped the pure philosophical attitude with the idea of the absolutely coherent discourse. He even leaves much of Hegel's conceptual apparatus in place, yet he differs from Hegel in important ways. Hegel's progression in *The Phenomenology of Spirit*, understood as the "science of the experience of consciousness," is built around the claim that consciousness must be explained using nothing other than the resources that consciousness itself can propose. This is a high demand, and this is why so many shapes of consciousness are surpassed: they simply cannot satisfy it. Hegel does not see this as problematic, rather he sees these shapes of consciousness as steps on the path that brings consciousness to recognize itself in its own work of becoming aware of the world. The culmination of this progression is the recursive circularity of philosophical justification. What consciousness finds in its experience is itself and this is what allows it to explain its progress with its own resources. Thought is an immanent process that unfolds from within itself. Following Hegel, Weil thinks justification must be recursive to get the job done, but he doubts that every attitude wants to justify itself, or that every attitude is seeking understanding and recognition. Rather Weil posits that the movement is not immanent. Because Weil frames both discourse and violence as a free choice, every step that Weil's system provides must be seen as a rupture, as a free "jump" that refuses the determined form of discourse that had up until then been in full force and effect. Each irreducible attitude is irreducible because it provides a form of coherence, and there is no slow and steady progression of reason. Rather, parts of it stutter forward while others never move or even regress. This is because people cling to the forms of coherence that their attitudes provide. This is, in part, why after Hegel the problem changes. In fact, after Hegel, Weil thinks the notion of philosophy itself changes. From the origins of Greek thought all the way through Hegel, philosophy has been seen as a discourse bearing on the structure of the world, as a discourse on being. This leads Hegel to the science of the experience of consciousness, which studies the way that this very experience unfolds. By characterizing attitudes as irreducible and the movement between them as jumps, Weil transforms the problem from a problem of consciousness and being into a problem of action and discourse.

In the Hegelian model, acting is acting for reasons and Weil accepts this. But he shows that the acting consciousness can give up the consciousness of its own activity in order for the activity to be pure activity. This means that the logic of philosophy is not a study of the experience of consciousness, but, as Weil presents it, the study of different possible human relationships to discourse. Consciousness, as self-consciousness in the Hegelian sense, emerges thanks to discourse, yes, but it also emerges because it chooses discourse. Weil presents Hegel's attitude as the culmination of the philosophical attitude, as a culmination of an attitude that proposes human satisfaction in terms of understanding. The philosophical attitude subsumes every previous attempt at understanding under this concept as different shapes of consciousness. Weil thinks Hegel adequately formulated the philosophical attitude, but Weil also wants to understand the violent one. Weil highlights that the violent attitude, in its purest form, does not seek understanding, but rather seeks to live in the immediacy of its feeling. That is why this attitude only becomes visible after Hegel. Before Hegel, each philosophical category found a way to bring violence into discourse by subsuming it under its own concepts. But pure violence is not conceptual, it is anti-conceptual, refusing justification, understanding, acting for reasons. Its activity is spontaneous no matter what the attitude of the person is when they are trying to understand. Pure violence outstrips understanding by going against every imperative that understanding places on the individual. It does not care if its activity is moral or good or true. Weil recognizes that human freedom can stubbornly stay in any attitude, even when it fully understands what other attitudes imply, and it is the violent attitude that teaches this lesson. The violent attitude stays in its attitude *because* it understands what the philosophical attitude implies. The philosophical attitude implies justifying, it implies argumentative practices, it implies submitting oneself to the normative weight of better reasons and accepting to modify one's position when better reasons hold. The violent attitude does not want to accept this change. It does not seek recognition, it wants to *be* the only consciousness in the world. All other consciousnesses are tools, are means, are the background noise and opposition that the violent attitude must overcome by any means possible. This is the attitude that the *Logic of Philosophy* understands under the category of *The Work*.

This is why it would be a mistake to see the *Logic of Philosophy* as merely a reworking of *The Phenomenology of Spirit*. Yes, Weil absorbs and keeps Hegel's main insights, and keeps the systematic structure, but Weil's critique of Hegel radicalizes the notion of freedom that Hegel is trying to coax out into the world. Following Kant, Hegel recognizes two types of freedom: negative and positive freedom. One of his goals in the *Phenomenology* is to bring about the advent of positive freedom by giving it a conceptual form that allows every individual to grasp it. Negative freedom is traditionally characterized as freedom *from* something; freedom from constraint; freedom from fear; freedom from authority. Positive freedom is characterized as freedom *to do* something, freedom to act as one sees fit, freedom to have a peaceful life, freedom to decide what authority to follow. Positive freedom, for Hegel, implies the recognition of the social historical context in which this freedom makes sense. It implies that individuals can and do recognize the norms that govern their lives, that individuals recognize what others in this social and historical context add to their freedom and to their understanding of their own situation. This is where the full force of Weil's critique of Hegel can be seen. This road from negative freedom to positive freedom is, for Hegel, the immanent experience that consciousness goes through for itself, but in coming to positive freedom, the individual is absorbed into the universal, because they know themselves to be individual thanks to the universal. Weil posits that the total refusal of discourse could

2.5 Hegel and the Categories of Philosophy

care less about *knowing* itself as an individual by being universal. It wants to *be* individual, wants to *feel* individual. Patrice Canivez has noted[21] how Weil's critique of Hegel turns on two different readings of the content of *Die Individualität, welche sich an und für sich selbst reel ist*.[22] For Hegel, the work (*Das Werk*) that the individual creates is an expression of their self-conscious activity and is part of their struggle for recognition. For Weil on the other hand, there exists a form of self-conscious activity that does not seek recognition, precisely because what it is refusing is the constraints, norms, and responsibilities that recognition implies. This critique points out how, in the Hegelian system, freedom only exists as a concept within understanding. What the individual rejects then, for Weil, is not the grasp of freedom as a concept, but rather the fact that this concept can add anything to their life. For them, the concept of freedom doesn't live up to its promise. Understanding doesn't make their life better, or fill their boredom, or overcome their individual dissatisfaction. They do not want to think freedom, and they do not want to be free only to the extent that they live in thought or conform to thought; they want to live their freedom freely.

Weil's work cannot be understood separate from this conceptualization of violence. It is this conceptualization that sets him apart from his philosophical forbearers. But this conceptualization is always undertaken by somebody in the philosophical attitude, somebody who seeks to understand. This is because the violent individual rejects all categorization for themself. To say that the violent individual is moved by the things that characterize attitudes, having a certain type of orientation that expresses itself as goals, being driven by a certain feeling about the world, is always to categorize the attitude of the violent individual from the outside. This is not what the violent person does. The refusal of discourse and of coherence must be considered a pure attitude because it can be grasped coherently in discourse, even if it is not by the person who lives within it.

All philosophical categories have grasped violence in order to understand it. They do so by characterizing violence as instinct, as evil, as madness, as passion, etc. The novelty of Weil's interpretation is in the way that he characterizes violence in relation to reason. He hypothesizes a shared source. Weil claims, "violence, and violence felt violently as such, is at the origin of all discourse which claims to be coherent. It is violence which, age after age, provides itself with what it can negate in discourse and which, grasping itself as freedom in its discourse and, at the same time, against its discourse, produces philosophy" (LP, 75). Weil thus argues that philosophy and violence cannot be dissociated because both spring from a shared source in human spontaneity. Therefore, violence and understanding can be seen as two different, but very human ways of interacting with the world. Here lie the radical implications. There is violence because there is reason. The choice to understand is a free choice. It sets itself violently against the world by refusing and negating it,

---

[21] Canivez (2013a).

[22] Section C of the chapter *Reason* in the *Phenomenology of Spirit*, which Terry Pinkard renders as "Individuality, which, to itself, is real in and for itself" Hegel (2018).

by being dissatisfied with the way the world presents itself as the immediacy of human experience. It thus posits that there is nothing immediate about this experience, and it makes the free choice to understand the totality of its experience against this world. It is a free choice that makes itself necessary by erecting an explanation of the world that justifies its dissatisfaction. But this choice, made necessary because made, can itself be abandoned. This is evident in the claim that violence and reason are two ways of interacting with the world. One can be satisfied with incoherence just as easily as one can be dissatisfied by a form of coherence and look to transform it. This puts all the fragility of understanding on display.

Roughly speaking, Weil distinguishes four possible ways of characterizing our relationship to discourse *as such* and they correspond to the categories *of* philosophy. They are: (1) the individual's *identification* with discourse (which culminates with Hegel's philosophy, understood under the category of the *Absolute*); (2) the violent *refusal* of discourse, of the very principle of giving and asking for reasons (category of the *Work*); (3) a practice that consists in *destroying* (or deconstructing) the coherence of discourse from within discourse itself (category of the *Finite*); (4) the *realization* of discourse in the transformation of the world through discourse (category of *Action*). The last two categories of the logic of philosophy, *Meaning* and *Wisdom*, recapitulate the entire process and elucidate its meaning, while grounding a *practice* of philosophy whose meaning and whose rational and reasonable character the *Logic of Philosophy* aims to make explicit: the logic of philosophy is the grounding logic of a practice that must be constantly renewed according to the specificity of concrete current *changing* historical situations. In order to analyze these categories, however, we will have to consider the overall organization of the *Logic of Philosophy*. This will be the topic of the next chapter. For the moment, we must introduce another concept that plays a key role in Weil's conception of philosophy. This concept, which is one of the most important of the *Logic of Philosophy*, is that of the *reprise*.[23]

2.6 Reprises

In its simplest form, the reprise is the grasp of one attitude or category under another. Under this simple form, the reprise helps us to understand the movement of the logic of philosophy. New attitudes separate from established ones in action and not in discourse. They take shape thanks to the pragmatic refusal of the logical norms of the established discourse, but they are understood in discourse (within the framework of a new discourse). This means that they start to develop before they are grasped. Initially, they have no discourse of their own, and so they are grasped under the language of the established category. This is because the conceptual work of elaborating a discourse that can grasp what is irreducible about the attitude takes

---

[23] The journal *Cultura* has dedicated an entire issue to the question of the reprise (Bernardo 2013).

much time and great effort. This effort is what shows that older concepts are inadequate to grasp what is irreducible about the new attitude. The concepts thus undergo major changes in order to make this new attitude understood. In this way, individual concepts *and* whole attitudes can be reprised.

There are numerous examples that can be taken from this history of philosophy, but a simple one is to be found in the way that intelligent design reprises the category of the *Condition* under that of *God*. That is, intelligent design subsumes the causally determined nature present in the experimental sciences under the notion of a divine creator that puts this causally determined nature into movement. We can also see how this works in the other direction. Explanations of faith as a psychological or socio-cultural mechanism reprise the category of *God* under that of the *Condition*. The cornerstone of religious belief is made sense of by transforming it to fit into an impersonal causally determined nature. Reprises thus play a central role in the coherence of categories. They allow attitudes to capture different phenomena and to give them a place within their discourse.

Because reprises can operate in a variety of ways between different discourses, they give way to the distinction between *justificatory* reprises and *evaluative* reprises. The difference between these two reprises is directional, one from the inside of a position and the other from outside of it.[24] Justificatory reprises are used when a person leaves an established attitude and tries to explain their new attitude to people living within a different one. Justificatory reprises try to make themselves understood and also try to make their new position coherent to those who do not yet understand it. Justificatory reprises are those that the individual provides facing "the tribunal of their own thought" (LP, 366). This is different from evaluative reprises. Weil notes that evaluative reprises are always adjectival. They add an attribute in order to understand and evaluate the attitudes of others. A *scientific* explanation of biblical events frames them in a way that allows the category of the *Condition* to grasp them coherently; ergotism, for example, can be hypothesized to explain prophecies and visions without giving up on the factuality of biblical events. Each attitude uses the reprises that allow them to understand phenomena because "the reprise, to use a Kantian concept, is the *schema* which makes the category applicable to reality" (LP, 82). This also means that concrete attitudes contain multiple reprises that are justificatory, explanative, and evaluative. The most basic reprises hold both aspects: when it is an older attitude that seeks to understand a newer one, it reprises this new attitude under its own language in order to evaluate and understand it. When a new attitude reprises itself in the language of an older one, it does so in order to justify its position and to make it understood. The reprise, at the most basic level, allows the forms of coherence in the categories to be applied to the real concrete attitudes that individuals hold in the world. In addition, there are two "meta-discursive" uses. First, it allows the progression of discourse to be *grasped* as a new category pulls away from other older ones in order to express itself. Second, once the entire journey through the logic of philosophy is complete, it allows

---

[24] Canivez (2013a).

understanding the *use* of the categories in a philosophical practice that opens once all the categories have been grasped in the formal categories of *Meaning* and *Wisdom*. From this second point of view, *to philosophize* is to understand the real as it presents itself to be grasped in a situation. This modifies the notion of understanding. Under this second perspective understanding becomes grasping meaning. This is both why the category of *Meaning* is central to Weil's work and why it is formal. In its comprehensiveness, it grasps every concrete meaning and includes them within itself. The reprise is therefore one of Weil's most important conceptual innovations and it plays a major hermeneutical role. It not only allows us to understand how individuals apply their discourse to their lives, it also allows us to understand how other discourses hang together and how they organize and hierarchize their concepts, just as much as how we do so for our own.

2.7 Systematicity and Openness

The *Logic of Philosophy* is an exploration of the act of understanding that hopes to ground that very act. It reframes this act in relation to violence because Weil thinks that understanding can only be grounded in relation to its other, and he posits violence as that other. This exploration asks what violence is, how violence impacts the way one grasps the real, how that real is understood once grasped, and the role discourse plays in that grasp. In order to flesh out this ambition, its rereading of the history of philosophy becomes a meta-discourse bearing on philosophy, or more importantly, on the act of doing philosophy, on philosophizing. For Weil, philosophy is the attempt to grasp the world coherently and universally through discourse. Philosophy, in the Weilian sense, therefore largely outstrips any professional discipline or school. It is born and reborn anytime an individual wants to understand themselves coherently, anytime they want to understand what bears not only on them, but rather on all people. It is the choice to understand particularity through universality. Because this choice starts from the particularity that it abandons, it has as many starting points as individuals. Because it aims at universality, philosophy seeks to overcome this particularity. When universality conceptualizes particularity, it can be seen as particular, as violent, as arbitrary, as contingent. Weil however doubts that this particularity can be overcome. This is because the choice to be reasonable can only be understood after it has already been made. The choice, arbitrary and contingent when made, can only retrospectively be understood as necessary. This choice thus remains free. By characterizing the choice of understanding as a retrospective process, Weil follows Hegel in implying that philosophy is circular, and thus systematic. But by characterizing particularity and freedom in terms of violence, he breaks from Hegel. The individual who seeks to understand themselves and to grasp themselves in the reality of their world must posit an explanation, and it is only when they have succeeded in grasping themselves that this explanation is seen to hold. However this systematicity cannot be closed and completed. The choice to understand oneself and the world is a free choice and is thus a continual effort that

2.7 Systematicity and Openness

anyone can start or stop at any moment. It is an a-reasonable and unjustified choice that is made and that is always threatened by violence. The a-reasonable choice to choose reason or violence does not however necessarily imply non-violence. In certain cases it can even be the choice to legitimize the use of violence. In the case of the Second World War it is clear that purely discursive means would in no way resolve the conflict that Hitler had triggered with the invasion of Poland. The only feasible response to this aggression was to take up arms.

For Weil, discourse is systematic when it tries to explain everything according to a central concept, according to something that it sees as essential. All coherent discourse is systematic because the coherence is constructed in terms of how concepts fit together inferentially. But Weil also characterizes the refusal of discourse. This shows that the central concepts are not restricted to the inferential relationships inside of discourse, but can also define a specific relationship to discourse, which is pragmatic. Weil articulates this theory in relation to the refusal of discourse to situate it between the individual's two major possibilities: (1) the individual who grasps what is essential from its particularity in order to explain it to others and (2) the individual who refuses this grasp and refuses all explanation. According to this model, when individuals try to explain what is essential to them, they enter into public argumentative practices where this essential is put to the judgment of others. When they do not, public argumentative practices have no hold over them.

The problem of the contingency of a choice and its retrospective necessity puts Weil in a tricky position. When the essential is grasped and explained, that is, when it is put into discourse, it is seen as a motivation, as an orientation, as a desire, as an interest, etc. But before this happens, it is merely the turbid depths of our experience. People already know too much and, desperately, not enough. This not enough, this lack of understanding is only clear however to the individual who decides to understand. For the rest of us, we are born in a community and our goals are already oriented by this community without us realizing it. This is why we know too much, we do not independently and as fully rational agents decide what is essential to us. It is a consequence of being part of a group, of a *we*, and *we* know how to act and what to do according to the contours of *our* society, *our* class, *our* gender, whether *we* are only children or come from a household crawling with siblings, whether *we* are rich or poor, etc. However, as soon as an individual seeks to understand, they are confronted by the radical insufficiencies of their own experience. Our knowledge seems solid but stands on sandy shoals, ready to be swallowed up by the slightest shift. Weil acknowledges this difficulty from the very first chapter, which starts: "[t]he defect of every beginning in philosophy is being the beginning: the choice of starting point is neither justified nor justifiable, since nothing is established" (LP, 89). He is not the first philosopher to have brought this problem forward. As Gilbert Kirscher notes, as far back as Parmenides' invocation of the Goddess, philosophers have had to deal with the problem of justifying the starting point of their philosophical gesture.[25] Weil, following Fichte, claims that the choice of starting point has to be understood as an act and this act has to be understood as free, arbitrary, and incomprehensible. It is precisely the process that keeps looking back over its shoulder to this incomprehensible choice that transforms it into a necessity.

Because individuals are born members of a community, there is an ambient authority that ranges over all the members. But there is no perfect adequacy between life experiences, between interests and desires, and so the understanding of what is supposed to establish this authority must be chewed over again and again. It must continually be reformulated. Weil's notion of systematicity is therefore both open and evolving. Weil's systematicity posits that when an individual has a coherent discourse, they grasp their life as a unity that has a place in a community that fits into the world as a united whole. It emphasizes the continuity of humanity with the rest of existence. Its openness comes from the fact that new things can always enter into the discourse that defines the unity of a life found within a human community, and its evolution, from the fact that individuals can respond to this novelty from the viewpoint of their interests and desires. Its openness and evolution are found in the way that discourse transforms the human community in which individuals find themselves. It is a systematicity that tries to organize the diverse human attitudes that are found in the world in order to understand them, but an openness that understands this systematicity as a project that can be shook to its deepest foundations or completely destroyed precisely by the individual's choice to live outside of discourse.

For all their similarities, it is the movement to understand life outside of discourse that separates the Hegelian project from the Weilian one. This also shows how the relationship to systematic philosophy differs from Weil to Hegel. For Hegel, everything is understood because it is understood within the system. For Weil, this remains true, to the extent that the *Logic of Philosophy* remains a system. But it is a system of the philosophical shapes of meaning that are also shapes of freedom, that must be taken up again and again in order to grasp every new production of meaning. This production of meaning is not merely recapitulative and discourse is only ever absolutely coherent formally and never concretely. Weil notes in the transcription of a roundtable discussion following a conference called "Philosophie et realité" that:

> Even in his *Logic* Hegel is required to distinguish between *Wircklichkeit* and *Dasein*, and to declare that the concept cannot penetrate the outer husk. In fact, when he works on the concrete, I believe that he does not at all maintain the pretention of absolute knowing. Absolute knowing is a knowledge of the structure and not of the structured. The structured is inexhaustible. He calls it *schlechte Wirklichkeit*, but because he calls it *schlechte* it is nonetheless real. (PR.I.49–50).

---

[25] The whole first part of Gilbert Kirscher's book on the *Logic of Philosophy* deals with the problem of the beginning of philosophy, both from a historical point of view, starting from the types of beginnings that have been elaborated in western thought, and from a logical point of view, that is, by examining the aporia of beginning, in Kirscher (1989).

2.7 Systematicity and Openness

To further cite Weil's response, "[t]here is the idea of absolute knowing, but absolute knowing itself does not exist, that is, philosophy always remains philosophizing" (PR.I.49). The system, in order to understand itself, must also accept that it is possible to live outside the system *and* be content. This opens Weil's project, which is systematic, to a philosophical practice that overflows every system. It creates an openness to all discourse, to all attitudes, that struggles to understand (philosophically) how these different attitudes are irreducible. The categories thus provide, for the individual who seeks to understand, who wants to remain a philosopher, a hermeneutical tool to understand how individuals shut themselves into different determined discourses. It leads to a practice of philosophy because the individual recognizes at the end of the *Logic of Philosophy* that nobody can be a pure Platonic, or Aristotelian, or Kantian, or Hegelian philosopher. This is because the situation in which these philosophers articulated meaning, and in which they grasped the meaning of the world, has changed (the greatest philosophers are even the central motors of that change). In this way, it is always necessary to modify the philosophy one finds in Plato, in Aristotle, in Kant, in Hegel, or in any other philosophical work, to make it applicable to one's concrete situation. Weil's understanding of systematicity is defined by an openness to the novelty that the social and natural worlds provide. According to this systematicity, different discourses are so many ways of grasping each situation as it presents itself in reality. Because of the singularity of each concrete situation, the major concepts of any discourse will always need to be reprised, that is, grasped under a variety of angles in order for those concepts to be applicable to this situation itself. This is because, in each person's life, the responsibility of orienting one's life, or giving it meaning, of grasping the meaning that they find in the world, falls on their own shoulders. No philosopher or philosophy can provide this orientation. It is for each person to create, with or without the help of philosophy. Different philosophies can help them to realize this orientation, but it cannot give it to them fully-formed and whole.

The *Logic of Philosophy* is thus a book about human discourse that opens the door to a practice of philosophy which seeks to articulate the identity between human discourse and human situations. Because this identity itself can only be concrete in the concrete world of human interaction and human understanding, it must take into account the possibility of failure that accompanies the very idea of this identity. This failure, as we have said, is linked to the possibility of violence. It is not merely the external violence of the natural or social world, it is also the real possibility of the refusal of understanding. It is the violence that lives in all of us because it is always one of our possibilities. It is the concrete individual, it is you and me, that can fail to be up to snuff, that can pull away from reasonable discourse and become violent. The *Logic of Philosophy* thus characterizes and develops the free choice that the act of understanding makes in order to refuse the incoherence and the violence that human individuals find in the world, but it also develops the ever-present possibility of choosing violence. In doing so, Weil claims that three major concepts constitute philosophical discourse, *attitudes*, *categories*, and *reprises*. However, in order for this to be true, it must also be true of Weil's discourse as it is presented therein. We must understand the *Logic of Philosophy* as the work of the philosophical attitude of understanding that attempts to constitute its own category by reprising the history of philosophy, that is, the history of philosophical discourses in order to apply meaning to concrete situations by understanding different individual relationships to discourse.

We can now present an initial overview of Weil's substantive philosophical concepts. The logic of philosophy develops an analysis of human discourse and the way that human discourse structures our conceptual landscape. Within this work, Weil does this by distinguishing the following ideas:

- **Violence**. The concept of violence is the formal grasp of the particular recognized in its particularity. It is brought into discourse (that is, it is formalized) by subsuming it under the logical role of contradiction.
- The **essential** and the **inessential**. The essential is defined as what is central to an attitude and what discourse is organized around. The inessential is what an attitude puts aside, places on the periphery, or refuses outright in order for its discourse to be coherent.
- **Attitudes** and **categories**. Attitudes are the diversity of human ways of being in the world. Pure attitudes are those attitudes that can be grasped in coherent discourse. All pure attitudes are ideal-types. They are not encountered in the world, rather they are articulated using those aspects that can be organized coherently and grasped thanks to a central concept. The category is the coherent development of the pure attitudes *as* a discourse. Pure attitudes are thus transformed into philosophical categories and not metaphysical ones.
- **Metaphysical categories** and **philosophical categories**. Metaphysical categories are the transversal concepts that are used by science in order to grasp reality as an object *inside* of an attitude. In this way they are ground-level articulating concepts. Philosophical categories are the unity of a concrete situation and a lived experience grasped *in* discourse. They are thus framework-articulating concepts. Because of this difference, metaphysical categories depend on philosophical categories for their orientation.
- **Concrete categories** and **formal categories**. Concrete categories are the categories that have a corresponding attitude. In this way, they constitute the concrete discourses of concrete individuals as they grasp the world, their situation, and their life in discourse. Formal categories ground the act of grasping the world. All individuals participate in this act when they try to grasp the world or their life in discourse. The formal category of *Meaning* grounds the formal possibility of having a discourse that grasps a human situation. The formal category of *Wisdom* grounds the formal possibility of the unity of life and discourse in the presence of a concrete situation.
- **Reprises**. Reprises are the grasp of one category or attitude under a different category. This grasp allows Weil to explain the development of the logic of philosophy as well as explain how individuals grasp their concrete situation. The reprise not only helps individuals to justify their action in order to make it understandable to others, it also gives individuals the hermeneutical tools to evaluate and grasp the actions and attitudes of others.

Thanks to these ideas we are now in a position to understand the main commitments Weil himself makes. In the next chapter, I will look at some of the major organizational structures of the *Logic of Philosophy* in order to help the reader to better situate themselves. These different organizational structures will be important as I present the substantive arguments of this work, and as I show what Weil's philosophical project can contribute to contemporary philosophy.

References

Aristophanes. 1996. *Wasps,* vol. 4. Trans. A. Sommerstein. Warminster: Aris & Phillips LTD.
Bernardo, L.M. ed. 2013. A retomada na filosofia. *Cultura: Revista de História e Teoria Das Ideias, 31*(II).
Bizeul, Y., ed. 2006. *Gewalt, Moral und Politik bei Eric Weil*. Hamburg: Lit Verlag.
Brandom, R. 2019. *A spirit of trust*. Cambridge, MA: Harvard University Press.
Burgio, A. 1990. Du discours à la violence: Avec Hegel, après Hegel. In *Discours, violence et langage: Un socractisme d'Éric Weil*, ed. P. Canivez and P.-J. Labarrière, 69–95. Paris: Éditions Osiris.
Caillois, R. 1953. Attitudes et catégories selon Éric Weil. *Revue de Métaphysique et de Morale 58* (3): 273–291.
Canivez, P. 1993. *Le politique et sa logique dans l'œuvre d'Éric Weil*. Paris: Éditions Kimé.
———. 1998. *Éric Weil ou la question du sens*. Paris: Ellipses.
———. 1999. *Weil*. Paris: Les Belles Lettres.
———. 2002. Le droit naturel chez Éric Weil. *Actes de l'Association Roumaine Des Chercheurs Francophones En Sciences Humaines 3*: 49–56.
———. 2013a. La notion de reprise et ses applications. *Cultura: Revista de História e Teoria Das Ideias 31* (II): 15–29.
Canivez, P., and P.-J. Labarrière, eds. 1990. *Discours, violence et langage: Un socratisme d'Éric Weil*. Paris: Éditions Osiris.
Gaitsch, P. 2014. *Eric Weils Logik der Philosophie: Eine phänomenologische Relektüre*. Freiburg: Verlag Karl Alber.
Ganty, É. 1997. *Penser la modernité*. Namur: Presses Universitaires de Namur.
Guibal, F. 2003. La condition historique du sens selon Éric Weil. *Revue Philosophique de Louvain 101* (4): 610–639.
———. 2009. *Le courage de la raison: La philosophie pratique d'Éric Weil*. Paris: Éditions du Félin.
———. 2011. *Le sens de la réalité: Logique et existence selon Éric Weil*. Paris: Éditions du Félin.
Hegel, G.W.F. 2018. *Phenomenology of spirit*. Trans. T. Pinkard. Cambridge, UK: Cambridge University Press.
Jarczyk, G., and P.-J. Labarrière. 1996. *De Kojève à Hegel: 150 ans de pensée hégélienne en France*. Paris: Albin Michel.
Juszezak, J. 1977. *L'anthropologie de Hegel à travers la pensée moderne*. Paris: Éditions Anthropos.
Kant, I. 1998. *Religion within the boundaries of mere reason and other writings*. Trans. A. Wood and G. Di Giovanni. Cambridge, UK: Cambridge University Press.
Kirscher, G. 1970. Absolu et sens dans la "Logique de la philosophie". *Archives de Philosophie 33* (3): 373–400.
———. 1989. *La philosophie d'Éric Weil*. Paris: Presses Universitaires de France.
———. 1992. *Figures de la violence et de la modernité*. Villeneuve-d'Ascq: Presses Universitaires de Lille.

———. 1999. *Éric Weil ou La raison de la philosophie*. Villeneuve-d'Ascq: Presses Universitaires du Septentrion.
Kluback, W. 1987. *Eric Weil: A fresh look at philosophy*. Lanham: University Press of America.
Livet, P. 1984. Après la fin de l'histoire. In *Actualité d'Éric Weil*, 83–91. Paris: Editions Beauchesne.
Marcelo, G. 2013. Paul Ricœur et Eric Weil. Histoire, vérité et conflit des interprétations. *Cultura. Revista de História e Teoria das Ideias 31*: 247–266. https://doi.org/10.4000/cultura.1881.
Perine, M. 1982. *Philosophie et violence: Sens et intention de la philosophie d'Éric Weil*. Trans. J.-M. Buée. Paris: Beauchesne.
———. 1987. *Filosofia e violencia. Sintese 49*: 55–64.
Plato. 1997a. *Gorgias* ed. J.M. Cooper; Trans. D.J. Zeyl. Indianapolis: Hackett Publishing Company.
———. 1997b. *Protagoras*, ed. J.M. Cooper; Trans. K. Bell and S. Lombardo. Indianapolis: Hackett Publishing Company.
Ricœur, P. 1984. De l'absolu à la sagesse par l'action. In *Actualité d'Éric Weil*, ed. C.É. Weil. Paris: Beauchesne.
Rockmore, T. 1984. Remarques sur Hegel vu par Weil. In *Actualité d'Éric Weil*, 361–368. Paris: Beauchesne.
Roth, M. 1988. *Knowing and history: Appropriations of Hegel in twentieth-century France*. Ithaca Cornell University Press.
Roy, J. 1975. Philosophie et violence chez Éric Weil. *Dialogue 14* (3): 502–512.
Savadogo, M. 2003. *Éric Weil et l'achèvement de la philosophie dans l'action*. Namur: Presses Universitaires de Namur.
Shepherd, W. 2019. *Persian war in Herodotus and other ancient voices*. Oxford: Osprey Publishing.
Strummiello, G. 2001. *Il logos violato: La violenza nella filosofia*. Bari: Edizioni Dedalo.
———. 2013. Ripresa, a priori storico, sistemi di pensiero. *Cultura: Revista de História e Teoria Das Ideias 31*: 195–212.
Taylor, C. 1989. *The sources of self*. Cambridge, MA: Harvard University Press.
Weil, E. 1950. *Logique de la philosophie*. Paris: Librairie Philosophique Vrin.
———. 1956. *Philosophie politique*. Paris: Librairie Philosophique Vrin.
———. 1970. *Problèmes kantiens*. 2nd ed. Paris: Librairie Philosophique Vrin.
———. 2003a. *Philosophie et réalité: Tome 1*. Paris: Beauchesne.
———. 2003b. *Philosophie et réalité: Tome 2, Inédits suivis de Le cas Heidegger*. Paris: Beauchesne.

Chapter 3
Logic as the Organization of Forms of Coherence

3.1 Introduction

In the last chapter, I claimed that the recognition of different forms of coherence present in human discourse leads Eric Weil not to any single overarching metaphysical principle, but rather to the possibility of a type of philosophical practice. Philosophy becomes one human possibility among others; the main other being the possibility of refusing all coherence and all understanding. This falls in line with the "anthropological" readings of the *Logic of Philosophy* proposed by Mahamadé Savadogo[1] and Francis Guibal.[2] Savadogo's reading sees philosophy as "the tale of human realizations" and sees the logic as "the forms of humanity's expression,"[3] whereas Guibal's sees philosophy as human self-understanding and self-realization in an "anthropo-logy within the whole of reality."[4] This helps us to understand what Weil means when he says that:

> *first philosophy* is not a theory of Being but the development of *logos*, of discourse, for itself and by itself, in the reality of human existence, an existence that is understood in its realizations, insofar as it *wants* to be understood. It is not ontology, it is logic, not of Being, but of concrete human discourse, of the discourses that form discourse in its unity (LP, 69).

According to such readings, the refusal of coherence and understanding is a free choice, just as understanding philosophically (coherently and totally) is. For this reason, the philosophical choice is what Weil calls an "absolute principle" (LP, 61). This description brings out the three concepts that will guide this chapter: coherence, totality, and ground. Together these three concepts help develop the notion of

---

[1] Savadogo (2003).
[2] Guibal (2011, 2015).
[3] Savadogo (2003), 78.
[4] Guibal (2015), 137.

comprehensiveness that Weil puts into place in order to understand the different shapes that discourse takes. Weil's position is the result of the historical development of these concepts and he organizes his own discourse in order to articulate the free choice to understand coherently and totally as what grounds philosophy. The individual who makes this choice and who chooses to understand philosophically does so by refusing incoherence and violence. Once they refuse incoherence, they posit a starting point—which can be anything, a first principle, a method, a certain metaphysical reality—and then they try to organize their discourse coherently around it. Together, refusing violence and positing some starting point constitute the opening philosophical gesture. The suite of categories is the history of the individuals (the philosophers) who have succeeded in elaborating discourses that allow a specific form of coherence to be grasped and understood from their starting points, from their fundamental concepts. Because they have succeeded, not only have they extracted a form of coherence that allows them to grasp the world and their experience, they have also articulated a form of coherence that can be used by others in their own grasp of the world. Philosophy is a possibility and an absolute principle for the individual who refuses to accept that the world is meaningless and that meaning is ungraspable. This refusal is the exercise of freedom that characterizes every coherent discourse.

The refusal that posits meaning is central to understanding the logic of philosophy. This is because the logic of philosophy, in being the organization of these different discourses, is not a logic in the terms that we are normally familiar with. Is it the study of the rules of thought? Yes, but it proposes multiple systems of thought that each see these rules differently. Is it the study of valid inference? Yes, but only in so far as valid inference allows us to distinguish between different forms of discourse. Is it the study of arguments? Yes, but first and foremost to show that argument is born of a choice that itself is not logical. Weil notes that the logic of philosophy is:

> not logic in the sense of non-contradiction, because it deals with contradictory, and self-contradicting, solutions; it is not a logic of science, because the logic of philosophy sees science as merely being one human possibility (sees it perhaps as not even being the first possibility, supposing that a first possibility is possible); it is the *logos of eternal discourse in its historicity* that has understood itself and that is understood as the human possibility that has chosen itself, but that is also aware of having chosen itself and aware that it would not be, were it capable of being necessary (LP, 77).

Weil thus presents the logic of philosophy as the organization of the different grasps of concrete forms of coherence that have *actually* held together in history. These grasps present themselves as coherent discourse. Different forms of coherence can be contradictory between themselves (and are), but they also build off each other and respond to each other.

Coherence is built in opposition, in the opposition to incoherence, to the nonchalance of partial coherence, to other forms of coherence that it doesn't accept. As it develops into different discourses, there are problems that appear and disappear; there are concepts that come to guide coherence and those that become errant. This is why concepts like being, freedom, truth, etc. have had long and varying fortunes.

3.1 Introduction

The logic of philosophy, as the organization of different philosophical discourses into a suite of categories according to their coherence and universality, helps us to understand these varying fortunes. Each category, by being the presentation of a form of coherence, is the articulation of a free choice to organize the act of understanding according to a central concept. Taken as autonomous free-standing forms of coherence, the categories are limited to the types of inferences that their central organizing concept allows or forbids. But, taken as a systematic whole, they are essential moments in the development of *all* forms of coherence. In other words, they are false on their own, but true as moments of the logic of philosophy. The different categories, with their different forms of coherence, and the different scopes of universality that each form proposes, highlight the role that orders of explanation plays in the logic of philosophy.

Different starting points and different orders of explanation provide different forms of coherence. In fact, if we look at Weil's three driving concepts (attitudes, categories, and reprises) according to the idea of orders of explanation we can better understand why Weil's project has the shape it does. He starts from attitudes because he wants to understand the human activity of individuals embedded in their lives. However, he highlights how objective understanding is always discursive, and thus he shows how attitudes can only make claims of objectivity *when* they are grasped thanks to discourse. As already noted, this difference between attitude and category is the difference between the production of meaning in language and action versus the organization of meaning in discourse. What separates language from discourse is that discourse, starting from its central concept, takes on an order of explanation that allows it to make a claim of coherence and universality. Each category *qua* shape of discourse does this. It is the reprise that allows us to grasp how these different shapes of coherence use the same concepts. Based on the type of order of explanation that they put into place, different concepts will be reprised in different ways.

Eric Weil uses a variety of means to explain and understand the role and place of violence in our conceptual apparatus: the difference between attitudes and categories, between types of categories, between language and discourse, as well as human spontaneity, reprises, orientation, etc. For Weil, this violence goes all the way down. Even if it is discernable from the act of understanding, it remains inseparable from it. By noting that the choice to understand is built in opposition, we recognize this violence. The choice to understand is the refusal and modification of different forms of coherence that *have* held together, that not only already propose understanding, but that also already form the understanding of the individual who refuses and modifies them. In other words, opposition does not happen in a vacuum, rather, the choice to understand implies the rejection and refusal of specific forms of coherence that are found in discourse.

The move from one form of coherence to another is a free jump, it is a leap where one tries to pull free from the constraints that hold them back while trying to build a stable landing out of these same constraints as they fall. It is a rupture, because in landing, these old constraints are used to climb higher in understanding. This rupture happens between each category, between each form of coherence, but Eric Weil also tries to understand how these different forms of coherence fit together. In this chapter, I will present the forms of coherence that Weil uses in the logic of philosophy and explain how they fit together. This presentation will not be exhaustive, rather it will be the minimum necessary to orient the arguments that I will develop in the rest of this work.[5] This work focuses on specific aspects of Eric Weil's arguments so it can in no way replace the study of the *Logic of Philosophy*. Nonetheless, with the objective of grasping specific arguments, I will draw out certain organizational and conceptual features that will help us to better understand the *Logic of Philosophy*.

3.2 Organizational Strategies of the *Logic of Philosophy*

There are multiple overlapping organizational possibilities in the logic of philosophy. This is normal: multiple historical and logical developments interlock in different ways and Weil tries to take them into account. This multiplicity also highlights why Weil thinks that all of the categories are necessary, and why every conceptual grasp deploys all the categories. To explain different things, different orders of explanation are needed and these different orders reduce the totality of meaning so as to bring out certain salient features. If this were not the case, the different organization features that Weil and his commentators deploy would be a confusing mess. Since Weil's insists on multiple points of view however, the different organizational strategies form part of a reasonable plurality if they are seen as participating in a grasp of meaning that requires the plurality of the different forms of coherence. With this in mind, we can look at the different organizational features that are present in the *Logic of Philosophy*. The most immediate and simplest division is between the different categories. Each category corresponds to a single chapter in the book. They are:

> *Truth, Meaninglessness, The True and the False, Certainty, The Discussion, The Object, The Self, God, Condition, Consciousness, Intelligence, Personality, The Absolute, The Work, The Finite, Action, Meaning, Wisdom.*

The next simple division is between concrete categories and formal categories, which breaks the work up as follows:

Concrete Categories

> *Truth, Meaninglessness, The True and the False, Certainty, The Discussion, The Object, The Self, God, Condition, Consciousness, Intelligence, Personality, The Absolute, The Work, The Finite, Action.*

Formal Categories

> *Meaning, Wisdom.*

---

[5] For full analyses of the suite of categories, see Kluback (1987); Kirscher (1989); Canivez (1999); Savadogo (2003); Guibal (2011).

This division separates the categories that have concrete attitudes from those that have no attitude but that explain the *possibility* of concrete attitudes, thus allowing a retrospective understanding of the logic of philosophy. When looking at the difference between concrete categories and formal categories, it is noteworthy that the content of the attitude and of the concrete category is not different. In fact, the category is nothing other than the irreducible features of a specific attitude given as a discursive shape. Labeling them (as Weil himself does on numerous occasions) attitude/categories instead of separating the two would therefore perhaps be more appropriate. This is because the development of the attitude (and therefore the understanding of the category) is the grasp of this development in all the particular aspects that make up the limited totality of its determined content.

The next division that Weil makes is between philosophical categories and the categories *of* philosophy. This division is useful but also problematic because it positions *The Absolute* as the first category *of* philosophy. Weil does not tell us whether the categories of philosophy are also philosophical categories, nor whether the formal categories are part of the categories *of* philosophy or not. Nonetheless, this division is useful because the categories *of* philosophy are the first to explicitly play a framework-explicating role; they characterize what philosophical discourse does, and not just its content. If we keep the division such as it is described by Weil, this division is as follows:

Philosophical Categories

> *Truth, Meaninglessness, The True and the False, Certainty, The Discussion, The Object, The Self, God, Condition, Consciousness, Intelligence, Personality.*

Categories of Philosophy

> *The Absolute, The Work, The Finite, Action, Meaning, Wisdom.*

This division is further complicated however because there is an ambiguity between the initial categories and the other philosophical categories. Weil claims that philosophy starts with *The Object*, that is, it starts in the development of classic ontology as exemplified by Plato and Aristotle. If this is the case, what is the status of the categories preceding *The Object*? Weil repeatedly calls the first categories "primitive" because when all is said and done, they remain pre-philosophical. Thus, are the "primitive" categories philosophical categories or not? He speaks of philosophical categories in *Certainty*, which is the last "primitive" category, so therefore it would seem that the primitive categories are philosophical to the extent that Weil sees them as necessary for the development of philosophy, but they are primitive because, strictly speaking, they do not themselves provide any philosophical reflection.

If the philosophical categories are those required for philosophical reflection, all the categories are philosophical categories but there are different subsets. However, if we follow this line of thought, *The Discussion* poses a problem. It is clearly not a "primitive" category. It is however pre-philosophical, since it precedes philosophy's own self-understanding—for Weil, philosophy only starts to understand itself *as* philosophy with *The Object*. Instead, *The Discussion* is political. It is the first category where the questions of rights and laws are explicitly posed. This political character is exemplified by the formal dialogical practices developed by Socrates. The dialogical practices that are put into place by this attitude/category do not aim at understanding reality in its totality; they aim at the agreement of different individuals inside of a political community. However, it is also clear that Socratic dialogical practices lay the groundwork for the categories that follow. We can therefore not say that it is primitive. According to this line of thought, the different subsets of philosophical categories can be divided as:

Primitive Philosophical Categories

Truth, Meaninglessness, The True and the False, Certainty.

Simple Philosophical Categories

The Discussion, The Object, The Self, God, Condition, Consciousness, Intelligence, Personality.

Categories of Philosophy

The Absolute, The Work, The Finite, Action.

Formal Philosophical Categories

Meaning, Wisdom.

Nonetheless, this organization is also complicated by the relationship between *Action* and the two formal categories, *Meaning* and *Wisdom*. Eric Weil develops the categories as the shapes human discourses on meaning have taken in history, however because he thinks that each new concrete shape provides something that an older one did not, the older shape is in this sense surpassed. Weil claims that *Action* is the last concrete category. This is because *Action* is the most fully realizable human attitude. It is the attitude of the individual who leaves the reflection on discourse and on reality to act on the same discourse and reality that presents itself in discourse *through discursive means*. It is the action that aims at the collective action of individuals to realize a world where discourse is real and effective. It thus is a return to a political attitude, but one that surpasses philosophy. It is the articulation of a philosophical attitude that gives itself the task of educating humankind. This leads Gilbert Kirscher, for instance, to claim that *Action*, *Meaning*, and *Wisdom* hold Weil's own philosophical attitude and, as such, this tryptic holds a place apart in the *Logic of Philosophy*.[6]

Does this however mean that we should divide the categories according to Weil's philosophical attitude? Does this mean that we are thus forced to recognize that Weil has fully explained the possibility of philosophy? Is that too bold of a claim? Maybe. It has been noted that Weil develops a philosophy of meaning and that this

---

[6] Kirscher (1992), 49–59.

philosophy "claims to be the last systematic discourse, of understanding, of understanding oneself and of making oneself understood."[7] However this claim has yet to be shown, and only history can show it. Again, within Weil's own discourse, there are a multitude of organizational strategies. And again, this is normal. Weil thinks that grasping meaning requires multiplying point of view and trying to bring this multitude together in a coherent and comprehensive unity. This also explains why different commentators have highlighted different articulations. Multiple commentators emphasize the way that Weil develops different logical moments from the Socratic dialectic to Hegelian conceptual logic (LP, 22–53) and then compare it to Weil's development of the contradiction between reason and violence (or truth and freedom, the grounds of this opposition).[8] This division can be presented as:

Prelogical Categories (in the sense of non-contradiction)

Truth, Meaninglessness, The True and the False, Certainty.

The Logic of Formal Dialogical Practices

The Discussion.

The Logic of Classic Ontology

The Object, The Self, God, Condition.

Transcendental Logic

Consciousness, Intelligence, Personality.

Hegelian Dialectical Logic

The Absolute.

The Logic of Reason and Violence (The opposition of truth and freedom)

The Work, The Finite, Action, Meaning, Wisdom.

This division is useful and is one Weil makes, however two categories, *Intelligence* and *Personality* seem difficult to situate. Are *Intelligence* (the category exemplified by Michel de Montaigne and Pierre Bayle) and *Personality* (exemplified by Friedrich Nietzsche) to be understood according to transcendental logic's opposition between nature and freedom as it is developed in *Consciousness* and as it is exemplified by Kant and Fichte? Placing them after *Consciousness* would lead us to say yes, because they reflect on freedom within a conditioned nature even though it is unclear whether Montaigne, Bayle, or Nietzsche would recognize themselves under these categories. In fact, for Michel de Montaigne and Pierre Bayle, it would be impossible to reflect on their discourse in terms of Kant's transcendental logic, precisely because they wrote before Kant. However, this highlights why Weil insists that attitudes "take precedence *in history*" (LP, 79) even though the logical order is

---

[7] Venditti (1984), 104.
[8] Kirscher (1992); Canivez (1993); Ganty (1997).

dependent on the categories. *Intelligence* reflects on something that *Consciousness* was the first to grasp coherently even though Montaigne and Bayle wrote before Kant.

The categories following the initial "primitive" categories have undergone different divisions. Gilbert Kirscher separates them according to Weil's distinction of the degrees of reflection that they allow (LP, 341–344), where Weil asks what categories grasp and how they grasp it.[9] Do they grasp the world? Yes or no? Do they grasp it partially or totally? Do they grasp the world *and* themselves? Yes or no? Do they grasp this unity partially or totally? A yes or no response to these questions distinguishes the degree of reflection each category has, from the simple pre-reflexive categories such as *The Discussion, The Object*, and *The Self*, which don't fully grasp the problems that the distinction between the subject and the object create, all the way to the categories of absolute reflection in *The Personality* and *The Absolute*, which seek to unite the subject and the object in a single discourse. Francis Guibal keeps this division but additionally insists on the relationship between the categories of Antiquity and of Modernity.[10] According to Guibal's division, the categories of Antiquity from *The Discussion* to *The Self* are grounded in reason, whereas those of Modernity, from *God* onwards are grounded in freedom. Weil however insists that *God*, as the junction of Greek and Judeo-Christian thought (ENHP, 15), straddles both. It is what he calls "the turning point of philosophical becoming, the most modern of the categories of antiquity, the most antiquated modern one" (LP, 188). How should it be understood then? Which division to use?

The problematic position of the category of *God* allows us to bring out another conceptual distinction that Weil makes and that Guibal highlights.[11] This is the distinction between the different "*sols*" of discourse. In using the term *sol*, Weil plays off the polysemy of a term in French that could alternately be translated as *floor, ground, soil*, or *earth*, but here it will be translated as "floor." The reason that floor is the translation used is to bring out certain conceptual distinctions while also restricting the term *fond* for use exclusively as a "ground," in the sense of what grounds reflection and thought, or what grounds justification. Additionally, floor also allows us to exploit the notion of a multi-story vertical structure where each floor is solid but not foundational. In this way, *The Discussion* is the floor of the categories of Antiquity, and the *Condition*, not *God*, is the floor of Modernity. Weil notes that:

> in each category, ordinary existence is recognized, under the title of unconscious life, life of the people, the mass, particularity, etc...., that the *condition*, as an attitude, is seen throughout as the soil [*sol*] out of which the new attitude blossoms, just as the new category grasps itself in the opposition to the one that immediately precedes it." (LP, 395).

Thus, the categories of *The Discussion* and *The Condition* highlight that the floors of discourse are defined by a type of social organization and a type of language. The

---

[9] Kirscher (1989).
[10] Guibal (2011).
[11] Guibal (2011), 121.

categories that follow *The Discussion*, the same as the categories that follow *The Condition*, are developed on and react to their discursive floor.

The notion of *sol* illustrates that there is something solid that supports later discourses. While it is true that every category builds off previous ones, we can exploit the architectural metaphor of a floor here and note that there are certain floors in buildings like landings or atriums that divide the building between what is below and what is above, and that the things above and below are understandable in relation to these specific floors. The discursive floors that I will speak of are thus important because the following categories interpret and understand themselves in relation to these floors. If we accept this, then the category of *Truth* can be seen as the ground of all discourse, because all discourse is articulated in relation to the truth that it proposes. The category of *Certainty* is understood in relation to truth, but it adds something new. It is the concrete discourse of any speaking and acting individual *before* they enter into the game of justifying and understanding, of giving and asking for reasons. It is the floor of tradition, of the normative structures that we unconsciously appropriate by being the member of a concrete community in a concrete situation. Because of this, every category is first lived as an attitude that reprises *Certainty*. *Certainty* can in this way be seen as the floor of any pre-reflexive, pre-philosophical understanding of the world, because all pre-philosophical attitudes are grasped according to the certainty that they provide to the individual. This distinction will become clearer in what follows; for the moment it is enough to highlight it. Following this notion, *The Discussion* is the floor of simple reason which has a critical reflection on the tradition, but is not itself reflexive. This is different from the reflexive total reflection on the world that takes shape in *The Condition* where the world is seen as a totality of conditions. The notion of discursive floors allows us to better understand why Kirscher insists on the degrees of reflection, and why Guibal and Kirscher analyze the *Logic of Philosophy* along the lines of what they call simple reason, which constitutes the categories of Antiquity, and freedom, which constitutes the categories of Modernity.[12] This allows the following articulation:

The Ground of Discourse

Truth.

Categories Interpreted in Relation to this Ground

Meaninglessness, The True and the False.

The Floor of the Tradition (The pre-reflexive understanding of all discourse from within an attitude)

Certainty.

The Floor of Antiquity

The Discussion.

---

[12] Kirscher (1989), 243; Guibal (2011), 80.

Categories Interpreted in Relation to this Floor

The Object, The Self.

Transitional Category Between Antiquity and Modernity

God.

The Floor of Modernity

The Condition.

Categories Interpreted in Relation to this Floor

Consciousness, Intelligence, Personality, The Absolute, The Work, The Finite, Action, Meaning, Wisdom.

The multiple divisions highlighted here are all present in the *Logic of Philosophy*. Their presence reinforces the reason that Weil thinks that a plurality of points of view is necessary in order to understand philosophically. What is clear in all of these divisions is that there are certain key junctions in the *Logic of Philosophy*. The key junctions that I will present are those that allow us to understand the *Logic of Philosophy* as a development of discursive resources, as a development of the resources that the categories add to coherent discourse. This approach is not new; most authors have in some way or another tried to bring these resources out and some authors have even done so explicitly.[13]

The division presented here will articulate the suite of categories according to the development of discursive resources. Thus, the primitive categories become the categories that present and develop the preconditions of argumentative coherent discourse. The simple philosophical categories are modified to be seen as the genesis and development of coherent discourse. By presenting the categories along the lines of the development of coherent discourse, *The Absolute*, which is seen as the completion of coherent discourse, falls into this grouping. The categories *of* philosophy that follow *The Absolute*—namely, *The Work, The Finite, Action*—multiply the points of view of coherent discourse and are thus understood as characterizing the individual's relationship to discourse itself. This is a major change from the other forms of organization because it allows Weil's difference from Hegel to become clearer. Furthermore, in this division, the formal philosophical categories are understood as formal, not only because they have no concrete attitude, but also because what they add to coherent discourse is the characterization and development of its possibility. This thus gives us the following organization:

The Background of Argumentative Discourse

Truth, Meaninglessness, The True and the False, Certainty.

---

[13] Quillien (1982); Kirscher (1989); Canivez (1999); Guibal (2011, 2012).

The Genesis and Development of Coherent Discourse

The Discussion, The Object, The Self, God, Condition, Consciousness, Intelligence, Personality, The Absolute.

Relationships to Coherent Discourse

The Work, The Finite, Action.

Reflection on the Formal Possibility of Coherent Discourse

Meaning, Wisdom.

Following this organizational strategy (while occasionally deploying the others) will allow us to avoid presenting a full commentary of the *Logic of Philosophy* (which, as I have said, has been done elsewhere) in order to focus on several key concepts that are present in the work. These concepts (ground, coherence, totality) are to be seen as the development of the different discursive floors. This chapter will therefore merely present certain articulations that allow these concepts to become clearer. First, it will present the initial categories from *Truth* to *Certainty*, which cover the preconditions of argumentative discourse. Next, it will present *Certainty, The Discussion,* and *The Object*, which will allow us to explore the transition between a prelogical understanding and the first two logical forms: formal dialogical practices and ontological logic. This will also allow us to present the discursive floor of reason and better define the categories of Antiquity. The next articulation that is presented is between *God, The Condition,* and *Consciousness*. This will allow us to explain the discursive floor of Modernity in freedom, the reflection on the totality of nature, and allow us to investigate the transition between ontological logic and transcendental logic. Afterwards, we will present the rupture between *The Absolute* and *Work*, which will allow us to see the transition between Hegelian logic and the logic of reason and violence, as well as the transition from the categories that develop coherent discourse and the categories that develop the relationship to discourse. Finally, we will examine the tryptic *Action, Meaning, Wisdom* which is the heart of Weil's own position.

3.3 The Background of Discourse

I have said that the reflection on orders of explanation is central to the *Logic of Philosophy*. This is clear as soon as Weil presents the first category, *Truth*. Weil posits that every philosophical starting point is a free act, unjustified and unjustifiable before the end. So, what do we learn at the end of the *Logic of Philosophy*? What justifies this starting point? We learn that Weil is seeking to understand the different shapes that coherent discourse has taken throughout its history in order to understand the free choice between violence and coherent discourse. The first category is curious because in it, Weil less explains the attitude and more reflects on the difficulty of starting. He thus chooses a starting point, notes that we should remain suspicious of it, but also notes that thought has to start somewhere. This starting point is that "[p]hilosophy is the search for truth and only the search for truth" (LP, 89). He then goes on to add that "the judgment 'Truth is everything' cannot be part of the doctrine; it is part of the explanation. The doctrine can only start with the single word *truth*. In other words, *any* judgment about truth is absurd" (LP, 90). This is important because it gives a key to unpacking his starting point.

The concepts of *doctrine* and *explanation* are, as Gilbert Kirscher shows, essential to understanding the *Logic of Philosophy* and are central concepts within the distinction that Eric Weil makes between attitudes and categories.[14] The doctrine is what is lived in the attitude. It is the meaning that the individual finds and creates. It is the center from which the individual thinks. It is what is implicit in the simple non-reflexive thinking and acting of the individual living in the world and grasping this world's meaning. Because this thinking and acting is non-reflexive and simple, it does not grasp itself (it will later, but here it is incapable of doing so). It remains invisible until another attitude that is different but that can also be grasped appears. The appearance of this difference is what leads to the explanation of the attitude. The explanation is thus the explicit content of the attitude; it is the reflexive grasp of what the attitude thinks and what the content of the attitude *means*. This allows us to reframe the reprise in terms of the doctrine and the explanation, in terms of the implicit and the explicit. The reprise is what permits a content to be made explicit. As soon as one starts to do so, by reprising the older language under a new attitude, the older attitude is changed into a category. This explains why, for Weil, "*reflection* precedes the *doctrine*. But the reflection only *is* within the doctrine, which is first" (LP, 92). The category is the starting point of *philosophical* understanding, but it is itself always mediated by discourse. Thus, for the "reflection of discourse actually started," saying that *Truth* "is a category of discourse is saying that it appears in its transcendental function (as the ground of discourse)." This is why "discourse is essentially reflexive and is only realized starting from the reflection on the fact of discourse."[15] Thus, to mobilize the concepts that I said would guide this reading, *Truth* is the ground of all discourse but it is not the ground of philosophy understood philosophically. This is because, in *Truth*, the questions of coherence and totality have not yet been asked. Whatever coherence there is, is lost in the totality of the pre-reflexive life lived as a total unity.

The discursive grasp of the attitude of *Truth* can only start from a single word, and in a way, the logic of philosophy is a development of the inferential unfolding of this single word. This is because the attitude of *Truth*, as a unity of the individual and the world, is silent and the grasp of the pure attitude in discourse cannot develop anything that has not yet been developed. There is no judgment because every predicate involves restricting truth's domain. There is no certainty because certainty involves the notion of subjectivity. In fact, not only is truth a silent attitude, it is unrecognizable to the person who lives in it because there is, as of yet, no contrast. This is why—for us, here and now—the reprise of truth is the background of our

---

[14] Kirscher (1989), 162–166.
[15] Kirscher (1989), 165.

3.3 The Background of Discourse

own attitudes. We don't recognize it because it is too "natural." It is only insofar as we each live embedded in the world and in the attitude of *Truth* that the world is taken to be factual, that it is the domain of facts. It nonetheless remains a reprise because we can only understand it thanks to notions such as *facts, attitudes, world,* etc. None of which is present in this first attitude.

The attitude of *Truth* is silent and yet Weil presents Parmenides in order to help the reader understand the category. This seems to be a contradiction. Parmenides spoke, he wrote, his poem has passed down through the generations. However, what Weil notes is that it is not Parmenides' teaching, nor his poem that is our guide, but rather it is the recognition of how he lived, as the mouthpiece of the Goddess, that allows us to understand the attitude of *Truth*. The content of the pure attitude grasped in discourse is a single word. This is why, in the presentation of the category, Weil does not elaborate any content, but rather gives a description of the difficulties and dead-ends that lie in wait for any reflection on the attitude. He warns that these difficulties are born from the fact that we come to this primordial category with all the conceptual determinations of our own modern attitudes, and that these are precisely the things we have to watch out for as we develop the category of *Truth*.

Because Weil hopes to avoid the difficulties of other philosophical projects, it is instructive to look at another starting point to see how it is different from Weil's. As already noted, Weil's project bears great similarities to Hegel's. We can thus look at two different starting points that Hegel uses to contrast them with Weil.[16] In the *Phenomenology of Spirit*, Hegel starts his presentation with an explanation of *Sense-certainty*, that is, he starts from the description of what he sees as the most primitive attitude of the knowing consciousness. In the *Science of Logic*, he claims that philosophy must start from "*being*, and nothing else, without further determination and filling."[17] In terms of starting points, Weil's *Logic* bears similarity to both Hegel's *Phenomenology* and to his *Logic*. In the first, Hegel is trying to show the *experience* of consciousness as it evolves from a purely subjective point of view into a socially articulated understanding where the individual recognizes their place in the whole thanks to that experience. In the second, he is trying to show the *nature* of thought as the development of the concept. Weil's project shares some aspects of both of these goals. In fact, we can say that *Truth* as an attitude can be compared with the attitude of *Sense-certainty* in the *Phenomenology,* whereas *Truth* as a category can be compared to *Being* in the *Logic*. Weil, like Hegel, is trying to say something both about the experience and the nature of his object, but his object is not the thought understood metaphysically. In a way, it is discourse understood empirically, that is, as a concrete and manipulable phenomenon. He is not looking to give the most basic shape of consciousness, but the most basic grasp of the world in discourse. This

---

[16] For a complementary but different reading of Hegel's place in the initial categories, see Renaud (2013).

[17] Hegel (2015), 47–48/GW 21.55–56. Throughout this work references to Hegel will provide the page number from the English translation used and then to *G.W.F. Hegel: Gesammelte Werke*, Deutsche Forschungsgemeinschaft (Hamburg: Meiner, 1968–), cited as *GW* followed by the volume and page number.

difference, added to the fact that for Hegel, Being leads to becoming, and thus to a type of immanence that Weil is seeking to avoid, helps to explain the difference between their starting points.

Weil circumnavigates the metaphysical question of Being and starts, like Hegel in the *Phenomenology*, from a human attitude. The difference here is that it is not the attitude of *Sense-certainty*, but rather the attitude of the individual that lives their experience in the world as *Truth*. This is because, *discursively*, in order to understand the problems of *Sense-certainty* we must already have a concept of truth in place, we must already make a distinction between what is true and what is false. The problem, in both cases, is that this philosophical starting point remains *discursive* and so Weil sees Hegel as not adequately investigating the conditions of discursivity. I mentioned in the last chapter how Weil's system goes beyond Hegel's because of the way that Weil seeks to understand the non-philosophical attitude. Here, at the beginning of his own *Logic*, Weil already distinguishes himself from Hegel. For Weil, it is the loss of meaning that opens the search for understanding, and not the confusion of sense-certainty that reveals its insufficiencies, as it is in the *Phenomenology*, nor the mediations of *Nothingness*, like in the beginning of Hegel's *Logic*. Weil thus posits that there is a more fundamental attitude than that of sense-certainty, that there is a unity more profound. Nonetheless, in positing a unity more fundamental than certainty, Weil also claims that when the individual tries to grasp it, they can only do so obliquely. It becomes fugitive as soon as discursive concepts are introduced. This is why Weil starts from a single word as well as why he makes a distinction between language and discourse. Language certainly did not start from a single word. Rather it seems that all the resources that we have in language had to be in place for language to be language. However, discourse, the coherent grasp of the world, starts somewhere else. This also explains why the early categories develop the preconditions of coherent discourse. These early categories are all *reconstructed* and make up part of all coherent discourse that follows.

This discursive starting point differentiates Weil from Hegel. Hegel's system, either as the experience of consciousness or as the nature of thought, depends on metaphysical and ontological claims that allow the system to be built but not interpreted. Any interpretation of the system, any *discursive* explanation of the system, keeps in place the deep divide between what thought or consciousness *is* and how we know it, how we defend that position, how we articulate it for others. In other words, the interpretation "falls outside the system" (LP, 340). Weil starts from a discursive position in order to defend a discursive position and thus starts from a single word as the whole of the discursive grasp, and goes through the work of unfolding how this discursive starting point holds up.

If the first category is understood as a discursive grasp of the individual as embedded in their world and living this world as a unity, then the attitude is one that knows no separation between the individual and their world. *Meaninglessness*, the next category, is the grasp of the individual separated from their world. *Meaninglessness*, like *Truth*, is silent. It refuses the meaning that is offered in *Truth* as a refusal of the meaning that is present in the world. But, because it is silent, it highlights that no one *has* to speak to refuse something that is given in experience.

3.3 The Background of Discourse

An animal strikes out when cornered or cajoled, an infant turns their head to refuse to eat. *Meaninglessness* holds our proto-discursive capacities to make ourselves understood and to understand through our refusal. However, this attitude is also the dissolution of the unity that is found in *Truth*. It is the attitude of dissolution in general, and when it is reprised, it is the attitude of every individual who can't see meaning around them, who lives their life as meaningless. Weil explains the difference between *Truth* and *Meaninglessness* by saying that "truth can be called the domain and whatever fills this domain and reveals the domain's existence to us is meaninglessness. Truth could be explained as the 'yes' and meaninglessness as the 'no.'" (LP, 95). This attitude characterizes individuals who refuse what had up to then been essential. *Truth* and *Meaninglessness* are both silent attitudes that are lived, but they can also both be seen as the *logical* and *pragmatic* grounds of all other discursive developments. If the categorial content of *Truth* cannot be more expansive than a single word, the same goes for the categorial content of *Meaninglessness*. The difference is the one's word is an affirmation and the other's, a negation. *Meaninglessness* is therefore the pragmatic gesture that refuses all meaning, but that does so without finding any new meaning. It is the attitude of the lost, of the adrift, and it needs a new concept if it is to re-anchor individuals to their lives.

Under *Meaninglessness*, the capacity to refuse the essential can itself be seen as what is essential to the attitude. This transformation allows *Meaninglessness* to be seen as meaningful. In other words, *Meaninglessness* can be reprised under *Truth*. The pair *Truth/Meaninglessness* are pragmatically essential in that they are *reprised* every time a new attitude opposes itself to an existing category. The existing category expresses a truth. This is the world in which a new attitude appears: the truth that the older category expresses is seen to be meaningless; it is a truth that leaves the individual unsatisfied. When this happens the truth changes. The *truth* of *Meaninglessness* is that everything is meaningless. The reprise alters the attitude. In the attitude of *Meaninglessness*, life has no meaning, it is empty of all sense, it is without direction. When individuals live in this attitude, whether they be violent or docile, they are stuck in the mire of their lives. This distinction allows us to shed light both on Weil's starting point and on the function of the reprise.

The transition from the unity of meaning in *Truth* to the lack of all meaning in *Meaninglessness* is violent, and there is no way of identifying all the specific ways that this can happen. In fact, the slide towards meaninglessness is possible at any moment, but the reprise of *Meaninglessness* under *Truth* helps to understand how the free act of understanding is also itself a violent act (which means, arbitrary and unjustified). When somebody refuses *Truth* they raise themself up against a determined meaning, but when they refuse *Meaninglessness*, they raise themself up against the lack of meaning in the world. They choose to understand, and in doing so they seek the meaning of meaninglessness, the *truth* of the *meaninglessness* that surrounds them. They seek to understand this meaninglessness, to give a positive content to the feeling of meaninglessness that inhabits their life. In this way, meaninglessness *becomes* a feeling that gives meaning, a feeling that, in turn, leads the individual to develop their own discourse, whose truth satisfies them. In doing so, they live meaninglessness as truth, and transform its content in order to understand it. The attitude of *Truth*, the unity of meaning and life, the embeddedness of an individual in their world, is what Weil calls presence. It is being outside of time because always in the present of one's life. In *Meaninglessness*, this presence is lost. For it to be found anew, the emptiness of *Meaninglessness* has to be interpreted as *Truth*. In this way, the individual understands and overcomes that feeling of meaningless: they give meaning to that emptiness. The presence that was lived in truth is now seen as being naïve because it doesn't satisfy the individual. It allowed the world to become meaningless, but this meaninglessness revealed the truth that underlies both of these positions, the truth that everything is meaningless. This reprise allows us to understand the pair *Truth/Meaninglessness* as the framework of the logical movement of the logic of philosophy. Each attitude is lived in truth and develops a discourse, each discourse brings out structural commitments and incompatibilities that can lead to a feeling of meaninglessness. The feeling of meaninglessness gropes around for meaning and in doing so lays the groundwork for a new attitude, which uses the old language to make itself understood through a reprise.

As attitudes, as ways of being in the world, both *Truth* and *Meaninglessness* are irrefutable. This is because *all* attitudes are irrefutable, but they can both be *refused*.[18] Any person can refuse any attitude and any category and can live in their refusal of all determined meaning, just as they can live in modern experimental science, just as they can live in their belief in any of the numerous representations of God or of the gods, just as they can live in the abnegation of their feelings and desires. As long as these positions remain attitudes, that is, as long as the people who live according to them do not seek to make them coherent or ignore the possibility of comparison, these positions are irrefutable and incommensurable. However, the philosophical attitude, as the refusal of incoherence and violence, is also always possible. The act of understanding transforms an attitude into a category and the categories can be refuted if the individual is seeking to understand coherently and totally. Categories, because they aim to grasp what is essential to an attitude in conceptual form, make claims of coherence and universality. They are thus subject to evaluative judgments and to argumentative practices that allow comparison and contrast, that allow refutation and validation. It is the attitude of *Meaninglessness* that allows the category of *Truth* to be taken as a category, as conceptual in a full-blooded sense. Weil notes, "[i]t is through the reprise that the attitude becomes category" (LP, 99). In its opposition with the category of *Truth*, the attitude of *Meaninglessness* allows *Truth* to be grasped. *Meaninglessness* allows *Truth's* essential concept to become visible, by reprising its attitude under *Truth*. *Truth* is the individual's silent affirmation of the world as an individual in the world, at one with the world, *Meaninglessness,* the pragmatic negation of any judgment that is asserted when the previously silent affirmation speaks. *Meaninglessness* understands that truth cannot be said because

---

[18] Weil makes the forceful distinction between refutation and refusal in the article "Les fondements de la philosophie," where he says that "philosophy has no absolute foundation, if by foundation one understands something that cannot be *refused*. Philosophy is only something that cannot be *refuted*" (PR.II.21–22).

3.3 The Background of Discourse

every utterance is particular and that truth, as the background of all meaning, is total. Every particular utterance is absurd. As Patrice Canivez notes, "the oldest form of [philosophical discourse] is the proposition that states the meaninglessness of every particular statement as such, of every determined statement that would claim to contain *the* truth, that is, to make an absolute of a particular thing."[19] *Truth* lives within its attitude's silence and *Meaninglessness* negates every particular utterance. Returning to the distinction between the doctrine and the explanation, between the attitude and the category, *Meaninglessness* is what allows this explanation to take place, it is what will allow the passage from a single word, *truth*, to propositions such as *this is not truth*, and *that is not truth*.

This difference becomes clearer in the category of *The True and the False*. The first two attitudes are silent. When we live our lives as a unity, we have no need to say anything, and when we face the dissolution of all meaning, the idea of saying anything is pointless. Their categorial analysis exists for us, for those who have chosen to speak and to understand. The category of *The True and the False* is the first logical *appearance* of discourse, in other words it is the first attitude where language is what is essential. *Truth* and *Meaninglessness* can (and do) use language, but language is not essential to these categories, what is essential is the lived feeling of unity or the lived feeling of meaninglessness. Weil's characterization of the use of language in the first two categories is instructive. For Weil, these attitudes do not discuss, they do not speak, they proclaim. They bequeath their word and their refusal. All refutation, all correction, all justification would be mysterious to them. In this way, both attitudes produce meaning, but it is as of yet free of the logical constraints *we* rely on. The classical rules of thought—the laws of contradiction, of the excluded middle, of identity—have no weight in these early attitudes. The category of *The True and the False* is the first where discourse is a necessity, and it is also here that the affirmation found in *Truth* and the negation found in *Meaninglessness* are subsumed under the rules of language and given logical roles. However, these logical roles are not yet those that we would recognize. Further logical developments are needed.

Truth is only grasped thanks to the development of its negation in *Meaninglessness*. This negation is itself transformed thanks to the reprise of *Truth* as meaninglessness and the reprise of *Meaninglessness* under *Truth*, where the truth is that everything is meaningless. *The True and the False* builds off these changes in order to sift through what is truly true and what is truly false. For Weil "[t]he true illustration of the two initial categories would have been what Parmenides and Buddha lived, not what they pronounced" (LP, 102). This is because language and discourse are not yet important to them. This is why *The True and the False* is the category "of the disciple who has become the master" (LP, 106). As Weil notes, even Parmenides, "Plato's dialogue master [...] sees himself as a disciple" (LP, 102) and this is the start of what can be called *serious conversation* where individuals "no longer speak 'lightly'" (LP, 103). For Weil, the disciple is "the human being who has pronounced

---

[19] Canivez (1999), 26.

and heard words and discourses, who did not know that the acts of pronouncing and listening were important, and who now hears *serious* discourse from the masters" (LP, 103). The individual who hears the discourse of a master who speaks from *Truth* becomes a disciple and uses discourse to give the *true* interpretation of the doctrine, and to rule out any *false* interpretation. This new category thus uses language to sort what is essential from what is inessential to discourse. However, because the person in this attitude does not see themselves as the mouthpiece of *Truth*, they recognize a separation between themselves and discourse. All they can do is promulgate or interpret what the master has revealed. Their own attitude is not a life lived as a meaningful unity, nor the concrete rejection of all particularity, it is the mixture of universality and particularity. This also allows us to reinterpret the first two categories. Discourse opens in the universality of *Truth* and then faces the particularity of *Meaninglessness*.

Weil starts from the attitude of *Truth* in order to develop the silent categories of *Truth* and *Meaninglessness*. These categories give way to the "primitive" category of *The True and the False*, where language and discourse first appear. By setting up this progression, the hope is to explain the logical possibility of reflective understanding, which itself is only communicated and developed in the activity of discourse. In the attitude of *The True and the False* the disciple speaks, but not as the master did. Language, which always says too much and never enough, needs to be interpreted, needs to be reformulated and corrected, and the disciple who takes on the mantle of the master does just that. Those who come after Parmenides are not mouthpieces of the Goddess, rather, they are interpreters of Parmenides, who was. This transition however already takes us further than *The True and The False* into the category of *Certainty*.

Certainty, as Weil notes, is the first "understandable" attitude (LP, 108). It is the attitude that characterizes all attitudes. Every attitude exists within the certainty of its content. No matter the discursive content, the attitude of the person within it, when they hold it sincerely, is that of certainty. *Certainty* thus allows us to understand why Weil characterizes the logic of philosophy as the historical development of discourse for itself. The three previous categories—like all categories—are all defined by their relationship to *Truth*. *Certainty* however is the first attitude of concrete truth. It is in *Certainty* that subjectivity is first developed, that the world is seen as such, as a world, as an organized whole (in the Greek sense of a *kosmos*). However, subjectivity and the world are both invisible to this ancient shape of certainty precisely because objectivity has not yet been developed. As Weil notes,

> certainty is essentially limited. It is what it is. To speak reflection's language, certainty is a for-itself that is not opposed to any in-itself, and we must carefully eliminate every in-itself (= for us) that is found on the side of content. In this way, certainty is the origin of subjectivity, the origin, but not subjectivity itself. Subjectivity does not exist without certainty, but certainty is insufficient for creating subjectivity. This is because this *pre-subjectivity* does not recognize objectivity as its opposite. But, from the viewpoint of later categories—which ours inevitably is—it can be said that certainty is, in itself, subjectivity. This is because, for us, the plurality of certainties is given and any certainty that is not total (which means, that is not our own) is, for us, only a particular opinion. Taking content into account, we distin-

3.3 The Background of Discourse

guish (and, by the same token, categorially identify) certainties that, for themselves, are completely separate and unrelated. (LP, 111–112).

It is thanks to this subjectivity that the notion of what is essential to a discourse comes to light. However, because the person living in naïve non-philosophical certainty does not see subjectivity and objectivity as inhabiting their discourse, they see subjectivity as nothing more than the false discourses that are held with certainty by others. For them, the others have just not yet seen what is essential to the world. An essential is what allows individuals to be certain about their discourse, and this certainty allows them to choose, decide, judge, act. *Certainty* is thus inextricably linked to the notions of commitment and orientation. It is when an individual is certain of what is essential to their discourse that they take a stance, that they can commit to something that allows them to orient themself in this world. This notion of orientation is of capital importance and it will return later as a central element of the argumentative character of Weil's theory that will be developed. Here, what we can note is the way that certainty is present in every attitude. Every category is of course present in every attitude, even if only as a refusal, however, certainty is present in a specific way. All concrete lived attitudes are lived under a reprise of certainty, no matter what other reprises they participate in, and no matter how these reprises are organized.

Truth is the background of all discourse, but in fact, because *Certainty* is the first attitude that we understand head-on and not just obliquely, all of the initial attitudes from *Truth* to *Certainty* can be seen as background attitudes that develop the preconditions of reasonable discourse. This now allows us to go back to Hegel's starting point in the *Phenomenology*. I said Weil's use of attitudes in his starting point is analogous to Hegel's starting point. However, there is also a very important difference. *Sense-certainty* is what Hegel sees as the most fundamental shape of consciousness, and indeed from the point of view of the modern consciousness it is, but this is because *Certainty* is the first attitude that uses a language we understand. It is not however the first position that can be reconstructed. Hegel's modern consciousness depends on distinctions such as subject/object, true/false, and these developments are only present once *Certainty* is, because certainty is intimately linked to its other, doubt. There is no doubt in the first attitudes. The person living in *Truth* really has a unity in their life, the person living in *Meaninglessness* really is unable to find any meaning to which to moor themselves, the person in *The True and the False* really is trying to excise the inessential in order to make the true clear and available to everyone. Anyone who speaks depends on all these tools to speak coherently. But it is precisely the recognition of the difference of their certainty from the certainty of others that forces them to examine their position. When *we* examine our position, it is the awareness that somebody can so blithely live in what we see as incoherent, as false, or even as a delusion that forces us to turn to ourselves and wonder whether our own position is justified, or if we are one of the blithe fools.

Any content can be lived in *truth* or as *meaningless*. *Every* attitude distinguishes between what is *true* and what is *false*, and *every* attitude is lived in the *certainty* of its content. As the background of discourse, they are present in every category as the logic of philosophy moves forward. This is important for two reasons, first is that it shows how, for Weil, multiple points of view are required from the beginning in order to make sense of conceptual content, and second because it shows the way that *Certainty*, by being the first truly recognizable attitude *in history*, bundles together all of these attitudes in order to form what Hegel would call the naïve consciousness. In the last chapter, I discussed how Weil places an emphasis on the way that the categories *of* philosophy multiply points of view. What the initial categories show is that this multiplication of points of view is present as soon as we can make ourselves explicitly understood. Yes, the attitudes of *Truth*, of *Meaninglessness*, of *The True and the False* exist, and we can recognize them, but we also interpret them from our point of view. This difference shows the importance of dialogical practices. We recognize these initial categories because we can live them, but we interpret them because they appear to us in the attitudes of others. Some aspect of our experience is always beyond all critique, because it is not even visible to us, it is what goes without saying. Some aspect of our experience is always denied out of hand as meaningless, in fact, it is so meaningless that we cannot even take it seriously as an option. We are always sifting through some aspect of our experience in order to decide what is factual and what is meaningless, and when we decide, we are certain about our decision, but we are just as certain as every other individual, even those who make choices, or who live in attitudes, that we see as not making sense or as being meaningless. We are only aware of these differences because we are embedded in a social context in which these differences become clear. We interpret the naïve form of consciousness under the category of *Certainty* because *Certainty* is the first attitude that brings out difference. It is the first category that has to recognize others and their positions. It is the first category where we can see what others add to our conceptual practices and because of this see ourselves. Weil thus interprets *Certainty* as the first attitude where discursive content matters to the category itself. However, this discourse is still pre-philosophical. The separation between the individual and their discourse has not yet taken place, *Certainty* is the content in which the individual *lives*, which is why it is not questioned, it is not yet a content that the individual *has*.

3.4 The Genesis of and Development of Coherent Discourse

The rupture with *Certainty* marks the genesis of coherent discourse. It is the jump from the prelogical categories that merely develop the background of discourse to the formal dialogical practices of *The Discussion* that are exemplified by Socrates and that are present in the Greek city-states. It is also the jump from the earlier attitudes reprised as *Certainty* and the pre-philosophical, pre-political tradition found in *Certainty* to reasonable discursive practices. This is because, historically, the movement towards truly political organization (organized around the questions of rights) and towards our own everyday pre-philosophical attitude both depend on

3.4 The Genesis of and Development of Coherent Discourse

reasonable discursive practices.[20] These practices, whether in their historical or modern form, present a new discursive floor, that of simple reason. Simple reason is born in *Discussion* and is developed in *The Object* and *The Self*. It is "the speech that is measured and justified in discussion, that elevates the individual to the universal and proves to be the decisive acting speech of the community on the subject of its good," which from a purely philosophical point of view means that "language/reason is all of reality and reality is established in its right, is justified."[21] This reason both logically and historically first appears in the public discourse of the community because it is available to everyone and is something in which everyone partakes. It is thus a reason that was invisible to the "primitive" categories, which were not bothered by the question of whether individuals have equal rights as participating members of the same community. In other words, the public discourse of *Discussion* marks the transition to reason, but a reason that sees itself as the only real and *knowable* thing. *Discussion* is born out of the failed traditional community of *Certainty*, a community that needs to be regrounded on reasonable principles because all the members of the community see themselves as legitimate potential heirs to the community's tradition, but also because they disagree about how the community should be governed. Unless the members of the community are ready to engage in open and potentially violent conflict, they discuss. Because it is seeking to reground the political community through discourse, *Discussion* is also radically aware of its own contingency, of its own fallibility, of its own precarious hold on its claims, and it is this awareness that gives rise to the specifically political attitude that Socrates exemplifies and that marks its difference with *Certainty*.

As a pure attitude, *Certainty* is the first category where human orientation and what is essential to discourse become visible as such. Because it is where the essential becomes visible, it is also the first place where the specific refusal of specific discourses are seen conceptually as forms of violence. As a category, it regroups all the other background categories under its own banner, and thus provides the initial interpretation of otherness. *Truth* and *Meaninglessness* are silent in their pure shapes, because their pure expression is lived. *The True and the False* is a speaking category, because language is essential to it, but this language has not yet been formulated in discourse. *Certainty* is also a speaking category, but one that marks the transition to discourse. Its content is central to it, but its discourse is not yet governed by the logical rules that will become essential. The same thing can be contradictory. It can be both true and untrue. It can both be and not be. All the forms of understanding that we, from our modern point of view, call magic and mythology fall outside of the classic laws of thought, and yet this poses no problem of efficacy to their practitioners, and in fact, it does not appear at the level of language and discourse, it appears at an ontological level. Everything is and is not.

---

[20] This is not to say that the political interpretation of *Certainty* does not exist. It does, and the communities that live in *Certainty* are both recognizable as political communities and are interpreted as such *by us*. What the distinction pre-political/political means here is that *Certainty* does not interpret itself that way. Rather *The Discussion* is the first category that is *essentially* political.

[21] Kirscher (1989), 245.

This ontological interpretation of discursive contradiction exists between all forms of certain discourse, but for the category of *Certainty* the existence of multiple discourses poses a different problem. Its certainty is the whole world, thus there can be no multiplicity of certain discourses, there are only enemies to eliminate. The attitude of *Certainty* has neither critical distance from itself, nor from the content of its discourse, which means that any difference has more often than not been historically dealt with through violence. The discourse of *Certainty* is the discourse of a worldview, of a community, of a tradition, and often, it sees its very existence as depending on the falsity of other discourses. The initial attitudes still exist insomuch as anyone can live their life embedded in a meaningful unity, can refuse any proposed unity as meaningless, can consciously grasp the essential of their life and separate out the inessential. But it is as a foreign certainty that different attitudes present themselves for the first time as truly foreign, and it is under *Certainty* that we grasp the earliest human civilizations in their political and social organization. These other civilizations seem so radically different from our own that, although we can marvel at their ingenuity, their military prowess, their technological sophistication, their way of life nonetheless seems impossible. This is not a question of the past either. Yes, innumerable civilizations have risen and fallen under the banner of their gods and their beliefs. Yes, innumerable ways of life have maintained that they depend on the destruction of another, foreign, heretical way of life, because this false way poses an existential threat. But this is certainty understood as a historic or social problem. What is important about Weil's articulation of *Certainty* and the jump to *The Discussion* is that it allows us to formulate a philosophical problem that will be the one that will be tackled head on at the end of this work in Chap. 8. This problem deals with the role certainty plays in argumentative practices and in the relationship between absolutism, relativism, and skepticism. The following formulation is not Weil's but is rather an important takeaway from reading Weil the way I do.

The problem is formulated as follows: an absolute discourse is absolute precisely because it either absorbs all others or it successfully refutes all others. *Certainty* lives in the absolute validity of its position. This is why the failure of certainty leads to either relativism or skepticism. Absolutism, relativism, and skepticism all depend on an incommensurability of discourse. *Either* only one discourse exists and all others are false, *or* many exist, but none can be judged and measured because they cannot be compared. When they can't be judged and compared, either all are accepted and seen as relatively true, or all are refused as being absolutely false, and the possibility of meaning itself is also refused. Absolutism, relativism, and skepticism are thus all structurally linked. In other words, relativism and skepticism are the nihilism of failed absolutism. They accept the material existence of other discourses, but differ in their reaction to them. Relativism refuses to give up on its own absolute and thus accepts all absolutes. Each discourse is built from a relatively true and incommunicable absolute. Skepticism gives up on its own absolute, but it thinks that because its own absolute has proven false, there can be nothing to replace it. Relativism and skepticism are born when the individual accepts the reality of multiple discourses, but refuse to compare them. They refuse because comparison

3.4 The Genesis of and Development of Coherent Discourse

forces individuals to submit their own discourse to the critical analysis that would potentially change it. When individuals refuse the incoherence and pessimism that go along with relativism and skepticism they enter into discussion.

This reading is different from (but not incompatible with) Weil's because it takes on the point of view of the (modern) individual. For Weil, the jump from *Certainty* to *Discussion* is just as radical but it takes place when different socio-cultural discursive *communities* are brought together into a new community. The loss of certainty is the consequence of one or more communities being subjugated to a foreign master. It is not individuals that recognize the multiplicity of discourse, it is the whole community that loses the right and the access to the discourse that had previously governed it. For Weil, individuals were forced to accept this new discourse precisely because the old discourse had become empty of values and had lost its force because of the domination of a foreign master. From our modern point of view, when faced with new possible and convincing discourses, if individuals do not want to remain in their naïve certainty they must submit their own discourse to modification. This happens because these individuals refuse to slip into meaninglessness. In other words, they make the choice to understand philosophically. From the historical point of view, we can see the forceful subjugation under a new discourse as making up part of the violent history of non-violence. The loss of certainty and the birth of discussion, which Weil situates as a consequence of the Greco-Persian wars, was a violent fact, but it did not wipe out the particularity of the already developing Greek thought, rather it transformed it. Under these historical conditions "simple *otherness*, their incommensurable and contactless existence, is changed into *difference* within a *common existence*: *the* content no longer exists, *many* contents do, and since multiple contents exist and since none of them can prove itself, no certain content exists." (LP, 122).

This passage introduces *dialogical controls*.[22] Dialogical controls are the discursive criteria that are developed by taking others to be genuine dialogue partners. They are what allow people to critically judge the contents of their discourse. Or, more correctly, what allows them to critically judge the contents of their discourse against that of others. The community is important here because dialogical controls are always socially articulated. The most basic dialogical control that Weil presents is the law of non-contradiction. Because different certain discourses present ontological contradictions, dialogue is the only way to eliminate them if one wants to refuse violence. This dialogical control allows for the first logical development that, for Weil, opens the possibility of identifying discourse with philosophy. In *Certainty*, violence is seen as a legitimate way of dealing with difference; individuals must

---

[22] The term "dialogical control" is borrowed from Harald Wohlrapp's *The Concept of Argument* (2014). The argumentative theory that I claim is present in the *Logic of Philosophy* has great affinity with the pragmatist theory of argumentation that Wohlrapp develops in that book. This is not surprising since Wohlrapp, in grounding what he calls "the Aristotelean foundation of Argumentation Theory," explicitly follows Weil's reading of Aristotle for certain key conceptual distinctions, notably the "relationship between the syllogistic and the dialectic," in Wohlrapp (2014), xxiii, n. 13.

either be converted to the true path or be eliminated as a threat. The authority of a discourse can be imposed or reinforced thanks to violence. In *Discussion*, no authority asserted through violence can be seen as valid. As soon as dialogical controls are in place, dialogue partners have to be seen as equals, and all authority must be established through discourse.

Weil notes that "certainty's content is not, necessarily, logical" (LP, 115). It does not rely on the law of non-contradiction to determine its content. Rather, it is the confrontation with other positions that are equally sure of where they stand in the world, and which are unable to simply be ignored or destroyed, that leads to a full development of the logical tools such as the law of non-contradiction. The importance of the transition from *Certainty* to *Discussion* cannot be overstated. Given that Weil presents the philosophical project as the choice, a choice to be reasonable, a choice to resolve substantial differences discursively and not violently, reprises of the jump from *Certainty* to *Discussion* are capital to reasonable discourse. In fact, because certainty is built into every attitude, it is a choice that individuals must constantly make. It is never a choice that is made once and for all. Each person can always come face to face with the limits of their concepts, and they can over and over again in their life. Most even do. This can happen facing a world that is changing because of new ways of articulating class, or race, or gender roles. This can happen facing new technology or new world views. This can happen when our friends and family change around us. As the world changes, we are pushed to resist it or change with it. Because of this, it is rare to experience no change and growth in the way we see the world. When we change, this change and growth are a consequence of being embedded in a world with other concept users who not only also present and defend the goodness of their claims, but with whom we refuse violent interaction, and who we see as adding something to our lives and to our understanding of the world.

Discussion is the category that gives birth to formal (though not formalized) logic, both as it applies to metaphysical categories, and as a novel step that allows for the development of the philosophical categories. Weil notes that "[l]ogic, in dialogue, prunes discourse," (LP, 24) and contradiction is central to revealing the differences that allow dialogue to take off. For Weil, the logic of philosophical categories is different from the logic of metaphysical categories. There is the difference that we have already mentioned, where the philosophical categories are framework explicating and metaphysical categories are the actual application of ground-level discursive content. There is also a logical difference. The logic of philosophical categories is understood in relation to violence, whereas the logic of metaphysical categories is not. The four types of logic that Weil highlights in order to establish his own logic shows this. Each of these logics brings violence into language by subsuming it under the role of contradiction, but none recognizes that it is doing so, because none recognizes its own philosophical category. If any did recognize its philosophical category, it would also be forced to recognize its discourse as being a particular point of view. This is why *Certainty* is not logical in the same way that the philosophical categories are. The differences that contradiction reveals still lead to violence. *Discussion* puts this violence at arm's length. In *The Discussion*,

3.4 The Genesis of and Development of Coherent Discourse

contradiction reveals, to the members of the community, that agreement has not yet been reached, and this is why a *law* of non-contradiction must be elaborated. This is not to say that the notions of contradiction and non-contradiction were never deployed before the development of this category. Rather, it means that non-contradiction is defined for the first time as the essential character of an attitude. In this way, non-contradiction and coherence become essential to discursive practices themselves for the first time.

From a modern point of view, once the individual has entered into discussion, belief gives way to reasons. This is one of the consequences of *Discussion*. It is no longer enough to assert something, rather it is necessary to have reasons for asserting it. This fact shows the distance that separates us from the pure attitude. For us (that is, in order to develop the guiding concepts of this presentation), we must establish the authority for our reasons and we do this by grounding them. The pure attitude of *Discussion* however does not yet see the need to ground reasons and so, showing formal contradiction in what an opponent holds is sufficient. This is why the dialogical practices of Socrates do more to reveal the instability of our beliefs than to assure their solidity, and this is why it is not yet properly speaking philosophical but political: it seeks the agreement of the community. In *Discussion* the stability that is to structure dialogue is merely formal and not yet substantive. It sees the need for grounding but has no solution. This attitude thus reveals the conflict in our discourse but it does nothing to resolve it. It proposes coherence and a form of totality that is the accordance with reason but that is all. This is still a monumental step forward.

The groundwork of the philosophical attitude as a free choice to understand is laid in *Discussion* (even though it is born in *The Object*) in the political discussion that seeks to re-ground the unity of the community by eliminating the contradictions that are tearing it apart. These are contradictions between traditional values and different diverse individual interests. These contradictions must be eliminated for the true values and interests of the community to have a hold on everyone. This constitutes a break with the earlier categories. The earlier categories are reconstitutions of the logical moments that make up the "primitive" attitudes that are lived and not discussed. *Discussion* refuses the naïve attitude of certainty, and thus opens all philosophical problems. Skepticism and relativism, for instance, as philosophical problems, are born within the destruction of the community (even though they also use other categories, *The Self* reprised under *Meaninglessness* for skepticism, and the *Intelligence* for relativism). This does not however mean that they were not present before, rather it means that their importance was limited. Here their role is seen as central and productive. Indeed, skepticism and relativism, as doubt and difference, are always present, and play a productive role every time someone moves from determined certainty to the discussion that follows. This productive role is thus present every time an individual leaves their certainty to place conflictual positions in relation and to see which hold up.

The presence of different discourses that can neither be eliminated nor ignored can be transformed into philosophical understanding because these differences provide a moment that relativizes one's own discourse. This relativization is essential to seeing one's own discourse as modifiable. If one's discourse is not seen as modifiable, the individual sees no reason to leave their certainty. Other discourses never even become visible as a possibility. When a discourse is seen as modifiable, it opens up a type of doubt that turns towards one's own discourse. This doubt undermines the previous certainty that the discourse had held. Together, doubt and difference open the individual up to the possibility of another way of life, to other beliefs, to other concrete positions. This type of relativism and skepticism is present in the reprise of the earlier categories under *Discussion*. For *Discussion*, when the individual in *Truth* recognizes doubt and difference, they are ripped out of *Truth* and thrown into *Meaninglessness*. In *Meaninglessness* they see doubt and difference as proof that everything *is* meaningless. Should they recognize the possibility of a discourse that can reestablish meaning, they convert to this discourse and become the master's acolyte, taking this new discourse on whole. In *The True and the False*, they thus separate doubt and difference out as what is inessential to their discourse in order to reach *Certainty*. In *Certainty* this doubt and difference is not only seen as inessential, but also as incommensurable. It is the external discourse of their enemies, enemies that must be converted to the true and certain discourse. When violent means are refused or impossible, the means of conversion changes and so do doubt and difference. In *Discussion*, where individuals see themselves as equals, all conversion must happen through *discursive* means. When individuals are seen as equals, doubt and difference are productive because each party is seen as adding something to the discovery of truth. Nonetheless, the category immediately shows its limits. Non-contradiction is a formal criterion and, as such, the resolution of contradiction is at most a formal agreement between dialogue partners. The whole of discourse must be made coherent for this agreement to hold, which means that discussion goes on forever.

Discussion thus stirs a need for grounding in philosophical discourse, but it does not provide it. It is *The Object*, the category that opens philosophical understanding, that provides the first ground, and so that moves logic to classic ontology, to the contradiction between reason and nature that is exemplified by the contemplative science of Plato and Aristotle. Each permutation of the philosophical attitude from *The Object* up to *The Absolute* is the same in that they seek something to ground discourse, but they differ in the way they choose to ground it. *Discussion* provides discourse with the concept of a totally coherent discourse but it does not present a ground. This problem presents itself in the indeterminacy of many of the early Platonic dialogues. Various definitions and positions are presented and tested in these dialogues, only for the most part to be rejected, shelved, or left completely open. The Good, the Just, the Beautiful are bushes we beat around without scaring out any game. A ground is needed, but what kind? *The Object, The Self, God, Condition, Intelligence, Personality,* and *The Absolute* each try to answer that question. This opens a reflection of the place of dissatisfaction in the *Logic of Philosophy*.

3.5 Immanence Versus Dissatisfaction

Each philosophical category is separated by a free jump. This is one of the primary differences that separates Weil's project from Hegel's. Because Hegel's project limits itself to the philosophical attitude of understanding, without developing the other possible attitudes an individual could have towards discourse (except perhaps the pre-philosophical one in order to show it insufficiency), its progression is immanent. For Hegel, the naïve consciousness in *Sense-certainty* is untenable. The *Phenomenology* shows how this consciousness develops into philosophical understanding thanks to the determinate negations that push it forward. The specific refusals of determinate negations can be seen as the inferential unfolding of the different determinations that show how concepts stand in relation to one another. By showing that philosophy is a non-necessary free choice that can start from anywhere *and* that can build itself out of specific refusals of specific aspects of discourse, Weil might seem to share Hegel's position. The difference lies in the fact that Weil sees philosophy's non-necessary character *and* its specific refusals as being downstream from the possibility of a total refusal of all discourse and coherence. This absolute refusal thus opposes itself to the immanence found in Hegel's model.

In the logic of philosophy, not only does Weil posit other attitudes that precede the attitude of certainty, he also notes how, thanks to the reprise, this certainty is found anew in every attitude. He shows that certainty is not the eternally unstable starting point that pushes people into philosophy, but rather that it is itself a conceptual development, and as such, it also provides each category with a certain level of stability. Each category proposes a form of coherence, but each form of coherence reprises all the initial background categories. They live in the certainty of truth and push away every other attitude as meaningless by separating the essential from the inessential. Weil characterizes the way that individuals can find human satisfaction in any attitude by refusing all other forms of coherence. The possibility of satisfaction through refusal undermines immanence because nothing can force an individual to leave a form of coherence where they are satisfied. Weil thus proposes dissatisfaction as the mechanism of philosophical movement because paradoxically it is what allows the individual to "maintain a distance between themself and the world, allows them to preserve the transcendence of their freedom and thus to avoid alienating themself in the things that they create."[23]

Dissatisfaction is to be seen as an explanatory mechanism and not as a metaphysical object. In other words, it is not a self-standing supersensible entity that is the source of meaning but rather part of the free act of understanding, the content of which changes in every specific concrete discourse. It is a real possibility, people can be dissatisfied, but as a possibility, it is on its own insufficient. It is a part of and a consequence of discourse and discursive practices. The individual must transform their feeling of dissatisfaction into a critical discourse for it to serve a discursive function. The ordinary individual is not *necessarily* pushed into the philosophical

---

[23] Savadogo (2003), 76.

attitude because of their dissatisfaction. Dissatisfaction can present itself in countless ways. It can always remain vague for example, or be temporary, or lead to *Meaninglessness*. When it remains vague, the individual does not know how to grasp their dissatisfaction, even if they recognize that they are dissatisfied. When it is temporary, it gives out faced with the more global satisfaction that the individual finds in their attitude. When it leads to *Meaninglessness*, the individual sees the world around them as immutable and their dissatisfaction is just a part of their condition. It only serves as an explanatory mechanism to the individual who makes the free choice to understand. This is because each form of coherence presents a form of satisfaction that allows individuals to live full human lives. The individual jumps from their "natural" attitude into a new (mediated) one when they refuse the determined form of satisfaction proposed therein *and* when they refuse meaninglessness.

When someone accepts meaninglessness because they suffer under the weight of dissatisfaction, they do not look to overcome it. They don't even see it as dissatisfaction. What they seek is respite. They seek different palliative forms of release to distract them. They participate in the gratuitous violence that is always possible, either against others, or against themselves. When they refuse meaninglessness, however, they see their dissatisfaction as what motivates them. Dissatisfaction as an explanatory mechanism is also a formal concept: the specificity of concrete dissatisfaction is defined by the specific forms of violence that individuals face. It will thus be different in each concrete situation and in each concrete life, and different categories characterize it differently. Even though dissatisfaction is a formal explanatory mechanism in the logic of philosophy, this structure allows different categories to see it is a metaphysical principle. This thus illustrates the difference that Weil makes between metaphysical categories and philosophical categories. The use of metaphysical categories helps us to see the shape of philosophical categories. Understood as part of the logic of philosophy, the differences in the contents of dissatisfaction help us to draw out the differences between different philosophical categories. This in turn helps to show how metaphysical categories are downstream from philosophical ones. Dissatisfaction changes from discourse to discourse. Dissatisfaction is part of an explanation only to the individual that seeks to grasp the whole coherently.

By framing the development of the logic of philosophy in terms of dissatisfaction, we can better understand the development and the order found therein. The different philosophical categories from *The Object* to the *Absolute* propose different grounds. Each ground is supposed to relieve the individual of their dissatisfaction by providing them with a coherent explanation of the world and of experience. As I have said I will not analyze each of these categories. Rather I will look at specific significative ruptures and articulations between categories, namely the articulation between *Discussion* and *The Object*, followed by that between *God, The Condition,* and *Consciousness*, and then between *The Absolute* and *The Work*.

The dissatisfaction of the individual who makes the jump from *The Discussion* to the next category, *The Object*, is two-fold. *Discussion* is formal and this can lead individuals to ask if non-contradiction is a sufficient criterion to orient human

3.5 Immanence Versus Dissatisfaction

action. In *Discussion*, individuals can come to absurd but coherent conclusions if they start from absurd premises. The community can agree to put Socrates, the individual who embodies the morality of agreement, to death. Discourse must thus both be formally coherent (non-contradictory) and in agreement with objective reality (the reality on which discourse bears). This is the first principle of science and of philosophy as first science. The initial dissatisfaction is not only that discussion goes on forever, but also the fact that the individual wants to be satisfied not in language but in their activity. Because *Discussion* is characterized by a merely formal agreement, the dissatisfaction that *The Object* is trying to overcome is the impotence of discussion. Purely formal discussion is impotent if it has no contact with the world. Weil notes that the greatest shock of Plato's life was watching the community execute somebody who was right (LP, 130). Discussion could not save Socrates, moreover, it was his participation in discussion that led to his death. The people around him, living in the certainty of their tradition, did not want to become aware of the glaring contradictions that existed in that very tradition. They did not want to recognize the tradition's contingency. I have said that *Certainty* is the floor of naïve, pre-philosophical certainty and that *The Discussion* is the floor of simple reason. We can now specify why *Certainty*, as the floor of naïve, pre-philosophical certainty, is the floor of tradition. Each individual, being born into a tradition and taking it for granted, does not see it as a tradition but merely as the way the world is. However, what the jumps from *Certainty* to *The Discussion* to *The Object* show is that:

> the tradition is insufficient as soon as it is a matter of making decisions, […][it] is only of value within the life of labor, where there are no decisions to make and where one can continue along the path that has always been followed. And yet they also observe that for as incapable as it is of justifying its way of doing things, this tradition achieves results in its realm that discussion is unable to equal. Tradition and common sense know without speaking; discussion speaks without knowing (LP, 141).

The Object seeks both to *speak* and to *know*. It is built out of *Discussion* and thus develops in relation to *Discussion* (this is what is meant by a floor: each category interprets the world in relation to the problems that its floor announces) but it modifies *Discussion*, and in doing so, opens the philosophical attitude of understanding. It develops *theoria*. In *theoria* the individual wants to "reach reality by means of language" (LP, 141) and to do so through universal judgments. *Theoria* is thus a "concrete and reasonable" science, "a total view of the totality of beings in their unity" (LP, 142). It is the immediate *sight* of this unity, not the sight of appearances, but rather the sight of the One, of the Being that underlies appearances. By positing this possibility, the individual of *The Object* surpasses the subjectivity of *Certainty* to posit the subject and the object, and to posit that their unity in discourse is what will allow individuals to overcome their dissatisfaction. In this way, *The Object* is the first category to recognize the importance of grounding discourse, of establishing its coherence by presenting a total unity. This is why it opens the philosophical attitude of understanding.

The Object posits that, to find satisfaction, the individual must leave the formal agreement of discussion and take reality into account. They must create a science that allows this reality to be grasped by any individual to avoid the mistakes of *Discussion*. This is the science that, born in the work of Plato and Aristotle, covers the discourse of classical ontology. Going back to the distinction that Weil makes between metaphysical categories and philosophical categories, it is in this category where philosophy and metaphysics is conflated, where philosophy is seen as first science. According to *The Object*, The Good, the Just, the Beautiful are only known thanks to the science of Being. Once this science is completed, satisfaction can be found in the contemplation of the One, and the individual can disappear into Being. This category inherits the notion of coherence from *The Discussion* and it develops the importance of grounding through its development of the ontological object. It does not have a sufficient notion of totality. The contradiction that structures this category, like all the categories of Antiquity, is that between simple reason and nature, or reason and desire. This desire though is something foreign to reason and so it is not understood: it must be excised. Because of this, the individual who is a mix of reason and desire cannot interpret themselves fully. A more sufficient notion of totality is needed. This is provided by the category *God*.

God is the first category of total reflection. The tradition of *Certainty* that is the floor of pre-philosophical understanding does not reflect; *Discussion*, the floor of the simple reason (and the categories that follow) reflects, but in a simple partial reflection that separates the individual and the world, reason and feeling. *God*, the transitional category between Antiquity and Modernity, takes the individual, the world, reason, and feeling and unites them all in a total reflection. This total reflection however remains outside the individual, because all these aspects are reflected in God. It is therefore a transitional category. It overcomes the difficulties that were insurmountable in the earlier categories, and in doing so, it opens the way for modern reflection, but it does not itself make the step into fully modern reflection. It does however add two essential pieces to the *Logic of Philosophy*: a sufficient concept of totality and the modern concept of freedom. This total reflection first happens by postulating an absolute creating self that is the immutable unity of feeling and reason because it is the source of both. The human individual understands this unity because they are made in its image. They understand it because they maintain a dialogical *I/Thou* relationship with God and with all the other members of the community of believers that love and trust each other thanks to their faith. This is the discourse of the great monotheistic religions. For the individual in this attitude, the word of God is *revealed* to the human being. In the attitude/category of *God*, the human being is free, but this freedom is only felt in the individual's disobedience to God's law. In other words, the individual discovers their freedom in their failure (such as in the doctrine of original sin) and must thus be forgiven and restored through God's forgiveness and the possibility of salvation. It is thus *in* God that the individual knows themself to be free, and this is where the individual and the world are totally reflected in God. It is a freedom and reflection that the individual feels in God's love, in God's mercy, and this love and mercy is what delivers the individual. In this attitude/category, feeling is the unity of reason and of nature. God is the source of all nature and God made nature reasonably. But God is also absolutely free and is absolute freedom as the source of all freedom. This starts the transition

3.5 Immanence Versus Dissatisfaction

to the categories of Modernity. The human being is free in God and because of God, but is also separate from God, who is impossibly far away. So, even though *God* starts the transition to the categories of Modernity, the individual's separation from God anchors the category to those of Antiquity. The human being understands the unity of reason and feeling, but is only its reflection. This is clear in Weil's interpretation of the attitude and the category. He splits them in two, and analyses the attitude of the believer and the development of the category in the elaboration of Christian theology separately. The elaboration of the category gives birth to the modern interpretation of the individual, and places this category halfway into Modernity, but the lived attitude of the believer and their separation from this totality also holds them back. This split is part of the birth of the reflexivity that is born in the category. The categorial interpretation of this form of theology (which is exemplified by St. Augustine) is the interpretation of its own attitude. For this interpretation, the individual is entirely absorbed into the unity of God, reason, feeling, and the world. It is in their "interdependence that they have their legitimacy."[24] This interdependence and this total reflection thus make this attitude/category the first place in the history of discourse that ground, coherence, and totality are fully united. Thus, this is where the modern notion of comprehensiveness that is essential to the understanding proposed in the *Logic of Philosophy* first sees the light of day. However, because this comprehensiveness is transcendent, the reflection of freedom and totality must be brought down to earth, so to speak. This is why *The Condition* and not *God* is the floor of all modern categories.

For Weil, discourse structures thought, it allows the individual to grasp their attitude and to grasp reality, but this means that reality is graspable in discourse.[25] There is however no direct grasp of *God*. There is no direct grasp of any metaphysical object, what the individual grasps when they grasp God, or their attitude, or their faith, or the certainty of their feeling is discourse. More precisely they grasp these things as mediated by discourse. This is another reason why Weil separates metaphysical categories and philosophical ones. The first are graspable only thanks to the second, but it is the first that reveal the second. It is discourse that allows the

---

[24] Kluback (1987), 81.

[25] Even though they do not state their position in the same way, Weil's position concerning this two-way relation bears great similarity to what Brandom calls "bimodal hylomorphic conceptual realism." According to this position, conceptual content takes two forms, both of which are determined by relations of incompatibility and consequences, in Brandom (2019). In Brandom's version, the first form is *alethic* relations of noncompossibility and necessitation. The second form is *deontic* relations of normative preclusion and consequential commitment. In other words, on the alethic side, determined content is determined because it is impossible for certain things to exist together and because some things are necessarily consequences of others. On the deontic side, subjects ought to not commit to incompatible commitments and ought to hold commitments that follow from others. For Weil, these alethic and deontic aspects are to be found in what he calls "discourse's deepest duality." In this duality, the "universal exists and is *one*, but it appears to the category in the attitude, to discourse in the situation (and, *as soon as it is interpreted*, to poetry in the world) under two aspects: as Freedom and as Truth" (LP, 442). In the long essay "*De la nature*," Weil further develops his theory of the relationship between normative and objective content and the way these two types of content line up, see (ENHP, 11–114).

individual to be in agreement with their feeling, and the category of *God* is the first discourse to do so. This explains the force and persistence of this discourse. It proposes an eternal discourse that allows the individual to explain all their present dissatisfaction as a trial, as a test, as part of a greater plan. This is a seductive option, but it is precisely what *The Condition* refuses. The dissatisfaction that raises itself up against the category of *God* is the dissatisfaction of the here and now. *God* proposes a form of satisfaction, but this satisfaction is found outside of the scope of human *life*. It is to be found in some great beyond. The faith that the individual must have is not just in *God*: it is also in themselves. The individual must have faith that their acts will provide them with the satisfaction that is to be found in *God*, but the life in which they hold that faith must also be lived. And it is lived not outside of time and space, but in the natural conditions of their own situation. The individual that is dissatisfied with the discourse of faith seeks a discourse that allows them to grasp this reality as it is lived.

The Condition, in a sense, reverses the discourse of *God*. It demands totality, but refuses transcendence instead of seeing totality within it. The structure of reflection for *The Condition* thus becomes the "indefinite movement whose totalization constitutes the world of the *condition*, the unachieved and unachievable system of conditional interdependencies"[26] where "rationality is no longer in search of any origin or end, foundation or meaning, it makes itself into a pure operational exploration of a universal relativity excluding any depth of essence."[27] In this category what the individual reflects totally is a "nature considered as a system of conditions, of phenomena conditioned by one another."[28] This category, exemplified by Auguste Comte and Voltaire, is the category of scientific positivism. Nature, and not reason, is seen as the ground of all thought and the source of all coherence, because nature is seen as an accessible comprehensive totality. This shows how the different possible articulations of the *Logic of Philosophy* overlap and multiply. *God* discovers the modern concept of freedom, but *The Condition* refuses it because freedom is not a knowable condition. Freedom is present but problematic. *The Condition* is the floor of all modern categories of Freedom, because each interprets itself in relation to it and must overcome the aporia of Freedom present in *The Condition*. Nonetheless, *The Condition* only retains the unity of ground, coherence, and totality found in *God* "at the price of a radical reduction."[29] Nature is the ground of discourse and any coherence must be in accord with nature, which is nothing other than the totality of conditions. The individual that is dissatisfied by the distance that separates them from God and by the mystery of His will, seeks to explain the life that happens down here, and consequently, any meaning that this life is to have must also be found at this level. In other words, *The Condition* corresponds to the individual's loss of faith. The individual in *The Condition* must face "the real insofar as real"

---

[26] Kirscher (1989), 268.
[27] Guibal (2011), 123.
[28] Canivez (1999), 48–49.
[29] Kirscher (1989), 269.

3.5 Immanence Versus Dissatisfaction

(LP, 213) and thus all that is real, the individual included, is merely understood as a totality of natural factors to which the science of calculating rationality applies its techniques. This allows the individual to have a total reflection but only as a quantifiable totality. Weil says that the tradition knows but doesn't speak, and that *Discussion* speaks but doesn't know and then shows how the development of the science of *The Object*, the science of contemplative reason, seeks to both speak and know. *The Condition* also develops a science; however the functions and goals of that science are radically modified by the union of a total reflection which fuses ground, coherence, and totality into a single comprehensiveness. The ground must be that which allows coherence and which leads to totality. *The Condition* is "not there to speak, but to act by means of language" (LP, 206). *The Condition* adds a dynamism that was missing in earlier discourses. Contemplation is no longer enough. Language tracks the changes in nature to generalize them and elaborate laws. Nonetheless, this discourse does not yet recognize its own dynamism as essential. In the condition "all the human being has in order to speak is this science. The human being undoubtedly is for themselves merely to the extent that they speak: but being for themselves signifies, for the human being, being for science, and being for science is not being language, but being opposed to language as objects are opposed to theory" (LP, 206).

In *The Condition*, the individual understands themselves as a conditioned thing in a conditioned nature. Their life is the totality of conditions, and if they want to be satisfied their discourse must grasp the totality of these conditions. They must participate in progress. Discourse must get rid of the contingent and traditional beliefs that litter our understanding: it must find the laws of nature. To do so, the individual must renounce their feeling and become a disinterested observer of nature in order to act on it. Humanity develops science and the individual understands themselves thanks to it. They understand themselves according to psychological, sociological, and biological conditions. This is the discourse of modern experimental science. It covers the attitude of the scientific researcher in their role as a researcher. It is the discourse of observation and hypothesis. It is the discourse of the mathematization of nature and of nature understood in measurement. Whatever cannot be measured and understood in terms of observation and hypothesis is ruled out. It is the attitude of progress, and humanity must progress by finding the facts. Progress is the only (invisible) value and so *The Condition* makes a hard value/fact distinction. Unless it can find a way to explain values in terms of (psychological, social, biological, etc.) facts, these values are considered false or empty.

Because the unity of ground, coherence, and totality is in the world, *The Condition* interprets the individual as part of this coherent totality of conditions, however in doing so it not only reduces all the values that make up the individual's life and makes life meaningful, it also reduces the individual. The world is a totality of conditions, but it lacks meaning, and yet, the individual still sees their life as meaningful. How does this happen? Is it merely a trick nature plays on us? In the category of *God*, the individual felt free in their ability to disobey God and that feeling of freedom does not disappear in *The Condition*, it becomes problematic. Freedom is not a condition. The categories of Antiquity separated nature and reason, in the categories of Modernity, nature and reason are united, but nature and freedom are not. *The Condition*'s solution is to reduce freedom, but for the individual that feels free, this reduction is inadmissible. According to Weil's reading of the different forms of logic as a reduction of different forms of violence, *Consciousness* moves us out of the logic of classic ontology and into Kant's transcendental logic. However, it still interprets itself in relation to *The Condition*. *Consciousness* demands a discourse that allows the contradiction between nature and freedom to be resolved. The category seeks to unite the individual's lived sentiment *and* their discourse, and it does so by "discovering the possibility of a discourse other than that of scientific knowledge."[30] This discovery is decisive because it is in the *Consciousness* that the ground of modern discourse changes. *Consciousness* seeks to elaborate a totally coherent discourse grounded in freedom reflected not in God, but in the individual. Here "science must be meaningful for a *consciousness* that essentially conceives of itself as moral consciousness, as the awareness of freedom."[31] This freedom is essentially negative, it negates the hold that conditions have on the individual and it shows how dissatisfaction plays a key role in the jump between categories.

As the floor of Modernity, all modern categories are interpreted in relation to *The Condition*, and thus it is also (through a reprise of *Certainty*) the floor of *our* tradition. It is the source of *our* naïve pre-philosophical attitude. The pull it has on us is thus massive. Anyone who is in this tradition, and who does not ask the question of their own meaning for themselves, sees the discourse that the tradition has elaborated as being "natural" and "given." If the individual chooses to reflect philosophically, that is, coherently and totally, and if they ask themself the question of what grounds this reflection, the question of freedom is nonetheless unavoidable. It is the thinking individual, the thinking consciousness that grasps that:

> [e]verything is discourse and only is discourse; but this *everything* is a silence that merely speaks to reprise all words within itself: Freedom is at the bottom of everything that is and everything that is merely is for freedom, for consciousness. Language is therefore not a *thing* in the world; it is a *way of speaking*, which conditions the world and, freely, conditions itself in the world (LP, 235–236).

It is in this rational activity that the individual determines themself, but only by taking the science of conditions into account and then by searching beyond external determinations. This is why, in the discourse of *Consciousness*:

> pure consciousness is, in this way, for itself the determination and knowledge of determination, and it is inseparably both. Free determination alone gets me to leave conditioned knowledge; only the reflection about the determining act as a transcendent possibility makes me to see the absolute that I am as *I*, but that I do not cognize in the condition (LP, 241).

It is this possibility that transforms the idea of reflection into an "access to the absolute" (LP, 241).

---

[30] Savadogo (2003), 141.
[31] Canivez (1999), 50.

3.5 Immanence Versus Dissatisfaction

The individual who jumps from *The Condition* to *Consciousness* jumps knowingly, jumps not because satisfaction is not possible in *The Condition*—it is—but jumps because they are conscious of the fact that they don't want to be satisfied in the manner that *The Condition* proposes. It is in *Consciousness* that the individual becomes aware of *meaning* and of the quest for meaning. The conditioned world provides no meaning because meaning transcends conditions. Meaning must be found by the individual and found in their life. *Consciousness* opens the possibility of the individual seeing themselves as the source of meaning. According to Weil, for *Consciousness*:

> [p]hilosophy is not the goal, it has a goal, and this goal is not speaking about freedom, it is leading the human being to determine themself as free. The human being is the being that surpasses the world of the *condition*—there is no other world—in order to enter into a world that now has *meaning*: it is the realm of human decision, of the confrontation between freedom and conditional necessity (LP, 243–244).

Consciousness is therefore the totality reflected into itself as a total reflection, but this total reflection is merely formal. This is why *Consciousness* is distrustful of reprises. In *Consciousness*:

> [t]he human being is made of ideas, which is an expression that must be taken literally; consciousness alone sees this fundamental *making*, which is not a fact, but is expressed in facts. Within the idea of a just God, the moral law exists for the human being that is free but unaware of their freedom, in the same way that the idea of the science governing conditions represents—but only represents for consciousness—reason's spontaneity, and the way that the idea of the universal kingdom of law prefigures free determination by suppressing individual interest, and the idea of wisdom announces the total reflection of the *self* in the *I*. For consciousness, the human being has always been trying to *make* themself within the condition and they have always betrayed themself in both meanings of the expression. They have betrayed themself by trying to abdicate their freedom and they have betrayed themself because they are not able to do so and because it is precisely their own attempt at self-objectification that demonstrates their fundamental spontaneity (LP, 255).

The contradiction between nature and freedom is internal to the individual themself. Each individual is both simultaneously nature and freedom, they are both an empirical and a transcendental self, and even though *Consciousness* only resolves this problem formally, it does open the path to its concrete resolution. Reflection becomes the idea of absolute reflection, the idea of a reflection that grasps both freedom and nature in philosophical speculation. This contradiction continues through *Intelligence* (exemplified by Michel de Montaigne and Pierre Bayle) and *Personality* (exemplified by Friedrich Nietzsche), which both interpret themselves not only in relation to *The Condition* but also in relation to *Consciousness*. It is resolved however in the category of *The Absolute*.

The Absolute is the culmination of the philosophical attitude. It is the pure attitude that unites ground, coherence, and totality in reflection and its fulfillment is what allows all the categories from *The Object* onward to be seen as permutations of the same overarching attitude. This allows us to clarify what we have already called *the philosophical attitude of understanding*. Eric Weil uses the term "philosophical attitude" twice in the *Logic of Philosophy*. The first is to critique certain types of philosophical attitudes (LP, 154) and the second is to give a definition of the usage itself (LP, 260). In *The Object*, Weil makes a distinction between the attitude of the "restricted common sense" that reprises *The Object* (the first category of the philosophical attitude of understanding) and the philosophical attitudes that this creates. Restricted common sense, for Weil, is marked by the fact that it "refuses transcendence" which:

> according to this common sense itself, leads to the most absurd *philosophical attitudes*.[32] Absolute skepticism, absolute materialism, absolute idealism can all ultimately be traced back to common sense's reprises of the category of the *object* using the category of discussion. These are scientific and not philosophical systems because they start out from the science of common sense in order to move to the absolute from the science of discussion, to move to the totality of theses arranged non-contradictorily. Each of them wants to explain how the human being is able to cognize reality—the only thing that, strictly speaking, does not need to be explained for philosophy (LP, 154).

We can interpret the attitude of common sense and the philosophical attitude as being distinguished by the way that the goal of explaining and understanding coherently and totally is understood. According to this reading, common sense is nothing more than the pre-philosophical attitude of the tradition. It does not seek to understand totally and coherently, and when it does, it reprises the initial category of philosophical understanding. The historical development of the philosophical attitude has already long surpassed these initial categories (even though it reprises them) in that it no longer takes the solutions and the satisfaction proposed by *Discussion* and *The Object* as being freestanding. They require reprises. This is why absolute skepticism, absolute materialism, absolute idealism are seen as absurd philosophical attitudes. They share the goals of the philosophical attitude of understanding but cut themselves off from any resolution to the aporia found in understanding. This implies that the philosophical attitude can take numerous shapes but that each shape shares the same goal, which is to understand.

As already mentioned, the second time that Weil highlights the philosophical attitude is to define the usage of the term. He defines it though negatively by showing why *Consciousness* in its pure form lacks any such attitude. Weil states:

> no philosophical attitude of consciousness exists (it is the word "philosophical" that matters), since there is no coherent discourse of the *I*, which is only present in the destruction of all coherence: the human being always is what they ought to not be, and this is the only way that they knows what they ought to be (LP, 260).

The philosophical attitude is therefore defined by its effort to organize discourse coherently. *Consciousness* is the attitude of pure transcendence that seeks to be "necessary coincidence of attitude and category" (LP, 255). But because it is merely the formal coincidence of these two things, in its purity, the attitude is not "philosophical." It is nothing other than the awareness of its self-grounding totality. This is not a contradiction in the sense that, for Weil, the *I* is a transitory state that evaporates every time it has to act, that it has to come face to face with the conditions of

---

[32] Highlighted by us.

3.5 Immanence Versus Dissatisfaction

the world. It is merely the *"ungraspable ground"* (LP, 256) of total reflection, an empty absolute, because it makes itself into a formal "absolute emptiness" (LP, 255). It therefore has no determined content to organize, since it merely acts negatively by destroying inadequate content.

The form of satisfaction that *The Absolute* proposes resolves this problem by filling this absolute emptiness of the empty absolute with real determined content. The individual is satisfied because they understand themself as a member of a community and a State, as a member of different associations, as the member of a family, and by understanding themself in those terms, which are universal, the individual in their particularity renounces that particularity in order to embrace the universal. But it is precisely this characteristic of *The Absolute* that will lead Weil to surpass it. By framing the development of the philosophical attitude in terms of satisfaction and dissatisfaction, it allows us to see the range of possibilities of human attitudes. We can see how attitudes resist change and how they jump forward. Individuals stay in their attitude when they are reasonably satisfied in it, or when they are unable to see the point of entering into the philosophical attitude for themselves, or when they don't want to accept any change to the content of their attitude. When they do take on the philosophical attitude, they develop their understanding. This however does not mean that they will go through all of the categorial developments that lead to *The Absolute*. They will not necessarily put their coherence to the test. In *Consciousness*, the category posits the coincidence between the attitude and the category, between life lived by the individual and their discourse bearing on this life, between the individual's feeling of freedom and reason, but it was unable to provide it. In *The Absolute* it is "no longer a matter of the *individual's* liberation and realization, but of *the human being's* freedom and reality" (LP, 321). The individual universalizes themself in *The Absolute* and in doing so the human being and Being "are *unified* in discourse" (LP, 322). *This* is the speculative attitude. Everything that is and that is understood is understood in discourse. This discourse takes in and understands every attitude as being moments of *The Absolute*, it sees them all as necessary for the realization of its content. It is the first category to consciously multiply points of view.

The Absolute becomes an attitude "that wants to be a category. It only—and totally—realizes itself by thinking itself. It is the universal attitude, the totality of attitudes, not juxtaposed and added together […] [but is] the whole of negativity, organizing itself." (LP, 327). *The Absolute* unites ground, coherence, and totality, but not as something transcendent like in *God*, nor as something reduced and external like in *The Condition*, nor as something formal and empty like in *Consciousness*. Here, freedom is the absolute ground of discourse. Discourse is coherent and its content is total. It is all content. The category is nothing more and nothing less than "the development of the attitudes" (LP, 327) that understands everything and itself. In fact, we can say *The Absolute* is the category that interprets itself as the philosophical attitude of understanding because it sees itself as the whole of discourse. In this whole, "[c]ategory after category, attitude after attitude are therefore revealed as what they are in the Absolute: the Absolute itself in its becoming." (LP, 328). From the naïve pre-philosophical, to the groundwork that is laid for philosophical understanding in *Discussion*, through its start in *The Object* and its development. Each moment is "the Absolute in its stages" (LP, 328) and is needed for absolute discourse to become aware of itself.

Each pure attitude can be taken independently. This is one of the things that defines its purity. But each attitude also includes reprises of every other one. In fact, it is *The Absolute* itself that allows us to identify two separate overarching attitudes. There is the "naïve" pre-philosophical attitude of *Certainty* and of the tradition that must be taken by the hand and led to philosophy, and there is the philosophical attitude of understanding. This second attitude regroups all the forms of coherence (each of which proposes a different metaphysical ground) that together make up the western philosophical tradition from Plato to Hegel. *Certainty* dominates the initial background attitudes because they all only become visible in *Certainty*. In other words, *we* recognize any attitude from *Truth* to *Certainty* as certainty. The same goes for the philosophical attitudes. Each can be taken independently because its determined content is freestanding, but once discourse has reached *The Absolute* they are all understood to be permutations of the same attitude because they all offer satisfaction in terms of understanding and reasonable discourse. These two attitudes are constantly mixing however. Both because as history marches forward, the naïve attitude is given access to the forms of coherence that are developed in coherent discourse, and because anyone who wants to understand reprises all the background attitudes in their concrete attitude. As I mentioned in the last chapter, the reproach that the categories after *The Absolute* present is that the philosophical attitude offers satisfaction in thought, in the act of thinking and of understanding, in speculative activity. It thus proposes that human satisfaction is itself the satisfaction of the individual as a thinking being, not as an individual understood in their individuality.

The categories following *The Absolute* don't want to understand satisfaction as it is grasped in discourse, their question is one of actual satisfaction. The jumps between *Certainty, Discussion,* and *The Object* radically alter discourse by opening the philosophical attitude. As the philosophical attitude evolves, it reveals forms of coherence that allow individuals to grasp themselves in the world. By framing this movement in terms of satisfaction and freedom, we are able to see how this evolution opens a range of possibilities to each individual. The philosophical attitude culminates in the freedom of thought, thought realized through its freedom, thought thinking satisfaction and its own freedom. The jump from *The Absolute* to the next category is a jump that is just as radical as the one between *Certainty* and *Discussion* because it also changes the orientation of discourse. *The Absolute* elaborates a discourse that offers satisfaction in the freedom *of* thought. *The Work* seeks satisfaction in freedom *from* thought. *The Work* refuses coherence, universality, reasonable discourse, and freedom itself to live, feel, and act.

3.6　The Individual's Relationship to Discourse

The dissatisfaction of the individual in *The Work* is a dissatisfaction with absolutely coherent discourse. However, this dissatisfaction cannot be reabsorbed into *The Absolute*, rather it presents discourse with a new shape and with new resources. The primitive categories are interpreted as the background of discourse because these categories develop the resources needed for discourse. For Weil, discourse starts from a purely pragmatic attitude of the unity of the individual and the world in *Truth* and then develops the productivity of the pragmatic negation in *Meaninglessness*. This difference allows Weil to distinguish between doctrine and explanation, implicit and explicit, attitude and category. *The True and the False* allows the reduction of the implicit to the explicit by distinguishing the true interpretation of the doctrine from all those that are false. *Certainty* develops the essential, which allows individuals to take up a commitment to a specific determined content in order to orient their life and their activity. In this way, these "primitive" categories are all pragmatic, but "naïvely" so. They are pre-philosophical. The logical tools that define coherence have not yet been fully and explicitly developed and so coherence has not yet been posited in terms of non-contradiction. The importance of grounding discourse has not yet been recognized. The possibility of a total discourse is still invisible. Discourse is thus not yet essential to the individual's attitude. *Discussion* develops the importance of coherence, but this coherence is merely formal. If *Truth* to *Certainty* are pragmatic, because they are characterized by their attitudes without any reference to specific content, and if *The Discussion* provides the logical resources to grasp determined content coherently, then the categories from *The Object* to *The Absolute* are semantic. They are semantic because each provides a coherent body of determined content and because any contradiction between these different categories happens at the ground level in that determined content. Their determined shape is nothing more than that determined content.

Each attitude reprises *Certainty*, which merely means that it is committed to something. By discovering "the form of content" (LP, 122), *Discussion* changes this by showing that being committed means committing to a specific thing. It shows that discourse must be filled with concrete determinedness. It discovers the formal notion of coherence but does not fill it with any content. It is ungrounded and it is not total. *The Object* posits a ground and allows a substantial determined discourse. Each category following *The Object* all the way to *The Absolute* posits a new ground and, in doing so, modifies content and provides discourse with additional resources. *The Absolute* adds resources by showing that, in order for discourse to be complete, it must be self-sufficient. Discourse is free in its realm. It is not grounded by anything other than the free choice to develop itself. What else is there? There is life. There is human struggle. There is violence. The transition from *Certainty* to *Discussion* is the difference between a naïve unthinking relationship to tradition and a critical one thanks to discourse. It is the passage from life into discourse. The attitudes from *The Object* to *The Absolute* see life only as it appears in discourse. Life, God, feeling, all these things are reduced to discourse. The passage from *The*

Absolute to *The Work* is the refusal of the satisfaction that is proposed in discourse, because it is the refusal to be mediated.[33] It is the attitude of pure particularity understood as particular. It is the attitude of revolt.[34] It is life without discourse. In this way it is a pragmatic attitude, like those at the start of the logic of philosophy and it develops no discourse for itself. However, because it adds something new to discourse and because its pure attitude is graspable in discourse, there is a category of *revolt*. This category reflects on the relationship the violent individual has to discourse, on the interplay between categories and attitudes, and in this way, it opens what we can call, following Robert Brandom (who uses it in a different context), the possibility of a *pragmatic metavocabulary*. Brandom notes that a pragmatic metavocabulary characterizes and develops the *"pragmatically mediated semantic* relation between vocabularies."[35] The category of *The Work* (characterized by the refusal of discourse and of coherence) is a metavocabulary in the sense that it characterized the pragmatic relationship that an attitude has towards the semantic content of different coherent discourses. In fact, what I want to suggest is that all of the categories *of* philosophy are best understood as pragmatic metavocabularies in that they characterize the different types of relationships that the individual can have towards discourse.

Every discourse makes room for violence. There is violence that is legitimate and violence that is illegitimate but both are understood in discourse. In *Certainty*, for example, what matters is the individual's (or the State's) certainty of their own discourse. Our certain discourse must be protected from the discourse of others, which for these others is equally certain. The best form of protection is to bring the others to see the truth of our unique discourse, even if by force. *Certainty* legitimizes its use of violence in order to create a unique world or at least to protect its certain discourse from attack. Violence is illegitimate when it puts this certainty at risk. *The Discussion* sees violence as illegitimate at the interior of the community, *because* this violence is what puts the community at risk. Each category uses discourse to decide what illegitimate violence is. This allows categories to decide what the legitimate use of violence is, whether it is defending the community from barbarians, converting infidels to the true faith, interpreting the recalcitrant elements of society as criminal or psychologically unsound. For *The Absolute*, violence is seen as a step on the individual's journey for recognition. This is clear from Hegel's interpretation of *Das Werk* in the *Phenomenology of Spirit*. However, *The Work* adds something new that cannot be reduced to *Das Werk*. It lives in violence and refuses discourse and so it does not separate legitimate use and illegitimate use. Because of this, it is *discourse* that is seen as inessential to life and not violence. This attitude thus refuses to allow its violence to be subsumed into language, refuses letting contradiction have any hold on it, refuses all forms of coherence. The individual living in *The Work* refuses to adhere to any discourse because they are not only the center

---

[33] Kluback (1987), 133.
[34] Kirscher (1989), 303; Ganty (1997), 669.
[35] Brandom (2010), 11.

of the world, their feeling is the whole world. The individual in this attitude does not recognize others as agents, as individuals, as peers, but only as obstacles or tools.

The Work allows Weil to theorize violence, but he goes farther than merely looking at violence on the individual level. He also uses *The Work* to make the leap to a political analysis of violence. *Certainty* uses violence rather than argument against other communities. Argument requires submitting oneself to specific dialogical controls whereby the best reasons take the day, even if they are the reasons of one's opponent. *Certainty* does not see the need to do so, because one's opponent is absolutely different and can be overcome or ignored. *Discussion* is born between the members of a single community where everyone is seen as equals and so can neither be overcome nor ignored. They are equals, and therefore they must discuss. *Certainty* is thus the category where the use of violence is seen as legitimate in order to force others to adhere to one's own discourse. Any other discourse that uses violence to do so, does so through a reprise of certainty. Each category provides a form of coherence that promises that once everyone adheres to it, violence will be reduced to a set of logical norms and pure violence will disappear. Even *Intelligence*, the first category that recognizes the irreducibility of other discourses, promises that violence will be overcome as soon as individuals see that it is relative to particular interests that cause violence. What the jump from *The Absolute* to *The Work* shows is that even if violence can be understood, it can never be overcome once and for all. It is the "remainder that remains."[36] *The Work* is the violence of the individual that is aware of being, and that wants to be individual. The individual who therefore recognizes no equals and no dialogical controls.

Violence cannot be overcome once and for all, because as *The Work* shows, violence itself can give meaning to the individual. This shows the importance of the free adhesion to discourse. There is nothing that grounds discourse *and* eliminates violence, except the free choice to exclude violence. Discourse is grounded in the free choice to understand, but this same freedom can be used to refuse or destroy discourse. In other words, *The Work* is the manifestation of a freedom that does not seek recognition.

At the individual level, the world that is reasonably organized and understood by *The Absolute* is a world where each individual is recognized in the roles they fill and in the path they take to be functioning members of society. *The Work* understands this organization and is born there but refuses it. It is the individual that accepts that education is necessary to individual development, but disdains education and refuses to be educated. It is the individual that accepts that each person is understood and recognized thanks to the role they fill as children and parents, employees and employers, friends and lovers, but refuses to be bound by these roles, and thus respects no duty that goes along with them. The freedom and satisfaction that *The Work* reaches for is the immediacy of feeling. It is the freedom to act, the satisfaction of doing something without reflection, and therefore it does not characterize its activity as seeking anything. It is the pure feeling of existing that is found in the

---

[36] Perine (1982), 190.

refusal itself. It is the presence of feeling outside of reasonable discourse. It knows that the others are there, and that acting correctly requires taking them into account, but it sees them as the malleable stuff of its own ends. It knows that discussion leads to reasons but that reasons lead it back into the endless spiral from which it wants to be free. There is no adhesion to a unique discourse that will satisfy the individual, and they do not seek to convert others to their discourse because they do not recognize them, not as individuals, not as equals, not as legitimate discursive partners that can help them to correct or purify their discourse. The others don't matter. The individual feels themselves individual in the act that no other individual can accomplish, because it is their own.

The others either keep the individual from their activity or help them accomplish it. This is why the individual does not want to convert others. The individual *uses* others. In this way, the others must adhere to the individual's project, and all trickery and cunning is allowed to bring them to do so. *The Work's* purest *political* expression is that of the totalitarian leader who seeks to reorganize the entire political structure to suit their own goals. Its project is to reshape the masses and the world. But as a project that has no goal other than the immediate satisfaction in its activity, it can never stop. There is no day after the revolution. The masses serve as tools for the individual in *The Work*, but as individuals they are individually taken into this project. This is because, as individuals, *they* are looking for meaning, *they* are looking to reasonably be fulfilled, and this is what the individual in *The Work* offers them. But it is an empty promise. The individual in *The Work* offers them a perfect meaningful world tomorrow, and to do so, it has to eradicate those who block the project today. Since the project depends on this, it can be accomplished by any means necessary.

The individual in *The Work* refuses reasonable discourse, but uses language, and uses all the forms of coherence that have been elaborated. They use this language to convince the others, but without being convinced of it themself. In this way, they can instrumentalize what reasonable discourse creates, and build an ersatz coherence that convinces others. *The Work* flies in the face of the philosophical attitude and in doing so it reveals that the earnest use of language, the use that sees understanding as the goal, is merely one of the types of stances the individual can take towards discourse. In fact, *The Work* reveals that there are multiple possible relationships to discourse. By showing that meaning develops in the free adhesion to discourse, and by showing that the individual is free to reorganize and use discourse as they see fit, *The Work* shows that there is no necessity outside of discourse because necessity has a conditional if/then structure that is only found in discourse. Discourse is a human affair and what it forms and reforms is human lives. This makes Weil's analysis of *The Absolute* anthropological and not metaphysical. He lived and wrote as *The Work* showed itself in its purity.[37]

Discourse and its refusal happen within human lives, there is nothing otherworldly about it. No single discourse can demand or require the adhesion of the

---

[37] Ricœur (1984), 408.

3.6 The Individual's Relationship to Discourse

totality of humanity. Discourse must multiply its point of views in order to face this plurality, to understand it, and more importantly, to act upon it. *The Absolute* is the first category *of* philosophy because it brings a specific relationship to discourse to its culmination; it takes the multiplicity of points of view and shows how they are moments of a single *absolute* point of view. It is *The Work* however that brings out the importance of the individual's relationship to discourse. *The Work* opposes itself to this Archimedean point by refusing to even enter into discourse. The other categories *of* philosophy weave these two strands together in different ways.

In *The Work*, the types of dialogical controls born in *Discussion* are ruled out. This individual is indifferent to objection, to rational argument, to reason itself. They are indifferent despite the fact that they understand it. They have freely chosen to refuse them and abandon reason. The individual in this attitude no longer seeks to understand, but rejects understanding because they already understand what reason implies. It implies being open to refutation, to counterexamples: it implies laying oneself bare before the normative weight of better reasons. It means abandoning their individuality, their particularity to opt for the universal. This possibility both secures the reality of philosophy as a free choice and opens a new philosophical question. This new question is neither ontological nor metaphysical. It does not bear on the constitution of reality, or at least not directly, but rather it bears on the reality of someone who stubbornly does not care about such questions. The question is about how discourse should be understood and about what should be done in the face of different understandings. The two categories *of* philosophy that follow the work answer it differently.

The Finite, exemplified for Weil by Martin Heidegger, Karl Jaspers, and the existentialists (and we could add the likes of Jacques Derrida), answers it by bringing the refusal of coherent discourse back into discourse. It recognizes concrete particularity, but it recognizes it in discourse. Each discourse however presents itself as the "*singular* act" that is aware of being singular and that understands its freedom in this act.[38] *The Finite* seeks to preserve the awareness of this freedom by the destruction and deconstruction of the coherence of discourse from the interior. This new attitude learns the lesson that *The Work* teaches. There is no necessity in philosophy and so it refuses the immanence that was proposed in *The Absolute*, just as *The Work* had done. But *The Finite* also refuses *The Work*. Not for "philosophical" reasons but rather because the individual doesn't believe in the project, because they don't want it. They refuse the purely violent interaction with the world because they don't want to be violent. *The Finite* refuses coherence but accepts discourse. In this way, it preserves discourse, but it preserves it in a refractory form. It is the attitude that destroys coherence in order to maintain the point of view of the individual performing this destruction. The single viewpoint sought by the tradition is refused because multiple viewpoints are needed. It is only thanks to these multiple viewpoints that individuals can recognize themselves as free and recognize the possibilities offered in discourse. Because *The Finite* refuses pure violence by opting for discourse, it

---

[38] Canivez (1999), 71.

discovers that the creative freedom felt in violence is also present in language. It is found in the poetic production of meaning that gives birth to discourse. The individual feels their freedom in their creation and see this creation as humanity's fundamental expression. What *The Finite* also recognizes is that this fundamental expression, this productive creation of meaning in a poetic language, this *poiesis*, is only understood thanks to discourse. The individual is alive and feels themself living in the contingency and finiteness of the life that only they can live, in the choices that only they can make, in the acts that only they can accomplish, but they recognize the situation because they have passed through discourse. The language that they recognize is the prelogical grasp of the meaning of their lives in the poetic creation of meaning itself. It is idiosyncratic, private, and fleeting. For it to be understood, the essential attitude must be mined out of this rich ore and refined into discourse, otherwise the meaning created disappears just as the individual does. Discourse is thus seen as the substance of understanding. It is what offers a fragile modicum of permanence. What *The Finite* refuses is that this permanence be absolute. There is no consolation for the finiteness of the individual, for the fleetingness of their activity, for the failure they inevitably face. In *The Finite* the individual is stripped of any consolation that the tradition offers.

All meaning is found in the singular creation of a singular individual, and the individual is free because they are finite. *The Finite* accepts that genuine meaning is the meaning created by the individual, and thus is limited by the limits of that individual, by the limits of all of humanity in their human condition. The limits of the individual's talent, of their means, of their life is the limit of their meaning and *The Finite* wants to grasp this limit in discourse. The coherence proposed by *The Absolute* is not merely rejected, this rejection is also explained. The total coherence proposed by *The Absolute* is seen to be impossible because we humans, as speaking acting creatures, are mired in the unforgiving thickness of our own lives. We cannot separate ourselves from our temporal nature, from our limited perspective, from the muddy opacity of ourselves. To see how this position is a departure from those found in the previous categories, looking at how the notion of the consolation of philosophy is treated in the categories before *The Absolute* and comparing them to those after suffices. Seneca's *On the Shortness of Life* (and the Stoics generally),[39] Boethius' *The Consolation of Philosophy*,[40] or the famous Book One, Chapter Nineteen in Montaigne's *Essays*,[41] entitled "That to Study Philosophy is To Learn to Die" are all examples of positions that present the philosophical act as the ultimate salve to human finitude. This can be compared to Simone de Beauvoir's closing reflections in her *Ethics of Ambiguity*. There, she rejects any such salve and it is a clear example of how the philosophical act is interpreted in *The Finite*. She states:

> Whatever one may do, one never realizes anything but a limited work, like existence itself which tries to establish itself through that work and which death also limits. It is the

---

[39] Seneca (2004).
[40] Boethius (1999).
[41] de Montaigne (1958).

3.6 The Individual's Relationship to Discourse

assertion of our finiteness which doubtless gives the doctrine which we have just evoked [that of Plato] its austerity and, in some eyes, its sadness. As soon as one considers a system abstractly and theoretically, one puts himself, in effect, on the place of the universal, thus of the infinite. This is why reading the Hegelian system is so comforting. I remember having experienced a great feeling of calm reading Hegel in the impersonal framework of the Bibliothèque Nationale in August 1940. But once I got into the street again, into my life, out of the system, beneath a real sky, the system was no longer of any use to me: what it had offered me, under the show of the infinite, was the consolations of death; and I again wanted to live in the midst of living men. I think that inversely, existentialism does not offer to the reader the consolations of an abstract evasion: existentialism proposes no evasion.[42]

The date she gives is telling. She rejects the consolation of philosophy because she is pressingly aware of the precarity of her situation. De Beauvoir goes back into a human world where the Parisian streets are newly filled with German soldiers. She does not turn away from the singularity of her situation. She is a single life facing the *real* possibility of death. In this context, one must steel their resolve and accept their finiteness in order to act meaningfully, even in the face of insurmountable odds and certain failure. She thus tries to show that this awareness of our finitude is instrumental to our awareness of our human freedom.

It is not the content of philosophy that is put into question, rather it is the relationship that the individual maintains with philosophy that is, specifically how that relationship affects human sensibility to that content. Different situations call for different philosophies. *The Absolute* proposes a single totally coherent discourse, a discourse by which the subject is a subject-for-itself, where the subject is its own object. This is supposed to hold a-temporally. *The Finite* refuses the possibility of a single totally coherent discourse because the singularity of every situation is what matters. Each individual is faced with a plurality of possible discourses in a singular situation, the individual must refuse coherence because coherence is the forgetfulness of our finitude. *The Finite* cannot propose real human satisfaction, and thus renounces the notion of satisfaction. All it can propose is the feeling of freedom that one has when looking their dissatisfaction and their inevitable failure in the face. The individual can find satisfaction in the awareness of freedom in their finiteness, but if they do, it's by chance. There is no necessary satisfaction to be had. It must be made. This is precisely what the last concrete attitude, *Action*, opposes to *The Finite*. The individual in *Action* refuses to live in a world where they are unsatisfied. But instead of refusing all coherence, it seeks to change the world reasonably and coherently so that their satisfaction can be realized.

Action, which is exemplified by Karl Marx (although one should refrain from seeing Weil's work as "Marxist"), is the attitude of the individual that sees themself as the junction of action, judgement, and the world. They recognize that this junction only makes sense in a world with other agents and within the embeddedness of their lives in social and political structures. Thus, Weil's account of *Action* looks to interpret and understand the world in order to change it. In this way, the philosophical "problem of action is the transformation of the social and political world in such

---

[42] de Beauvoir (2015), 158.

a way that the individual can freely seek satisfaction within it."[43] The world is modifiable because it is understandable and understood, but this world is a world filled with others. This is why the attitude does not merely look to recognize the natural, social and political structures of the world like *The Absolute*, why it does not see action as individual within the framework of the realization of an individual project, like *The Finite*, but sees action as collective. The attitude of *Action*, and the category that grasps it, posits the possibility of an individual who, because they understand their actual situation as being the consequence of a historic process, aligns their discourse with this situation in order to bring others into meaningful action. They seek to know the world in order to act and they know how to act upon the historical conditions in the world in order to modify them. In other words, their goal is to modify the situation to align with discourse.

This modification of the world is different from the type of activity that is undertaken within the attitude of *The Work*. Within *The Work* the individual does not worry about the validity of their project, because they are unconcerned with understanding, and because they feel alive in the refusal of coherence. Within the category of *Action,* the individual presents a discourse that makes claims of coherence and universality. This discourse is thus still open to refutation and modification. That is, the individual still submits themself to the types of dialogical control that happen in discussion, but they have the content that *Discussion* lacks. They inscribe themselves in a theory of history. They understand that the world has been grasped through discourse and that there are facts. These facts not only help the individual to grasp their situation, but they also condition it. The person wants their action to be reasonable, that is, they want to know why, how, and when to act, but they also want it to be transparent to others. They want their reasons for acting to be taken up and appropriated by others; they want their reasons for acting to be coherent and universal, and thus become reasons for everyone.

The category of *Action* completes the political analysis that was started in *The Work*. Discourse works on humanity and humanity is formed through discourse, thus for real satisfaction to be possible, the world must be *made* reasonable for the universal satisfaction of the whole of humanity. This is discourse's task. As discourse elaborates this task, it allows individuals to understand themselves and their situation and allows them to freely organize their goals and act upon them. This is thus the last concrete category, because it is the last pure attitude. The discourse of *Action* "saturates the philosopher's requirement of universality" because they "no longer only aim at the universality of discourse for all thinking individuals, they aim at the realization of a world where thinking would be a real possibility for the universality of individuals."[44] This real possibility of thinking is only possible when individuals have real autonomy articulated in civil and political rights, thus it is realized through the social and political action that reduces the violence of the world for thinking and acting individuals.

---

[43] Canivez (1999), 75.
[44] Canivez (1999), 78.

3.6 The Individual's Relationship to Discourse

We are now in a position to understand the different attitudes that Weil treats. The initial attitudes, from *Truth* to *Certainty*, are background attitudes because they accompany all other human attitudes. They are regrouped in *Certainty* as the precritical or pre-philosophical attitude. *Discussion* opens the search for coherence but does not ground it. *The Object* proposes the initial ground that opens philosophy. All the "semantic" attitudes from *The Object* to *The Absolute* are permutations of this philosophical attitude which have different semantic contents. These categories provide different logical points of view based on different ways of grounding understanding. Each category thus reveals a different irreducible attitude because it offers a different order of explanation that provides different scopes of comprehensiveness and universality. *The Absolute* brings the idea of total understanding in the absolutely coherent discourse to a close in its universality. However, it reduces the actual freedom of the particular individual. The attitude of *The Work* reveals that this freedom is irreducible by seeking a life outside of discourse. *The Finite* accepts particularity and discourse but as a particularity that is only maintained by destroying coherence from inside of discourse. *Action* is the attitude that seeks to make the world a place where universality is effectively universal, to modify discourse to transform it into something that can transform the world thanks to its universality. The categories *of* philosophy, from *The Absolute* to *Action*, all characterize different relationships that the individual can have with discourse. They all reprise the different forms of coherence that are found in the philosophical attitudes, and those found in the pre-philosophical background attitudes. The way that they combine their reprises, mixed with the way that they position themself towards discourse, and the aspects of their own discourse that are pre-critical, define the specificity of *each* person's concrete attitude. This is what allows people to act for reasons.

Action is the start of the theoretical crux, which along with the categories *Meaning* and *Wisdom*, defines Weil's own philosophical project. The attitude of *Action* is thus different from the category of *Action*. The individual acts in the attitude but understands thanks to the category. With this understanding Weil refuses a simple return to *The Absolute*. He wants to understand the possibility of understanding in the face of the refusal of discourse, just as he wants to understand the possibility of living a meaningful life outside of discourse. In order to do this Weil embarks on a "transcendental" reflection in *Meaning* and *Wisdom*. These two final categories bear on the two possibilities that Weil seeks to understand and they complete his project.

None of the concrete attitudes hold the totality of meaning. In fact, meaning depends on the interaction of all human attitudes and it is created anew in every human life. It is created in violence and in language, in violence by presenting the specificity that reasonable discourse will raise itself against, and in language by creating the stuff of discourse. The category of *Meaning* thus gives us the concepts that are necessary to understand all the appearances of concrete meaning. Language produces meaning and discourse organizes it in a given situation. Thus, for Weil, meaning is understood formally as the concrete expression of human freedom organized to grasp a specific human situation by a specific individual. *All* meaning takes on this form. The additional concepts that Weil develops—attitudes, categories, reprises—are used to understand how this form of meaning is articulated is specific situations. In human attitudes individuals produce meaning in their freedom, they grasp it thanks to the categories and they apply it to their concrete situation with the help of the reprise. The reprise thus highlights the way that all concrete meanings participate in meaning. Additionally, Weil uses the notion of satisfaction and dissatisfaction to understand how people situate themselves in attitudes. When an individual is satisfied, there is no movement, the individual lives their life as a unity. Satisfaction however is a rare thing. When they are dissatisfied they *can* articulate a new meaning in their attitude. This meaning becomes visible in reality and when the reality of this meaning is seen as making up a part of reality, *philosophers* seek to grasp it in the form of coherent discourse.[45]

Philosophers understand this unity, but they do not necessarily live it. Another category, *Wisdom*, is needed to explain how individuals live their lives as a unity. The union of reasonable discourse and life is thought in *Meaning*, but is lived in *Wisdom*. In other words, *Wisdom* provides the form that reasonable life outside of discourse takes. It is a return to the attitude after the thinking and understanding of the categories. It is also this reflection that allows Weil to see the logic of philosophy as complete. The acting individual uses discourse because they have understood it. They know what to do precisely because they have passed through it. But what do they find when they leave discourse? They find the attitude of *Truth*. They find the unity that was left at the starting point of reflection in their action, in their life, the unity of their feeling of presence. *Wisdom* is the formal *category* that reflects on the possibility of rediscovering this attitude. As a formal category however, this means that the idea of wisdom depends on the concrete appearances of wisdom. In each form of coherence, in each logical point of view, the individual can find this unity and can return to the attitude of *Truth* but without its previous naivety. Each concrete individual can find a coherent discourse that grasps their singular situation and that guides their action so that they can find plenitude in their reasonable feeling. In other words, if the formal category of *Meaning* reflects on "the unity between coherent discourse and coherent reality" (LP, 413), the formal category of *Wisdom* reflects on the unity of life lived as a coherent whole. This life is a life that is lived in the universal, but among other individuals, and so is able to unfold the meaning that it has found and created in the world.

---

[45] This is what makes them philosophers. Artists for instance do something very similar, but they do not aim at universal coherence and justification. Scientists also do something similar but they do not worry about the well-groundedness of their theory. Or alternatively, artists and scientists do not worry about such things in their activity as artists and scientists, when they worry about them they become philosophers.

3.7 Conclusion – The Beginning Is at the End

The Logic of Philosophy closes with a reflection on life, a reflection on the meaning that is created in human action, and how that meaning should be understood. This is why the final reflection is formal. There is no normative prescription that can cover the meaning that has not yet been created, and that humanity is always in the middle of creating. Weil's thought therefore leads to a philosophical practice understood as a *discursive* practice. It is also why *Action* saturates the philosophers' demand for universality. The categories are the totality of discursive shapes that coherently grasp meaning as it is lived in the world. *Action* unites these discursive shapes with a discursive activity by recognizing the plurality of discursive shapes as the plurality of forms of meaning. Because of this, the individual that reaches *Action* cannot properly said be a Weilian philosopher, just as they can also no longer be an Aristotelian, a Kantian, a Nietzschean, a Hegelian, or a Marxian philosopher. We put aside our books to reflect on our concrete situation and to grasp it in discourse. The individual who passes to the attitude of *Action* becomes their own philosopher by deploying the plurality of discursive shapes to grasp their situation, and they do so to elaborate a coherent discourse that will allow others to do the same *for themselves*. Philosophy thus becomes an argumentative and educative practice. It deploys the plurality of the shapes of meaning in the plurality of their discursive shapes because each individual is faced with other individuals with other situations. This plurality is needed to maintain reasonable discursive practices with these individuals. Argument does not *necessarily* bring individuals to see their own choice to participate in this reasonable practice. Individuals must freely choose to refuse meaninglessness, violence, and incoherence. But once they choose reasonable argumentative practices, individuals lift themselves up to the philosophical attitude of understanding by deploying the multiple forms of coherence that are available for grasping the singularity of their life. In doing so they grasp meaning and create meaning. They modify the world by modifying their own practice and by modifying the practices of others reasonably. This is the highest goal that humanity can give to itself: to live reasonably with others in a world that is understandable and understood, to act to make the world ever more reasonable. The relationships between life, action, meaning, practice, satisfaction, feeling, etc. can be articulated in multiple ways, and Eric Weil presents a way to understand such relationships, a way to understand them that helps others to grasp themselves coherently and reasonably thanks to them. In this way, Weil's discourse unites ground, coherence, and totality in a comprehensive *open* discourse. Freedom is seen as the ground discourse, but only in its initial opposition to truth. In discourse, it is the perpetual effort to resolve this opposition in each life that is *mine* and *yours* that allows us to see our coherence as total. This is because such discourse multiplies perspectives to include an ever-expanding circle of reasonable and potentially reasonable agents. It is because discourse will only be coherent when all perspectives are included within it and when their order and scope is understood; because it will only be satisfied if it concretely allows any potentially reasonable agent to grasp themselves reasonably. It aims at a comprehensive comprehensiveness.

Weil is certainly not alone in trying to understand these relationships. In fact, as I will argue throughout this work, the comparison between the way that Weil treats these themes and the way that they are dealt with in the American pragmatist tradition is particularly felicitous. From pragmatism's origins in the work of Charles Sanders Peirce, this tradition has grappled with the general problem of understanding and how understanding is linked to human action. In the next chapter, I will present my reading of pragmatism and its main threads in order to establish a dialogue between Weil's work and the work of pragmatist thinkers.

References

Boethius, A. 1999. *The consolation of philosophy*. Trans. V. Watts, rev. ed. New York: Penguin Books.
Brandom, R. 2010. *Between saying and doing: Towards an analytic pragmatism*. Oxford: Oxford University Press.
———. 2019. *A spirit of trust*. Cambridge, MA: Harvard University Press.
Canivez, P. 1993. *Le politique et sa logique dans l'œuvre d'Éric Weil*. Paris: Éditions Kimé.
———. 1999. *Weil*. Paris: Les Belles Lettres.
de Beauvoir, S. 2015. *The ethics of ambiguity*. Trans. B. Frechtman, rev. ed. New York: Philosophical Library/Open Road.
de Montaigne, M. 1958. *The complete essays of Montaigne*. Trans. D.M. Frame. Stanford: Stanford University Press.
Ganty, É. 1997. *Penser la modernité*. Namur: Presses Universitaires de Namur.
Guibal, F. 2011. *Le sens de la réalité: Logique et existence selon Éric Weil*. Paris: Éditions du Félin.
———. 2012. Langage, discours, réalité: Le sens de la philosophie selon Éric Weil. *Laval Théologique et Philosophique 68* (3): 593–617.
———. 2015. *Figures de la pensée contemporaine*. Paris: Hermann.
Hegel, G.W.F. 2015. *Georg Wilhelm Friedrich Hegel: The science of logic*. Trans. G. Di Giovanni. rev. ed. Cambridge, UK: Cambridge University Press.
Kirscher, G. 1989. *La philosophie d'Éric Weil*. Paris: Presses Universitaires de France.
———. 1992. *Figures de la violence et de la modernité*. Villeneuve-d'Ascq: Presses Universitaires de Lille.
Kluback, W. 1987. *Eric Weil: A fresh look at philosophy*. Lanham: University Press of America.
Perine, M. 1982. *Philosophie et violence: Sens et intention de la philosophie d'Éric Weil*. Trans. J.-M. Buée. Paris: Beauchesne.
Quillien, J. 1982. La cohérence et la négation: Essai d'interprétation des premières catégories de la *Logique de la Philosophie*. In *Sept études sur Éric Weil*, ed. G. Kirscher and J. Quillien, 145–185. Villeneuve-d'Ascq: Presses Universitaires de Lille.
Renaud, M. 2013. La confrontation des trois premières catégories de la *Logique de la philosophie* d'Éric Weil avec la dialectique hégélienne. *Cultura: Revista de História e Teoria Das Ideias 31*: 63–69.
Ricœur, P. 1984. De l'absolu à la sagesse par l'action. In *Actualité d'Éric Weil*, ed. C.É. Weil. Beauchesne.
Savadogo, M. 2003. *Éric Weil et l'achèvement de la philosophie dans l'action*. Namur: Presses Universitaires de Namur.

References

Seneca. 2004. *On the shortness of life*. Trans. C.D.N. Costa. New York: Penguin Books.
Venditti, P. 1984. La philosophie du sens. In *Actualité d'Éric Weil*, ed. C.É. Weil. Paris: Beauchesne.
Weil, E. 1950. *Logique de la philosophie*. Paris: Librairie Philosophique Vrin.
———. 1999. *Essais sur la nature, l'histoire et la politique*. Villeneuve-d'Ascq: Presses Universitaires du Septentrion.
———. 2003. *Philosophie et réalité: Tome 2, Inédits suivis de Le cas Heidegger*. Paris: Beauchesne.
Wohlrapp, H.R. 2014. *The concept of argument: A philosophical foundation*. Dordrecht: Springer.

Chapter 4
Pragmatism, Inferentialism, and Expressivism

4.1 Introduction – Orders of Explanation

In the first two chapters, I presented the main driving concepts of the *Logic of Philosophy*, an overview of its structure, and its goal. The *Logic of Philosophy* presents a development of historical forms of coherence as they are found in discourse and as they can be logically structured according to the universality and coherence, the comprehensiveness, of their content. Weil claims that these different forms of coherence have the categorial structures that they do because they organize conceptually what is essential to a lived attitude, thus providing an understanding of concrete lived situations. Because categories allow us to understand how claims are structured within different forms of discourse, Weil's use of the term category is meta-conceptual. It picks out and develops the consequences of different ground-level commitments. This meta-conceptuality is important because several different strands of modern philosophy when taken together—namely pragmatism, expressivism, and inferentialism—also insist on this meta-conceptuality (under the name of a *pragmatic metavocabulary*). Robert Brandom's inferential expressive pragmatism is thus a natural dialogue partner with Weil's philosophical position and it is precisely this meta-conceptual character that I will draw out of Brandom's work.

In this chapter, I will present an overview of this position in order to place Weil's theory in relation to it. What I will claim is that the primary concern of the strain of pragmatism defended by Brandom, like in Weil's own theory, is a certain practice of philosophy (even though Weil's theory has a political destination that is hitherto underdeveloped in this strain of pragmatism). This philosophical practice primarily aims at understanding what is *done* when one makes substantive claims about the world. To do so, it presents the substantive ontological and metaphysical claims made in discourse as explainable in terms of the kinds of practices that are involved in holding claims as true. Saying that claims made in discourse are explainable in terms of practices puts the individual's relationship to discourse front and center.

This is one of the main bridges that I am going to build between Weil's theory and pragmatism. This explanation is thus itself meta-philosophical. However, in order to build this bridge, a word must first be said about explanation.

As argued last chapter, orders of explanation are at the center of the *Logic of Philosophy* and Weil uses the term explanation in a specific technical sense where explanation is paired with doctrine. Remember, a doctrine, for Weil, is an implicit lived grasp of meaning. Explanation, on the other hand, is the reflexive work of making what is implicit in the doctrine explicit in discourse. Explanation therefore makes up part of what Gilbert Kirscher calls "the critical reduction of appearances."[1] This is where, by "elimination" and by "progressively destroying untenable interpretations,"[2] the doctrine is reduced to its essential commitments. These commitments are essential because they have allowed violence to be reduced and have allowed pure attitudes to be grasped. However, Weil also insists on the plurality of discursive positions. In this context, explanation allows individuals to bring diverse points of view together to see which hold up. Thus, as a technical term, *explanation* aims at (1) developing all of the consequences of a discourse so that the individual knows what they are committing to when they hold a position, (2) making the plurality of discursive positions explicit in order to understand the diverse paths that can lead to shared conclusions.

Explanation is thus understood as having a pedagogical and an argumentative function. In its pedagogical function, explanation helps individuals to understand the consequences of concepts they may not have encountered and/or have difficulty understanding. In its argumentative function, explanation acts as a type of dialogical control that allows individuals to understand where difference and disagreement fall. Difference and disagreement are seen as essential components of understanding because they allow us to shake the slough off our concepts by showing what is yet not understood, what needs to be clarified, what needs to be taken from a different angle, what needs to be *explained* further.

However, despite referring to explanation in terms of the critical reduction of appearances (and of violence) it must be highlighted that Weil's position is stubbornly non-reductive. In other words, Weil remains a pluralist. The reduction found in the critical reduction of appearances is always limited and never absolute. For Weil, the need for explanation implies a certain distance. It arises when individuals do not immediately *see* what is in front of them, because of multiple reasonable options. This plurality can be reduced but only to a certain degree. The effort of reduction allows the philosopher to act in good conscience (LP, 65). That is, it allows them to understand their own commitments and what these commitments mean faced with a plurality of other possible commitments. Explanation thus aims at being a step in an integrative process. Explanation leads to understanding, understanding leads to judgment, judgment decides whether the content of the new

---

[1] Kirscher (1989), 127.
[2] Kirscher (1989), 131. Kirscher also notes that despite Hegel's deep influence on Weil's work, Weil's insistence on the critical reduction of appearances owes more to Fichte than to Hegel. It is also at the center of Weil's critique of constructivism.

4.1 Introduction – Orders of Explanation

explanation will be taken up or not. An individual understands the thing being explained when they understand how it fits in with other concepts, that is, what it excludes and entails. Therefore, an individual can understand thanks to explanation but still refuse the thing being explained *because* there are other options. Remember that, for Weil, meaning takes form in the *application* of a specific concrete discourse to a specific concrete situation. Weil highlights that there is a plurality of possible discourse and situations. Because of this, there is also a plurality of possible ways that meaning can be articulated and a plurality of explanations and understandings. In other words, no single *prima facie* explanation is privileged. Rather, explanations become privileged through argumentative practices, and they *only* become privileged to the extent that they allow for more coherent, more universally communicable explanations of concepts and concept-use. The plurality of explanations though implies that we also play a role in choosing which explanation we are going to pursue, and this choice likewise cannot be eliminated. Things are turned in a variety of ways and multiple perspectives are used in order to bring out understanding. Explanation must exploit this diversity.

Explanation, understood this way, falls under the concept of the *reprise*.[3] According to the reprise, the individual evaluates and justifies their position in terms of others, and other positions in terms of their own. They then try to see whether their position can be understood under another discourse and how these positions fit together in the history of discourse. This falls in line with what Weil says in his *Problèmes kantiens*, where he argues that in the act of understanding, individuals should both tackle concepts in their strongest, most robust, most cogent form, and take their interlocutor seriously, seeing them as real dialogue partners.[4] In this way, the individual engaging in the act of understanding has the best chances of being sure that they actually understand. In addition, following this head-on confrontation with a robust, cogent explanation of things, the individual that is not convinced, if they want to remain in discourse, must be unconvinced for reasons. This shifts the burden of proof and engages interlocutors in genuine dialogical practices. This itself is linked to the articulation I have made between the normative weight of better reasons and the possibility of the radical refusal of discourse. In other words, we can recall that norms are not external necessities (even though they can often feel that way), but rather internal necessities that we submit ourselves to and that we give to ourselves. In order to stay in discourse, individuals must enter into real dialogue when there are differences and disagreements about concepts. Explanation, in its

---

[3] Looking ahead, I will argue that the reprise (and Weil's distinction between evaluative and justificatory reprises) fills a similar role in Weil's work as Brandom's three main ascription types, *de re*, *de dicto*, and *de traditione*.

[4] Weil states, "why study an author unless we are ready to get something out of it, ready to consider them, therefore, as someone we can learn something from if we seek not their weaknesses but their strength" (PK, 18). The reprise is one of the things that allows us to do this, and this aspect of the reprise can be read as a hermeneutic principle in the same family as the *principle of charity*, see Quine (1960) and Davidson (1984a). For a good overview of the evolution of this principle and the differences between Quine's and Davidson's use, see Delpla (2001).

argumentative function, is thus itself the result of difference and disagreement. It is also another way of understanding one of the principle functions of the reprise. In *Problèmes kantiens*, Weil describes the reprise as:

> [a] fundamental phenomenon in the history of thought and in history full-stop. It is the grasp of the new in an older language, the only one available to the innovator (who nonetheless transforms it). More importantly, it is the only one that they can use to make themself heard by their contemporaries, with the risk, which is certainty's neighbor, of only being understood with considerable effort by the posterity that has itself benefitted from the reprise's contribution to the development of a new language (a new conceptual system) (PK, 18, n. 4).

Categories, as meta-concepts, thus play an essential role in explanation by sculpting the pure forms of coherence that are concretely present in the history of thought. These pure forms are nothing more than irreducible coherent explanations of the world and descriptions of how people position themselves within them. In an important way, the content of a category is the part of previous explanations that has gone all the way through the integrative process mentioned above. It is born thanks to a reprise that seeks to explain an attitude. This new attitude has become visible by opposing itself to the category in place. It gives way to a new category *because* it grasps (explains, understands, and integrates) the pure attitude in discourse. The reprise grasps pure attitudes in discourse and thus allows new categorial articulations to emerge. This is the argumentative function. This process, like all processes in the logic of philosophy, is dynamic. The explanatory function of the reprise exploits its justificatory and evaluative functions in order to judge the way in which explanation will hold and how best to reach one's interlocutor. The reprise allows us to see our interlocutor's reasons as reasons. It thus allows us to apply explanation in both its pedagogical and in its argumentative function.

Explanation, in Weil's work, is one aspect of an integrative process that slowly and progressively makes explicit both the content of determined ground-level concepts *and* the structure that allows using such ground-level concepts in the first place. It is in this way that it is meta-philosophical. Weil's recursive conception of explanation thus allows us to both characterize the practice of philosophy and to show the role that different practices play in philosophy. This is a thread that Weil's philosophy shares with inferential expressive pragmatism. The strategy I will pursue in this chapter will be to give an argument about how pragmatism, expressivism, and inferentialism should be understood. It is essential not to hem and adjust these positions in such a way that they fit Weil's project, rather I must show them as freestanding, and *then* see if similar commitments can plausibly be extracted from Weil's position. As already noted, Robert Brandom's work is going to be the key to doing so. Not only does Brandom make a strong case that these positions fit together, but he also convincingly presents them as independent positions that nonetheless mutually support each other.

We will be working from Brandom's definition, which states that pragmatism "is a generic expression that picks out a family of views asserting various senses in which practices and the practical may be taken to deserve explanatory pride of

4.1 Introduction – Orders of Explanation

place."[5] The generality of this definition is going to be important because Brandom, like Richard Rorty before him, applies pragmatism far beyond the classic American pragmatist, Peirce, James, and Dewey. In fact, even though he has a deep respect for the importance of the classic pragmatist thinkers, Brandom thinks that we should look elsewhere to develop the kind of pragmatism that he himself is defending.[6] The pragmatism that Brandom defends hinges on a pragmatist order of explanation. This order of explanation places practices, understood as specific types of *doings*, at the center. For Brandom, such conceptual pragmatism implies that "what confers conceptual content on acts, attitudes, and linguistic expressions is the role they play in the practices their subjects engage in."[7] In this way, metaphysical and ontological claims, for example, are not to be taken to be explanatory primitives, but are themselves seen to be explainable in terms of the role they play in reasoning and the kinds of practices that are involved in holding these claims to be true. To do this, Brandom develops a pragmatic meta-vocabulary that allows us to understand the kinds of substantive claims that are made in descriptive first-order vocabularies, such as the vocabulary of empirical science. This pragmatic meta-vocabulary is to be our starting point.

Brandom starts by claiming that, roughly speaking, practices should be given explanatory pride of place and that contents are defined by their role in such practices. This differs most significantly from philosophical positions that start from immediately (non-inferentially) known first principles. Pragmatism thus refuses to *deduce* the content of beliefs from any set of such first principles. This is because pragmatism holds that any principle can itself only be understood as resulting from the effort to understand the content that is supposed to follow from the first principle in question. First principles are thus best thought of as explanatory candidates, as the result of the integrative process of explanation, and not as their starting points. In other words, instead of justifying all explanation *prima facie*, they open the possibility of re-explanation. How does this change our understanding? If we take an example, say Platonic Ideas or Forms, we can give a first-principle reading or a pragmatist reading. According to the first-principle reading, Forms are taken to be what grounds our knowledge about the world because they are what is unchanging behind appearances.[8] The first-principle reading however leaves the Forms in a difficult position. As first principles, they are supposed to ground knowledge, but they are radically different from the knowledge that they are to ground. This leads to them being interpreted as ontological or metaphysical objects that are present to intuition, that are immediately known, and that ground our discursive claims, even though it is unclear how they can enter into contact with the kind of inferentially articulated claims that we use in discourse. According to the kind of pragmatist

---

[5] Brandom (2011), 58.

[6] Brandom (2004).

[7] Brandom (2019), 3.

[8] In Weilian terms, the first principle reading corresponds to the *content* of the category of *The Object* in the *Logic of Philosophy*, the pragmatist reading, to the *role* that this category plays in argumentative practices.

reading suggested here, the Forms are better understood as the results of reasoning, as the final development of a specific commitment that *something* must ground our knowledge. Starting from this discursive commitment, Plato can be seen as developing the consequences of this commitment (along with other concomitant ones) until he arrives at the need for something eternal and unchanging behind appearances. The Forms can therefore be seen as a candidate explanatory meta-concept used to explain the *structure* of thought and belief but not any specific content. This is why they are empty and yet why all content participates in them. The pragmatist reading allows us to see how a particular just act, for instance, falls under the concept of justice, instead of trying to describe justice as an ontological and metaphysical substrate of reality. The first-principle reading has a character of defeasibility that risks invalidating the first principle itself. Because each first principle is incompatible with every other one, a wrong first principle invalidates everything that is said to follow from it. But under the pragmatist reading, mischaracterizing the explanatory candidate (the first principle) does not invalidate all the reasoning that led to it, rather it opens the path to re-evaluation and repair. It allows us to single out problematic commitments at different moments in our reasoning and to test alternative candidates, without overthrowing *all* of our understanding of reality.

A side-effect of the pragmatist reading is that different candidates can be seen as essential moments in the development of our other discursive commitments. This means that the Forms can be seen as playing an important role in the development of later explanatory models and can continue to be rich resources for considering our own modern positions, all while containing other elements that we no longer take to be plausible. One such element is that, in this Platonic model (which can also be used as a generic term to cover a whole strain of thought throughout western philosophy), individuals are seen as passive receptors of content and not at all as the active fashioners of content. Pragmatism refuses this position because it is interested in showing how the commitments, endorsements, and entitlements taken on and conferred in discourse play a structural role in defining conceptual content itself. For pragmatists, content is shaped in discourse and through discourse by the types of stances individuals take towards discourse itself, and through the incompatibilities and consequences of these commitments. However, once it is understood as a way of positioning oneself towards discourse, pragmatism does not escape the question of the kind of substantive claims that a pragmatist should hold.[9] It is all well and good to say that ontological, metaphysical, and even semantic claims should be analyzed in terms of discursive practices, but this is not what worries theorists. What worries them is the *content* of these claims and the *nature* of language. Theorists are right to worry about such things and different solutions must be explored. One solution, representationalism, focuses on reference and representation. Generically, representationalism is the idea that cognitive and semantic content stands in a word-world, or idea-world, relationship. Words and ideas represent

---

[9] Christopher J. Voparil, for instance, claims that Brandom gives ontological priority to "the social," in Voparil (2011).

the world and representations *refer* to that same world. In this model, representation and reference are taken to be *primitive* semantic concepts. We cannot go any further down. This response has gotten a lot of traction in the twentieth century, both because word-world relations intuitively seem to explain content and because the success of representational models in the cognitive sciences seems to shed new light on the nature of language. Representationalism however also holds many dead-ends. These dead-ends have given rise to rival models. It is in this context that inferentialism and expressivism will be defended as candidate explanatory commitments that make the content and nature of language intelligible. Inferentialism will be seen then as offering a substantive claim about semantic *content* and expressivism, a substantive claim about the *role* of language use, and together, these positions will be seen as making a substantive claim about the *nature* of language. If representationalism can be seen as generically claiming that the goal of language is to represent non-linguistic objects, then expressivism can be generically seen as claiming that the goal of language is to express something. Even by minimally characterizing the difference in this way, it should be clear that we do more in language than just characterize how things stand to each other in the non-linguistic world, and so a broader explanatory theory seems to be needed.

Expressivism in philosophy of language can thus be understood as a conceptual commitment to explain language use in all its forms and variety. The kind of expressivism in philosophy of language that is defended here, and that I am claiming is present in *Logic of Philosophy*, aims to provide a conceptual framework within which this form and variety can indeed be understood. However, it is, taken alone, insufficient to understand the mechanisms that make individual sounds and signs meaningful. A more robust articulation is needed in order to understand how, starting from language use, we can understand language use itself. That is, a recursive, self-critiquing, self-correcting definition of the mechanisms of language use is needed. What I claim is that Robert Brandom's articulation of inferentialism provides a robust framework within which the mechanisms of language use, and not merely its variety, can be understood. What is particular about this articulation is that it itself depends on a pragmatic meta-vocabulary that explains conceptual content starting from the kind of linguistic practices concept-users engage in. Therefore, it will be helpful to start from pragmatism.

4.2 Pragmatism's Narrative

As announced, the goal of this work is to bring Weil into fruitful dialogue with three different commitments, pragmatism, expressivism, and inferentialism. In order to do so, it is important to show what is specific about each of these commitments in Brandom's system and also show how they interlock in order to make a coherent picture. This implies that pragmatism, expressivism and inferentialism all have different roles. With that in mind, pragmatism is being asked to ground a type of order of explanation and to be the grounding commitment of the metavocabulary that allows expressivism and inferentialism to be *grasped*. The type of order of explanation that pragmatism is asked to ground is one that focuses on what people *do* in discursive practices. It claims that semantic content is explainable, is made intelligible, by focusing on this. It provides an order of explanation that moves from linguistic doings to semantic content. By starting from a pragmatic metavocabulary, this order of explanation claims that differences in semantic content cannot *merely* be explained away by appealing to other semantic content. Rather, when disagreement about semantic content arises, one way out is to look at the practice of appealing itself (justification, reasoned argumentative practices, etc.). In this way, there is a constant dialectical movement between the content of ground-level claims and the analysis of the framework within which such claims are made. Such a dialectical movement hold two key advantages.

First, by looking at what people do in discursive practices, the pragmatist order of explanation puts an emphasis on a *public* kind of doing. While this is not to say that such doings are simple (a lot goes into characterizing what counts as such a doing), they are analyzable in a way that appeals less directly to the content of prior commitments than the first principle model does. Looking at the act of committing to content before looking at the goodness of content allows speaking in a subjunctively robust conditional mode. It allows us to look at different contents and say *"if* somebody were committed to such and such content x, *then* they would be required to adopt this or that consequence y (or this or that consequence z would be incompatible)." By characterizing the form of subjunctively robust claims in abstraction from their specific content, the idea is that pragmatism's order has greater "expressive" force. That is, it allows us to say more. The greater the expressive force, the greater the scope, the more comprehensive the discourse. This expressive force is going to be important because it will be at the center of the defense of expressivism. If representationalism claims that language's role is to represent (mirror) a static and predefined world, expressivism makes a more open-ended claim. It claims that language is used to express something, however (and this is where the claim is open-ended), expressive goals are not predefined. They are dynamic and are elaborated progressively. In a sense we can look at pragmatism and expressivism as bookends. Pragmatism makes a claim about what is done in language and expressivism makes a claim about what can be done.

By starting from a pragmatist order of explanation, the notion of pragmatism is already larger and narrower than traditional pragmatism. It is larger because under this definition, the types of thinkers that fall under pragmatism expands. A more diverse set of thinkers than traditional pragmatism allows can be collected under this umbrella. However, it is at the same time narrower because the work that pragmatism is being asked to do is more specific. In order to see how this type of pragmatism differs from the classical characterization of pragmatism, it is important to look at what the classic characterization is. This characterization itself is a subject of controversy. Richard Bernstein has, after all, claimed that pragmatism is "a

4.2 Pragmatism's Narrative

conflict of narratives."[10] And indeed, there has never been more than a vague consensus about what pragmatism itself is. This is already clear in the years immediately following James's early broad defense of the philosophical movement. In a famous article, Arthur Lovejoy identifies at least thirteen different strains of pragmatism in the works of the early pragmatists.[11] Worse, he claims that not only are these strains not coherent between them, but moreover, that they cannot be reconciled. The question of whether pragmatism should be thought of as a unified school with a unified doctrine thus has to be asked.

Looking at some of the garden varieties of pragmatism, there seems to be little in common between them. Robert Brandom's neo-analytical linguistic pragmatism and Cornell West's theologically-grounded pragmatist social critique, for example, seem difficult to reconcile. And yet, both equally claim to be drawing influence from the classical pragmatists. Is the focus on practice enough to link them? Bernstein might say yes, Lovejoy, no. I will go on to defend Brandom's position, but it is nonetheless important to give some indications to how we got here. This problem itself is in part linked to the development of pragmatism and to its reception. The term was first brought to public attention through a series of lectures given by William James, even though the movement that is now known as pragmatism started well before that. As James himself indicates, pragmatism was born from an informal discussion group at Harvard and its founding document is the article "How to Make Our Ideas Clear" by Charles Sanders Peirce.[12] Already in this paper, many of the features that would go on to define pragmatism are present. There is a critique of Cartesian representationalism, there is an emphasis on the practical and functional nature of our beliefs claims, and there is an attempt to analyze conceptual meaning in terms of use. Peirce would then go on to develop and refine his picture of pragmatism at the same time that other thinkers rallied to the pragmatist banner. These thinkers, such as William James and John Dewey, took up Peirce's insistence on the practical character of concept use and modified it to suit their own projects. James's use of the concept is varied. At times he treated it, like Peirce, as a method, and at others, as a substantive theory that made robust metaphysical and ontological claims. Such claims were used, for example, to describe how different psychological characteristics gave way to different philosophical beliefs. He could then use these psychological characteristics to explain the pluralism of philosophical beliefs and to make room for religious and moral claims in a world described in scientific terms. James however adhered to Peirce's emphasis on the practical character of concept use, and saw human knowledge as adaptive and evolving. They both saw human knowledge and human concept use not as a thing that mirrored a fixed and eternal reality or that represented it, but as something that is deeply embedded in a reality that is itself adaptive and evolving. John Dewey would exploit this aspect of pragmatism to great effect, while placing even more emphasis on the social character

---

[10] Bernstein (1995).
[11] Lovejoy (1908).
[12] James (2000), 25.

of knowledge and thought. While all pragmatists, by starting from human practices, are aware of thought's social character, Dewey, who was deeply influenced by Hegel in his student days, exemplifies this thrust better than any of the other classical pragmatists. This becomes clear when we see how his pragmatism (which he preferred to refer to as instrumentalism) was tightly linked to his theory of education and of democracy.[13] For Dewey, education and democracy are bound to pragmatism because they all reflect the kind of social embeddedness that characterizes concept use in general, and it is through the development, promotion, and refinement of education and democracy that good concept use is fostered.

Dewey's place and influence as a public intellectual seemed to secure pragmatism's importance as a homegrown philosophy and as a live option for solving a variety of theoretical and practical problems. However, this was not to last. The sudden irruption of the Second World War led many of the finest German-language philosophers to flee Europe and take up residence in the United Kingdom or the United States and this led, in the United States, to pragmatism becoming overshadowed and displaced by the technically more robust and seemingly more innovative nascent "analytical" philosophy.[14] Pragmatism was eclipsed and went into hibernation until its concomitant but independent rediscovery by Richard Rorty and Hilary Putnam. This version of the story leads to what Robert Talisse and Scott Aikin have called the "eclipse narrative." Rorty himself was a defender of the eclipse narrative. He says that, "[a]mong contemporary philosophers, pragmatism is usually regarded as an outdated philosophical movement—one which flourished in the early years of this century in a rather provincial atmosphere, and which has now been either refuted of *aufgehoben*."[15]

Despite Rorty's defense, there are clear problems with the eclipse narrative of pragmatism. Talisse and Aikin note that one of the problems of this narrative is that it distorts the relationship between classical and contemporary pragmatists.[16] According to the eclipse narrative, contemporary philosophers need to look back to the classical pragmatists in order to "retrieve" their philosophical program. This implies that pragmatism itself has not evolved past these earlier articulations. If pragmatism has not evolved, we are, according to Talisse and Aikin, faced with two separate problems. The first is that, if pragmatism has not evolved, its usefulness to contemporary philosophical debates is merely historical. A return to classical pragmatists allows us to see how contemporary debates formed and thus provides important background information in order to fully understand arguments being made today. This option seems clearly false. Contemporary pragmatists, even those with the most historical bents, are not making this claim. Rather, they are saying that there is something vital in pragmatism. However, this leads us to the second problem. If there is something vital in pragmatism and if it has to be retrieved, this

---

[13] Dewey (1916, 1927).
[14] Dummett (1994).
[15] Rorty (1982), xvii.
[16] Talisse and Aikin (2008), 5.

implies that contemporary philosophy made a wrong turn somewhere and that to correct that wrong turn, one must look to the classical pragmatists. This errs in the other direction.

The first option claims that contemporary philosophy needs pragmatism only to fill in historical details, and the second option claims only classical pragmatism, and not the various other forms of contemporary philosophy, can move us forward. Both claims seem too strong and too narrow. Rather, contemporary pragmatists are saying that pragmatism is vital both as a body of philosophical questions, and as a *participant* in contemporary philosophical debates. Refusing the first problem by insisting on pragmatism's relevance and vitality allows us to clearly see the second problem. The eclipse narrative suggests a rupture, two separate pragmatist moments in philosophy that are connected because certain contemporary philosophers were able to retrieve pragmatist commitments to apply them to contemporary debates. However, again following Talisse and Aikin, if we insist on pragmatism as a living body of questions, as a vital philosophical position, we are more apt to see the development of pragmatism not as a rupture but as a continuity. This allows us to understand how certain pragmatist positions evolved and entered into contemporary philosophy.

However there does seem to be a genuine renewal to be found in Rorty's articulation of pragmatism. If that is the case *and* if the eclipse narrative is misled, then what is this specific Rortyan contribution that allows us to see pragmatism as having taken a step forward? A plausible answer could actually be found in the rise of analytical philosophy. Wilfrid Sellars, one of the key figures in Rorty's retelling of pragmatism, remarks through the title of one of his papers that analytical philosophy ushered in a "new way of words." Analytic philosophy was able, for the first time, to productively isolate specifically *semantic* concerns from metaphysical, ontological, or epistemological ones. This allowed thinkers on this side of the linguistic turn, like Rorty, to better clarify the central role language plays in shaping our conceptual lives. This also allows us to see how the two main problems with the eclipse narrative can be overcome. First, pragmatism is seen as interacting with the claims made by different philosophical positions, and also, as absorbing them. In this way, there is no need to cry for a "return to pragmatism." It has never left. Second, because it has never left, and because it sees specific claims made by different philosophical schools as meriting absorption, it does not see contemporary philosophy as having taken a radically wrong turn, rather it sees it as having essential but incomplete insights, insights that can potentially be completed by pragmatism. The interaction between philosophical positions thus becomes an important correction to one-sided concerns.

Another move that might allow us to overcome the eclipse narrative but still see Rorty as adding something specific and essential is to draw the distinction between the theorist and the practitioner.[17] In broad strokes, theorists worry about the framework and meta-vocabulary questions concerning a specific position. Practitioners,

---

[17] Brandom (2020).

on the other hand, work from central commitments that characterize the theory. Theorists look to give the criteria that allow practitioners to fall under a given heading. Practitioners work from within those criteria (and may even do so unwittingly). Most theorists then are also practitioners, but this is not always necessarily the case. And even though practitioners usually also become theorists when they look to ground their practice, nothing requires this to happen. Louis Menand, for instance, is a theorist of pragmatism, insofar as he has acted as an important historian for the movement, but he is not, properly speaking, a philosophical practitioner of pragmatism.[18] Wilfrid Sellars was a practitioner of pragmatism, using the criterion given here, without being himself a theorist of pragmatism. In fact, he refused this term. Despite that though, he adopted pragmatist positions and was even comfortable using pragmatist terminology (he even adopted the term pragmatics and used it to characterize certain concepts in philosophy of language well before it entered into the linguistic mainstream in the late sixties).[19]

It is from the point of view of theorists that the eclipse narrative is the truest. In this case, the middle years of pragmatism were indeed lean years, and Rorty (and Putnam) did in fact do a great deal to restore the luster to pragmatism's name. However, a more useful way of understanding pragmatism is to look at practitioners.[20] Rorty, as a practitioner, develops pragmatism in a variety of ways. One such way was to combine his "ironist" position (where ironists are the "sort of person who faces up to the contingency of his or her own most central beliefs and desires")[21] with "solidarity" (where each individual is constantly working to incorporate others into an ever more expansive notion of "us"). What is important here is the way that Rorty thinks that both moves belong to the critical examination of the linguistic practices that happens in what he calls "vocabularies." Vocabularies are the content and consequence of shared normative discursive practices. They are the contents we are committed to and the consequences we are willing to accept based on those contents.[22] In this way, we can see exactly how, as both a practitioner and as a theorist, Rorty finds himself on the near side of the linguistic turn. He starts from specific practices yes, but the practices that matter most are discursive. Individuals are to identify the contingent features of their own vocabulary, and then analyze whether such features ground what they are actually committed to. It is in this way that his

---

[18] Menand (2001).

[19] He himself notes that he read pragmatism through the eyes of his father, the important critical realist philosopher, Roy Wood Sellars, who saw pragmatism as "shifty, ambiguous, and indecisive" Sellars (1996), 9.

[20] We will not go into this story here, but one has only to look Cheryl Misak's retelling of the course traced by pragmatism in the United States and Great Britain, in Misak (2013, 2016), to see that the eclipse narrative does not tell the whole story. One could also look at the course that pragmatism took in mid-twentieth-century Germany to see that this story is incomplete. Habermas and Apel, for example, were both practitioners and theorists of pragmatism and argued from pragmatist positions while incorporating different (analytic, hermeneutic, phenomenological) elements from various other philosophical schools.

[21] Rorty (1989), xv.

[22] Rorty's vocabularies thus play a similar role to Weil's categories.

4.2 Pragmatism's Narrative

position as a practitioner, who sees the work he is doing as falling under the pragmatist banner, allows Rorty the theorist to unite Sellars, the Hegel of the *Phenomenology of Spirit*, Donald Davidson, the "second" Wittgenstein, Jacques Derrida with the "classical" pragmatists, Peirce, James, Dewey. By bringing together these diverse positions under a single banner, Rorty was himself able to tell a broader story about the kind of things that people do in language. Importantly, this allowed him to absorb the changes in his own thought, which had moved from a relatively sober form of philosophical analysis to a sweeping claim about the role of history and philosophy as stories that humanity tells to itself. Rorty is a theorist and a practitioner on our side of the linguistic turn. His attack on representationalism and foundationalism is, in fact, an attack on specific semantic and epistemic orders of explanation. The pragmatist order of explanation has to therefore offer something different. This is what that his student Robert Brandom has been working to provide.

In the terms to be defended in this work, and following Robert Brandom, pragmatism is the metatheoretical framework in which ground-level language use is to be understood. In this way, it is first and foremost a commitment to a specific type of order of explanation. This is the commitment to explain meaning in terms of use. It claims that, instead of looking at what an assertion is, one should look at the act of *asserting*, instead of the content of a judgment, the act of *judging*, etc. Practice is seen as the most basic explanatory concept within that order of explanation and the practice of articulating an order of explanation is seen as a central practice. Semantic pragmatism thinks that this can only be done by giving an account of the discursive practices necessary for such a second-level practice to be possible. It thus, in a sense, has to be recursive. The pragmatist order of explanation contrasts then with other orders of explanations, such as the Platonic example found earlier in this chapter, or the representational order of explanation, which will be tackled again later on. Both lack the type of recursiveness that the pragmatist order of explanation is hoping to provide. Because the pragmatist order of explanation takes actual practices into account, it can be thought of as a *role-functional* vocabulary. Like the name implies, the goal of role-functional vocabularies is to understand how different vocabularies play different roles at different levels of discourse.

It will be useful to say a word here about the specific kind of *normative functionalism* that Brandom defends. As we have already argued, one of the key pragmatist moves is to explain meaning, understood as semantic contents, in terms of use, understood as discursive practices. But this functionalism is not only articulated at the level of *practices*, it is also articulated at the level of *contents*. At the level of practices, roles are defined by the way they articulate, and are responsive to, norms. Thus, as we shall see, the kind of pragmatic functional roles that are essential center around commitment. Taking on a commitment means inscribing oneself into a normative space. It means being subject to the assessment of others while also being the kind of creature that can provide assessments that other such creatures within the normative space are subject to. Commitments have the role they do both because they can be acknowledged and because they can be attributed. This is why Brandom's functionalism is a *normative* functionalism. Its greatest concern is explicating the role of normative statuses, as they are instituted by normative attitudes, and normative attitudes, as they are shaped by normative statuses. This is different from the classic functionalism that is to be found in philosophy of mind.

The functionalist model in philosophy of mind is not looking at normative roles, but rather, at causal ones. It looks at the way that mental states are caused by and responsive to physical states, without being reduced to them. It defines mental states in *relational* terms and then looks to cash out these relations by picking out the roles that different constellations of relations play. In this way, it seeks to avoid the pitfall of naïve materialism that reduces the mind to predetermined physical states, and the pitfall of dualism that explains mental states by appeal to some sort of unknown and unknowable metaphysical entity such as the mind. By looking at the functional role different analyzable physical states play, we are able to see mental states as resulting from physical states, but also able to avoid reducing them to such physical states. A role is a new kind of characterization that cannot be deduced from its composite parts, even though the role can be analyzed into its composite parts.

This guiding insight allows normative functionalism to do something very similar. Instead of looking at causal relations, it looks at how normative attitudes attribute normative statuses, and how normative statuses influence normative attitudes. This is cashed out in terms of the way discursive practitioners take on, acknowledge, and attribute commitments. Thus, the fact that these different practices can stand in productive relationships to each other allows them to take on the specific normative roles that they do. Pragmatic normative relations play a framework-explicating role. However, one of the attractive features of a role-functional explanation is that it can also be used, starting from the practice of inferring, to explain the determinate contents of ground-level concepts. In other words, semantic contents can also be seen in functional terms. Under such a model, semantic content is to be understood at this level as giving us rules for application. When one infers from the content of a commitment, understood as the premise of a reasoning, they are being sensitive to a whole network of inferences. Some provide the incompatible inferences, whereas others provide the permissible or necessary inferences that are consequences of the initial commitment. In this way, claiming that something is red demands that one acknowledges that they are prohibited from also claiming that it is green, precisely because green and red are incompatible. It also demands that one acknowledge that red is a color because being a color is a consequence of being red. These just are features of the concept of red. What the game of giving and asking for reasons does is it draws out further incompatibilities and consequences. A good example is Wilfrid Sellars's comparison between "red" and *rot*. Red and *rot* can be seen as having the same meaning not because they pick out the same color in the world but because they have the same rules of application, one of which is picking out that color. Therefore red has the same meaning as *rot* if and only if these two words play the same role in their respective languages.[23]

---

[23] One of the most frustrating things a second language learner encounters is trying to learn from *translation* because so many words in one language have a different scope of application in another. Some even allow whole different sets of permissible inferences to go along with the single targeted corresponding application, thus leading to clunky or humorous sentences.

Such a functionalist reading implies both a pluralist and a holist account of meaning. It is pluralist in that it recognizes that different types of language use play different roles and have different scopes and applications. It is holist in three important ways. First, it is holist because of the way that concepts rely on each other for their content. One cannot know a single content in isolation, one must know many to know one. Second, even though *all* discourse cannot yet be said to be unified, different levels of discourse must at least minimally interact with each other. This is because commitments at one level of discourse can be shown to effect those at other levels of discourse. Individuals slip from one level of discourse to another (often without being aware of it) and only slowly and in public discursive practices are able to unfold this interconnectedness. Third, it is holist because, once public discursive practices are seen as the starting point, this kind of order of explanation must describe the *kind* of practices that allow cashing out on this insight. Such practices: commitments, acknowledgements, and endorsements teach us that semantic content is relational. It acts on and is acted on by other conceptually articulated contents. This, as will be developed later on, is central to inferentialism. It is the idea that semantic content is, at the core, a series of incompatibilities and consequences in relation to other such incompatibilities and consequences.

4.3 Semantic Pragmatism

Because Brandom's pragmatism starts from "an account of what one is *doing* in making a claim, [...][which] seeks to elaborate from it an account of what is *said*, the content or proposition—something that can be thought of in terms of truth conditions—to which one commits oneself by such a speech act"[24] Brandom can be seen as defending a form of linguistic pragmatism whereby an explanation of linguistic practices allows for a robust description of conceptual content. This is why his order of explanation takes on the form that it does. He denies that truth, or any other strictly ontological object such as representation, should be considered a primitive semantic concept. Rather, he holds that one should look at the practice of ascribing, judging, and holding conceptual contents as true in order to know if these contents were formed in reliable ways. Pragmatics comes before semantics. Following this notion of normative functionalism, there are two key concepts that are necessary to understand Brandom's position. The first is Rorty's already mentioned concept of vocabularies, the second is Wilfrid Sellars's development of the pragmatic meta-concept of the space of reasons.

Rorty's notion of vocabularies is important, but it would be incomplete for understanding Brandom's position without the additional development of the space of reasons. To develop this thought, Brandom constantly directs readers to a passage in Sellars, "Empiricism and the Philosophy of Mind" where Sellars says, "[in]

---

[24] Brandom (2001), 12.

characterizing an episode or a state as a knowing, we are not giving an empirical description of that episode or state; we are placing it in the logical space of reasons, of justifying and being able to justify what one says."[25] For Sellars, and Brandom, the logical space of reasons plays a normative, structural role in concept use. By focusing on *how* one places things into the space of reasons, and what counts as a correct and incorrect placing, Sellars starts to develop the pragmatic metavocabulary that Brandom will exploit. According to this metavocabulary, the content of descriptive language use, such as someone saying "this is a tree" or "this is an oak" or "this is a live oak" is not to be understood *essentially* in terms of an object in the world but rather as fleshing out the contours of the space of reasons, as a certain practice of categorization. The inferential articulation of a concept gives us the rules for applying concepts in judgment.

John McDowell makes this point clearly when he notes that "the conceptual apparatus we employ when we place things in the logical space of reasons is irreducible to any conceptual apparatus that does not serve to place things in the logical space of reasons. So the master thought [of the space of reasons] as it were draws a line; above the line are placings in the logical space of reasons, and below it are characterizations that do not do that."[26] McDowell's characterization of Sellars's position allows us to see that there is a rupture between our non-conceptual and our conceptual experience. Using this characterization, we can call this rupture, *the Sellars line*. To apply what McDowell is saying to our example, we can argue that even basic descriptive vocabularies, which involve claims like "this tree is a live oak," themselves have to be understood according to the practice of categorization, or the placing in the space of reasons. The observations that are made about the world thus depend on the conceptual framework within which those observations are made. However, the analysis of the framework itself cannot be made in the same language-register as the observation without running aground in a confusion of eternal regresses and vicious circularities.

Taking the example of the hypernym "live oak." We can note that in English this term refers to certain evergreen species of oak. We can then go on to note that such a hypernym is not universal. In fact, it is entirely missing in some languages and in others multiple terms are needed to do the work that "live oak" does. If we take one language, say French, as an example we can see this. Between "chêne," the general word for an oak, and the individual species of oak that, in English fall under the term "live oak,"[27] such as "cork oak"/"chêne liège," two different terms, "vivace" and

---

[25] Sellars (1997), §36.

[26] McDowell (2013), 5.

[27] George Lakoff, in his seminal work, *Women, Fire, and Dangerous Things*, notes how reliable basic, *genus* levels of categorization are because of how context sensitive they are. Thus, to paraphrase Gertrude Stein, an oak is an oak is an oak. Lakoff insists however that this reliability breaks down as we move up or down into superordinate or subordinate categorization, Lakoff (1987), 199–200. This is an important discovery, because, as he highlights, a representational model *should* have the same articulation across different granularities of fineness of categorization. Thus, *genus*-level categories should be confirmed as we move through superordinate and subordinate

4.3 Semantic Pragmatism

"pérenne," are needed to do the work that the English term "live oak" does. So, while an analysis of the concept CORK OAK[28] would show that "chêne-liège" and "cork oak" both correctly cover the concept, an analysis of the concept LIVE OAK is more difficult. Thus, an analysis of the concept LIVE OAK says just as much, if not more, about the conceptual commitments of colloquial English arboriculture than it does about the trees themselves. A proper analysis of the meaning of LIVE OAK thus looks neither exclusively nor primarily to a specific thing in the world, but rather to the way that incompatibilities and consequences carve up different concepts in different spaces of reasons. In other words, to say anything about the meaning of this concept, a metavocabulary is needed to analyze the practice of ascription within a space of reasons, in this case, that of colloquial English arboriculture. These practices start from the notion of discursive commitment.

In order to make sense of the notion of commitment, Brandom builds off of David Lewis's notion of scorekeeping.[29] As a basic notion, scorekeeping is the idea that we can track our interlocutors' language use as one would track the score in a game. According to Brandom, in language games, there are two basic aspects of linguistic practices that we track, commitments and entitlements. Tracking commitments builds off the responsibility we take on when we make a judgment. We are responsible for the conceptual content that goes along with what we assert. This is what it means to commit. Thus, when someone standing in a field says that the tree out in front of them is a live oak, they commit themselves to the content of the inferences that accompany the concept LIVE OAK. In this case, the success or failure of the language user's claims define the implicit score that is attributed to that individual's knowledge in colloquial American arboriculture. Commitments pair symmetrically with entitlements. Entitlements are the inferences that the individual is allowed to make based on the commitments that they take on. Entitlements allow the individual to make additional claims that are not explicitly contained in the judgment "this is a live oak." By saying that the tree out in the field is a live oak, the individual is entitled to judgments such that, in normal conditions, this tree will retain its leaves throughout the entire year, or that it will produce acorns. These are the types of inferences that allow us to move from one claim, that such or such thing is a live oak, to other claims that we have not made. This also adds a third essential concept to Brandom's inferentialism, namely, endorsements. The role of endorsements is to guarantee the intersubjective nature of Brandom's position by including larger social practices within the practice of inferring. When one commits oneself to a content, one endorses the content and places it in the social sphere as a candidate to be endorsed by others. Recognizing entitlements to a content, in turn leads to

---

categories. The live oak example however shows how quickly categorization breaks down as we move across languages and levels of categorization, an experience which I am sure any frustrated second language learner can attest to.

[28] Throughout this work small uppercase letters will be used to refer to the central incompatibilities and consequences of a concept that is being highlighted when it changes languages or when it is articulated differently according to various reprises.

[29] Lewis (1979).

endorsing commitments. By saying something is a live oak, I commit to it being an oak and being evergreen. I am entitled to say that it will keep its leaves and that it will produce acorns. But I may not be able to distinguish between two live oaks, between a white oak and a cork oak. If my friend claims that something is a cork oak, because I consider her a reliable reporter on arboriculture matters, I may endorse her claim and thus see her as entitled to other claims. When I endorse her claim, I am saying that her judgment is such that I can adopt it in my own reasoning. If she gives me criteria that allow me to distinguish between white oak and cork oak, I can consequently take up those criteria, and independently share them with others.

While it is convenient to separate these three concepts—commitments, entitlements, and endorsements—in order to bring out their specificity, it is important to note that they are in reality interlocking. When we commit to something, we are endorsing something and taking on new sets of entitlements, just as when we endorse something, we attribute entitlements and take on commitments. If our claim that a certain tree being a live oak is endorsed by others, to remain coherent in that endorsement, they must also endorse the claim that it is a hardwood and that it is an Angiosperm, as those claims are implicit in the concept LIVE OAK. By saying that they must also endorse the claims that are implicit in the concept, we highlight the normative structure of concept use. Commitments and entitlements structure the correct use of concepts. Claims are implicit in concepts and by making them explicit, the individual makes good on their inferential entitlements. By taking responsibility for a judgment the individual is committing to a content. Individuals implicitly keep score of their own commitments and entitlements as well as those of others. This double scorekeeping allows us to keep track of the general shape of spaces of reasons. This means that certain people will be considered reliable reporters of tree species but not of sports, or of classical French literature, but not of classical Chinese literature. We can thus come to rely on some people for certain types of information and not for others, and we can see people as being good at some things in concept use and not at others. We track individuals' use of concepts and recognize when they use them correctly, this allows us to endorse their concept use, which in turn allows us to use their reasons as our owns. At the same time, others are doing the same thing, including with us. When we endorse someone's claim, we recognize that we can use that claim in our own reasoning. When we assert a claim, we are committing to its goodness, claiming that others can use it in their reasoning. This is the lynchpin of "the game of giving and asking for reasons." It is precisely giving our reasons and demanding reasons from others that brings out the shape of commitments and entitlements.

Reliable users of specific concepts allow us to gauge the assurance with which we use them ourselves. They will act as potential correctives when we use them poorly and will help us to whet our judgment. This will also effect the authority that I attribute to others. I will more likely take the word of a friend who knows a great deal about arboriculture when they tell me that the tree we are looking at is a cork oak than I would of a friend who has never shown any interest in trees before. This does not mean that this second friend does not have this information, rather it means that I have not yet myself made a judgment about their reliability, so I am hesitant to endorse their claim. This shows that judgments are housed in other judgments, which themselves concurrently work at multiple levels. There are judgments that are tracking what my friend says about the tree while these judgments are being compared to other times that we have spoken about plants. There will be, at the same time, judgments tracking my general confidence in their reliability about other non-tree-related claims. This will go hand in hand with the judgments that track my own knowledge about trees, and what I myself feel responsible for and entitled to, and whether I feel competent to endorse their claims as good claims.

4.4 Inferentialism

The language of commitments and entitlements allows us to make sense of what we are doing within discursive practices but it does not yet provide a full picture of *conceptual content*. Rather, this is the role that inferentialist semantics plays. As already noted, inferring is to be seen as the key practice that allows us to talk about specific determinate contents. Above, we spoke about how we take on commitments and how we acknowledge and attribute entitlements, all within the social practice of scorekeeping. This practice belongs to the pragmatist metavocabulary that grounds inferentialism. Underlying these practices however is the additional notion of inferential relations and the distinction between logical inferences and material ones. These inferential relations are what is seen as constituting conceptual content itself. In other words, in the inferentialist picture, content just is this relation of incompatibilities and consequences. Seeing conceptual content in this way allows us to overcome the dead-ends found in the representationalist model and its dependence on reference. The representational model, following Descartes, focuses on the epistemological concept of certain knowledge and, with it, the semantic concept of truth-values. This is built into the role representationalist models see references playing. In such models, what reference does is allow us to pick out an aspect of the world that corresponds to our representation. Reference is thus seen role functionally, but representations are not. Brandom's inferentialist semantics tries to help us think about reference, inference, representations, and content all role functionally. Content is therefore analyzable in terms of inference. It provides rules of application. These rules are themselves defined by the inferential relations of consequence and incompatibility. It is only after that Brandom goes about explaining reference and representation. What matters here is that both reference and representation are *social* practices and their most primitive role is communicational. Under the inferentialist model, reference and representation are fundamentally dialogical concepts. In this way, reference is used to draw the attention of others to specific features of discourse or the world and representation is used to communicate the content of those features meaningfully to others. So, a goal of offering an alternative dialogical and pragmatist order of explanation to representationalism is to clear up what work it is that representations do. One of the main problems of representationalism *and* one of its main draws is found precisely in this ambiguity. In fact, different representational theories ask representations to do different things, and within the representationalist tradition there seems to be no clear picture of what exactly a representation is. Is it a mental item with semantic qualities? A mental process making use of symbols? The mapping of features of the world into an appropriate mental or semantic item (concepts? ideas? words?).[30] Again, different theories that swear allegiance to representationalism will respond differently. "Representation" thus seems to be a big baggy term that holds lots of different things within it. And this bagginess may, in fact, be both its appeal and the source of its confusion. If this is the case, then one of the initial draws of representationalism is that it allows us to slide, almost seamlessly, from one domain of discourse to another, using a readily available and overarching concept (representation) to do work in all these different domains, despite the fact that the way that the concept is articulated in each domain is quite different. This is what makes representations hard to pin down. A by-product of the pragmatist (and dialogical) order of explanation must then include a robust description of the work representations do and a good working definition of the concept. Representationalism runs together multiple notions of representation. This ambiguity either allows representations to play some fundamental role in explanation without clearly defining what this role is or it allows representation to play a great many roles in explanation by appealing to some "intuitive" notion of representation that itself is confused. Thus, getting clear about representations would require picking apart these different threads that representationalists run together.

Letting these threads run together leads to what Huw Price calls (big R) Representationalism.[31] To avoid (big R) Representationalism, Price thinks there are two distinct concepts of representation that have to be kept separate. So, what is (big R) Representationalism, and what are the two versions of representation that need to be kept separate? According to Price, (big R) Representationalism is a "proto-theory about language" where "the function of language is to 'represent' worldly states of affairs and that true statements succeed in doing so."[32] (Big R) Representationalism depends on the idea that what we are doing with language is first and foremost labelling parts of the world or matching statements about the world with the facts that make these statements true. This proto-theory for Price rests on a commonly held assumption, namely, that "linguistic items [...] 'stand for' or 'represent' something

---

[30] This last question is going to fall under what Brandom calls invidious Eddingtonian realism, see Brandom (2018), 176. Brandom uses Eddington's famous two tables example, which distinguishes the solid, colored, extended thing that is available to our perception (and thus represented according to the representationalist model) and the aggregate of particles that theoretical physics uses to describe the table. Another example could be sounds, should we think of sounds as waves that we are representing as moments of auditory experience, or should we take the wave to be a way of representing our auditory experience? Which way the representation should be seen as going highlights the point Price makes about e-representations and i-representations, in Price (2013).

[31] Oddly enough Price does not give any characterization of (small r) representationalism. Is (small r) representationalism to be found in Brandom's attempt to rebuild "[r]epresentationalism on pragmatist foundations" Price (2013), 35? Is it Price's own single "cheer for representationalism?"

[32] Price (2013), 24.

4.4 Inferentialism

non-linguistic."[33] At the heart of this assumption is a confusion about two distinct *types* of representation, e-representations, or the type of representations that, roughly speaking, track the external aspects of the environment, and i-representations, representations that are internal to a specific idiom and that designate inferentially articulated dimension of representations *within* that idiom. Price clearly thinks that both types of representation play a role and that both roles are essential. He nonetheless also thinks that the problem comes when we reduce one form of representation to the other, namely when i-representations are seen as needing to be explained in terms of e-representations. This is the major fault of (big R) Representationalism, but again, without such a distinction, it is not clear why. Because both roles are essential, we cannot just do away with them, but when they are confused, we give them an undue place in our order of explanation.

If we look at both e-representations' and i-representations' role functionally, then it becomes clearer why e-representations cannot play the role that we want representations to play *semantically*. This lines up with Brandom's inferentialism. We want our language to be informative, but for it to be, it must not only pick out the features of the world. It must also tell us what things are not, what follows from what, what is possible. E-representations do no such thing: this is the role of i-representations, the role of the inferential articulation of concepts. Therefore, instead of trying to start from an explanation of how language and the world line up, and then explaining how they form conceptual content, inferentialism is trying to clearly distinguish the realm of the conceptual itself. To see why this matters, it will be helpful to look at Brandom's development of the different levels of *awareness*. Brandom's articulation of awareness allows us to see that an observational vocabulary depends in many ways on a pragmatic metavocabulary. If we look at non-inferential reporting sentences, such as "this is a live oak", the (big R) Representationalist tendency is to assign the term "live oak" a labeling role. That is, the term labels a particular object in the world, and the sentence then reports a state of affairs.

Besides highlighting certain objectional ontological claims that go along with this notion of states of affairs and particulars, Brandom's strategy is to show that many things can be considered to have reliable differential responses to their environment without themselves being able to manipulate and share concepts, without being, to use Brandom's apt turn of phrase, concept-mongers. To do so, Brandom distinguishes three different levels that are required for full awareness. These levels are "reliable differential response dispositions," "sentience," and "sapience." The first element marks out things that respond to elements of the environment without necessarily being aware. Thus, iron responds in a reliable way to the presence of humidity by rusting, but there is no claim that iron is aware. However, while reliable differential response dispositions *do* play a role in awareness, they do not themselves additively amount to awareness. Awareness belongs to living creatures. This type of awareness, which contains environment-tracking e-representations, is itself

---

[33] Price (2013), 7–8.

different however from *discursive* awareness. All creatures that are aware depend on their reliable differential responses in their awareness to navigate their environment, some can even be trained to use these reliable differential dispositions to give *specific* responses to their environment, such as the way a parrot can be trained to squawk "red" in the presence of red things. Awareness at this level is what Brandom calls sentience, and it is this type of awareness that we share with other non-human animals. Sentience also plays a role in the specifically human kind of awareness that Brandom calls sapience. Sapience is specifically discursive awareness, and it is the level where agents can mobilize i-representations. In other words, it involves the capacity of mobilizing reasons to *explain* one's behavior. It involves discursive understanding and discursive intelligence. It is something that we humans have a hand in shaping, because we are able to mobilize a *history* of reasons that surpasses the scope of our own lives and that characterizes us as part of a community.

We can imagine an iron-based device that tracks the humidity levels in the air, but it would be hard to argue that such a device is aware. Tracking the environment in this way relies on reliable differential responses but in no way can be assimilated to awareness. Likewise, sentient and sapient creatures track their environment and this is part and parcel of our constitution as living things. However, this fact, and the fact that it is shared with a variety of sentient non-sapient beings, shows that there is something different going on with sapience. Brandom explains that one can teach a parrot to say "red" every time it is in front of a red object and one can see iron's rusting as reliably responding to ambient humidity. But these reliable responses are dispositional, they are not in themselves concept use. The parrot, just like a pig of iron, is not responding conceptually to the environment. They are not using these dispositions and responses as concepts. This use requires knowing at least some of the incompatibilities and consequences that accompany concepts themselves. To make non-inferential reports *as* reports, one must also be able to exploit and use such inferential connections. Iron produces reports of ambient humidity. Parrots produce reports of red. Both only do so however derivatively. For such things to be reports, they have to be interpreted. This, for Brandom, is the work of "concept-mongers," of beings that grasp inferential consequences and incompatibilities. This is why we cannot properly attribute any full-fledged notion of conceptuality to animals like parrots or to artifacts such as pigs of iron. Such things reliably respond to different characteristics of the environment but lack a mastery of the inferential connectedness that defines concept use. Thus, as we have noted before, to distinguish a live oak, one must master *at least* part of the concept. They must, at the observational level, master some of the incompatibilities of the concept, such that a live oak is neither a conifer nor a deciduous flowering plant, and the consequences, such as the production of acorns. They must be aware of these differences. They must also be able to master, at the framework level, the kinds of inferential entitlements that go along with knowing that a certain tree is a live oak. This means that, when someone is able to identify that this or that tree is a live oak, they are also able to see themselves as being entitled to certain inferences that are judged permissible by this information.

4.4 Inferentialism

This does not just matter in discourse, it also matters *materially*. The fact that certain types of trees produce acorns while others do not allow us to determine and categorize. It is these specific differences that matter. Being able to identify such material features is thus part of what is entailed by a grasp of determinate content. A directional concept such as WEST is in large part defined in relation to other directional concepts. For instance, a key feature of this concept is its opposition to the concept EAST. The two concepts quite literally run in different directions. Thus a materially good inference is that if Lille is west of Berlin then Berlin is east of Lille. In the same way, Lille being west of Berlin is incompatible (in standard use) with Lille being east of Berlin (unless one is willing to go all the way around the world to get there). In the example of our live oak, the concept itself is nothing more than the consequences and incompatibilities that can be drawn out of the materially good inferential relations. If these things were different, it would be a different concept, because it would also be a different tree. This does not mean that *all* the material features of a concept are fixed, or are even in some way fixable. In fact, a lot of what we do as concept users is wrangle with each other over just what incompatibilities and consequences should be held within specific contents. This partially accounts for why concepts have become so much materially richer over time. People are constantly coming up with new criteria that allow us to distinguish specific material differences.

At the most basic level, using the concept LIVE OAK would allow one to infer that the specific oak is an evergreen tree, that it is a hardwood, that it produces acorns, etc. Brandom points out however that there are concepts that allow us to establish continuities as well as discontinuities. The concept OAK allows us to create a continuity between trees that produce acorns, that have a specific type of foliage, that reproduce in a specific way etc. The discontinuities allow us to distinguish trees that do not do so, and thus that should not be considered oaks. The concept EVERGREEN allows us to establish continuities with the trees whose foliage remains functional throughout the year and allows us to establish discontinuities with trees that do not. Applying these two concepts together provides us with a subset of trees within the oak family that in colloquial American arboriculture has become a concept in its own right, LIVE OAK. Such continuities and discontinuities are established across our conceptual landscape. Within awareness SENTIENCE and SAPIENCE are thus concepts that allow us to do this same work. By focusing on the parrot's perceptual capacity to reliably distinguish aspects of its environment, we can note that the parrot, and all other animals, share this capacity with human beings. By reliably distinguishing aspects of its environment through its sensuous capacities, we can say that the parrot is *sentient*. Human beings are also sentient, but our *sapience* overlies our sentience. Brandom defines sapience as "a status achieved within a structure of mutual recognition: of holding and being held responsible, of acknowledging and exercising authority."[34] Sapience, according to Brandom, who equates it with the faculty of judgement, is essential to our self-consciousness. This faculty is built out

---

[34] Brandom (1994), 275.

of our sensitivity to reasons. This mean that we act not only according to sensuous stimulation but also according to conceptually articulated propositions. For instance, standing in a field, one does not have a determined reaction to the live oak, as the iron would to the ambient humidity, but rather one has a panel of ways of interacting with the tree and this will follow from the way that individuals organize their goals, their desires, and their needs, for instance. If a person goes over to the live oak to sit below it, it is because they want shade, or are tired, or they like the smell, or think that trees are the appropriate poetic backdrop for sitting, and they can thus give a reason that explains *why* they do what they do. The parrot or the pig of iron cannot explain the *why* of their activity and because of this we classify it as purely reactive. This is the way sapience overlies sentience, the why of our activity binds us to certain commitments.

Distinguishing between these two kinds of awareness, sentience and sapience, helps to flesh out the motivation of inferentialism, but another way to do so would be to contrast it with the atomist picture of semantic meaning found in representationalism. According to such atomism, there are fundamental and fundamentally discrete conceptual or ontological items, and these items can be held or deployed independently. By insisting on inferential semantic holism, Brandom makes two major claims. First, he takes up the Sellarsian idea that in order to understand one concept, one must be able to also access a multitude of concepts that are inferentially linked to the target concept. Second, he claims that the proposition is the minimal semantic unit. Atomism, on the other hand, claims that the word (or some particular) is the minimal semantic unity. However, what Brandom underlines is that single words, used alone, are not useful in reasonings. Even when single words are uttered in isolation in reasonings such as red in the presence of red things, they only make sense if we can access sundry contextual incompatibilities and consequences that allow the role of the single word to emerge. This, Brandom claims, is because the sentence, a complete proposition, expresses a judgement, and the judgement is the minimal unit for which we can hold ourselves, or hold others, responsible. It is starting from the judgment that we are able to define the space of reasons that is being deployed, because it is from a judgment, articulated in a proposition, that we can see the inferential commitments that are involved in the reasoning.[35]

These judgments themselves all happen underground, so to speak, and one thing that discursive practices do is to bring them out. Furthermore, by defending that claims do not initially have reporting roles, but must enter into the game of giving and asking for reasons in order to have reporting roles, we are uncovering some of the work sapience does. Before claims are endorsed as having reporting roles, they are subject to greater scrutiny, they are treated as hypotheses. These hypotheses can

---

[35] Weil makes a similar move in the jump from *Truth* to *Meaninglessness*. The doctrine of *Truth* can only start from a single word, but that sense is meaningless from the point of view of judgment. *Meaningless* is the attitude that claims that each judgment that claims to assert the truth in its totality is meaningless, thus it pragmatically negates all judgments. Nonetheless, the truth can have an expressive meaning, but it is one that is constituted retrospectively, that is, after all the semantic and logical tools necessary to understand propositions are in place.

4.4 Inferentialism

have lower or greater levels of verisimilitude and credibility. It is at this level, the level of scrutinizing claims, that sapience is fully operational. When claims take on reporting roles, it is because they are endorsed and because the scrutiny is terminated and the work of sapience is relaxed. Claims can always undergo a new period of scrutiny when new information is introduced, however, normally they have no need to. When the period of scrutiny is over and when claims take on reporting roles, it is at this moment that they become part of the structure that holds our conceptual motor in place. It is also at this moment however that they run the risk of becoming hypostasized.

A hypostasized concept is a concept that is so structural that it resists scrutiny. This allows us to operate on autopilot, so to speak. But it also means that we are no longer sensitive to the different ways that concepts are used by different interlocutors. To recall the distinction that Weil makes between metaphysical categories and philosophical categories: when a metaphysical concept, such as that of causality, becomes hypostasized according to a specific philosophical category, it is resistant to the use of the same metaphysical concept by another philosophical category. Thus, the world of magical thinking that is present in the category of *Certainty* uses the concept of causality, but this use is foreign to someone who uses the discourse of experimental science that is found in the category of *The Condition*. Nonetheless, both are explaining things in relation to the temporal appearance of an antecedent and a consequent that structures the concept of causality. The risk is that, when people are operating on autopilot thanks to a hypostasized grasp of a concept, they no longer make the effort to try and grasp what is meaningful in what their interlocutor says, which allows them to refuse the discourse out of hand. This is a major impediment to reasonable practices because it means that individual commitments can become dogmatic certainties. When this happens, individuals are no longer operating at the level of sapience. In fact, because hypotheses can evolve to take on reporting roles, individuals do not always need to operate at the level of sapience. In fact, even with concepts, individuals can (and probably most often do) operate at the level of sentience. This also means that to be a fully-fledged agent, to be sapient, one must not only be able to operate at the level of claims, they must actually do so. They must make their own claims as well as evaluate their own claims and those of others. In addition, they must be able to see others as adding something to their own ability to make claims.

Once an individual learns to identify something, such as a live oak, and learns to distinguish it from other things that are similar, such as deciduous oaks or other members of the same family such as beeches and chestnuts, they no longer need to evaluate the criteria that go into the concept, nor to go through the checklist of those criteria in order to identify the thing as a live oak: they can do so non-inferentially. Non-inferential identification, which is precisely something human beings share with sentient beings, holds a complicated place in sapient practices. It is easy to confound sentient identification that is non-conceptual, with sapient identification. This is why Price's distinction between e-representations and i-representations is so important. Both humans and non-propositional animals non-inferentially identify things, because both can have reliable differential responses towards those things.

That is, they can act the specific ways in the presence of the thing. However, both human and non-propositional animals can also make mistakes in their dispositions. They can see food, eat it, only to get sick. They can see an icy surface, walk on it, only to fall through the ice. Both can even see things as errors and correct them, and learn from others through reciprocal processes. The difference is that the discursive practices found in i-representations allow us to generalize these corrections and share them indifferently with others because we grasp their incompatibilities and consequences. Sapient practices bring out conceptual commitments and entitlements, but normally we do not need them, because normally we have a strong enough grasp on our environment to be able to navigate it without worry. This grasp, in humans, is born and develops thanks to i-representations. We learn to grasp the world conceptually through the social practice of language learning and practice. It is when our grasp of our conceptual landscape is less sure that we must reason, argue, and discuss. It is at this point that we play the game of giving and asking for reasons until we can settle back into the "instinctive" confidence of our concept use. This we do with others. We do this with others because, on the one hand, it is others that can show us the limits and weakness of our commitments and entitlements. And we do this with others because, on the other hand, social argumentative practices and interlocutors provide the dialogical controls that open wide the field of our entitlements. This is the key advance of Brandom's position. It makes explicit a certain notion of discursive commitment and puts it at the center of language use. The notion of discursive commitment is essential both to explain the way that certain individuals willingly assume the binding aspect of concept use and to explain how there can be error in concept use. Error here is not to be seen as crippling to concept use, but rather as one of the main elements that brings discursive practices out into the light of day and that explains why sapience is distinct from sentience. It is the recognition of error that demands that concept use correct error itself. It is this recognition of error as error that is at the base of our order of explanation that moves us away from certainty and into a dynamic notion of conceptuality. It is also why e-representations are insufficient to explain semantic content.

4.5 The Two Sources of Contemporary Expressivism

The pragmatist order of explanation allows us to understand what people do in their discursive practices and inferentialism allows us to understand semantic content. While it may seem evident that language practices should be at the center of the understanding of language use, this is not actually always the case. Indeed, there have been a variety of formal semantic projects that place pragmatic considerations in the back seat.[36] One reason for the different conceptions can be found in the role

---

[36] Noam Chomsky's generative grammar for instance, insists that there are universal rules that are hardwired into our brains and that are sufficient to *generate* all meaningful sentences, see Chomsky (1957). Not only does this position put pragmatic considerations into the back seat, it also puts a

4.5 The Two Sources of Contemporary Expressivism

different theories see language use playing. Following Charles Taylor, we can characterize two major models of language use and call one the *designative* tradition and the other the *expressive* tradition.[37] According to this distinction, the designative tradition—which Simon Blackburn[38] alternatively calls the descriptive tradition—claims that the role of language is to designate something out in the world. Thus, reference is seen to be the primitive semantic concept. According to Taylor's argument, something is only meaningful in the designative model if it assures a word-world relationship. Using our example of the live oak, the statement, "this is a live oak" or "there is a live oak in the field" is meaningful as long as the thing I am pointing my language towards, the thing out in the field, *is* a live oak. Taylor's complaint is that, while this relationship holds up pretty well in ideal designative-type sentences, there is a plethora of other language uses that human agents take to be meaningful that does not fall under this kind of designative situation. Sentences that express value judgements, for example, are often taken to be meaningful (and often to be much more informative than designative sentences) but it is difficult to see how there is a simple designation in a sentence such as "live oaks are the most sublime evergreens." However, precisely because this sentence is taken to be meaningful, the meaning must lie elsewhere.

The expressive tradition looks to respond to this problem by proposing that the most basic role of language is not in fact to designate something, but rather that it is to express something. This does not mean that designation is not involved in this language use, or even that its role is not essential. Rather, it means that when trying to establish an order of explanation that grasps the diverse ways that individuals use language, reference and representation are not the basic unproblematic starting points that the designative tradition has taken them to be. The expressive model of language use claims that this designative character matters *because* of the way it is used in other judgments, rather than seeing humanity to be merely continuing the adamic endeavor of going around giving names to all things under the sun. Thus, the designative role of the statement "this is a live oak" is itself embedded in a rolling mess of arguments, judgments, and claims. It becomes important because it is followed by another claim, such as "live oaks are the most sublime evergreens," or because it can be used to settle a previous disagreement, such as *"This* is a live oak, the oak we saw earlier is deciduous."

Simon Blackburn notes the importance of expressivism as a meta-ethical position and says that "the point of expressive theories is to avoid the metaphysical and epistemological problems which realist theories of ethics [...] are supposed to bring along with them."[39] While this is certainly true in Blackburn's reading of expressivism it seems less clearly obvious in Taylor's reading. This highlights the two separate

---

clear limit on what meaningfulness is, thus also creating criteria that exclude forms of expression that do not fit into its paradigm.

[37] Taylor (1985).
[38] Blackburn (1984).
[39] Blackburn (1984), 169.

origins of contemporary expressivism. One of the origins of expressivism follows Blackburn's line and was initially limited to meta-ethical statements dating back to Hume's position in the *Treatise of Human Nature*, and thus can appropriately be called Humean expressivism. The second origin is linked to the German Enlightenment and to what Isaiah Berlin calls the Counter-Enlightenment.[40] Here, expressivism starts to take form in the work of Johann Gottfried Herder and Johann Georg Hamann and then moves through German thought from Hegel and Wilhelm von Humboldt through later neo-Kantians such as Ernst Cassirer. For this reason it can be called German expressivism.

While these two currents seem to be coming closer and closer together, as is seen in the work of Huw Price,[41] who claims that Robert Brandom's German expressivism lines up well with Blackburn's Humean expressivism, their initial impetus nonetheless remains radically different. Hume's moral expressivism is difficult to square with his own theory of language use which remains firmly anchored in the so-called "way of ideas" that offers a representational picture of content, and opposes a truly expressivist understanding of language use. Humean expressivism is based on an emotivist reading of Hume. According to this reading, starting from his famous distinction that "is" in no way entails "ought,"[42] emotivists claim that there is an unsanctioned leap from descriptive to evaluative claims. The emotivists read Hume to be saying that moral claims, because they express certain emotive dispositions towards states of things, do not state facts and are thus not subject to truth conditions. Saying something is good or bad relates subjective preferences and not qualities bound up in the objects or states of affair to be evaluated. Even though Hume's moral theory was waylaid by the rise of Kantian deontic ethics and utilitarianism, early analytic philosophers, looking to overcome G.E. Moore's naturalist fallacy while nonetheless naturalizing moral consideration found an easy ally in Hume's emotivist moral position. For example, in *Language, Truth, and Logic*, A.J. Ayer defends a position whereby only empirical or causal claims can pretend to have the status of genuine propositions. Ethical claims, because they present a normative content, are thus emotive, they are used "to express feelings about certain objects, but not to make any assertions about them."[43]

An easy way to distinguish between Humean and German expressivism is to look at the scope of the initial expressivist projects. In A.J. Ayer's reading, as well as that of C.L. Stevenson,[44] and R.M. Hare after him,[45] Humean expressivism is specifically meta-ethical. It maintains a representational picture of conceptual content that is inherited from Descartes and taken up by Hume himself, while presenting a model of this representational picture that can be applied to normative

---

[40] Berlin (1979).
[41] Price (2011, 2013).
[42] Hume (2000), T 3.1.1.27.
[43] Ayer (1949), 108.
[44] Stevenson (1944).
[45] Hare (1952).

4.5 The Two Sources of Contemporary Expressivism

content.[46] Expressivism is thus used as a way to naturalize moral claims by explaining them according to an empirically realist paradigm. Meaningful claims are claims that allow descriptions of causally structured relations. The causally structured relationships that carry over from moral claims are psychological, they are expressive claims about individual sentiments on states of affairs while saying nothing about the states of affairs themselves.

The German expressivist project is, from the beginning, far more ambitious. In contrast with the initial Humean expressivist motivation, German expressivism looked from the start to overthrow the representationalist picture of conceptual content. In order to do so, the German expressivists, notably Herder and Hamann, claim that *all* language use is primarily expressive. According to this model, meaning itself is not dependent on external entities such as Forms, nor internal entities such as ideas, but rather meaning is bound up in language use. The idea that meaning is bound up in language use itself and is not *dependent* on non-linguistic factors is one of the key elements of Herder's expressivism. In fact, according to Michael Forster, these are two of the three key doctrines to Herder's picture of language use. These doctrines argue that:

1. thought is dependent on and bounded by language—that is, one cannot think unless one has a language and one can only think what one can express linguistically.
2. *meanings* or *concepts* are [not] to be equated with [...] items, in principal autonomous of language, [...] for example, the objects to which they refer, Platonic "forms", or mental "ideas" [but are rather equated] with *usages of words*.
3. Meanings, or concepts [...] are of their nature based in (perceptual or affective) sensation.[47]

While the third doctrine is one that Hume would share, his own notion of concept use clearly goes against these first two doctrines. So how does Herder's expressivism link these aspects? First of all, he sees the language of sensation as being in continuity with the vocal production of other animals. In his *Treatise on the Origins of Language*, he says, "already as an animal the human being has a language,"[48] and for Herder, this language is the language of sensation, it is the common language of all feeling creatures, and his claim is that humans as animals are sensuous beings before becoming reasoning beings. In fact he notes that "the human being is feeling through and through."[49] Thus, we can read Herder's account of language use as trying to create a holist image of human beings, as opposed to the dualist picture that goes along with pure representational theories. This holist image of human beings

---

[46] Ayer states that this applies "*mutatis mutandis*, to the case of aesthetic statements also," in Ayer (1949), 103.
[47] Forster (2012), 56–72.
[48] Herder (2008), 65.
[49] Herder (2008), 111.

emphasizes human embeddedness in the natural world, thus showing how humanity is more in continuity with nature than in rupture from it.

According to the picture presented in the emotivist reading, Hume still maintains the rigid dualism between the rational and the sensuous aspects of the human being, between the philosophical and the vulgar aspects of human life. This reading completely ignores the normative content of meaning and of concepts. In the emotivist reading, Hume has a descriptive language that makes genuine claims about the world, and an expressive one that does not. The descriptive language is based on sensation (or more correctly, on the transformation of sensuous impressions into ideas). It has to itself depend on some higher function—which nonetheless goes unexplained—that transforms impressions into ideas and ideas into the linguistic material from which languages are built.[50] While the Humean expressive language is also based on impressions, that is, the impression of certain moral feelings, preferences, aversions, etc., this language does not add any actual content to concepts. Thus, according to this reading, Herder's first two doctrines do not hold up: thought is not bound up by language, because this implies that language is logically prior to thought, or that they are at least concomitant developments, and meaning *is* independent from language.

In Hume, since one works back up to the source impression to get to meaning, language itself must be thought of as arbitrary sounds that express the content that is represented in the impression. It thus only serves to uncover the content of that impression. It would then be custom and habit that link these sounds to the meaning that they have, however these meanings are understood as logically prior to language itself. The Humean picture assumes a preexisting structure of thought that explains how it should be that human beings acquire meanings at all. In other words, for the Humean expressivist, thought would have to precede language. Even though Hume does not exploit this option, he clearly distinguishes between thinking and feeling as two separate faculties. Herder, on the other hand, seems to be saying that thinking grows out of feeling. In order to show this, he claims in the *Treatise on the Origin of Language* that the expressive language that reports emotional states is shared with all animals and it is from this origin that human language developed. Because he claims that thought is bound by language, Herder commits himself to the idea that language is a social practice and that meaning is out loud, so to speak, before being in our heads, this is something which expressivist readings of Hume do not have to commit themselves to.[51]

However Herder himself also has a tension specific to his own model. He emphasizes the social character of language use but also claims that language grows out of

---

[50] This is expressed in the famous copy principle whereby "All our simple ideas in their first appearance are deriv'd from simple impressions, which are correspondent to them, and which they exactly represent," in Hume (2000), T 1.1.1.7. This principle is however itself insufficient to explain how this transformation happens.

[51] These two options seem to present the two branches of expressivism as a strict either/or choice, however I will show later on, current developments in expressivism overcome this strict division, and they do so through what can be characterized as a reprise.

4.5 The Two Sources of Contemporary Expressivism

feeling, which itself is not public. Does Herder resolve this tension? Partially, yes. But even though he was unable to completely resolve it, he does give us the tools to do so, tools that would be taken up independently and developed by Sellars's own version of expressivism. Why is Herder unable to fully resolve this tension? One reason is the way that he conceives of the human individual in relation to the human being as a social animal. We have mentioned how, for Herder, the human being already has a language as an animal. What is important to note is that this language, the language of a sensing feeling creature—a language that each animal species has in its own measure—is radically different from the propositionally articulated language that defines our language as being specifically human. This second language is not purely natural, but is cultural. It is a language that has a history and a history that has slowly and progressively made it richer. In fact, given the sentience/sapience distinction made earlier, it might be more appropriate to call this first natural language sentient communication, since it lacks the characteristics that accompany full-fledged sapient language use. Herder is clear about this, he states that animal languages, "all stand completely and incommensurably apart from human language."[52] Here, however, is a contradiction within Herder's work that he is not able to resolve. On the one hand he asserts that our human language is different in kind from the animal language of feeling, that it is cultural despite having grown out of the natural language of feeling, that it develops through socialization and transmission. But he *also* asserts that the individual would develop a language just by being open to the world. In this way, with many of his philosophical forebearers, he still sees language primarily as an individual faculty, and not as a social one. Nonetheless, Herder does seem to provide the resources to overcome this tension. Herder notes that "[r]eason and language took a timid step together, and nature came to meet them half-way through *hearing*"[53] and that "the *progress of language through reason* and of *reason* through language."[54] Herder's argument shares features with Donald Davidson's argument whereby to be a competent language user one must first be an interpreter of the language of others.[55] It cannot however be assimilated to Davidson's argument because Herder does not yet mobilize interpretation but instead relies exclusively on hearing. From the sounds of the world, the human being creates language, and a language that is already meaningful. The difference then between these two positions is that interpretation already mobilizes normative features, the interpretation can be endorsed or rejected by the speaker being interpreted.

In the Davidson model—and this will be exploited by Brandom—an interpreter is needed to take a sound as meaningful. This opens the game of giving and asking for reasons whereby *individuals* together recognize each other as saying meaningful things, and so search to understand the content of the speech act. By recognizing the

---

[52] Herder (2008), 96.
[53] Herder (2008), 98.
[54] Herder (2008), 125.
[55] Davidson (1984b), 156–170.

other as indeed saying something meaningful, they can then endorse that content and commit to it themselves or reject it. In Herder's model, it is telling that hearing connects to the natural world, to the non-rational features of it, features which are unable to endorse anything. In this way, Herder sets us on the path but does not take the step himself. Herder almost sees this because he provides an additional resource for understanding the kind of expressive language use being defended here, but again he does not fully exploit it. This is our social character. For Herder, language *develops* thanks to us being members of families, clans, tribes, and nations. Within these different structures we can create fruitful bonds with people but we can also be in conflictual relations, this dialectic of mutual aid and conflict is the main mechanism of language development in Herder's model, but again, he does not take a full step into a social model of language *acquisition* because he remains convinced that language would spring from the isolated individual. He states, "I cannot think the first human thought, cannot set up the first aware judgment in a sequence, without engaging in dialogue, or striving to engage in dialogue in my soul. Hence the first human thought by its very nature prepares one to be able to engage in dialogue with others."[56] This is where the expressivism to be developed in the following pages pulls away from Herderian expressivism. The logical expressivism to be developed starts from dialogue-like interactions between distinct individuals and only then is a specific individual able to interpret their own thought as participating in the kind of internal dialogue that characterizes the Herderian model.

Given the tension within the Herderian model of German expressivism and the limited initial scope of Humean expressivism, it is unsure that these two forms of expressivism can be as easily united as Huw Price would like to claim, at least in its earliest iterations. If they can be brought together, it is because expressivists working today have abandoned a certain number of commitments which seem to be central to one of the positions or to the other. And if they can be brought together it is certainly because of the social emphasis of the role of language use. This emphasis, which is explicitly present but secondary in Herder, lines up better with the pragmatist order of explanation. Because this conception of meaning is use-based, the analysis of meaning must pass through an analysis of social linguistic practices in order to present a convincing picture of semantic content. Here we can thus see that although Humean expressivism and Herderian expressivism share a similar goal, to naturalize our understanding of language use,[57] this is done in strikingly different ways. On the one hand, the expressivist reading of Hume is based on an initial meta-ethical position, which tries to describe what is meant by the use of moral sentences. Herderian expressivism, on the other hand, makes more substantial claims about the nature of mind and language. However, these two forms of expressivism have the same goal in mind, to explain language use in non-representational, non-truth-conditional ways. For the Humean expressivist, up until

---

[56] Herder (2008), 97.

[57] It is important to note that expressivism does not need to be *necessarily* naturalist, and that both Weil's and Brandom's expressivism are non-naturalist.

Simon Blackburn, this explanation of language was limited in scope. For Herder, this claim amounts to an affirmation that the primary role of language is neither to represent, nor to know, nor to designate, but to express. Expressivism and pragmatism thus share similar features because they share similar goals. Their goal is to better explain actual human practices, which of course include description and designation, but which are seen as more problematic when description and designation are given a primitive status in explanation. This goal implies upturning the notion of correspondence and replacing the notion of representation as the starting point to explain language use. It displaces truth as the conceptually primitive notion by opening up a meta-discourse that looks to explain what an individual does when they use a descriptive language.

4.6 The Taxonomy of Expressivism

These goals, especially as they are articulated in Herder's expressivist project, were vitally important for the development of German Idealism. There nonetheless remains quite a bit of debate concerning how clearly we can describe German Idealists, Hegel for instance,[58] as expressivists. The story of the development and legacy of Herder's expressivist thought has been masterfully told in two companion volumes on German philosophy of language by Michael Forster.[59] Therefore, I will not retell the story that he does. This story goes from Herder and Hamann, through Hegel and Humboldt all the way to Frege and Wittgenstein. What I do want to do however is use his taxonomy in order to distinguish between different types of expressivism. Forster distinguished between what he calls broad and narrow expressivism. According to Forster, the three criteria given above are characteristic of narrow expressivism, thus Herder is the archetypal narrow expressivist. As a reminder, these criteria are (1) the dependence of thought on language, (2) the rejection of external metaphysical entities to explain meaning and (3) the sensual origin of meanings. According to Forster, narrow expressivism is sensitive to the expressive powers of other forms of communication outside of language, and wants to be able to explain their expressive force. However, it claims that there is something qualitatively different about language use itself.

What Forster goes on to claim is that narrow expressivism denies non-linguistic forms of expression full autonomy. That is, gestural expressions, dance, non-textual music, bodily signals, as well as visual expressions, painting, drawing, scratches on surfaces, are all only fully meaningful because language has already instantiated meanings. While the shapes of natural expression certainly exist well before the emergences of language, these things themselves must be understood as

---

[58] Charles Taylor's book *Hegel* inaugurates the debate (and much contemporary thinking about expressivism) that has since turned into a small cottage industry of scholarship, see Taylor (1977). For a critique of this position, see also, Buchwalter (1994).

[59] Forster (2012, 2014). For a critical continuation of this position, see Englander (2013).

proto-conceptual up until the point that there is a language to instantiate the meaning that ranges over them. Language thus allows these proto-conceptual elements to emerge as such, but they require the presence of thought and meaning already bound up in language to be understood as such.[60] Thus, narrow expressivist defends a position whereby language is the necessary key to understanding the possibility of meaning that is found in other forms of expression.

Forster contrasts this position with what he calls broad expressivism. Broad expressivism is, according to Forster, committed to the same principles as narrow expressivism, however where they differ is in the definition of the notion of "language." Language is thus to be understood as "drawing, painting and music."[61] All forms of expression are put on an equal footing, and equally responsible for the conceptual jump between animals as feeling, reacting things, and animals as reasoning, acting things, language is just one of the forms of this conceptual development. According to Forster, Hamann is the archetypal broad expressivist, but he is not alone. Hegel, both in Charles Taylor's development of the expressive themes found in his work, and in Forster's interpretation, is to be seen as a broad expressivist. Taylor, who does not make the distinction between broad and narrow expressivism, and who himself seems to defend a form of broad expressivism, places Hegel's expressivism under a form that must be considered broad expressivism. Forster however sees Hegel as shifting towards broad expressivism. For Forster, the work of Hegel in the *Phenomenology of Spirit* falls under narrow expressivism, but he claims that Hegel evolved towards a position of broad expressivism as he continued to reflect on aesthetic questions.

The twentieth century saw Wilfrid Sellars develop a sophisticated form of narrow expressivism in "Empiricism and the Philosophy of Mind."[62] This form of narrow expressivism will allow us to overcome the tension in the heart of the Herderian model pointed out above, and will also show why Herder's insistence on the sensuous origin of meaning is misplaced. In "Empiricism and the Philosophy of Mind" Sellars tells a story that he calls "the myth of Jones." In the myth of Jones, we are invited to imagine a society of people who follow a certain behavioristic paradigm. That is, the intelligibility of the members of the society depends on overt behavior. They have no theoretical framework with which to speak about inner episodes such as thoughts, emotions, beliefs, dreams, etc. In this story, a member of the society, Jones, comes up with a way of talking about such inner episodes. He proposes that we model inner episodes on external episodes such as overt linguistic expression. In other words, Sellars proposes that we model thought on speech as a way of analyzing and understanding thought. Jones therefore proposes that individuals interpret

---

[60] While narrow expressivism claims that thought is bound up in language, I would argue that it does not imply propositionalism, the idea that all intentional states are propositional states. Rather it implies that non-propositional states, attention, boredom, desires, emotions, only become clear as intentional states because there are *also* propositional states. For a clear critique of propositionalism, see Montague (2007).

[61] Forster (2014), 184.

[62] Sellars (1997).

4.6 The Taxonomy of Expressivism

the other individuals of their society based on the overt public behavior of linguistic episodes. The idea is that doing so will allow them to understand intelligent-seeming behavior even when there is no overt reasoning like the kind that happens in linguistic episodes.

There are two benefits to modelling thought on speech that need to be highlighted to understand how Sellars's myth of Jones links into the expressivist project at large. First, he is proposing a model of cognitive episodes that insists that thought can be understood thanks to discursive episodes, and thus thanks to basic semantic categories. Second, by claiming that thinking is learned in conjecture with speech, he is also claiming that the basic semantic categories of thought are learned with the semantic categories of linguistic behavior. Thus, he can be seen as arguing against the notion of a universal grammar that is to be found in Noam Chomsky's work, as well as against forms of dualism that are to be found in the Cartesian model of thought.[63]

Sellars goes a step further and claims that thinking only happens after speaking has been mastered. He notes that Jones's theory "is perfectly compatible with the idea that the ability to have thoughts is acquired in the process of acquiring overt speech and that only after overt speech is well established, can 'inner speech' occur without its overt culmination."[64] His position, that "thoughts are *linguistic episodes*,"[65] must thus be thought of as defending the first claim of narrow expressivism, namely that thought is bound by and dependent on language. Sellars then goes on to defend the second criterion of narrow expressivism. Jones's theory gives us a model for speaking about non-empirical entities without transforming them into metaphysical unexplained explainers. This is clear in the way that the members of the society in the myth of Jones initially lack any way of discussing inner episodes. Thought is not seen as the unexplained explainer of speech, rather it is the very thing that Sellars is looking to explain. To do so, inner episodes are postulated along the lines of overt linguistic behavior in order to explain other behavior, namely intelligent behavior that itself is overt without the use of the direct reasoning that accompanies overt linguistic behavior. What distinguishes Jones's theory, and what lines up with the second claim of narrow expressivism, is that Sellars does not propose any metaphysical entities. The entities are methodological. He is not claiming that there is such a thing as thoughts and that they are made up of such and such matter and that they function in such and such way. Rather he is proposing that in order to explain certain behavior, certain mechanisms need to be postulated. However, the mechanism or the entities that are postulated are methodologically conservative extensions of an already existing theory. That is, they do not make claims that outstrip their explanatory needs.

The step to a type of inner speech called thought does not itself sanction the jump to metaphysical entities with specific describable characteristics such as Ideas and

---

[63] Chomsky's *Cartesian Linguistics* explicitly combines these two elements, in Chomsky (1966).
[64] Sellars (1997), § 58.
[65] Sellars (1997), § 47.

Forms. Thus, linguistic meanings are not explained by inner speech, rather inner speech extends aspects of the theory that are already taken for granted. This conservative extension is itself subject to test and discussion, which highlights another essential aspect of Sellars's expressivism, its intersubjective nature. In order to solidify their intersubjective nature, Sellars notes how certain methodologically sanctioned conservative extensions of working concepts take on a reporting role in a theory. Thus, initially, inner speech is postulated in order to explain the intelligent behavior of members of Jones's society. Other members of the society can however take up Jones's theory and use it both to accurately describe, and understand, their own behavior and that of others. Once they have taken up the theory of inner speech, they can take it as no longer being a hypothesis, but as a working part of the theory. Thus, thoughts are used to report certain behavior and to accurately describe it. They can be used, for example, to understand the privileged access that each individual in the society seems to demonstrate towards their own inner speech as well as the idea of rational motivation that accompanies non-verbal but understandable behavior. When theoretical entities, such as thought in the myth of Jones, take on reporting roles, they can be used as reasons in argumentative practices and as part of the general framework of concepts that are mobilized by dialogue partners. Thus, the transition from a conservative extension to a theoretical entity that plays a reporting role "constitutes a dimension of the use of these concepts which is *built on* and *presupposes* this intersubjective status," and so "language is essentially an *inter-subjective* achievement, and is learned in an inter-subjective context."[66]

It should be noted that Sellars does not come to his expressivism as Herder does, by trying to understand the origins of language use. Rather he comes to his expressivism the way Humean expressivists do, as understanding that certain questions cannot be solved without taking a meta-theoretical position. His initial goal is to say something about what happens in thought, and how a scientific reporting language, the language of observation, can be squared with the theoretical framework which is necessary for the observation itself to make sense, the normative meta-language. Thus, his expressivism, while structurally more similar to Herder's, because it clearly distinguishes itself as a form of narrow expressivism, also resembles Humean expressivism, because it uses a similar technique to answer a different set of questions. In the case of Humean expressivism, the set of questions is (or *was*, since the scope has since grown, and since there are more and more philosophers who marry the two questions) how to understand and explain moral claims, whereas in Sellars case, the question is how to understand and explain scientific claims.

This is also where Sellars's expressivism separates itself from Herder's. As already noted, Forster gives us a set of criteria to distinguish narrow expressivism from broad expressivism. However, Sellars's expressivism is even narrower than Herder's in that he does not share the third criterion, namely, the sensuous origin of meaning. Sellars's expressivism is not looking to understand how *private* sensuous experience is transformed into linguistic activity. Rather, he is interested in understanding how *public* linguistic activity, language, has the expressive force that it

---

[66] Sellars (1997), § 59.

4.6 The Taxonomy of Expressivism

does. He is interested in understanding what language allows us to say. This is already clear within the myth of Jones. Here, Sellars is giving a model that allows us to understand how language users can interpret their inner episodes. These episodes, of course, may be the "linguistic" episodes of thought, or they may be the sensuous episodes of feelings, desires, etc. This is the opposite direction from the one Herder takes. As already shown, Herder starts from a dialogue that one has with oneself that allows us to prepare the ground for the dialogues that we have with others. In Sellars, one starts from social discursive practices and the kinds of dialogues we have with others, and it is on the model of these dialogues that we learn to interpret ourselves. In this way, our sensuous episodes do not *immediately* give us content. Rather, whatever content they have is progressively elaborated through public discursive practices. We learn conceptual tools that allow us to identify our feelings, and thanks to these tools we interpret our feelings. Feelings do not give us any content fully formed. This goes along with the minimization of metaphysical entities of narrow expressivism, but against the sensuous origin of meaning to be found in the specifically Herderian version of narrow expressivism. No feeling is freestanding, it requires conceptual articulation to be grasped *as* a feeling.

Humean expressivism refuses that thought is bound by language, but both Humean and Herderian expressivism were looking to minimize the multiplication of metaphysical entities while giving robust explanations of actual practices that themselves cannot suitably be described in their own observation language. Both also, at least in their initial forms, accept the sensuous origin of meaning. Sellars, standing in an essential middle position to understanding the historical development of the contemporary pragmatist and expressivist programs developed here, provides us the tools to see why the sensuous origins of meaning should be refused. By focusing on the public intersubjective nature of language use, Sellars allows us to productively explain meaning without recourse to any sensuous origin. He allows us to provide a functional explanation of language that responds to the second criterion of narrow expressivism as an explanation that focuses on use. These developments motivate an important part of Brandom's *inferentialist* program.

Brandom sees his own expressivism as a descendent, by way of Hegel, of Herderian (or as he calls it, Romantic) expressivism. However, in addition to Sellars, the most important aspect of Brandom's expressivism is his expressivist reading of Frege. His expressivism, which he calls logical expressivism, can also be seen as a species of narrow expressivism. He states that the goal of logical expressivism is "not to *prove* something, but to *say* something."[67] This lines up with previous expressivist programs that shift from a concentration on the kind of knowledge that can be represented in our language to a concentration on the diversity of the human experience that can be expressed in language. What Brandom hopes to show is not only that the role of language is expressive, but more pressingly, that the advances of modern philosophy of language, as well as the developments of contemporary logic, can be accommodated within an expressivist program.

It is not sufficient, for Brandom's project, to say that language has an expressive role, rather he wants to say that that this expressive role is not at odds with logic,

---

[67] Brandom (1988), 267.

which *has* historically been taken to *prove* something. Thus, he has to develop the expressive role that logic is to play, but in order to do so he must clear out the brush in the tangled forest of the philosophy of language.[68] He thus claims that the role of a logical vocabulary is to make explicit the conceptual content that is implicit in natural language use. The question then becomes, how exactly does a logical vocabulary make explicit the conceptual content that is explicit in natural language? Here, we can see the importance of the pragmatist order of explanation. This order of explanation must look to the practices present in natural language. Brandom does this not by trying to analyze complex concepts into their simpler composite parts, but rather by using the logical vocabulary as a practical metavocabulary that brings out what one commits themselves to when they use certain terms or concepts. This leaves concepts as complex as they are outside of a logical way of speaking, all the while showing their embeddedness in other conceptual commitments.

The designative paradigm of language, by focusing on a word-world (or mind-world) correspondence,[69] thus places truth and knowledge at the center of its philosophical concerns. The expressive paradigm of language, by focusing on expression, places understanding and intelligibility front and center. Brandom extends the expressivist paradigm by focusing on the expressive roles of certain logical operators, namely the conditional and the negation. These are the operators that allow us to make explicit the incompatibilities and consequences of determined contents. Here, Brandom situates himself as a narrow expressivist, because he sees certain practices, specifically linguistic and logical practices, as being central to the intelligibility of other practices. So, just as for Herder, language allows other forms of expression to be understood as meaningful, for Brandom, within language use, the conditional and the negation are the resources necessary in order to see other language use, other speech acts, as meaningful. He reinforces this position when he claims, *pace* Wittgenstein's claim that language has no downtown, that it in fact does, that there is a "region around which all the rest of discourse is arrayed as dependent suburbs."[70] This downtown, through which all the other commerce and transport of language passes, is what Brandom calls "the game of giving and asking for reasons". Within this "game" assertion has place of pride because, according to Brandom, other speech acts—referring, naming, asking questions, giving commands—are all "in an important sense derivative from or parasitic on speech acts involving sentences, paradigmatically claiming, asserting, or putting forward as true."[71] Brandom importantly does not reduce all meaningful speech acts to assertion,

---

[68] It is significative that recently, Brandom has insisted that the goal must now shift from *logical expressivism* to an *expressivist logic*, in Brandom (2018).

[69] It is interesting to note that this model could perhaps also be interpreted as a form of expressivism, it is trying to express what designation does, but because it does so starting from the objects to be designated and not from what the designation is trying to accomplish, it cannot interpret itself in this way.

[70] Brandom (2009), 120

[71] Brandom (1994), 82. This type of claim which is present throughout Brandom leads Quill Kukla (writing as Rebecca Kukla) and Mark Lance to claim that Brandom falls into what they call,

4.6 The Taxonomy of Expressivism

rather he presents assertion as a qualitative threshold that discloses other speech acts as in fact being speech acts. As logical operators, the negation and the conditional become necessary resources. This is because the negation and the conditional are the resources needed for assertions to have *full* expressive force. That is, in order for assertions to do all the things we claim that they do.

Brandom's expressivism is not only narrow, but follows the general criterial structure of narrow expressivism at each level. That is, at each level there are certain paradigmatic functions that allow the level's other functions to become visible as actually being functions. In this way, logical operators such as the negation and the conditional, are only *seen* as meaningful because of their role in speech acts. Speech acts are only *seen* as meaningful because they are *seen* as part of the same category of acts as assertions. Assertions are only seen as paradigmatic because they are the speech act that best exemplify sentences. Sentences are *seen* as paradigmatic because they allow us to understand and explain the normative practices of being responsible for content, for taking something as true. It is, in turn, these types of normative practices that allow us to see ourselves as having agency and as being the kind of things in the world that we are. And finally, for Brandom, it is the discursive practices which are central to language that allow other forms of expression to be *seen* as meaningful. It is only thanks to these discursive practices that we can recognize meaningful behavior and attribute it to others.

So, just as Sellars develops a form of narrow expressivism to show how Jones attributes reasonable activity to his peers in his myth, Brandom develops a multi-layered system of dependencies that all have the main feature of narrow expressivism. There are thus certain thresholds that have to be attained in order to see the constituent parts as actually constituting the activity. Although narrow expressivism highlights and emphasizes thresholds, it is important to note that it is dialectic. An easy analogy is found in learning processes. There are aspects of learning a technique or a skill that only become clear after the skill has been learned. Thus,

---

following Nuel Belnap, the "declarative fallacy." This fallacy presumes that "semantic content in general could be understood entirely in terms of declarative content," in Kukla and Lance (2008). They go on to state that "It isn't that Brandom and others fail to notice the existence of imperatives, interrogatives, etc., but they feel confident that these will fall into (their secondary) place once the account of declaratives is completed," in Kukla and Lance (2008), 11–12. Their account attacks the declarative fallacy in order to defend their claim that observative such as "Lo, a rabbit!" and vocatives such as "Yo, Fiona!" play critical roles in an embodied theory of the recognition of pragmatic normative commitments we *actually* take on. For them, "[t]he appropriate response to the utterance 'Lo, a rabbit!' is not, then, merely to believe the consequent declarative, but to *look and see* the rabbit for yourself. Thus lo-claims call people into just those intersubjective practices of observation that constitute the necessary framework supporting declarative truth-claiming and epistemic inquiry. In a lo-claim, we explicitly mark the intersubjective character of observatives by calling others to shared attention in a public world," in Kukla and Lance (2008), 81. Because of the emphasis that Eric Weil places on the pragmatic roles of imperatives (LP, 363) his analysis of *language* seems partially at least to line up more with that of Kukla and Lance than that of Brandom, however, because of the reflexive role that *discourse* plays in understanding, the declarative, or what Weil terms serious conversation, seems to line up with Brandom. This must remain at least in this chapter an open question.

learning to blacksmith, for example, requires learning how to hold a hammer, learning how to strike the metal correctly so the force of the hammer is translated into the desired effect in the heated stock. However, where the process shows itself to be dialectic is where we can see how single concepts are parasitic on other concepts. Learning one's way around the forge will mobilize a whole battery of practical and conceptual skills that the individual has already mastered and integrated into their capacity to navigate the world. The initial gestures will necessarily be crude, even if the whole series of movements are explained in a language that the individual understands. It is only once the gesture as a whole is mastered that one can retrospectively look back at what is involved and *understand* how the parts fit together. Learning involves multiple steps of partial mastery that allow the learner to move forward. It is only because the individual acquires a partial mastery of all the parts involved that they can identify and correct what is lacking, or that they can ameliorate their skill. Thus, mastery involves different thresholds that allow us to retrospectively look over our shoulder in order to understand what we are doing.

These thresholds are themselves then the result of dialectic processes that already use the conceptual capacities that need to be mastered before they are fully *understood*. This is also what allows concepts to be explained at different grains of fineness and at different levels of complexity. Each new level of complexity incorporates what has been learned and what is essential from the preceding level, and in fact takes it for granted. While this seems paradoxical, the deeper paradox is that it is this dialectic process itself that allows us to take acquired skills for granted and thus also to mischaracterize them. Once we have a skill, because we can see its constituent moving parts, we think that the skill has always had the form it does when we try to characterize it. However, autonomy transforms processes. This is what makes teaching such a difficult practice. One must find the appropriate level of fineness in order to explain a concept, and must continue to evolve their explanations with the evolution of the student's understanding of the complexity that is contained in the concept. An apprentice blacksmith will blindly follow what they are told to do long before they understand how and why they do it, just as a child learning a language will speak long before they are able to understand what their speaking implies. Thus, narrow expressivism always implies a reflexive moment that *discloses* the activity of language as meaningful in itself, just as learning processes imply a reflexive moment that discloses the activity to the learner. But in language this reflexive moment only happens after the speaker has already been using language for so long that they have integrated its use. This disclosure allows one to recognize the parts as being parts *of* the activity. These levels of disclosure are like Matryoshka dolls. If one had only the innermost doll, its painted approximative forms might be unrecognizable. However, with a complete doll, when we move towards the innermost doll, we can still recognize its features, its flowers and designs, just as we recognize meaningful moves in language and thought as we move into its finer-grained layers. So, it is not just that, without the most basic mechanisms, we would not have a language recognized as such, it is moreover, without crossing a certain threshold that allows for a retrospective, recursive point of view, language would not be language, but would only be the noisy orchestra of instinct. Because narrow expressivism implies that we are only able to recognize parts when the whole is present, our recognition depends on a holistic picture of language use.

4.7 Conclusion – Pragmatism and Eric Weil

In the first chapters I claimed that Eric Weil's *Logic of Philosophy* is a work that confronts us with the problem of understanding as *the* problem of philosophical discourse. In this chapter I showed that this problem is not unique to him, but has been a central concern to a variety of philosophical positions. In recent years, thanks to philosophers working in the expressivist and the pragmatist idioms, this problem even seems to have come back to the philosophical fore. The argument thus seeks to show that this is a perpetual problem that human beings confront *whenever* they seek to understand meaning and understand the meaning of understanding. The strategy used by Robert Brandom to answer this question is to start from a pragmatist *order of explanation*. This order starts from practices, specifically linguistic practices, because it is within such practices that the question itself can be asked. It is also only within such practices that the question can be answered. Brandom's answer develops a pragmatist metavocabulary, the goal of which is to explicate the framework within which this question makes sense. He presents a theory of discursive commitment to explain the kind of practices necessary for making semantic content intelligible. These practices are themselves enriched by the practice of inference. If commitments, entitlements, and endorsements are necessary for understanding the framework within which semantic content makes sense, inferential relations are themselves essential to understanding *specific* determined content. These relations allow us to make conceptual content explicit by determining the incompatibilities and consequences that define a given concept. Together, Brandom's pragmatism and inferentialism motivate his expressivism. Looking at linguistic practices, notably the practice of determining conceptual contents by means of their inferential relations, undermines the static representationalist model. The fundamental role given to language practices in the representationalist model, that of establishing a word-world correspondence, leaves many types of language use poorly explained. The goal then of expressivism is to provide a more robust dynamic model of the role of language use in our conceptual lives. This is essential if we want to understand human discourse, which, for Weil, is *the* philosophical problem, the one that animates philosophy understood in the largest possible terms. In the chapters that follow, I will make good on the claim that similar commitments are present in Weil's work. I will also develop what I see as being his key achievement in terms of diagnosing this philosophical problem, that is, the fundamental entanglement between language and violence. By developing Weil's arguments concerning this aspect of concept use, I will show how he has much to teach contemporary philosophy, both at large, but also, in the specific branches, such as philosophy of language, epistemology, and philosophy of action.

References

Ayer, A.J. 1949. *Language, truth and logic*. 2nd ed. London: Victor Gollancz.
Berlin, I. 1979. *Against the current: Essays in the history of ideas*. Princeton: Princeton University Press.
Bernstein, R. 1995. American pragmatism: The conflict of narratives. In *Rorty and pragmatism*, ed. H. Saatkamp Jr., 54–67. Nashville: Vanderbilt University Press.
Blackburn, S. 1984. *Spreading the word*. Oxford: Oxford University Press.
Brandom, R. 1988. Inference, expression, and induction. *Philosophical Studies 54* (2): 257–285.
———. 1994. *Making it explicit – Reasoning, representing & discursive commitment*. Cambridge, MA: Harvard University Press.
———. 2001. *Articulating reasons – An introduction to inferentialism*. Cambridge, MA: Harvard University Press.
———. 2004. The pragmatist enlightenment (and its problematic semantics). *European Journal of Philosophy 12* (1): 1–16.
———. 2009. *Reason in philosophy: Animating ideas*. Cambridge, MA: Belknap Press.
———. 2011. *Perspectives on pragmatism: Classic, recent, and contemporary*. Cambridge, MA: Harvard University Press.
———. 2018. From logical expressivism to expressivist logic: Sketch of a program and some implementations. *Philosophical Issues 28* (1): 70–88. https://doi.org/10.1111/phis.12116.
———. 2019. *A spirit of trust*. Cambridge, MA: Harvard University Press.
———. 2020. Rorty on vocabularies. In *Revisiting Richard Rorty*, ed. P.G. Moreira, 1–24. Vernon Press.
Buchwalter, A. 1994. Hegel and the doctrine of expressivism. In *Artifacts, representations and social practice: Essays for Marx Wartofsky*, ed. C.C. Gould and R.S. Cohen, 163–183. Dordrecht: Springer. https://doi.org/10.1007/978-94-011-0902-4_10.
Chomsky, N. 1957. *Syntactic structures*. The Hague: Mouton & Co.
———. 1966. *Cartesian linguistics*. New York: Harper & Row.
Davidson, D. 1984a. *Inquiries into truth and interpretation*. Oxford: Clarendon Press.
———. 1984b. Thought and talk. In *Inquiries into truth and interpretation*, 156–170. Clarendon Press.
Delpla, I. 2001. *Quine, Davidson: Le principe de charité*. Paris: Presses Universitaires de France.
Dewey, J. 1916. *Democracy and education*. New York: Macmillan.
———. 1927. *The public and its problems*. New York: Holt.
Dummett, M. 1994. *Origins of analytical philosophy*. Oxford: Oxford University Press.
Englander, A. 2013. Herder's 'expressivist' metaphysics and the origins of German idealism. *British Journal for the History of Philosophy 21* (5): 902–924. https://doi.org/10.1080/09608788.2013.805120.
Forster, M.N. 2012. *After Herder: Philosophy of language in the German tradition* (Reprint edition). Oxford: Oxford University Press.
———. 2014. *German philosophy of language: From Schlegel to Hegel and beyond* (Reprint edition). Oxford: Oxford University Press.
Hare, R.M. 1952. *The language of morals*. Oxford: Oxford University Press.
Herder, J.G. 2008. *Herder: Philosophical writings*. Trans. M.N. Forster. Cambridge, UK: Cambridge University Press.
Hume, D. 2000. *A treatise of human nature (Oxford philosophical texts)*. Oxford: Oxford University Press.
James, W. 2000. *Pragmatism and other writings* (New Edition). New York: Penguin Classics.
Kirscher, G. 1989. *La philosophie d'Éric Weil*. Paris: Presses Universitaires de France.
Kukla, R., and M. Lance. 2008. *"Yo" and "lo": The pragmatic topography of the space of reasons*. Cambridge, MA: Harvard University Press.
Lakoff, G. 1987. *Women, fire, and dangerous things*. Chicago: University of Chicago Press.
Lewis, D. 1979. Scorekeeping in a language game. *Journal of Philosophical Logic 8* (1): 339–359.

References

Lovejoy, A.O. 1908. The thirteen pragmatisms. I. *The Journal of Philosophy, Psychology and Scientific Methods* 5 (1): 5–12. https://doi.org/10.2307/2012277.

McDowell, J. 2013. *Having the world in view – Essays on Kant, Hegel, and Sellars (reprint)*. Cambridge, MA: Harvard University Press.

Menand, L. 2001. *The metaphysical club*. Flamingo.

Misak, C. 2013. *The American pragmatists*. Oxford: Oxford University Press.

———. 2016. *Cambridge pragmatism: From Peirce and James to Ramsey and Wittgenstein*. Oxford: Oxford University Press.

Montague, M. 2007. Against propositionalism. *Noûs 41* (3): 503–518.

Price, H. 2011. Expressivism in two voices. In *Pragmatism, science and naturalism*, ed. J. Knowles and H. Rydenfelt, 87–113. Frankfurt am Main: Peter Lang GmbH, Internationaler Verlag der Wissenschaften.

———. 2013. *Expressivism, pragmatism and representationalism*. Cambridge UK: Cambridge University Press.

Quine, W.V.O. 1960. *Word and object*. Cambridge, MA: MIT Press.

Rorty, R. 1982. *Consequences of pragmatism: Essays 1972–1980*. Minneapolis: University of Minnesota Press.

———. 1989. *Contingency, irony, and solidarity*. Cambridge UK: Cambridge University Press.

Sellars, W. 1997. *Empiricism & the philosophy of mind*. Cambridge MA: Harvard University Press.

———. 1996. *Naturalism and ontology*. Atascadero, CA: Ridgeview Publishing Company.

Stevenson, C.L. 1944. *Ethics and language*. New Haven: Yale University Press.

Talisse, R.B., and S. Aikin. 2008. *Pragmatism: A guide for the perplexed*. London: Continuum.

Taylor, C. 1977. *Hegel*. Cambridge UK: Cambridge University Press.

———. 1985. *Human agency and language*. Cambridge University Press.

Voparil, C.J. 2011. Rorty and Brandom: Pragmatism and the ontological priority of the social. *Pragmatism Today 2* (1): 133–143.

Weil, E. 1950. *Logique de la philosophie*. Paris: Librairie Philosophique Vrin.

———. 1970. *Problèmes kantiens*. 2nd ed. Paris: Librairie Philosophique Vrin.

Chapter 5
Pragmatism, Expressivism, and Inferentialism in the *Logic of Philosophy*

5.1 Introduction

My main argument is that reading Weil along pragmatist, expressivist, and inferentialist lines helps to better understand what Weil himself was doing. In this chapter I will focus on developing these commitments as they appear in Weil's work. After, in Chap. 6, I will argue that Weil's position also helps us to understand certain problems and positions within the pragmatist, expressivist, and inferentialist programs. The question that must be asked, now that both Weil and Brandom's positions have been presented, is how well Weil's philosophical program and Brandom's actually fit together. To that end, in this chapter I will directly develop the aspects of Weil's thought that fit with this program and claim that these aspects are central to a more profound understanding of Weil's work. In the next chapter I will apply this understanding and Weil's presentation of violence to the inferentialist position itself.

The first question is how to position Weil in relation to pragmatism. To return to the distinction made last chapter between theorists and practitioners, it is clear that as a theorist Weil has very little to say about pragmatism. He at least read James closely, but he has very little to say about other pragmatists.[1] He does also occasionally speak about pragmatism in his work, but these mentions are idiosyncratic. The standard practice among theorists of pragmatism is to start from the classical pragmatists (Peirce, James, Dewey) and then to enrich the reading according to one's goals and definitions.[2] Weil however, with the exception of Hermann Lotze (LP,

---

[1] The Institute Éric Weil, which houses Weil's personal library, has both James's *Pragmatism* and *Varieties of Religious Experiences*, the latter is heavily annotated. Weil also cites James when dealing with pragmatism in his article, "Pratique et Praxis," *Encyclopædia Universalis*, accessed June 10, 2020, http://www.universalis-edu.com/encyclopedie/pratique-et-praxis/.

[2] For examples of this practice see Rorty (1982); Tiercelin (1993); Rescher (2005); Talisse and Aikin (2008); Bernstein (2010); Cometti (2010); Brandom (2011); Bacon (2012).

© The Author(s), under exclusive license to Springer Nature Switzerland AG 2023
S. Yiaueki, *Action, Meaning, and Argument in Eric Weil's Logic of Philosophy*, Logic, Argumentation & Reasoning 32,
https://doi.org/10.1007/978-3-031-24082-9_5

223, n. 1), never tells us who the pragmatists are. All that he ever gives us is a rather flat and cursory overview of pragmatism (the place of interested theory in human practices, the idea that what is true is what works, and an empirically motivated notion of progress). Weil, in fact, sees pragmatism as being incapable of asking and answering the question that interests him most, the question of meaning. Worse, by lumping pragmatism in with historicism, relativism, and skepticism, he critiques it as a form of positivism that sacrifices "the autonomy of moral reflection" (PP, 41). In this way, he sees pragmatism as unable to think through the real implications of autonomy. In other words, he seems to either mischaracterize pragmatism, or to dismiss it too easily. Why?

The start of Weil's professional career as a philosopher took place in the Germany of the late 1920s. At that time, pragmatism was still the dominant philosophical school in the United States and had already been introduced into Germany. William James, for instance, had direct interactions with and a direct influence on Wilhelm Wundt and Ernst Mach.[3] Because of the war however, any burgeoning interest in pragmatism seems to have disappeared. In fact, after the war the influence of pragmatism has been characterized as "a long chain of misunderstandings and misconceptions [...], originating from some of the most eminent German philosophers, and passed on with an amazingly uncritical self-assurance to others."[4] Heidegger, for example is one of the philosophers distrustful of pragmatism, but the prevailing thought among the immigrant German philosophers that went to the United States, and thus confronted pragmatism head on, is that "the sensational reception accorded to [...] [*Sein und Zeit*] by the German philosophical world in 1927 would have been tempered—without detracting from Heidegger's achievement—had Germans been more familiar with the pragmatist tradition.[5] The thought that there is a specific pragmatist strain in Heidegger's work has been reinforced repeatedly by Richard Rorty,[6] and has been dealt with in great detail by Mark Okrent.[7] Weil came to age philosophically in this context and he sees Heidegger's work as adding something essential to the history of philosophy. In fact, because he interprets Heidegger as one of the prime representatives of *The Finite*, the second to last concrete category, he sees Heidegger's work as an essential modern step that allows a full grasp of the concept of action and that allows reflection on the possibility of meaning itself. But because of this historical context, he may have merely adopted the "uncritical misunderstandings" that were prevalent in the German academic context of his time. Nonetheless, he may also have absorbed (in a way similar to Heidegger, and perhaps by way of Heidegger) a certain pragmatist bent. His characterization of *praxis* certainly gives credence to this possibility. For Weil, praxis is "the activity of the human

---

[3] It is interesting to note that Weil claims that the "*Methodologists*, such as Mach or H. Poincaré" (LP, 223, n. 1) share certain commitments with pragmatists, namely the way that methodological reflection opens the way to scientific progress.

[4] Oehler (1981), 27.

[5] Oehler (1981), 30.

[6] Rorty (1989, 1991).

[7] Okrent (1988).

being who, in their struggle with nature, wants to act reasonably within nature" (LP, 41) and thus praxis always precedes theory. He says that "no matter where and when the human being has lived, they have done so in and through *praxis*" (LP, 42). In fact, both humanity's production of meaning in language as *poiesis*, and its discursive grasp of this meaning (and of itself) constantly "refers back to *praxis*" (LP, 43). Therefore, even if Weil was in no way a theorist of pragmatism, there is a strong case to be made that he was a practitioner of pragmatism. Like the pragmatists, he builds his thought on a constant reflection of the concrete human practices that are found in concrete human situations. These practices, as meaningful practices, are seen as the throbbing heart of philosophical reflection. If this aspect of pragmatism is present in his work, it remains to be seen if he shares the main criteria that I am attributing to semantic pragmatism, namely a metavocabulary that focuses on orders of explanation that explicate the framework of meaning.

5.2 The Role of Error in the *Logic of Philosophy*

In Chap. 3, I touched on the jump from *Certainty* to *Discussion*. Therein I claimed that discussion plays the essential role of relativizing beliefs. It is only once beliefs are relativized that they can be seen as claims and not as mere descriptions of the world. Difference and doubt are therefore essential elements of claim-making. This relativization plays a key role in the conceptual development present in the logic of philosophy and it is only through this progression that, for Weil, we can see the role that concept use plays. It allows us to see the structural features of the logic of philosophy, to understand the work that the different types of categories play and the importance that Weil places on orders of explanation, and to see the logic of philosophy as providing a pragmatic metavocabulary that seeks to explain the possibility of meaning and life as a meaningful unity. Without difference and doubt there is no need to distinguish between knowledge and error, between claims that are well-grounded and those that are not. More importantly, without difference and doubt discursive content does not even appear as content, thus difference and doubt both play essential epistemological and semantic roles. If there were only one thing to do, all would do it. If there were one thing to know, all would know it. Without multiple reasonable choices, discussion never starts, because there is no doubt about what to do. This doubt leads to the demand of justification that opens the argumentative moves that happen in discussion, and discussion is the place where discursive content develops and unfolds. Weil notes that:

> Logic, the science of dialogue, applies to what both interlocutors share; its sole purpose is to eliminate the *remaining* contradictions, thus helping interlocutors put together a coherent discourse on a given subject, pushing them to get rid of the contradictions that they had not noticed when they were defending one individual statement after another but that they now find themselves needing to defend simultaneously. This results in them either needing to abandon one of the statements or to demonstrate that it is possible to reconcile all of them.

Logic does not make up discourse, it makes discourse coherent by purifying it of its contradictions (LP, 25).

According to Weil then, *Discussion*'s goal is to settle debate, to reset the bases of belief, to end enquiry so that people can get back to the business of living. To do so however, individuals must excise error from discourse, must identify what is faulty in the conceptual content that they commit to and must therefore repair their concepts so that their positions are coherent. Discussion is therefore, in the strongest sense, the space of the conceptual. Discussion pursues the end of inquiry, where the dust settles and all is clear and known and justified, but this is also, for Weil, merely a nostalgia for lost certainty, because a world once lost is never reclaimed. Instead the relativization of beliefs that happens in the jump from *Certainty* to *Discussion* is part of the motor of the development of semantic content. It is a condition for making claims of coherence and universality.

The philosophical position of relativism is defined by the incommensurability of criteria between different contents, whether it be moral relativism, epistemological relativism, or semantic relativism. Weil, by arguing that there are different discursive centers that are irreducible, would fall into relativism unless he were able to offer substantive criteria to distinguish between these positions and show their coordination. In some sense, this is a goal of the logic of philosophy. Yes, some discourses are irreducible, but they can nonetheless be compared by a set of criteria. They are irreducible but not incommensurable. This is why the logic of philosophy is presented as a suite of categories that make growing claims of comprehensiveness. Weil shows both the possibility of multiple forms of comprehensiveness within which claims of universality and coherence make sense *and* how concrete individuals can move between these very forms of comprehensiveness. Weil thus wants to defend a position that puts plurality front and center, while not folding into relativism.

In a manuscript dating from around 1939, which comprises structural notes and ideas for the *Logic of Philosophy*, Weil sketches some key positions that he would work through in the book. Notably this text shows some of the difficulties that Weil hoped to resolve in the *Logic*. One such difficulty bears on his starting point. He looks to overcome the problems linked to two common starting points in the philosophical tradition, subjective interest and a metaphysical concept of truth. Weil states, "If we start with interest, we start with a for-itself that only leads to action. If we start with truth, we remain in an in-itself that is merely identical to itself. One will need to start with the fact of the human being thinking about the false and the possibility of error" (PR.II.228). This is important for two reasons. First, it shows that Weil seeks to avoid a possible tension that leads to either a purely instrumental theory of action or of a theory of truth that folds into an ontological notion of Being. Second, it shows that his solution is to focus on an order of explanation that places human error at its center.

The reason that Weil seeks to avoid the tension between an instrumental theory of action and an ontologically grounded theory of truth can be redrawn according to Weil's commitment to a plurality of human discourses understood as the distinction

5.2 The Role of Error in the *Logic of Philosophy*

between relativism and skepticism. Eric Weil's goal is to navigate past one without falling into the other, to avoid the gaping maws of both Charybdis and Scylla. The problem with purely instrumental theories is that they collapse into subjectivism and relativism. When the individual's interest is the sole criteria for acting, action becomes uniquely a subjective endeavor. Each interest becomes an equally valid reason to act, thus leading to the philosophical form of relativism: the criterion of each interest is incommensurable with that of all others since it is grounded in personal interests that can be understood as free from all dialogical control. On the other side, there is the problem of skepticism. Ontological theories of truth lead to skepticism because they create a gap between the object outside the mind in the world and the representation of that object inside the mind that it is unable to overcome. The link between these two things can always be attacked as arbitrary and thus can always undermine any possible certainty and set off a tilt-a-whirl of doubt. This creates a problem because, as stated, Weil thinks that doubt and difference—the roots of philosophical skepticism and philosophical relativism—are necessary conditions in order for the jump from *Certainty* to *Discussion* to be possible, however he also insists that these *necessary* conditions are far from being sufficient. Rather the jump (and every reprise of this jump) depend on specific historical conditions. Without doubt and difference playing a productive role, philosophical inquiry would never be born out of the naïve attitude of *Certainty*.

As already mentioned, the attitude of *Discussion* alone (and not dialogical practices more largely construed) shows itself unsatisfactory to reestablish certainty. The type of discussion that happens under the philosophical category that bears that name—the discussion illustrated in Socratic dialogue—establishes nothing.[8] Instead, it leaves the initial questions unresolved while opening more questions. One question leads to another, and to another, and to another. The original question, which needed to be resolved in order to know what to do, leads to an interminable discussion. Classical foundationalist claims aim to stop this infinite regress by providing something external to discussion, something that itself cannot be put into doubt, something that is immediately known and understood. Foundationalist claims seek to *ground* discussion in something that can be immediately and non-inferentially admitted as being true. However, because one of the main points of Weil's work is to show that there is a real plurality of discourses that can be organized in a coherent manner, he cannot accept the foundational claim because of this very monism.

A key feature of monism is its absolutism. The jump from *Certainty* to *Discussion* happens precisely when the original monism of *Certainty* is no longer operable. Before this jump, the world is a single meaningful unified whole. When the single meaningful unified world falls to the wayside, more and more distinctions are made that are translated into the various domains. These domains give rise to different distinctions, whether they are epistemological, ontological, semantic or otherwise.

---

[8] Even though we call this Socratic dialogue it is merely exemplified by Socrates. For Weil, this type of dialogue characterizes the whole practice of discussion in the Greek city-states of Antiquity.

Foundationalist programs seek to re-articulate this unity by grounding discourse on a single condition. Foundationalism's monism is put into peril by the existence of other discourses and monism finds itself in a weak position. It is far easier to show that one possibility is wrong than to show that only one possibility is correct. The monist discourse must show that the world cannot be organized in any other way, otherwise monism collapses into relativism or skepticism. That is, if there is no single discourse that can be said to be all-encompassing, then monism fails *because* there are a plurality of discourses. Once this pluralism is accepted there seems to be two options. On the one hand, as long as these discourses claim to be coherent on their own while remaining incommensurable, the absolutist claim risks becoming relativist. And on the other, if all claims are refused precisely because the real plurality of positions is recognized, then the absolute claim risks falling into skepticism.

Weil recognizes the dual dangers, and his solution is not to overcome them in order to rule them out but rather to integrate them into discourse by showing the productive role they play. He shows how the failure of beliefs at the most fundamental level, the level where beliefs allow individuals to succeed in their endeavors, relativizes the beliefs themselves. This failure that leads to relativization by recognizing differences has a world-disclosing function. The shape of our concepts become visible thanks to difference. This difference, in turn, casts doubt on the well-foundedness of those concepts that before were not even visible and reveals them as making up one human possibility among many. This highlights the free choice to understand. On their own, argumentative practices can lead to full-blown philosophical relativism or skepticism if the individual chooses not to give up on the absolute validity of their own position. Argumentative practices however also stand as a bulwark to relativism and skepticism while profiting from their productive roles. These productive roles are present in the ability to form coherent discourse from older failures, to repair error and to develop materially richer semantic content. This shows that the effectiveness of discourse itself is built off the failure of certainty. In other words, failure is real inasmuch as discourse is real and failure only happens in light of discourse, in light of things being held as certain.

One can accept the failure of discourse that leads to skepticism and relativism, just as one can refuse it. Both are real possibilities. Many a philosopher have bitten many a bullet and have accepted skepticism or relativism. In fact, each moment of the historical development of philosophical discourse, each of the philosophical categories, has its own skeptics and relativists. When one does not accept skepticism and relativism, it means that they are still committed to the possibility of a single unified discourse that involves the possibility of the thing that the skeptic denies, the possibility of knowledge, of values, of meaning, and the thing that the relativist denies, the criteria by which we can judge different possibilities. I said that the movement from the attitude of *Certainty* to that of *Discussion* destroyed the faith in the certainty of one's own position. This does not however mean that it leads to the philosophical positions of skepticism and relativism. Rather, skepticism and relativism are both possible, but unstable, terminal points of two necessary aspects of human reason. Doubt and difference, as the openness to other positions and

5.2 The Role of Error in the *Logic of Philosophy*

comparison, are essential dialogical controls and both are used in discussion to get things right.

The experience of failure teaches the individual—philosopher or otherwise—that certainty can be put into doubt; the experience of other people having different reasons for doing things leads the philosopher to compare their position to that of others. It is a bit puerile—though understandable—to move from one's own failure, and one's own awareness that there are multiple reasonable positions, to a claim that all knowledge is impossible and that nothing can unify such divergent positions. Weil's solution is to refuse an instrumental theory of action built on interest, and to refuse an ontologically-grounded theory of truth, for a position built on the real possibility of human error. This, for Weil, grounds the formal unity of discourse. In other words, he takes this failure as a learning lesson instead of as the world's failure. What pushes the individual to continue to seek a reasonable position, or to develop new criteria, when their previously reasonable position has failed? For Weil, the individual makes a choice, but it is a choice that is confirmed at every corner.

Weil notes that the attitude of certainty accompanies every concrete attitude. He states: "The human being is always living in a world. This is the anthropological expression of certainty. There are no detached objects, no isolated values, no independent thoughts; everything holds together" (LP, 116). The individual is only capable of living in the certainty of their world if they do not massively face failure. If they do massively face it, it wears away at more than just certainty. It wears away at meaning itself. When it has sufficiently worn away at meaning, meaning collapses into *Meaninglessness* and individuals live their life there. That is, they become unable to see any concepts as playing a structuring role. Without certainty, concepts turn idly. Therefore, along with doubt and difference, certainty also plays a productive role. It structures commitments and allows them to resist scrutiny. Weil notes that "in everyday life, far from turning to theory, no one even asks questions. The concrete certainty of *this* naturally following *that* is so strong that it is not even felt. There needs to be a failure or an unforeseen event for certainty to become visible as what is missing" (LP, 117). So, failure, for Weil, marks the entry into the philosophical attitude, but as he also notes, the bulk of our lives happens in certainty, and thus, outside of the philosophical attitude. Weil highlights this by saying that the "surest thing, the best 'known' science, is at the same time the farthest thing from consciousness: know-how. Even if the human being recognizes their world's essential in and through their life, they are not necessarily able to designate it in their theory" (LP, 117). It is know-how, the implicit certainty that the individual exhibits and experiences every day, that keeps them from accepting the route of skepticism and relativism. This is because skepticism and relativism are of a piece with the philosophical attitude, and because most people spend most of their lives outside of this attitude. This insight is pivotal to Weil's work. By abandoning certainty as an absolute criterion, Weil presents the development of the different categories as different forms of ground-level explanations that develop semantic content differently. He abandons the epistemological criterion of certainty in order to show the way that certainty, in the form of commitments, plays an essential pragmatic role. It allows people to commit. Each different category articulates a different conceptual commitment and thus participates in the development of semantic content. Different philosophical categories are thus the different articulations of different conceptual contents, and the logic of philosophy as a whole is the framework that allows philosophical categories to play this structuring role. The logic of philosophy is an order of explanation that seeks to organize all these different contents in such a way that understanding itself makes sense. To do so, Weil places human error at its center, however into doing so, he transforms the notion of error.

For Weil, error is always intra-discursive and retrospective. It is intra-discursive because what is considered false or erroneous depends on the fundamental commitments that are provided by a category. This is what an individual grasps by having an attitude. For Weil, the philosophical tradition has characterized error as a "deficient mode [...] of reality" (LP, 17). However, this presentation of error, for Weil, is problematic. For error to be error, it must true, that is, it must truly be error and thus it "falls within truth" (LP, 91). This is the basis of the category of *The True and the False*, where what is true and what is false mix in discourse. Before discourse nothing is false and nothing is impossible, both what is false and what is impossible are based on a necessity that is determined in discourse itself. Thus, in this category, error is seen as what is inessential to a discourse, as what keeps the discourse from grasping the world coherently. The goal of the philosopher is therefore to purify "their discourse of the errors that disfigure it and that keep it from being reasonable and from grasping truth" (LP, 32). The pre-philosophical attitude, such as we recognize it, is marked by its certainty. For this pre-philosophical attitude, and in a constantly evolving present tense, in its progression of nows "error does not exist: the present (outside of projecting into a future that anticipatorily allows watching the present as a past) only knows certainty" (LP, 110). One of the things that marks the move from the pre-philosophical attitude to the philosophical one is its awareness of the possibility of error. However, within the structure of the logic of philosophy, error is also always retrospective for another reason. When the individual moves out of one attitude and into another, when they refuse the coherence of one attitude because it does not comprehensively grasp what they want to understand, they grasp the older attitude as a category. In this way, they grasp what didn't satisfy them in the older category *as* error. This error is what the new category is trying to correct. By presenting error this way, Weil transforms error into a retrospective grasp of the explanatory mechanism of dissatisfaction. It is this mechanism that allows us to grasp the movement of the logic of philosophy itself as the development of ever more comprehensive, materially richer, discourses. In this way, we can interpret Weil's insistence that philosophy starts from thinking the false and from the possibility as error within the logic of philosophy as the way that the individual grasps their dissatisfaction in order to transform it into a coherent discourse. Dissatisfaction on its own is insufficient to account for the movement of the logic of philosophy. Individuals can always be dissatisfied without seeking to grasp that dissatisfaction coherently *because* they are always within an attitude that is structured by a coherent discourse. Philosophy therefore starts from the possibility of claiming that this unsatisfying coherence is not just unsatisfying, but also misses something, does not state the whole truth. Somewhere, it is wrong. This is the movement of the

5.2 The Role of Error in the *Logic of Philosophy*

development of semantic content. To give but a single example, for *Consciousness*, *The Condition*'s error is not in the way that it describes nature, it is that *The Condition* ignores the free self-determination of the moral consciousness. By characterizing this specific error this way, *Consciousness* is able to provide new criteria that do indeed grasp this free-determination, and that therefore make discourse materially richer.

Thus, the philosophical progression of the logic of philosophy conceptualizes a truth that the non-philosophical attitude always implicitly understood, that error is "nothing more than the source of failure in the pursuit of satisfactions" (LP, 17). The difference however is in how the philosophical attitude conceptualizes it and this highlights the other reason that Weil interprets error as starting in dissatisfaction. The concrete categories do not see error as undermining their overall position, they merely see it as something to correct. However, from the viewpoint of another category, any error is a sign that the fundamental concept of every other position is in some way inherently flawed. From the viewpoint of the formal reflection on the possibility of meaning, this error is *semantically* seen as a structural feature of the development of meaning, because it is the mechanism that allows determined conceptual content to be materially enriched. *Epistemologically*, it also implies that the possibility of error leads to a certain fallibilism towards determined contents themselves. In genuine argumentative practices, such as those characterized by *Discussion* and its reprises, we are constantly relativizing our beliefs. We must accept that our position may be wrong in order to see our dialogue partners as genuinely adding something to what we know and to our grasp of the world. Our goal is to reach new commitments that, semantically, are defined by materially richer concepts and that, epistemologically, allow us to re-ground our certainty. This seems however to lead to a contradiction in Weil's work because he claims to have found a discourse that encompasses the possibility of discourse. Should we see his categories as the final word, as an ultimate table of categories to which nothing can be added? If this is the case, how does he avoid the danger of merely creating another overarching superdiscourse that is blind to its own possibility of failure? A discourse that itself falls into monism because it claims to be total, but is thus also subject to the problems of relativism and skepticism. A construction, but nothing more. In other words, is this merely the discourse that allowed Eric Weil, the individual, to understand the meaning in his life, but that goes no further? This is a problem because even though Eric Weil tries to understand the possibility of dialogue between discourses, he unites all of them into a single discourse which seems itself to necessarily absorb all other discourse. In other words, how does Weil avoid falling prey to the very problem he is trying to understand?

The answer to this question must be found in Weil's notion of systematic openness. I have already claimed that Weil's theory opens the door to a practice of philosophy. By positing *Action* as the last concrete discourse, and by positing a formal "transcendental" reflection on meaning and on the possibility of a life lived as a meaningful unity, Weil highlights the way that, in order to have a concrete discourse that allows one to be oriented in the world and in their thought, the individual must reprise the totality of discourse in order to apply it to their concrete situation. Weil therefore sees the logic of philosophy as explicating the framework or structure of discourse. It is in this way that Weil's theory provides a recursive pragmatic metavocabulary that allows concrete discourses to be grasped. The systematic openness of the logic of philosophy means that there will be no end to the kinds of concrete discourses that human beings can elaborate, but it also means that the logic of philosophy is not the final word. This implies that if someone takes the question of the logic of philosophy seriously and is unsatisfied by it, the only thing they can do is the actual work of providing a discourse that surpasses it. This is where Weil's systematic openness comes into play. Any new discourse must, in turn, also be taken seriously. It must be seen as a viable candidate, both as possibly offering correction and as materially enriching the discourse of the logic of philosophy. Weil's discourse is open because in order to have a coherent discourse that grasps the possibility of coherent discourses, that grasps the possibility of philosophical possibility, it has to be. It must seek to grasp the meanings that individuals articulate in the world and see them as meaningful, thus as possibly adding something to the logic of philosophy itself.

At this level, epistemological and semantic concerns are entangled. One cannot abandon certainty without abandoning meaning, and we only look for meaning because it is everywhere. This opens what, following Weil, we can call the paradox of certainty (LP, 117–118). According to Weil, certainty only becomes a criterion in the face of doubt and difference. This is because doubt and difference disclose the world by showing us the limits of our concepts. They allow the world's conceptual features to become visible first by making us doubt our commitments and then by showing other possible commitments that may reasonably be held. We can only look for certainty, as an epistemological criterion, because we are no longer certain. But certainty, in its productive form, plays a semantic role. It determines the concept (or concepts) that we are committed to and that we are looking to repair. In other words, certainty is what we are trying to establish. So we are certain that something can be established and this is why our research is oriented. This orientation is itself based on a new certainty that is not yet disclosed but that moves us. It is implicit in our practice and the conceptual work that we need to do is make it explicit in our discourse. Thus one can only *become* philosophically certain about a claim through the loss of pre-philosophical certainty. This is because it is the loss of pre-philosophical certainty that allows claims to be tested, that allows the problems of our conceptual content to be identified, and where need be, repaired. But a claim can also only be tested if one is at least in part certain. Thus, the paradox of certainty is defined by the gap between the epistemological criterion of certainty and the practice of committing to a determined content. In other words, the individual is looking for something they already have. What they are looking for—this know-how, this essential—is found in the everyday commitments that define what Weil calls "the fluent activity of daily life" (LP, 117).

5.3 The Paradox of Certainty

For Weil, certainty is part of the dynamic conceptual motor that allows for inquiry along with doubt and difference. It is the mixture of doubt and certainty in their productive roles that allows discourse to jump into the discussion that inaugurates the philosophical attitude. In this way *Certainty* and *Discussion* can both be read as pragmatic categories. Each provides a specific type of practice. *Certainty* thematizes the practice of taking on commitments and *Discussion* thematizes a specific type of argumentative practice. This practice, and the way that it inaugurates the philosophical attitude of understanding will be essential for understanding why we should read the *Logic of Philosophy* as providing a pragmatic metavocabulary based on the development of a specific type of order of explanation. Or, more precisely, it is the jump between *Certainty* and *Discussion*, a jump that is constantly reprised, that allows us to read the *Logic of Philosophy* this way. As already mentioned, doubt and certainty both play productive roles in the development of conceptual content. However, it is certainty and not doubt that can attain categorial purity. There are two reasons that skepticism does not reach categorial purity, one practical and one logical. First, categorial purity depends on recognizing something that is essential in the *fluent activity of everyday life* and philosophical skepticism is born in the philosophical attitude, thus outside of this fluent activity. In this way, skepticism is always parasitic on the pure categorial form that has failed it, or that it is looking to refute. Here we can think of the distinction David Hume makes between the philosophical and the vulgar. The philosophical can posit a pure form of doubt, but the vulgar overrides it in the practical actions of one's daily life, in their fluent activity. Thus, skepticism never *practically* reaches categorial purity. *Logically*, it doesn't reach categorial purity either. This is what the paradox of certainty shows. Skepticism, as a philosophical position, says that everything must be doubted, but as a philosophical position, it is sure of where it stands. Thus, skepticism only exists in the attitude of certainty and, as such, contradicts itself. As Weil notes, this doesn't convince the skeptic, but this is precisely because they are certain. *All* discursive commitments are confirmed in a free choice and the skeptic, like any other individual, can decide to remain in their position. We must take the productive role that Weil gives to certainty seriously. It is this productive role, this recognition of our own certainty in our activity, that allows philosophers to refuse skepticism and relativism, and to seek understanding and unity. By recognizing the productive role of certainty we are already on the path to resolving the problem of the multiplicity of discourses and the possibility of failure.

It is within attitudes, and as an attitude, that certainty has a productive role. This role therefore is invisible to the category because the category has not yet accepted the productive role of doubt and difference. In the category of *Certainty* the world appears as a united whole for the first time. But, because this united whole is particular, held only by this community or that, *Certainty* also sees difference for the first time, without recognizing the role that it will come to play in the relativization of beliefs. In this way, *Certainty* is the attitude of discursive commitments. It is in

Certainty that individuals commit. In fact, before the acceptance of the relativization of beliefs in *Discussion*, speaking is nothing more than a statement of fact. Weil notes that *Certainty* "is so sure of itself that it is unable to understand how someone could not accept it; there must be something within them other than just opinion's speaking, a quality that does not depend on their thought and their language, a stubborn and wicked *character*, a *force* that is foreign to their humanity, a psychic, physical, astrological *misfortune*, an evil *demon*, the *devil*: for certainty, the human being *must* be open to its content" (LP, 112).[9] The plurality of discursive contents is recognized in certainty but this plurality also poses a very real existential threat. This threat must be eliminated. Since the world is seen in discourse as a united whole for the first time, the failure of this discourse signifies the end of *their* world, which for them is the equivalent of the end of *the* world. The individual's certainty depends on their commitment to the ontological and metaphysical positions that structure the world. But these claims are made in discourse. If the world were not ontologically and metaphysically structured in this way, the individual in *Certainty* would be at a loss to understand how the world could be meaningful, because this is precisely what, for them, gives the world meaning. But for this same individual, this does not yet happen at the level of claims. Here we can see how two separate aspects of what I said in Chap. 3 come back with full force. First, the category of *Discussion* plays a key role in relativizing the certainty that different forms of life hold. Second, the jump between one category and the next is always free and unjustified. It is thus only once the individual has passed to *Discussion* that they can see that the failure of their doctrine was not *the* end of the world, but only *an* end to *a* world, that it was a matter of discourse. In *Certainty*, however, the end of *one's* world remains identical to the end of *the* world.

The attitude of certainty sees these external influences, be they demon or devil, as what keeps the individual from being able to access truth. Thus certainty, like all other pure attitudes, presents a universal character. All individuals can access truth if the path is cleared for them. It is just sometimes the obstructions are too large or too imposing for them to see this immediately, through intuition, or as given, and so the only way to guarantee that each individual has access to this path is to clear the way for them, by force if need be. The path has to be leveled and any means are legitimate so that the unfortunate (who do not yet see that they are in the false) can be led to truth. The problem is that certainty can reinforce certainty. An individual that is certain of being right, that leaves no margin for difference, can push their opponent to double down and dig their heels deeper into their own certainty. For anyone, this can be better than giving way to a despotic foreign certainty that misses what they see as essential. Such certainty blinds people to the possibility of seeing each other as potential dialogue partners that have something to contribute to one another's conceptual content. In other words, seeing them as possible sources of

---

[9] This is different from the type of certainty that is found in Weil's own position of systematic openness. In this position, it is not that others must be open to our certainty, that is something we must work to achieve, it is that we must be open to the possibility that their positions will provide something essential to our own.

5.3 The Paradox of Certainty

dialogical controls becomes more and more difficult. As Weil says, "the human being of certainty only knows one way of behaving towards anyone who does not share their truth: if the sermon does not force the adhesion of their fellow human beings (the content of course still needs to allow conversion), all that remains is the destruction of the infidel who, through their stubbornness itself, has shown that they are a human being in appearance alone and that, in reality, they are the most dangerous of animals" (LP, 113).

The jump to *Discussion* thus plays a key role because it allows people to relativize their claims. However, it does not just change the individual's posture towards content. The jump to *Discussion* also plays a key role in altering one's interaction with others. Because it opens dialogical controls, others are seen as equal and autonomous partners who add something to discourse. This is precisely the reason that discussion establishes dialogue as the domain of non-violence. One does not act violently towards an autonomous equal who adds something to their lives. Weil thus claims that dialogue is impossible without a commitment to non-violence (LP, 24). This commitment to non-violence is the initial meta-commitment that individuals explicitly take on. In this way, *Certainty* is the category that develops the idea of discursive commitment, and *Discussion*, the meta-commitment to non-violence. As will be shown later in this chapter, it is this meta-commitment that allows people to enter into the recognitive relations with others that are translated into entitlements and endorsements. It also highlights the difference between the relativization of claims in discussion and the philosophical position of relativism. In other words, the incommensurability of discourses is different from the local relativization of claims. The incommensurability of discourses makes discussion futile, while the local relativization of claims structures the possibility of grasping multiple point of views. In this way, such local relativization is implicit in the structure of discussion. This is then translated into entitlements and endorsements because entitlements and endorsements are used to identify what commitments people actually hold, which is how the different points of view within this plurality are structured. Without this relativization, individuals see each other not as potential dialogue partners, but as potential opponents. *Discussion* presupposes that for the most part, the parties concerned agree. This is the crux of Weil's claim that non-violence structures the domain of dialogue. This local relativization is seen as local, and thus as productive, only after one takes on the meta-commitment to non-violent (reasonable) argumentative practices. The role of dialogue (as logic) is to identify the agreement in the difference and then to settle disagreement by bringing opponents to define what they hold, what follows from it, what is incompatible with it, all in such a way that the disagreement is settled.[10] *Discussion* thus alters discursive practices because it alters the role that others have: each interlocutor is taken to be essential.

The relationship between partners and opponents is philosophically subtler than it initially seems. It is easy to see one as a positive relationship and the other as a

---

[10] It is important to note that the *category* of *Discussion* opens this path, but does not itself lead to agreement because it is built around the formal practice of dialogue and does not itself provide any content.

negative one, however, in accordance to the Hegelian influence that is present throughout Weil's work, it is more correct to see them as dialectic, and thus the poles of positivity and negativity can easily be reversed. Weil ironically quips, "Individuals struggle because they agree, as François I was in actual agreement with Charles V about the value of Milan" (LP, 289). Weil uses the historical example of the rivalry between these two kings during the so-called Italian Wars to show how their deep difference revealed a deeper agreement. Both kings agreed that wielding a strong influence on European affairs was essential. What they disagreed on was who should wield it and how it should be wielded. The struggle to control Milan can thus be seen as representative of that agreement: both saw it to be of central strategic importance. Here, it is the opposition that allows the contested aspect of their agreement to come to light. Conflict, by revealing what is essential to a disagreement, also reveals what is essential because of the disagreement. Conflict and difference reveal what is to be overcome. This is another way of understanding the crucial jump from *Certainty* to *Discussion*. Weil notes that we "can ask what virtue is, but only if we agree that virtue exists; we can contradict one another about the sacred character of this act or that phenomenon only once we both have agreed on the fact that something is sacred" (LP, 25). *Certainty* is unable to see this because it reduces these values and this sacred to the thing valued or sacralized. By focusing on things valued and sacralized, certainty fetters the search for what these things share. *Discussion*, on the other hand, seeks to render this disagreement productive by highlighting the need for a common ground. Precisely because seeking a common ground involves recognition, one must see opponents as partners linked in their conflict. The conflict itself reveals what is essential to both disagreement and agreement. Once this happens, once opponents recognize each other as real dialogue partners, they can then examine what their commitments are. They can see what is incompatible with their commitments, and see what the consequences of those same commitments are. In other words, this is the first step to recognizing the entitlements that go along with these commitments.

When individuals accept the possibility of seeing opponents as partners, they legitimize their place in discourse and thus also recognize them as making up part of the same community. Discussion binds people to discursive norms, which are only recognized if individuals see themselves as being bound by the same customs and traditions, as being equals before the normative weight of better reasons. Weil thematizes this community as initially being understood as the community of "genuine human beings" (LP, 26) as genuine participants in the dialogue that resolves conflict.[11] This form of recognition is defined by non-violence. Certainty leads to violence when violence is seen as a solution to resolving conflict. If one decides to avoid violence, there must be another way to settle conflict. Weil uses *Discussion* to

---

[11] As already noted, Weil is not endorsing this claim. He is merely highlighting that the Greeks characterized themselves as genuine human beings in relation to the non-Greek "barbarians." For the Greeks, non-Greeks were not genuine human beings precisely because they did not recognize the same sacred as the Greeks and because their relationship to the Greeks was mediated by violence.

5.3 The Paradox of Certainty

show how argumentative practices become a viable way of avoiding violence to settle conflict. This does nothing to change the fact however that one must freely enter into argumentative practices for them to hold any sway. It is only once individuals freely enter argumentative practices that they are willing to accept the common character that is under discussion. Conflict shows what is essential, but the goal of argumentative practices is to end conflict. In order for argumentative practices to come to term and thus to settle the conflict, all recourse to violence must be refused. That is, individuals must be willing to abandon violence. This however is merely a necessary condition and not a sufficient one. There is no sufficient condition. There is no sufficient condition because nothing guarantees that people won't choose violence. Philosophy is taken to be the free choice to refuse incoherence and to seek understanding, but this also means that the free choice to opt for violence is just as much always present. This opposition of free choices reminds us that there is no sufficient condition possible. Necessity, possibility, sufficient conditions, all happen inside of discourse and thus do not affect the decision to enter discourse.

Individuals find themselves in a paradoxical position, they are looking to avoid being submitted to violence, but in order to do so, they must themselves be willing to abandon violence. They must be willing to abandon violence with no guarantee that others will also do so. This position is built, not out of a single refusal of violence, but out of a continual refusal of recourse to further violence. Individuals have already shown themselves partially willing to do this by looking to resolve a conflict by non-violent means. But in order to recognize opponents as equal dialogue partners, one must willingly abandon violence from within violence. Thus, conflict reveals a deep agreement, but it only does so by first presenting itself as conflict. This conflict comes about because the attitude in which every individual lives is the attitude of certainty. But there is naïve certainty and there is what Weil calls reasonable certainty (LP, 33), but which we can also call *mature* certainty.[12] This allows us to give a second formulation to the paradox of certainty: one only arrives at mature certainty by abandoning the violence that defines naïve certainty. In its first formulation, the paradox of certainty states that because we must account for the possibility of error, things can only be put into doubt because of a deeper certainty. We lose certainty when we are faced with difference, but this loss is never total, and we lean on some deeper certainty to justify ourselves, to live, to repair whatever certainty we have lost. To do so, we must be willing to abandon naïve certainty in order to put it to the test. But we can only put it to the test because we *are* certain that this is the way to re-achieve certainty. Thus, we open the relativization of certainty in order to compare different certainties from within certainty itself. When we have accomplished this task and justified our certainty, we have transformed it. This transformation reveals that this deeper certainty is what actually grounds the one that had been naïve. In the second formulation, this deeper certainty is only disclosed because of

---

[12] I am calling this development *mature* in part because for Weil, reasonable certainty is the product of the mature consciousness (LP, 429), and in part because of the way that reasonable certainty and the mature consciousness overlap with what Kenneth Westphal calls mature judgment, in Westphal (2003). The notion of mature judgment will appear again in Chap. 8.

the conflict that forces one to see the possibility of error that defines the initial formulation. Thus, the paradox of certainty is only a paradox epistemologically. It is a paradox for anyone who is reflecting on it from naïve certainty but who wants to resolve conflicts non-violently. For the person who has found mature certainty there is no paradox because they have done the work to understand themselves and the world. For the violent individual, there is no paradox either, but for different reasons. There is no paradox because there is only another determined content that is not their own and that must be eliminated. In some ways, this second formulation of the paradox is more primordial than the first, however, logically they happen simultaneously. In order to be recognized as an equal partner by someone, one must recognize what that individual has to say as potentially valid and as potentially true. Without this, discussion is not the means of resolving conflict. This means that one must willingly abandon their own certainty and violence in order to recognize their partners as having potentially good reasons, reasons that can help to establish mature certainty. Here is the greatest paradox. The paradox of certainty only exists for the person who is caught between naïve certainty and mature certainty. What reflection shows is that this person caught between naïve certainty and mature certainty turns out to be all of us, again and again. We can always choose to understand just like we can always choose violence because our lives are constantly wrought by new situations and our understanding is continually surpassed by our own hand. What we do is the material of the human world. The question is, what does mature certainty look like to Weil?

What the second formulation shows us is that the paradox of certainty also deals with the way that violence is to be overcome by means of argumentative practices. For Weil, the partial resolution to this paradox is to be found in the category of *Action*. It is in this category that individuals understand their concrete situation and look to transform the world in such a way that individuals, themselves and others, no longer need to turn to violence in order to settle disputes. They look to transform a violent world so that others can see themselves as belonging to a world that is reasonably organized. This resolution always remains partial however because it is always in a violent world that the individual seeks to act reasonably and because, as a free choice, it is itself violent (that is, particular and recognized as such). This world needs to be reasonably organized because that is the condition for the individual to carry out reasonable action. This also shows that the world is already reasonably organized, precisely because in *Action* the individual acts reasonably. What they find though is that its organization is only partially coherent, and so the goal of action is to make the partially coherent world ever more so. Reasonable action thus happens against the background of the partial coherence of a reasonably ordered world that the individual seeks to change by presenting a discourse that allows others to grasp what is still incoherent about the world's organization. This formulation is in fact just a way of unpacking what goes into the concept of a *pseudo-nature* (which is Weil's preferred term for the concept of a second nature), a concept that plays a critical role in the category of *Action*, and formally, in *Meaning* and in Weil's philosophical project in general.

5.3 The Paradox of Certainty

The pseudo-nature governs our social lives, it is what causes us to live our social lives as external to us and imposed upon us from the outside. It is the depository of ancient discourses, of former actions, of historic organizations, of accepted norms. It is what appears as given to the individual when they enter into the world and it is what they can refuse in their free activity. It is what overlays the natural world and with it, what makes up human reality. It appears to us as external, and thus as given, because, as Weil notes, "it is not the same human being that thinks reality and that constitutes it" (LP, 402). In this way, the pseudo-nature makes up the naïve certainty that the philosopher looks to overcome. It appears to the individual as external, as inhuman, as hostile, as violent. Mature certainty thus presents itself in the recognition of this pseudo-nature as the condition for human action, as being violent, but constituted of a violence that can be grasped and reduced, as being hostile, but hospitable enough for humanity to make a home there, as inhuman when it is seen as external, but as inimitably human when it is recognized as something that makes us the kind of creatures that we are. This *pseudo-nature* is not just the domain of individual's activity (the interaction of a conditioned thing with the other natural conditions existing in the world), it is the domain of their action (the transformation of their activity through the reasonable application of discourse). Here, action is acting for reasons and so the question of how reasons are constituted becomes all important. The transformation of the world in *Action* is undertaken to create the real social and historical conditions that allow every individual to present their action as reasonable, and thus as a reason to act for every other individual. This action is social, not only because it targets the rest of humanity, but because it targets the understanding that humanity has of itself and of its place in the world. It targets human understanding. It targets the normative structures that allow individuals to understand the world in which they live so that their activity becomes action, so that their action in turn is able to act on the normative categorial structures that allow the real to be grasped in discourse. Mature certainty reveals itself at this point of reflection to be what Weil also calls *wisdom* or "the certainty of understanding and of reasonable action" (LP, 442).

The paradox of certainty disappears when it is resolved in the mature certainty of action *or* when it is left unseen in the naïve certainty that precedes the relativization of belief in the jump to *Discussion*. It is a paradox when individuals recognize their certainty but are led to undermine it through philosophical discourse. By recognizing the possibility of error at the beginning of his philosophical enterprise, and by interpreting it according to the explanatory mechanism of dissatisfaction, Weil gives us a key to resolve the paradox as it presents itself in our own lives. It is only partially resolved in *Action* because the category shows the plurality of ways that it can be resolved by the concrete individual's concrete action in their concrete life. It is only fully resolved by me and by you when we know what to do because we have worked through our concepts, because we have a discourse that holds together and that allows us to make a reasoned stand. Error is therefore not a deficient form of reality, it is the concrete individual's recognition that a given form of coherence does not satisfy them. It is a failure of discourse in a world structured by discourse and it is real. It is not an illusion. It is a self-standing part of human activity in the real world. As such, it is what allows individuals to orient their activity and their thought. This is what is sought in coherent beliefs, a way to avoid error because of its *real* consequences, a way to find a satisfying discourse that allows the individual to grasp the world and their life concretely. But error also shows possibility as possibility. It allows us to doubt our discourse and to compare it to others. It allows us to stop seeing the world as given in an a-temporal sense and to see it as made up of conditions which we can shape and alter. Weil recognizes that each person has a hand in making the human world and so argues that we must recognize both the possibility of success and of failure in individuals' discourses and in their practices.

Together, the recognition of error and the paradox of certainty play key roles in Weil's philosophical system. They are also the elements that allow us to see an analogy with Brandom's pragmatic metavocabulary that focuses on orders of explanation. *Discussion*, dialogical argumentative practices, is the starting point of philosophical explanation. It starts from the identification of multiple contents and the force that different individuals' commitments to these contents have. These commitments can be so strong that individuals are willing to die and kill for them. The argumentative practices found in *Discussion* start from a meta-commitment to reasonable non-violent practices, to dialogue, and the goal of dialogue is to draw out the commitments. It does so though by looking to make explicit what is implicit in the social pseudo-nature of our institutions and normative practices. Individuals can constantly be dissatisfied with what presents itself as given in this pseudo-nature and can lift themselves up to refuse it and to refashion it and to make the world over, over and again. The goal is to articulate the mature certainty where the individual recognizes the place they have in redefining the conditions they found in the world, where they understand the scope of their action in its limits and in its breadth because they recognize the place of error and doubt in their certainty. People recognize error in the fluent activity of their daily lives and this is why Weil defends its place in philosophy. For philosophy to understand itself philosophically, it must constantly hem closer and closer to actual human practices. Error allows individuals to recognize the limits of beliefs and the scope of discourse. The scope of discourse is important because each discourse is defined by the scope of their essential and their consequent inessential and because these discourses are compared in terms of their relative scope and ordered based on the coherence and universality of that relative scope. The order of explanation chosen will allow different internal and comparative scopes to be articulated because it sees discourse as a dynamic process that constantly seeks to recognize what is amidst different claims of what must be. This distinction, as I said earlier, is one of the reasons to defend an expressivist reading of the *Logic of Philosophy*.

5.4 Weil's Expressivism and the Placement Problem

In the last chapter, expressivism was contrasted with representationalism. However, in Eric Weil's defense of expressivism, he does not directly critique representationalism. One reason for this may be that "the equivocality of the term is […] total, given the multiplicity of the domains under which it falls (image, signification, concept and finally thought)."[13] Or, it may be because Weil takes the critiques of representationalism found in Fichte and Hegel to be decisive. Or perhaps it is because, as Cassirer's student, he took the German expressivist tradition for granted. Whatever the case, the concept of representation almost never appears in the *Logic of Philosophy*, and when it does it is never defended as a primitive explanatory concept. It is always a mediated position. Because of this, we cannot approach Weil's expressivism based on any critique of representationalism. This however is not a problem given the expressive resources that Weil himself provides in his work. In fact, his texts are brimming with descriptions of our expressive use of language. In the clearest statement of his defense of expression, Weil states: "Language is not an instrument destined to state what is, but to express what leaves the human being unsatisfied and to formulate what they desire; its content is not formed by what is, but by what is not" (LP, 8). It is important to remember however that dissatisfaction is used methodologically, it plays an explanatory role. This is clear in the way that he describes this dissatisfaction. He states:

> language is negativity's tool; every judgment bearing on the present is false as a judgment and true only to the extent that it expresses human interest, human desire, human discontent, and the philosopher's speaking can be no different. If the human being is the being who is not satisfied by the given, then their own given being, which consists in negating the given, will not satisfy them either. As soon as any human *nature* is given, it will be transformed by human activity; as soon as the human being's character is given—which happens in and through the philosopher's language—the human being, as what negates every given, is discontent with this being that claims to be their own. They only express it to surpass it, to transform it, to negate it—to negate themself; as soon as they understand their own life as the active expression of their discontent, they will rise up against this discontent and against this very activity: they will no longer seek to rid themself of what displeases them, but will seek to create contentment through the victory over discontent itself and over negativity (LP, 9).

As we can see, the human being must grasp themself in language (and discourse) to understand themself, and this language is not uniquely their own, it is a language that is built out of already existing and conflictual discourses, it is the language of the community. Here, Weil is refusing to give primacy to the designative role of language by placing its expressive role in the forefront. Weil insists that language in its expressive capacity is used to interpret what dissatisfies the human being and to give voice to that dissatisfaction. He sharpens his thought by insisting on the role of negativity. In this way, it is precisely the expression of dissatisfaction and desire that triggers the conceptual movement that defines the type of concept use that

---

[13] Thomas-Fogiel (2000), 8.

transforms language into coherent discourse. We can see how this thought is clarified further when Weil calls language the tool of negativity. Thus, even though it is a lived human feeling that language expresses, what matters most to conceptual content is the negativity that transforms the feeling. In this way, thanks to Brandom's articulation of pragmatism as a species of functionalism, we are in a better position to understand Weil's insistence on human feeling. Feeling is to be understood role-functionally, it is the particularity that resists universality. The individual expresses dissatisfaction in order to transform it. In this way the negativity of language is transformed into the positivity of content. The individual determines a content by refusing another content, by clarifying what has been said, by giving criteria in order to understand, by limiting and delimiting the determinations that they posit. Weil presents a form of expressivism that leaves a place for representation, but this place is limited in scope. For instance, in *The Logic of Philosophy*, it is people that are representative, they represent attitudes, stances, interests, actions, others, all when faced with an opponent that is also, on their side, a representative of such things. In other words, representation for Weil belongs to a certain type of public social interaction, one that is central to us being the kind of discursive creatures we are, but is not the whole story. It is expression that plays the role of an explanatory primitive.

By recognizing Weil as defending expression as an explanatory primitive concept, we can look at how Weil's expressivism lines up at the two distinct levels of analysis that we put into place in the last chapter. These levels first distinguish between Humean and German expressivism and then between broad and narrow expressivism. Remember, in the last chapter, I claimed that expressivism falls into two distinct currents, one Humean, and the other German. The hallmark of Humean expressivism is to limit the amount of metaphysical entities that need to be posited in order to explain certain concepts, namely, in the Humean meta-ethical example, those concepts that are used in moral judgments. The goal of German expressivism, as I have said, is quite different. It seeks to create a holistic picture of humanity by examining the roles of language and cognition in our lives. In a certain sense, Weil's project does look to limit the number of metaphysical objects that are mobilized in order to explain things, even though he is working from the German tradition. His project limits metaphysical objects precisely because he is looking to trace their correct scope. This takes the form of seeing how different metaphysical categories allow us to determine the shape of different philosophical categories, but he does this by explicitly rejecting the Humean position.

Humean expressivism is built out of what has been called the "bifurcation thesis."[14] According to this thesis, a clear distinction can be made between descriptive and non-descriptive language, between facts and values. The Humean expressivist thus places expressive language on the side of non-descriptive language while allowing descriptive language to do the heavy lifting, thus preserving the classical representational model. The bifurcation thesis has the advantage of allowing

---

[14] Kraut (1990).

5.4 Weil's Expressivism and the Placement Problem

Humean expressivists to minimize the metaphysical concerns present in moral and normative vocabularies (even though most classical Humean expressivists do end up falling into the realist metaphysics trap in their descriptive language) while still recognizing that there *are* moral and normative vocabularies. But in resolving one problem it opens another. Humean expressivism is exposed to what is known as the placement problem. The placement problem asks where to put or place the kind of practices or concepts that fall outside of the scope of a theoretical framework. In other words, it asks what must be rejected or reformulated so that discourse remains coherent. For example, in a causally determined representational framework of language, moral and normative language is an uneasy fit. Therefore these models seek to place normative language outside of its framework in order to "save" the framework. Humean expressivism's solution is to describe moral and normative language in terms of feelings or dispositions, in terms of attitudes. This allows the causally determined representational framework to accord a subordinate place to the work normative language does while removing and minimizing the incoherencies that could trip up the representational model.

Weil rejects classical Humean expressivism, or, more correctly, he rejects the bifurcation thesis, even though he recognizes the placement problem (as is clear in his argument that each philosophical category's coherence is defined by its essential and its inessential). Weil notes that "at least since Hume's days"[15] the following thesis has been formulated over and over: "there is no path from fact to value. Science is concerned with facts exclusively, and science alone is qualified to distinguish what is a fact from what is not. Value judgments are not scientific nor can they become so."[16] But then he asks, "whether this purely negative fact is sufficient to elucidate the relations between facts and values"[17] because even if "[i]t is certainly true that values do not follow from facts [...] it now appears that facts become relevant only through values."[18] By looking at Weil's characterization of what is essential and inessential in terms of the placement problem each philosophical category can in fact be understood as different ways of characterizing a central discursive commitment. Each discursive commitment will therefore define different things that are to be taken out of discourse in order for it to remain coherent. Using this strategy, we can claim that Weil sees the bifurcation thesis as a specific response to the placement problem. Likewise, Humean expressivism becomes a specific solution (falling, in Weilian terms, under the category of the *Condition*) that tries to keep the bifurcation thesis in place, while making room for normative language. German expressivism shows that this is not the only solution possible. In fact, the tension between German expressivism and Humean expressivism shows that there may be a better solution available. By placing expression at the root of language use, German expressivism minimizes the threat of the placement problem, but it faces its

---

[15] Weil (1965), 180.
[16] Weil (1965), 180.
[17] Weil (1965), 180.
[18] Weil (1965), 182.

own problems. It potentially trivializes language use by blurring the distinction between different forms of expression, and some of its iterations even seem to allow the multiplication of metaphysical entities. However, this does not mean that these two forms of expressivism cannot be brought together. It will thus be helpful to look at Huw Price's efforts to do so in order to see more clearly what the problems are and how Weil's position relates to this solution.

Price presents what we can call a "deflationist" expressivism. Price's deflationist expressivism presents Humean expressivism and the Brandomian articulation of German expressivism as being reconcilable because he claims that the differences are in fact only superficial.[19] While this may be true, it is important to notice however that Price makes significant changes to both Humean and German expressivism in order to make them fit, thus in their pure form, they are less reconcilable. Remember, the Humean expressivist's goal is to explain certain kinds of evaluative attitudes that fall outside of a purely designative language use, while not appealing to metaphysical objects. In this way, Humean expressivism is locally restricted. It only deals with certain aspects of language use. Price's first step to reconciling the two strands of expressivism is to abandon the local restrictedness of Humean expressivism. By unrestricting the role of expressive language and making it global, the bifurcation thesis loses much of its force. In fact, unrestricting this role also modifies the scope of expressivism in terms of the placement problem. Modifying the scope of the placement problem, a problem that is one of the motivating factors of Humean expressivism, shows how Humean expressivism is surpassed. Unrestricting this form of expressivism already moves it closer to German expressivism. However, Price does not jump headlong into German expressivism because there are elements of Humean expressivism that he wants to save.

One of the key elements that Price hopes to maintain is the minimization of metaphysical entities, and even if Herder's narrow expressivism also minimizes metaphysical entities, this is far from being the case in German expressivism widely understood. Price will thus be insisting on this element as he advances to show that the two forms of expressivism can be reconciled. And indeed this is the point that needs to be reconciled, because once Humean expressivism has become a global expressivism, possible metaphysical commitments are the only thing that keeps these two forms of expressivism from being the same. Price focuses on the place of metaphysics specifically in Brandom's form of German expressivism. What Price suggests is that, at least in Brandom's case, the project is far less metaphysical than it seems (he may however have made less of the criteria of minimizing metaphysical entities if he had also treated Herder's expressivism). Price's claim is that Brandom mischaracterizes his own project when he defends a metaphysical position. In fact, Price says that all this hangs on what we understand by metaphysics. Price argues that if we understand metaphysics as a description about the *deep nature* of extralinguistic entities then there is good reason to be a Humean and not German expressivist. However, if we understand Brandom's metaphysical project anthropologically,

---

[19] Price (2011).

5.4 Weil's Expressivism and the Placement Problem

as Price clearly does, and as an "account of the *attribution of terms*—'truth', 'reference', 'represents', etc.—not of the properties or relations,"[20] not as revealing the deep nature of truth, reference, and representation, then the Humean expressivist has far less to object to.[21] Price reconciles the two positions in tension, but only by modifying certain key commitments in order to find a new position.[22] By changing the scope of both projects, Price is able to reconcile them, and thus present a type of global expressivism that minimizes the need to resort to metaphysical entities.

Weil's project shares certain aspects of Price's project, because even though he rejects classical Humean expressivism, his position is far less metaphysical than classical German expressivism. He rejects Humean expressivism, because he sees the expressive and evaluative role of language use as more fundamental than its designative, and therefore, representative role. Remember, metaphysical categories and concepts are a consequence of the stances and commitments that we take in discourse and thus do not uncover the deep nature of reality, but rather present an anthropological character: our understanding of nature is tied to our capacity to grasp it in discourse. In this way, the fortunes of metaphysical concepts change from discourse to discourse. Sometimes they are minimized and deflated, sometimes they are eliminated altogether. Their presence is a consequence of the explanatory needs of discourse and they are born in discourse to grasp the world. They are not the eternal and really real substrata of existence, and Weil clearly thinks that expression provides a more comprehensive explanation of language use than designation. Price holds a deep commitment to Humean expressivism and tries to generalize it using the insights of German expressivism. Weil on the other hand is an heir to the German expressivist tradition but elaborates certain commitments that bear a similarity to Humean expressivism, namely a deflationary approach to metaphysics and a clear-sighted recognition of the placement problem.

Weil's approach to the placement problem becomes clearer as we try to situate him in the German expressivist tradition and try to decide if he should be considered a broad or a narrow expressivist. German expressivism is a global program. It hopes to explain all language use according to the expressive paradigm. Because of its unrestricted scope, the German expressivist program does not face the bifurcation thesis, but it has its own difficulties. By claiming that language is initially expressive and not representational, Herder and Hamann (reacting to Kant) saw no need to make a clear distinction between descriptive and non-descriptive language, but German expressivism does still have to make a distinction between expression in language and other forms of expression. Broad expressivism puts all expression at the same level, whereas narrow expressivism seeks to hierarchize different types of expression. As we saw in the last chapter, by completely unrestricting the notion of expression as well as unrestricting the notion of language use, broad expressivism

---

[20] Price (2011), 19.

[21] As already noted, the anthropological reading prevails in Weil scholarship. For explicit defenses of the idea that Weil should be read as giving an account of what we do when we argue from a content, instead of giving us a description of that content itself, see Savadogo (2003); Guibal (2011)

[22] He in fact sublates both positions to defend a new modified position.

risks trivializing the notion of language. Everything that is expression is language. It does not face the bifurcation thesis and has a less restricted approach to the placement problem, but because of this, it also risks losing some key features that we normally associate with language, namely representing and referring. The tension between broad and narrow expressivism is precisely a tension between different scopes of the concept of language itself.

I have already stated that Weil should be considered a narrow expressivist. I will thus be examining how closely Weil's philosophical project fits into narrow expressivism such as Michael Forster describes it. As a reminder, Forster gave three criteria for narrow expressivism, the dependence of thought on language, the rejection of metaphysical entities to explain meaning, and the sensuous origin of meanings. In the last chapter, as I looked at contemporary forms of narrow expressivism, I also insisted on the notion of thresholds. This is something that Forster touches on as a consequence of narrow expressivism, but that I want to bring more fully to the forefront as an element of Weil's expressivism. Narrow expressivism denies non-linguistic forms of expression full autonomy. This threshold is itself only conflictually present in Herder's expressivism. Herder still places the source of meaning exclusively in the individual's internal private sensuous language and merely places its development in the external public communicative language that defines our social lives. It is Sellars that has given the resources necessary for a "narrower" narrow expressivism. In fact, Sellars abandons the third criteria altogether because he treats language role-functionally. In a role-functional methodological form of expressivism, all forms of expression, including our sensuous expression, depend on the instantiation of meaning in language to be *seen* as meaningful. This also means that under a certain threshold one has to wonder whether one can speak of meaning at all. This is a controversial topic, and as the sciences advance, more and more conceptual capacities are attributed to non-human animals, because of their capacity to anticipate changes, their ability to demonstrate moral capacities such as altruism and trust, their ability to make their needs known. So here we must tread lightly and be rather conservative in our claims. Herder's expressivism, by focusing on what animals share with us, allows us to be seen as being in continuity with nature. Sellars, Brandom, and Weil however are more interested in the discontinuity between human animals and non-human animals. This allows them to side-step this question.

Under the Herderian model, the tension between the idea that thought is dependent on language and the idea that meanings have a sensuous, empirical *origin*, is never truly resolved. Nonetheless, his position concerning the *development* of language provides the resources to overcome the problem, despite that fact that he did not exploit them himself. Herder is not proposing a simple theory of mental causation. Herder is claiming that the content of our sensations and the content of our thought are mutually dependent. As our cognitive lives proceed, we distinguish differences that we then *form* into the content of meaning. We do so thanks to language. In this way, what we feel is partially determined by what we think and what we think is partially determined by what we feel, and language is the way that individuals act upon both. They are mutually dependent, but now we see that they

5.4 Weil's Expressivism and the Placement Problem

are also mutually structuring. Thanks to Herder's first criteria (that thought is bound to language) we can see meaning as usage based. But this meaning thus starts vague and only progressively becomes finer. It does not start from discrete elements that are clear and that only then become confused when combined. We grope around for meaning from the get go. This implies two things. First, there is no privileged path to meaning. Individuals must mobilize a whole variety of contextually sensitive and pragmatically respondent capacities not only in order to understand each other, but also in order to understand themselves. Second, individuals are deploying meaning before they know what they mean. So other forms of expression are meaningful, but they require language to be seen as such. There is no autonomy before the instantiation of meaning in language. This ties in well with Sellars's claim that one must have a whole battery of concepts in order to have any. It means that what is identified and identifiable as meaning is identifiable because we have crossed that threshold. However, once this threshold is crossed, it also means that we are able to attribute meaning to gestures and acts that do not autonomously have it, and *this* is important.

The central concept underlying this form of expressivism—and present in the notion of thresholds—is freedom. In an entirely determined model, there is no need to explain novelty, spontaneity, individuality, etc. The tension with which the early Humean expressivists struggle is how to square the representational model of language use, and a correspondence theory of truth, with moral language. By focusing on the problem of human freedom we can easily see why *fully* representational models and correspondence theories of truth struggle so much with the placement problem. In fact, if we were able to work out all the consequences of these theories, they would eliminate any discussion of freedom. The gap of indeterminateness that allows for possibility would be shown to be false, and thus inoperative. However, if it is shown to be false, it would, according to their model, always have been false and thus the problem of freedom should never have even become visible *as* a problem. Thus, what was a convenient way to maintain the designative model of language use, with its representational underpinnings, while accounting for moral language in the Humean case, is itself the root of freedom in the Herderian case. Expression is freedom of expression. The unboundedness of expression is the field that discloses freedom to individuals. They understand themselves because they can apply the negativity of their language to anything. They can say no. The notion of thresholds only makes sense in relation to this notion of freedom. Weil's philosophical project is based on freedom, and it is understood thanks to expression. He calls a specific discourse in a specific situation the "form" of meaning. He notes that discourse does not create this meaning, but merely organizes it. It is created in the individual's particular spontaneous expression, born of violence. It is, as he notes, "violence which, age after age, provides itself with what it can negate in discourse and which, grasping itself as freedom in its discourse and, at the same time, against its discourse, produces philosophy" (LP, 75). Violence thus creates the specificity of the human situation that individuals can raise themselves up against, and it is the violent refusal of violence that is the step towards the kind of meaning that we traditionally deal with. In this way, non-violence is the first of a series of thresholds that Weil highlights in order to show how content develops, how concepts form, and how thought and feeling mutually depend on and structure each other through language.

5.5 The Necessity in Discourse and Narrow Expressivism

Weil's nuanced position concerning human freedom is central to his philosophical project, and it is also what allows us to see the thresholds that define his narrow expressivism. Freedom is, in a certain sense, the goal of his project. Weil freely seeks to present freedom in such a way that each individual can see freedom as the goal of action (in Weil's particular political sense). The idea is that, in action, each individual can access real autonomy through discourse. However, it is only if philosophy is grounded on freedom that the philosopher can find freedom at the end of discourse. Weil thus seeks to show that all discourse presupposes freedom, even when it denies it (as is the case in *The Condition*). It is the presupposition of freedom that makes it an achievable goal for philosophy. Discourse shows the human individual what they already possess implicitly in their deployment of discourse. This is why Weil states that "what is first in itself, the foundation and the essential, is the last for us in the order of discovery."[23] It would however be a mistake to see Weil's conception of freedom as metaphysical. There is no freedom unless the individual realizes it thanks to discourse. In this way, its full grasp derives from discourse. But because of the way that it is found in discourse, it can be seen as always having been present. Weil's project thus seeks a discourse that opens the path to freedom, a path that anyone can take in order to grasp their own freedom. The achievement of this goal is what allows the individual to understand themselves as conditioned, as embedded in social structures, as natural, but also as free. Free, because philosophy is future-facing. It turns towards the past to understand the present, and it situates itself in the present to act upon the future. Philosophy brings the individual to the acting presence of the present. This is one of the central reasons that Weil places expression at the wheel: it explains freedom. It also reinforces the claim that Weil's position should be understood as a narrow form of expressivism.

We have already stated why Weil starts from the transformation of dissatisfaction into error. This is what allows for the development of semantic content. This, in fact, is one of the ways that Weil is able to refuse the Enlightenment's dependence of representation. According to Enlightenment thinkers, there is a duality that exists in nature, between the objects and subjects, precisely because of the way that subjects are apart from nature. This thought takes to its fullest form in the theoretical work of Kant.[24] According to this picture, there is the reality of things out in the world,

---

[23] Weil (1973), 51.

[24] However, as I have already said, Kant, as a transitional figure, is both the fullest expression of certain Enlightenment positions and the first step beyond them. Weil's position is to place Kant's

5.5 The Necessity in Discourse and Narrow Expressivism

and there is the representation of this reality that happens in subjects as the form of phenomena, which nonetheless are insufficient to give subjects any access to that reality because humans are unable to *represent* it. We thus have no access to the reality of things in themselves even though they are in some way supposed to be causally effective thanks to our intuition of representational phenomena. There is an aspect of this thought that is often overlooked even though it has been central to many debates that try to make sense of the question of freedom. That aspect is the determinism of representationalism. Representationalism tries to *fix* reference so that there is a single monist description of the world that holds in all situations. Once that reference is fixed, the things that can be said about the world are also supposed to be fixed, and that *determines* what is considered to be true and false. When truth-conditionality is placed at the center of the explanation, the specific Humean version of the placement problem comes rushing back in with full force. How do we explain what falls outside of representation? We do so by claiming that representations are a lesser, defective form of reality. This allows us to reduce false statements to errors in the subject and not in the object. This is done to *save* reality from human error. But this inverses the real goal. This move is not trying to save reality, it is trying to salvage human knowledge by guaranteeing that it corresponds to the objects in the world. Weil thus thinks that reality needs no saving from human error. Humanity is a part of nature, and it is only as it is human that nature is interested in humanity. Weil even doubts that extra-human nature can properly be called nature, and to the extent that it can be, it is indifferent to humanity. This is not to say that there is nothing outside of humanity, rather it is claiming that the concept of nature is a historic concept that has a human timeline.

So representationalism has a tacit underlying commitment to causal determination that expressivism is able to circumnavigate. What shape, according to Weil, does this give to human freedom? For Weil, negativity is at the center of human freedom. Because we can express negativity through our dissatisfaction, we can start the positive project of setting goals and eliminating contingencies. We are free because the way that we express our dissatisfaction—the fact that we express it at all—is in no way necessary. In fact, understanding the way that Weil characterizes necessity is helpful for contextualizing his position on human freedom. This is a theme Weil comes back to again and again outside of the *Logic of Philosophy*. In his short essay "Philosophie et réalité" Weil makes the following claims, (1) the philosophical tradition, at least since Plato, has seen philosophy as dealing with necessity head on; (2) this same tradition has claimed that philosophy is conceived of as a formally coherent discourse whose "principle task is to separate what is essential from what is not, to reject this inessential into the realm of shadows, of illusions, of epiphenomena" (PR.I.26). In other words, the philosophical tradition fixes what is essential and determines necessity from that essential. However, when things are relegated to illusions or epiphenomena, discourse is not seen as being a part of

---

most important moves as being on our side of that transition, thus to see him as the midwife of all modern treatments of the question.

reality, but as being a separate thing. It is seen as an inessential addition to the real. For Weil, whether discourse is seen as part of reality or as something added on to it has deep consequences. If discourse is an add-on to reality and necessity is in the world, then everything is determined, and we are merely clarifying things in order to ease our consciousness, but it is unclear what effect discourse is supposed to have on our actions. If discourse is a part of reality and if necessity is only found in discourse, then our discourse matters, and it matters because it influences what we see as possible and as necessary, and thus how we act. For Weil, necessity is a quality of judgments, not of facts or events, except derivatively (PR.II.42). This again highlights the difference that Weil makes between metaphysical and philosophical categories. Within a discourse, thanks to a metaphysical category, things *are* seen as necessary. If a wire is made of copper, then it necessarily conducts electricity. However these claims depend on this discourse and nothing requires that an individual hold a discourse that affirms the material implication of copper's conductivity. In fact, for Weil, one is only bound to this deontic status if they hold a discourse that instantiates it. It is defined by the presuppositions of coherent discourse and thus is not experienced "naturally" so to speak. Rather, it is conditioned by the discourse that individuals hold. Weil notes that "animals know constraint, but they do not know necessity given that they are immediate to their surroundings" (PR.I.27). Mediation starts, for Weil, as soon as the individual leaves the attitude of *Truth*, but this same mediation is conceptualized in the jump from *Certainty* to *Discussion*, and is realized in *The Object*. This does not mean that earlier discourses didn't grasp the separation between the object and the subject, but again, they didn't explicitly conceptualize it. It is by explicitly conceptualizing this distinction that *The Object* places a wedge between the subject and the object that becomes a problem to be overcome. By doing so, it uncovers the difficulty that representational systems face head on. *The Object* discovers this mediation, but it nonetheless ignores that this wedge is a human product. Weil states that "[a]nimals do not have the abstract negation at their disposal, they do not think what is not as such (they can have dreams and hallucinations, but this is not thinking what is not, it is feeling it as what is) they do not think the possible (although they have, but for our eyes only, possibilities at their disposal and know how to take advantage of them) the necessary is complementary and opposed to the possible, as that which cannot be" (PR.I.28). The abstract negation is thus, for Weil, a threshold that allows us to distinguish between non-human animals and human animals. But as with all thresholds, there is an element of rupture *and* an element of continuity. We can thus situate the rupture at the level of the *abstract* negation, at the level of speaking about what is not. This however is itself born out of the *pragmatic* negation that allows us to refuse anything that is presented to us. The pragmatic negation is what allows us to establish continuity with the natural world whereas the abstract negation is what allows us to differentiate what is specific and special about human language use.

For Weil this holds two major consequences, first, it means that philosophy does not deal with what is necessary, but rather with what *is*, what the individual finds before them in their life. Second, this means that the individual is free because they are conditioned. Because they find the world before them, they are free to act upon

5.5 The Necessity in Discourse and Narrow Expressivism

that world. These two consequences are at the center of Weil's expressivism. Weil claims that there is no necessity *as such* in philosophy, but rather that necessity is a consequence of the structural architecture of the individual's discourse. This discourse however is not pulled out of thin air, rather as Weil notes, it is found and it is historical. This allows Weil to refine his notion of language. Language is both the space of human freedom and the depository of human freedom. It is the space of human freedom because it is language that allows individuals to be future-facing in our specifically human way, because it is language that pulls us out of the flow of experience and into time. Weil here is not speaking about planning for the future and anticipating the future, other animals do that, but as seeing the future as the space of human action. It gives meaning to human action because it allows that meaning to come about and to be a continuation of beliefs and goals. It is however also the depository of human freedom because language holds the sedimentation of individual human acts of freedom. It holds the sedimentation of the ways in which human individuals have raised themselves up against the world and opposed it. It holds and collects the ways that individuals have imposed their negativity on the world by saying no to the condition and the ways they have tried to elaborate coherent discourse to justify that negativity, to justify that no. Weil notes that the philosopher:

> does not start thought, thought preexists them and precedes them. It is insufficient, primitive, mythical, but always prior to their personal undertaking, a condition that is as much restricting as it is grounding. The freedom of those who have preceded the philosopher has been deposited in language, in the discourses that the philosopher accepts or refuses, but that they could not even refuse if they did not find them in their world: whether the philosopher thinks with the others or against them, they cannot avoid referring to what is (PR.I.32).

This extract helps us to situate the two levels of Weil's position. There is no necessity without discourse because discourse imposes necessity on the world. However, discourse itself depends on something that is larger and deeper than itself. Thus, language encompasses discourse, because it is the domain in which all these discourses make sense. This also shows us the importance of reference. Weil denies reference the role of a conceptual primitive because as this quote shows, prior uses of language structure it. He does however show that within the expressive role of language use, reference plays an essential role. To speak meaningfully, the philosopher must speak about reality. However, because Weil sees language and discourse as making up part of reality, this referring role is neither limited to the spatial extended external world, nor does it *primarily* refer to this.

Language is the domain of freedom and discourse is the domain of necessity. Once discourse has been put into place, the logical development that allows for necessity opens the possibility of philosophical discourse. It is there, in this possibility, that reference and representation can take on the role that philosophy gives them. They allow us to correct our discourse by referring to the way that others grasp the world, by taking error into account, by grasping whatever can be shared discursively, that is, can be represented. When we correct our discourse we do not correct the world, we rethink the world, but we can only do so once we have taken up position at the interior of a discourse. This is why, for Weil, all the attitudes that precede the category of *Discussion* present themselves to us as certainty. Without the elevation of the law of non-contradiction to a central structuring role in our discourse, necessity cannot take hold.

Expression is more conceptually primitive than representation because, for Weil, representation and necessity only make sense based on other commitments. These commitments form the philosophical categories that govern metaphysical concepts like representation and necessity. There is thus a plurality of shapes that representation and necessity can take based on the different philosophical categories and together this plurality makes up the sedimentation of language that each individual finds. This expression however is not independent, it depends on the articulation of discourse to disclose its meaning. Weil's expressivism thus gives discourse a structuring role because it is discourse that progressively shapes the expression of language, just as the creative spontaneity of language constantly pushes back against discourse. This mutual pushback is reciprocally structuring. This is also why Weil presents the logic of philosophy as a suite of categories. Each new category, by adding something new and irreducible to our understanding, can be seen as an independent threshold that enriches what we can say. Reference and representation are central features of this account, without being primitive features of it.

Representation and reference, as I have mentioned, have an implicit determinism, and this is also one of their most important functions. It is thanks to representation and reference that we can make claims of necessity that hold for every individual, and it is thanks to these structures that we can act upon nature and change it to suit our needs. Thanks to representation and reference we can make objective claims, the type of claims that hold up in science, and so we can predict the behavior of the world. But this is exactly why Weil places expression at the base of his understanding of language. We cannot deduce human actions. We cannot deduce the questions individuals will ask. Any new action, any new question can surge up at any moment. Anything can be refused, even something that never had been refused before. The failure to deduce future events or future action puts what we know into doubt and relativizes it. It requires us to be open to this novelty. It is what creates the possibility of reevaluating theories and changing them. Philosophy is future-facing because, standing in the present, it looks to the past to act on the future. This also means that the future is undetermined. No quantity of knowledge about the past can allow us to deduce a free human act. This is because it is born of the *no* that any individual can present to any situation, and it develops with the discourses that individuals elaborate to justify their no.[25]

One of the corollaries of Weil's treatment of necessity is that because all necessity starts in discourse, there is no necessity in the individual's choice of discourse. Science and philosophy are only necessary for those that have chosen them, and only for as long as they are what the individual chooses. Science and philosophy are

---

[25] The ability to say no highlights the dialogical nature of the argumentative structures that I will be developing out of Weil's work. Although one can scream no out into the emptiness, or oppose oneself to the totality of nature. These extreme acts are themselves exaggerations of the more measured no's that happen in dialogue. They also depend on discourse to be seen as meaningful.

both born of human expression, just as art, religion, and society are. They are born there, but once they are born, they are reduced to the conditions that humans find in the world. Nobody needs to refuse violence, nobody needs to elaborate discourses, no one needs to refuse their condition as unsatisfying and work to change it. No one needs to become a philosopher and no one needs to stay one, except for the person who builds that necessity into their own discourse. Weil thus identifies expression as what allows individuals to make the free choice to understand the meaning they find and the meaning they create, and all other commitments are downstream from there.

5.6 A Case for Inferentialism

5.6.1 Weil's Critique of Reference

In presenting Weil's position, I have insisted that his defense of expression implies that he is barred from seeing representation and reference as conceptual primitives. I think that it is at this level that Robert Brandom's inferentialism is particularly fruitful for understanding why Weil refuses to see designation as a conceptual primitive. Brandom's position is articulated around the notion of discursive commitment just as Weil's is. In the last chapter I insisted on Brandom's use of David Lewis's notion of scorekeeping and how it allows us to track entitlements, commitments, and endorsements in the language game. I also insisted on his use of Wilfrid Sellars's "space of reasons" to define how discourse only makes sense inside of a normative space of giving and asking for reasons. These are two moves that allow Brandom to explain reference in terms of inference and thus allows inference to be seen as the more conceptually primitive of the two. What I will suggest is that the philosophical categories of the logic of philosophy play a similar role. They can be defined as the different spaces of reasons. Each such space of reasons, each category, is structured by the commitments, entitlements, and endorsements that follow from its specific central concept. It is in this context that the concept of reference should be defined.

There are several major moves that Weil makes that allow us to build a case for an inferentialist reading of the logic of philosophy. I will highlight three of these moves in this section. First, there is a critic of the kind of direct reference that is the bread and butter of representational models of language use. Second, there is a positive claim about what reference does do and how it is built into other claims and commitments. Third, there is the notion of responsibility that Weil develops in defense of the normative character of philosophy. Together, these three moves allow us to look at the development of the suite of categories in the logic of philosophy under a different light. I have already argued that each category presents new thresholds that allows different concepts to become visible. What we can add here is that some of these concepts play important inferential roles. By reading the development of the categories as containing the development of different inferential concepts, this will allow us to look at the importance of incompatibilities to the articulation of meaning and will build us a bridge to seeing what Weil's theory can add to inferentialism.

Weil's critique of direct reference is two-pronged. He presents the classic designative model of language use as being built on the notion of pointing to things out in the world and labeling them. The first prong of Weil's critique is that, under this model, language use itself would cause us to continually falsify language, and the second prong is that if pointing and labeling were the ultimate goal of language use, we would have little to say. The first point is part and parcel of what the Humean expressivist is trying to overcome with their solution to the placement problem. Since pointing to things out in the world and labeling them is not the only thing we do with language, the designative model has to find a way to explain what we do with the language that does fall outside of pointing and labeling. As long as we stay in the limits of these goals, all other language use either falsifies or corrupts language. Weil notes that for theories of direct reference:

> all judgment that isn't a judgment of identity (and who formulates such judgments?) is a lie, when we take it as a judgment and not as an expression of a human feeling, of a desire, of a passion, of some interest: a lion is not a felid, it is not even a lion, it is *that there*, and to tell the lie that it is a lion only makes sense when refuting another coarser lie according to which *that there* would be an eagle in the snake family (LP, 8).

Because the classical model of direct reference assumes that there is some conceptually whole content that is given in perception, Weil claims that, in this model, language that isn't a judgment of identity would force the speaker to go beyond the limits of correct language use. This falls into line with Sellars's critique of the given that I highlighted in the last chapter. Weil is not critiquing the role of perception in the acquisition of conceptual content, because the use of indexicals *this* and *there* implies the intervention of perception. Rather he is critiquing that this content be already *given* as such in the perception itself. He shows that from an initial perception of an object, which seems to fall under the concept of LION we are dependent on *inferential relations* that are not themselves given in the perception. In order to have knowledge of the lion and to be able to categorize it correctly, we cannot depend on the perception alone. Rather, we have to pull from other background assumptions that accompany the judgement:

x is a lion therefore *x is a felid.*

Without inferential relations, all perception can provide is a bare observation of a unified object in a specific piece of space, a *this there*. However, the thing must be determined by noting the incompatibilities in what is said. It is not positively built up from this bare observation, without incompatibilities the string of things *this there* could be is endless. Thus Weil highlights the way that we use incompatibilities in order to eliminate or exclude more problematic inferences. In this way, even the *this there* draws on inferential relations because, as indexical, *this there* depends on contextual and pragmatic indications that are put into relation with other commitments in order to identify what the *this there* is. This is in part the structural role that the categories fill; they put things in their place. The individual does not have

5.6 A Case for Inferentialism

unmediated reference to the world because they are always imbedded in a social, historical, and normatively structured world, in a *pseudo-nature*, that is part of the dialectic between a discourse and a situation. For Weil, the confusion is born out of the fact that this pseudo-nature presents itself to us as given precisely because we have carved out our understanding of the world in its terms. What Weil critiques in direct reference is thus neither the role of perception, nor the fact that things are "given" in experience, but rather that perception provides us with a conceptually autonomous, a-temporal content. Weil thinks that thought needs some ground in order to be determined, but he rejects that this ground be in some way outside of the world or unknowable. The ground that Weil defends is historical and cultural: it is the sedimentation of discourses and practices that are present in the life of the community.[26]

The second prong of Weil's critique of direct reference asks why we speak. Throughout his work, Weil maintains that when language is used in its specific tool-like function, as soon as the task at hand is completed, we set the tool aside. In other words, when we have said what we had to say, we stop speaking. Direct reference is based on the tool-like function of pointing and labeling. For Weil, this means that whenever someone points to something or labels something, they should exhaust the task and thus fall silent, however most times people do not stop speaking. This is because pointing and labeling, the role of direct reference, is only understood within the larger context of reasoning and judging. We do not stop with reference, rather we use reference in judgments that allow us to continue to discuss, to justify, to question. Because reference only makes sense in the larger context of judging, we never even exhaust language's overall tool-like function, we only ever exhaust specific tasks. Language as the tool of our negativity, allows us to express what dissatisfies us, to change our gregarious behavior into discourse, and thus to produce a constant stream of new tasks. This is why for Weil, "the human being spends their life in discussion" (LP, 138). Discussion is where these new tasks present themselves. Reference plays a critical role in language use, but it can't be the whole story. This is why Weil claims that reference (and thus representation) only make sense inside of a discourse that is already structured and only with a limited scope. Direct reference is thus a very specific confined use of language and not its most fundamental building block. In fact, for Weil, referring to objects in the external world is not even the most conceptually basic form of reference.

Weil's positive claim is that the most basic form of reference does not point to single items out in the world but rather points to commitments and claims that are found in discourse. For Weil, direct reference only makes sense once discourse is already structured. Direct reference points to something outside of discourse but discourse determines what will be pointed at and how, precisely because of the way the thing pointed at is used as an element of judgment. Weil notes that, "[l]ived reflection has shown (it has not *demonstrated* this, since it does not *demonstrate*

---

[26] This critique of direct reference share certain similarities with C.I. Lewis's articulation of the pragmatic *a priori* (as Sellars's critique of the given also does), in Lewis (1923).

anything) language's importance. In addition, it shows that language refers (taking the meaning of this term as formally and vaguely as possible) to the situation, because the human being, speaking of meaninglessness and living it, *takes a stance"* (LP, 100). Thus, the most primitive form of reference that Weil defends is not to a given out in the world but to what he calls the situation.[27] Remember, the situation is one side of the "form" of meaning, which is the grasp of a concrete situation in a concrete discourse. It is a complex of commitments, goals, satisfactions, dissatisfactions, questions, hypotheses, theories etc.… It is built into a social world and a natural world that the individual grasps in order to overcome. It is the overlapping of multiple points of view that are found in this social world and that make us aware of our differences. In this way, all involved define the situation together. It holds coherent discourses. It holds determined refusals of discourse and the absolute refusal of discourse in violence. It is partially coherent. It is meaningful *and* riddled with meaninglessness, but with a meaninglessness that can be transformed into meaning. For Weil, language always refers back to the situation and to its complex of commitments because this is what structures the judgments and reasonings that use direct reference. When one disagrees with something pointed at in direct reference, they rarely resort to just saying the same word and pointing to something else. They refer to other commitments. They refer to the complex of inferentially articulated moves that allow the judgment to happen in the first place. Reference and representation are thus deployed within the inferential relationships of the discourse that an individual holds, based on the stance they take in it, based on the category that guides it and the collections of reprises that are put in place. In other words, it is in discourse that the individual grasps a situation, and it is thanks to the situation that an individual has a discourse. Thus, reference does not point to something in an a-temporal world that is deformed in discourse, but points to the reality that is structured by discourse and that discourse is a part of, a reality that Weil calls the situation.

If discourse is real and if it plays a role in structuring reality then there are real consequences to discourse. In other words, we are not the passive patients of something that is *really* real and that we grasp in a deficient form, rather we are active agents in reality itself. This, for Weil, is important because it means that discourse conditions the freedom that we exercise in language. This leads to the third move that Weil makes that can be read as inferentialist, which is to highlight the specific kinds of responsibility that are found in discourse. Because discourse conditions the freedom that we and others exercise, we are in a special way responsible for our discourse. It is a responsibility that we give to ourselves by organizing, hierarchizing, and purifying our discourse. In his distinction between sapience and sentience, Brandom also highlights the role of responsibility in the normative character of

---

[27] The formalization of the concept of *the situation* is one of the essential resources that existentialism (specifically Sartre's existentialism) adds to discourse. And while Weil sees existentialism's position as legitimate, he also sees it as insufficient (LP, 61–64). In the useful glossary of terms in her translation of *L'être et le néant*, Hazel E. Barnes describes Sartre's use of the situation as "[t]he For-itself's engagement in the world. It is the product of both facticity and the For-itself's way of accepting and acting upon its facticity," in Sartre (1992), 806.

5.6 A Case for Inferentialism

concept use. For Brandom, what separates us from other animals is our sensitivity to rules, the fact that we can give reasons for what we do, and the fact that we ask for reasons from others, that we take on responsibility for what we say and do and that we demand that others do as well.[28] For Weil, there is nothing necessary about language, no one needs to speak. But once one speaks and once one wants to say something true about the world, they submit themselves to specifically governed argumentative practices that are defined by the individual's conflict with others. The individual creates and defines the necessity that will guide their thought and their action. Again, for Weil, all necessity is found at the interior of discourse, it is built into conditional judgments, and as such is inferentially articulated.

We are defined by the responsibility we take on in discourse, by the premise and conclusions of our judgments, by what we say and how we say it, but we are defined this way by ourselves. Thus this responsibility starts deeper for Weil; it starts in the free choice to speak and to understand. He notes that once that choice is made (which no one knows that they are making) we find ourselves sifting through the essential and the inessential in order to make a coherent discourse that holds up. But he also notes that this necessity only holds up as long as the free choice to speak and to understand is upheld. Remember, a key aspect of Weil's theory is that the individual can always quit reasonable discourse, but they always do so in a world that is defined by discourse and that is structured by discourse. This is what gives a special character to Weil's notion of responsibility. Responsibility is not born of necessity but of possibility. It is only because the possibility of throwing off the constraints of discourse—of no longer submitting oneself to the normative weight of better reasons—exists that individuals can hold themselves responsible. They are responsible for what they say and do because they could just as well not say and do it. Philosophy can be thought of as the continued effort to shoulder the responsibility of our discourse, to refuse meaninglessness and to seek to explain and justify what we do in the world. The responsibility that we take on starts from the free choice to organize one's discourse coherently, to excise contradictions and to eliminate incompatibilities. This gives credence to an inferentialist reading of Weil.

Recognizing inferential relationships means recognizing networks of commitments and entitlements that structure the normative stance that each individual takes to render their discourse coherent. For Weil, we freely choose a ground, then we work to unfold the consequences of that conceptual ground and commit to these consequences. We are thus not the patients of meanings that are in some way independent of discourse, rather we are the participants (and the heirs of other participants) in the gradual and dialectically articulated production of meaning. The main difference between these two positions is that, in the first model, if we are merely a patient of meaning, the meaning itself would already be structured independently of discourse. It would be a meaning that enters into discourse through reference and representation. In other words, we would understand the whole of meaning immediately. This is not the case in inferentialism. As participants in the production of

---

[28] Brandom (1994), 275–277.

meaning, we grasp meaning but only partially. We do not fully understand it. In order to understand it we must work through it, and in doing so we modify the meaning that we have grasped. This second, inferentialist, model reminds us that the initial creation of meaning is only subsequently understood *as* understanding when it is made explicit in discourse. We are the agents of this initial creation of meaning that we grasp thanks to our negative use of language, but that does not mean that we will immediately grasp that meaning or immediately understand our dissatisfaction. Weil's critique of reference and his defense of the role of discursive responsibility thus puts him in a good position to be read along inferentialist lines, however this is just one aspect of a possible comparison between inferentialism and Weil. The other is a rereading of the first categories, not only as the development of pure attitudes, but also as the development of the resources of coherent discourse. What this reading suggests is that these resources can be understood as inferential concepts.

5.6.2 The Development of Inferential Concepts in the Initial Categories

The development of the logic of philosophy is the development of different forms of coherence based on their central organizing concepts. These different forms of coherence define the way that individuals will grasp their situation in order to understand it. By way of his critique of direct reference, we can see that it is not far-fetched to read Weil as an inferentialist. By showing that there is a special type of responsibility that we take on in discourse and that this responsibility shapes the types of inferences that follow from our free choice to understand, we can characterize the logic of philosophy as a catalogue of different spaces of reasons. These spaces of reasons (the philosophical categories) are each defined by the inferential scope of their central concept, their response to the placement problem, and by the ensuing concepts that they make visible. In other words, we can see the philosophical category as a concept that is structured by commitments. It also structures commitments because the content of each category has different determined content based on their different fundamental concepts. In each category what is essential and inessential changes and what people are bound to commit to changes as well. Each philosophical category is therefore defined by the types of inferences that are permissible or incompatible in a discourse: the category's content is that concept's inferential articulation. Thus, the resources that the initial categories add to discourse can be understood as a development of the specific concepts and the specific inferences needed for full-blooded reflexive philosophical discourse.

As already noted, the first two categories, *Truth* and *Meaninglessness*, are the backgrounds of all discourse and can be described as its *yes* and its *no*. They thus form a logical framework that allows us to understand the *Logic of Philosophy* as the structured grasp of different progressive unities of meaning and their determined refusals. By claiming that *Truth* is the *yes* of discourse, Weil is already starting from

5.6 A Case for Inferentialism

a non-representational point of view. He reminds us that "there is nothing that 'corresponds' to truth, that is truth's 'other'" (LP, 90). In other words, already in this first category, there is nothing that refers to the external world, that points outside of discourse. The most basic reference is to the complex constituting a situation, and here Weil refers to the attitude of the individual in unity with the concrete situation of their life. As Weil notes, this category does not itself develop a discourse, it has no doctrine that is discursively articulated. At most, the entire content of its doctrine is a single word: *truth*. But this is not how it appears in the attitude itself. Rather, the category is the conceptual reconstruction of the attitude that is undertaken by the logician of philosophy. I have already mentioned that the logic of philosophy as a whole can be understood as the inferential unfolding of this word, by looking at the initial categories as steps in developing inferential concepts, we will be able to see how this plays out.

Following this argument, we can see *Truth* as placing the origin of discourse in a pragmatic attitude. The attitude of *Truth* is unbounded. It accepts everything that *is* as it is. Because it is unbounded, it has no determined content. This is why the category can't propose an articulated discourse: the contents of discourse are built in opposition. Nothing is outside of *Truth* and so it is without contour. Truth presents itself as empty. This empty character shows how important negativity is to Weil's theory. Endless things are permissible so long as incompatibilities and limits have not been established. Incompatibilities define spaces of reasons by being the opposition that gives discourse determined content. This opposition is found in the category of *Meaninglessness*. By opposing itself to *Truth*, *Meaninglessness* can be thought of as the birthplace of incompatibility, but under the form of the pragmatic negation that is found in the attitude. Incompatibilities are not yet seen as such since, in its opposition, *Meaninglessness* merely refuses all content. Remember, I said that this pure attitude is the pragmatic refusal of the world, of all determined content, as being meaningless. Because this negation is pragmatic, it is not yet necessarily discursive. That is, it does not yet need to take the form of the abstract negation that for Weil separates us from other animals, that allows us to give determined refusals to determined content. It nonetheless remains the birthplace of incompatibility. Incompatibilities give definition to the space of reasons by limiting which inferences are permissible, but it does not try to organize them. In order for this to happen the idea of scope is needed.

In its pure form, *Meaninglessness* refuses *all* determined content. Therefore, no inferences are permissible. In *The True and the False*, this changes. Some inferences are permissible and some are not. This is because here, "[t]ruth and meaninglessness become entangled in language" (LP, 102). Without reflecting on what it does, *The True and the False* nonetheless uses the abstract negation to fix the notion of judgement that is present in inference. The abstract negation is different from the pragmatic one in that it is anchored in language and so is not just negative but is also positive. It does not merely refuse meaning to see the world as meaningless, but it has the tools to transform the individual's dissatisfaction into determined content. This is why the scope of discourse is so important, it is only thanks to the capacity to fix incompatibilities that permissible inferences grasp a concrete situation in its singularity *and* in its universality. With the abstract negation, the individual changes the given character of discourse and grasps what is universal in *their* situation. They negate previous discourses and then turn to language in order to elaborate a new discourse that grasps the world. This transformation, from negativity to the negation of negativity, is, for Weil, what allows individuals to be "reasonably reasonable" (LP, 10).

By sorting through the essential and the inessential, by identifying incompatibilities, *The True and the False* establishes the scope of permissible inferences. But just as *Meaninglessness* is the root of incompatibility that is not yet understood as such, *The True and the False* is the root of inferential scope without yet seeing itself as such. Further developments are needed. In fact, I would argue that it is only in *Discussion* that these developments take on full-blooded logical roles. *The True and the False* cannot yet see its development of inferential scope because the notion of commitment has not yet been fully developed. This does not mean that there is no commitment in these early categories. In fact, the *yes* of *Truth* is already a commitment, but it is not until the category of *Certainty* that the concept of commitment becomes explicit. Scope allows us to see what shape a discourse has, it allows us to see what is permissible and incompatible in discourse, but the notion of the essential and of commitment have not been fully developed.

Certainty is what Weil calls "the constitutive category of the world" (LP, 108). In *Certainty*, individuals commit themself to the content of their discourse, by grasping "the essential as an essential" (LP, 107) and this commitment is what defines them. In other words, the individual is bound to the scope of their discourse in *Certainty*. The individual declares the certainty of *their* certainty "[a]mid uncertain opinions" (LP, 108), and in doing so commits to the goodness of their discourse. Once the essential is grasped, this central concept allows the individual to organize their discourse, and permissible and incompatible inferences allow the individual to orient their activity, because they know what they are committed to. This is also why the paradox of certainty takes the form that it does, certainty only appears in doubt. For this category, other certainties appear as aberrations instead of being other possible reasonable contents. Nonetheless, the commitment that is developed in *Certainty*, when it is reprised by other categories, makes other commitments explicit thanks to the scope its permissible inferences and incompatibilities define. It is however, *Discussion* and the transition to *The Object* that show how these concepts come together in a way similar to inferentialism and show how Weil's critique of direct reference has an inferentialist background.

Discussion's primary mission is political: it seeks to recast the community that has fractured through the relativization of its content and the ensuing doubt that this relativization brings on. In this way, *Discussion* not only thematizes the dialogue of two opposing contents held by two opposing people, it also thematizes the whole community as a community of potential judges. For Weil, this happens because this discourse establishes procedural rules that allow the positions of different opponents to be heard, and that allow the whole community to decide (LP, 127). *Discussion*, because it is political, follows the model of political trials that establish the scope of rights and property between opposing parties. Rights and properties

5.6 A Case for Inferentialism

help to determine what share an individual has in and of the community and thus is useful for tracking what individuals or parties are responsible for. In this model, individuals use discourse to help other community members decide who is right within the framework of the individual's determined complaints against their specific opponents. For Weil, the individual does this by demonstrating where they stand, by showing that they are a good citizen, that they defend and uphold the tradition, whereas their opponent does not (LP, 126). The goal of these procedural rules is to bring out and make explicit what the individual's *actual* commitments are through a process of legitimate question and response. However, even though the goal in the category of *Discussion* itself is political, we can see these procedural rules as being analogues to deontic scorekeeping.

In the *Logic of Philosophy*, judgement and judging is a sophisticated logical development that depends on ruling out violence, recognizing others as equals, recognizing the productive roles of difference, doubt, *and* certainty, taking positions, attributing statuses, taking on responsibility, etc. In our own lives, this same development is just as sophisticated and depends on many social and cognitive factors. By seeing Weil's development in *Discussion* as an analogous development to scorekeeping we can also see this category as opening a process analogous to the game of giving and asking for reasons. It is where individuals take themselves and others to be responsible for what they say in language and what they do in the world. The political model of trials is helpful not only because it allows us to see how Weil's notions of discussion and of dialogue are normatively articulated from the get go, but also because it allows us to see how, for him, this leads into the development of formal logic and to an order of explanation that gives inference a more basic conceptual role than reference.

Certainty is a category of value systems, of organized social labor, of certain modalities for resolving conflicts but, because, for us, it predates *Discussion*, its language use is found in modes of production and of organization, in different rites and rituals that act on the world. In *Discussion*, because the language of trials acts on individuals and not on the world, the individual does not need to leave language in order to establish their rights and lay claim to their share of the community (LP, 129). Rather, the individual needs to study language in order "to allow the pure identity of words to remain in the identity of their relations" (LP, 129). This pushes the inferences found in predication towards those found in conditional judgment. Weil notes that the type of relations that are studied are the "this is that" of an assertion and the "this is not that" of a counter-assertion (LP, 129). He goes on to note however that this assertion and counter-assertion teach us nothing (LP, 129). We can however modify this claim based on what he has already said about judgments of identity in his critique of direct reference. Assertions and counter-assertions do indeed teach us something. When these empty forms are filled with content, they teach us the commitments of the individuals speaking. This is essential for discussion to start, but it remains insufficient to bring discussion to a close. A new relation is needed, that of conditional judgments. Conditional judgments allow us to draw out what is essential to our claims, what qualities we are looking to highlight, what our goals are, to anticipate similar conditions in order to determine terms by limiting them. In other words, the inference that is present in predication is codified thanks to conditional judgment. Through conditional judgments however the *Discussion* transforms the tradition that it is trying to salvage. In the trial before the community, Weil sees the substantive values of the tradition as being deployed to defend individual interests. Thus in trials, conditional judgments lead to diverse interpretations of the tradition itself. What is at stake in these interpretations however are the substantive values themselves. In his attempt to stem this transformation by seeking to reconstitute the community's fundamental values, Socrates becomes *Discussion*'s central figure. He institutes a formally coherent discourse based on non-contradiction, but this discourse is unable to decide the conflict present in trials precisely because formal discourse is silent concerning conflictual grounding principles. This is one of the great paradoxes in the transition between *Certainty* and *Discussion*. *Certainty* holds commitments but its language is obscure and protean, *Discussion* clarifies language but it has no ground-level commitments. Its only commitment is in fact a meta-commitment, the meta-commitment to non-violent reasonable argumentative practices.

In *Certainty*, because it appears to us as the category of magical thinking and as a closed system of values, only the initiated have access to a language that acts on the world. In *Discussion* equals square off against each other before their peers and thus effective language is in the purview of every citizen. But *Discussion* does not make language effective. Commitment does. This has tremendous consequences. For Weil, *Discussion* is born in the dissolution of *Certainty* that is the dissolution of tradition. It is because the tradition and the convictions that accompany it have been undermined that the presence of differences reveals multiple reasonable possibilities. *Discussion*'s only goal is reestablishing conviction, is giving people true commitments that allow the community to hold together. Initially though, things are merely hypothetically posited in order to create enough room to allow for the ancient certainty to discuss its principles and goals. Socrates not only exemplifies this attitude, he even finds "the possibility of formally coherent discourse" in language (LP, 132). He is unable however to ground it. Discourse bears on everything, is valid for everyone, but these two conditions do nothing to guarantee that discourse is true or that it comes to a successful and satisfying conclusion. The failures of language show that everyone can agree and still be wrong, as was the case, for example, with Socrates' execution. The conditional judgment that surpasses *Discussion* thus becomes: *if* error is in language *then* there must be something outside of language that grounds discourse. Again, the elaboration of a discourse that transforms dissatisfaction into error is, for Weil, at the start of all philosophical projects. It is essential to his order of explanation, and this transition, which in the order of the logic of philosophy is the transition from *Discussion* to *The Object*, marks the beginning of western philosophy. I have said that *Discussion* is at the genesis of the philosophical attitude of understanding, but that, as a transitional category, it merely points towards the possibility of philosophy. *The Object* marks the free choice not just to understand but also to explain the world coherently starting from the ontological correspondence between external reality and discourse. It seeks to ground discourse and thus assigns direct reference a philosophical role. In doing so, it creates philosophy (and science) out of the recognition of error and the effort to overcome this very error by coming up with an order of explanation that permits a coherent grasp of the world. It starts philosophy, but this start is incomplete. Many other concepts will be needed in order to understand our own situation and these are what the *Logic of Philosophy* claims to offer.

5.7 Conclusion

By looking at the initial categories as the progressive development of inferential concepts, we can see that Weil posits *Truth* as the initial grasp of the *pragmatic* character of discourse, starting from the concept of the individual who lives their life as a meaningful unity. In *Truth* however, discourse has not yet developed the content of this unity. Further categories will be needed for content to be developed. This development, this movement, requires another pragmatic category to set it off. This is what the pragmatic negation in the category *Meaninglessness* provides. These two initial pragmatic positions are transformed into the inferential roles of permissibility and incompatibility in *The True and the False* because this category defines the scope of discourse. *Certainty* adds the concept of commitment and *Discussion* brings these developments together in order to create a set of procedural rules that bear strong similarities to Brandom's game of giving and asking for reasons. All these developments are already in place and prefigure the development of reference and representation, a development that is only grasped in the categories that develop concrete content. These early categories are part of the reconstruction that Weil thinks explains the possibility of meaning, therefore they were not themselves deployed as categories. This is because their pure attitudes lacked the metavocabulary needed to grasp them as such. These reconstructions are thus in a sense pragmatic. They describe specific discursive practices such as assertion, negation, inference, and specific framework-explicating features, notably commitments and procedural rules. The subsequent categories, from *The Object* to *The Absolute*, are the different shapes that the philosophical attitude of understanding takes on based on different specific grounding concepts. In this sense, they are semantic: they provide determined ground-level content.

All the categories are used in language and in philosophical discourse. Nonetheless, reprising these initial categories as the development of inferential concepts, and the later categories as the *specific* shapes of *philosophical* discourse, reinforces Weil's goal to understand both philosophical language and discourse, as well as the language and the discourses that are neither in themselves nor for themselves philosophical. This shows that Weil's critique of direct reference (and thus representation) is not tied to the *use* that philosophy has given it, but to the *scope*. This fits in with his pragmatic order of explanation and his expressivism. Reference (and representation) are essential to specific types of discourse but are in themselves insufficient to ground the totality of language. The logic of philosophy allows us to trace the scope of these concepts by seeing the types of discourse, the types of spaces of reasons, the types of philosophical categories that directly depend on reference. However, when this reference faces conflict or incompatibilities, one must appeal to the human possibility of creating a discourse that transforms their dissatisfaction into error and one must thus look outside of reference and representation. The source of this conflict itself is grounded in the human capacity to express dissatisfaction. This capacity, for Weil, is regimented by discourse (which can be referential and representational) but is born of human spontaneity. This spontaneity is at the heart of what can be called *the fundamental entanglement between language and violence*. In this chapter I sought to articulate Weil's theory in a way that connects it to inferential expressive pragmatism. In the next chapter, I will develop what Weil's theory can add to this position.

References

Bacon, M. 2012. *Pragmatism: An introduction*. Cambridge, UK: Polity Press.
Bernstein, R. 2010. *The pragmatic turn*. Cambridge, UK: Polity Press.
Brandom, R. 1994. *Making it explicit – Reasoning, representing & discursive commitment*. Cambridge, MA: Harvard University Press.
———. 2011. *Perspectives on pragmatism: Classic, recent, and contemporary*. Cambridge, MA: Harvard University Press.
Cometti, J.-P. 2010. *Qu'est-ce que le pragmatisme?* Paris: Gallimard.
Guibal, F. 2011. *Le sens de la réalité: Logique et existence selon Éric Weil*. Paris: Éditions du Félin.
Kraut, R. 1990. Varieties of pragmatism. *Mind* 99 (394): 157–183.
Lewis, C.I. 1923. A pragmatic conception of the a priori. *The Journal of Philosophy* 20 (7): 169–177. https://doi.org/10.2307/2939833.
Oehler, K. 1981. Notes on the reception of American pragmatism in Germany, 1899–1952. *Transactions of the Charles S. Peirce Society* 17 (1): 25–35.
Okrent, M. 1988. *Heidegger's pragmatism: Understanding, being, and the critique of metaphysics*. Ithaca: Cornell University Press.
Price, H. 2011. Expressivism in two voices. In *Pragmatism, science and naturalism*, ed. J. Knowles and H. Rydenfelt, 87–113. Frankfurt am Main: Peter Lang GmbH, Internationaler Verlag der Wissenschaften.
Rescher, N. 2005. *Studies in pragmatism*. Frankfurt: Ontos Verlag.
Rorty, R. 1982. *Consequences of pragmatism: Essays 1972–1980*. Minneapolis: University of Minnesota Press.
———. 1989. *Contingency, irony, and solidarity*. Cambridge, UK: Cambridge University Press.
———. 1991. *Essays on Heidegger and others*. Cambridge, UK: Cambridge University Press.
Sartre, J.-P. 1992. *Being and nothingness*. Trans. H. E. Barnes. New York: Washington Square Press.
Savadogo, M. 2003. *Éric Weil et l'achèvement de la philosophie dans l'action*. Namur: Presses Universitaires de Namur.
Talisse, R.B., and S. Aikin. 2008. *Pragmatism: A guide for the perplexed*. London: Continuum.
Thomas-Fogiel, I. 2000. *Critique de la représentation: Étude sur Fichte*. Paris: Librairie Philosophique J. Vrin.
Tiercelin, C. 1993. *C.S. Peirce et le pragmatisme*. Paris: Presses Universitaires de France.
Weil, E. 1950. *Logique de la philosophie*. Paris: Librairie Philosophique Vrin.
———. 1956. *Philosophie politique*. Paris: Librairie Philosophique Vrin.
———. 1965. Science in modern culture, or the meaning of meaninglessness. *Daedalus* 94 (1): 171–189.

―――. 1973. The Hegelian dialectic. In *The legacy of Hegel: Proceedings of the Marquette Hegel symposium 1970*, ed. J.J. O'Malley, K.W. Algozin, H.P. Kainz, and L.C. Rice. The Hague: Martinus Nijhoff.

―――. 2003a. *Philosophie et réalité: Tome 1*. Paris: Beauchesne.

―――. 2003b. *Philosophie et réalité: Tome 2, Inédits suivis de Le cas Heidegger*. Paris: Beauchesne.

―――. 2020. Pratique et praxis. Encyclopædia Universalis. Retrieved 10 June 2020, from http://www.universalis-edu.com/encyclopedie/pratique-et-praxis/

Westphal, K.R. 2003. *Hegel's epistemology*. Indianapolis: Hackett Publishing Company.

Chapter 6
The Language of Conflict and Violence

6.1 Introduction

In the previous chapters, I proposed that both Weil and the expressive inferential pragmatism that I am defending here should be understood as presenting us with an underlying theory about orders of explanation. According to this position, these theories, by starting from a certain conception of orders of explanation, place the emphasis on discursive commitments and thus do not look outside of discourse to ground themselves. Orders of explanation matter because they define the kind of explanatory force a discursive commitment will have. In both Weil and this brand of pragmatism, the goal of the order of explanation is to explain the framework within which the development of semantic content makes sense. This is important if we want to understand the possibility of meaning, of reasonable behavior, and of understanding itself. Additionally, I have claimed that both positions place an emphasis on how these discursive commitments are initially implicit, and that for both positions the work of philosophy is to make them explicit. For Weil, this is the distinction that he makes between attitudes and categories. For Robert Brandom, this is found in his inferential semantics and his pragmatic metavocabulary. By showing how implicit content (content that is lived in our lives without being reflexively grasped) is brought out into the light of a structured discourse, these two positions place a great deal of emphasis on the essential role that discursive categories play in structuring our cognitive experience in the world. Discursive categories are seen as structuring the content of our language and the content of our commitments, whether these be the Sellarsian meta-categories of spaces of reasons or the Weilian philosophical categories. I then worked out how different orders of explanation favor different types of positions. This is helpful in two ways. One, it shows how orders of explanation play an essential role in understanding different philosophical positions, and two, it shows how Weil and expressive inferential pragmatism's orders of explanations justify why certain aspects of a commitment are weighted differently than others. We can exploit the shared emphasis on characterizing orders of explanations to better distinguish the divergences between Weil and Brandom's position.

One similarity I have been looking to draw out of these two orders of explanation is the claim that an expressivist and an inferentialist model of language use has greater explanatory force than a representational and designative model. This is because the key representational and designative insights can be captured thanks to an expressivist inferentialist model, but on the other hand, a representational designative model struggles to capture what is right about the expressivist inferentialist model. Now I will present what Weil's discourse allows us to grasp comprehensively that this pragmatism does not—namely violence and the radical refusal of discourse. Violence is a concrete expression of human spontaneity. In that capacity it is fundamentally entangled with language. Language and violence are two of the forms that the creative production of meaning can take. In this chapter then, I will focus on the divergence between Weil's position and the pragmatism that is exemplified by Brandom's inferentialism. Following Weil, I will argue that any philosophical tradition that sees the individual as an essentially rational being overlooks the fundamental entanglement of language and violence, and that this entanglement is a blind spot in modern inferentialism.

I have argued that modern inferentialists (Sellars and Brandom, as well as sympathetic commentators such as Huw Price and Jaroslav Peregrin) have provided an expansive explanation of language use. Despite this, they do not see violence as *the* limit to discursive reason that Weil does. This is not a weakness of their theory. A great part of philosophical tradition has missed this point. Even theories that do grasp the importance of violence, like different forms of irrationalism, only do so obliquely because they do not take coherent discourse into account. Weil refuses irrationalism, but nonetheless grasps the importance of its critique against the rational tradition. Like irrationalists, he sees the importance of concrete violence, but unlike them, he self-consciously tries to explain this importance rationally. The conceptualization of the fundamental entanglement of language and violence must be seen as Weil's greatest contribution to philosophy. I am therefore not arguing that this blind spot is a fatal flaw in inferentialism. Rather, I am arguing that inferentialists are in a better position to absorb Weil's insights because they explain semantic content by appealling to discursive practices. The fact that they are so well-positioned to absorb these insights highlights the full force of the critique that Weil provides. By formulating discursive practices in terms of commitments, inferentialists must face Weil's problem head-on. They cannot sidestep it. With that in mind, I will present three major arguments in this chapter:

1. Brandom's inferentialism is vulnerable to Weil's critique precisely because of the way that Brandom reads the distinction between sapience and sentience.
2. The language of commitments and entitlements does not dodge this problem, but rather runs into it headlong.
3. The space of reasons is a nebulous concept in its present form and, without further definition, its usefulness as a metaphor may wane.

These arguments have two goals: first, to provide a critique that inferentialism must answer, and second, to highlight what Weil's theory can add to inferentialism. Weil's critique however does not merely touch inferentialism. It applies to the philosophical project in general. In doing so however, it also provides a role-functional grasp of violence in philosophical, logical, and semantic terms. The fact that Weil's answer fits so easily into an inferentialist program is a merit and not a demerit of inferentialism, given how fatal Weil's critique is to so many other programs. Both Brandom and Weil insist on discontinuities in their work, what I will argue is that the main difference, the difference that counts, is where they situate these discontinuities, and nowhere is this truer than in the scope and status of sapience. In fact, the greatest divergence between Weil and Brandom is to be found within this scope and status. On these points, I will defend Weil's order of explanation over Brandom's while at the same time showing that incorporating these changes would not weaken Brandom's position, but rather, would strengthen it.

6.2 Sentience and Sapience

Eric Weil does not use the pair sentience/sapience since it is a pair that came into the philosophical mainstream after his time. These terms however are anchored in a tradition that he does exploit. This is the tradition of characterizing the human being as a rational animal, as an animal whose reason overlays its animality. Weil nonetheless modifies that traditional usage and, from the beginning, places the emphasis on a certain model of language use. He reformulates the tradition's characterization and states that the tradition understands the human being "as an animal endowed with reason and language, or more precisely, endowed with reasonable language" (LP, 3). This modification might seem slight but it is important because it highlights the way that Weil, like Brandom, uses discursive practices to trace the discontinuity between an animal existence and a human one. For Weil, reasonable language is language that aims at coherence and universality, that is regimented according to the logical roles of conditionals and negations. Reasonable language is discourse. As such, it has been used throughout the philosophical tradition to define the human being and to mark what distinguishes us from other animals. It is, according to that tradition, the most important dividing line that we can draw. By describing sapience as something that overlays sentience, Brandom distinguishes creatures that manipulate concepts from other things that do not. This places him clearly in the rational tradition. It is also why Weil's top to bottom reformulation of philosophy in relation to violence touches Brandom's position. To show why this is the case, I will again present Brandom's characterization of sapience and then highlight how Weil's critique effects it.

In Brandom's use, sapience not only contrasts with sentience but also with reliable differential response dispositions. Brandom uses these three concepts in order to create a hierarchy that allows us to characterize human sensitivity to reasons and to understand what is distinctive about this sensitivity. Brandom's philosophical position contains the sophisticated nesting of progressive discontinuities in order to identify the qualitative thresholds that allow us to characterize different phenomena as autonomous at different grains of fineness. Thus, to correctly characterize sapience (which is his goal), he must distinguish the different concepts that are contained within it. He must also show that they are comprehensible separately at other grains of fineness. Brandom uses the concepts of reliable differential responsiveness, sentience, and sapience in order to respectively distinguish between things that respond to their environment, things that are aware of their environment, and things that can conceptualize their experience of their environment. Human beings can do all these things. But not all the things that respond to their environment, or that are aware of it, can grasp their experience discursively. In this way, reliable differential response dispositions and sentience are contained in sapience but are insufficient to explain it.[1]

According to Brandom, reliable differential responses are nothing more than dispositions to respond to an environment (or to changes in that environment) in reliable and thus predictable ways. This capacity is an important aspect of sapience, insofar as the reasons that sapient things mobilize include what Brandom calls non-inferential reports. Non-inferential reports are in no way limited to human beings. They are however only grasped as *reports* when they are brought into discursive practices. It is trivially true that everything is constantly a reliable reporter of different aspects of its environment. Brandom notes that a thermostat will give a reliable report of the temperature of a room.[2] Iron responds to humidity by rusting. Water responds to changes in temperature by freezing and evaporating. Ears respond to sounds by vibrating, and so on. What makes these responses salient is when they are mobilized by conceptual beings to do specific things. Conceptual beings can use the temperature of a room to decide to put on a sweater, the solidity of the ice as an indicator of whether or not it will support their weight in order to go skating, or whether the pain caused by the vibrations of sounds at a concert are reason enough to put in earplugs. Sapient things also have the capacity of making claims that are sharable based on these observations: they can advise someone to put on a sweater, not to go on the ice, or to remember their earplugs when going to a concert. There is clearly a great gap between just differentially responding to things in a reliable way, responding to specific things, and further using these things inferentially as premises and conclusions.

While reliable differential responses are contained in sentience and sapience, sentience is a threshold that adds something new to the disposition to respond reliably to an environment. It includes a level of irritability and arousal that is linked to being "aware in the sense of being awake."[3] This, for Brandom, is merely a "factual matter of biology" and so is different from the kind of thing that sapient things can

---

[1] Brandom (1994), 87.
[2] Brandom (2001), 167.
[3] Brandom (2001), 157.

6.2 Sentience and Sapience

do.[4] Certain animals for instance can be trained thanks to their sentience to reliably respond to *specific* aspects of their environment. Brandom's favoritve example of this is the parrot that reacts to the presence of red things.[5] Brandom sees reliable responsiveness and sentience as making up sapience, but also as being more limited in scope. The properties of a thermostat make it respond to the environment and the parrot can be trained to respond reliably to the presence of red things. Neither are capable however of connecting these reports to judgments and reasonings. This implies an additional awareness, an awareness of normative force and the inferential articulation of concepts. Again, Brandom is highlighting the way that responsiveness to our environment is a necessary, but far from sufficient, condition for sapience. What matters is not just our awareness of our environment, but this additional awareness of concepts and of the way they hold sway over us. This is what is particular about sapience. Human concept users mobilize their differential responses and their natural environmental awareness in a way that artifacts and sentient beings do not. Sapient things are sensitive to conceptual content and to its inferential articulation and they mobilize them both. The conceptual is thus, for Brandom, a realm of laws that cannot be reduced to the natural. Sapient things transform non-inferential reports arising from their responsiveness to and their awareness of their environment by bringing them into this realm of laws as the premises and conclusions of judgments. These are the salient differences that separate us from the mercury used in thermostats to indicate temperature and from the irritability and arousal in animals that can be trained to respond reliably to the presence of *specific* stimuli. Sapience highlights our capacity to submit ourselves to reasons, to take on normative weight.

This is why Brandom separates sapience from sentience and reliable differential responses. However, inside of sapience, he makes another key distinction as he assimilates sapience to rational behavior. Brandom initially focuses on the way that, for Kant, being rational "means being bound by rules."[6] But as he develops the more historical aspect of his thought, Brandom starts to more clearly make a distinction within sapience itself. This is the distinction between *Verstand* and *Vernunft*. For Brandom, these two ideas are what he calls meta-metaconcepts where the difference is between representational thinking (*Verstand*) and conceptual thinking (*Vernunft*).[7] This distinction is important. Following Hegel, Brandom argues that it is what allows us to think of the "determinateness of conceptual content in terms of […] a *process*, rather than in terms of the *property* of having sharp complete boundaries."[8] It is also what allows us to see *Vernunft* as "a dynamic account of the *process* of determi*ning* those contents."[9] This is different from the merely static relationship

---

[4] Brandom (2009), 3.
[5] Brandom (2001), 48.
[6] Brandom (1994), 50.
[7] Brandom (2019), 7.
[8] Brandom (2019), 7.
[9] Brandom (2009), 89.

between contents that is found in *Verstand*. Brandom claims that *Vernunft* is a specific type of *expressive* rationality that contains both inferential and historic rationality and that involves giving and asking for reasons. Inferential and historic rationality is thus used to make conceptual content explicit. Once this content is explicit, we are able to see the inferential and the historic use of reasons as the "progressive form of the gradual, cumulative unfolding into explicitness of what shows up retrospectively as having been all along already implicit in the tradition."[10] *Vernunft* is seen as a rational retrospective reconstruction of the history and use of reason itself. The distinction between *Verstand* and *Vernunft* however can also be read as a distinction between the rational and the reasonable. Brandom admits this possibility and drolly notes that despite the fact that he places the emphasis on rationality "[o]ne might object that 'reasonable' and 'rational' are not synonyms in English. Being relentlessly, excessively, or inappropriately rational can be a way of being *un*reasonable (Just ask anyone who lives with a philosopher!)" nonetheless he goes on to insist that even though the rational and the reasonable have "different dimensions of normative appraisal, judgments of how rational a belief, commitment, action, or person is do nonetheless have normative consequences."[11] He thus seems more worried to show the normative dimension of rationality than of reasonability. Because of this, it must be asked whether he authentically speaks from *Vernunft* or whether, in speaking about *Vernunft*, he remains in the language of *Verstand*. Whatever the response to that question, it is exactly along these lines that he and Weil diverge.

Weil clearly separates the rational and the reasonable, and his separation focuses on the human individual insofar as they are a moral being. When this moral dimension is not taken into account, Weil thinks we miss something essential about judgment and action. It is because the individual seeks rules that they can give to themselves and can use to guide their action that they are led to moral reflection and it is thanks to this moral reflection that they can give themself rules. Weil notes that:

> [a]n amoral being, a being that not only knows nothing about the concrete rules of a given morality, but that also knows nothing about the concept of a rule, will, from the moral point of view, merely be an animal since the human being is defined at this level as the living being that has, or that at least seeks, a rule that allows them to choose between the possibilities that are presented to their action (PM, 19).

Therefore, Weil thinks that if we obscure the reasonable (moral) dimension of action we miss both why people act and how they act. This also leads us to miss the possibility of refusing determined norms in determined situations *and* the radical possibility of refusing all normative constraint. Normative constraints are something that the individual gives to themselves, something that they determine. For Weil however individuals only become aware of this through moral reflection. In Weil's model, the rational is born in our conflict and competition as both natural and social creatures. The reasonable on the other hand plays the role of an all-important

---

[10] Brandom (2002), 12.

[11] Brandom (2009), 2.

6.2 Sentience and Sapience

threshold that allows this conflict and competition to be resolved according to rules. This is why Weil sees the progressive rationalization of society, along the lines of means and ends, as being in conflict with the reasonable reflection of the *individual*. For Weil, the individual's social second nature is a matter of "acting rationally and determining oneself reasonably" (PP, 103). It is however our capacity to determine ourselves that is to be seen as more conceptually primitive than our rational activity, because without this reasonable determination, our rational behavior would not even be present to us. There would be no "us." This reasonable self-determination is a fundamental threshold that discloses other grains of fineness to us. It is the most basic fully autonomous characterization. All other characterizations must be thought of as proto- or sub-reasonable. The history of humanity's rational activity is therefore downhill from this reasonable self-determination. Self-determination falls under the reasonable (moral) reflection on the universal that "gives meaning to the individual's reasonable life" (PP, 105). It is according to this meaning that the individual determines what is rational and reasonable, both in a given situation and as concepts. For the individual who has not gone through moral reflection, the reasonable and the rational intermingle in the ambient norms of their historic situation's concrete determinations. For the individual who thinks through their moral possibilities, who demands what they *should* do in a world determined by the past and by other potentially reasonable beings, it is not only a question of being rational, but also—and above all—of being reasonable. In other words, it is only a reasonable moral individual that can ask the question of meaning for themself, that can seek to understand, and understand comprehensively thanks to that meaning. Without this dimension, rational effectiveness is not just hollow, it is deadly (as the example of any efficiently organized genocide shows). In a sense, the rational is our first contact with the universal, because society asks us to act rationally. But again, this concept depends on reasonability. It is *for ourselves* that we act reasonably within an open community of reasonable beings and it is through our reflection on reasonable action that we *understand* the rational demands of our social situation. We decide for ourselves in view of a more human world. It is in this sense that rationality is derivative of reasonability. By understanding *Verstand* and *Vernunft* as two different *types* of rationality, Brandom is trying to capture this element. However, by focusing on rationality, he obscures or ignores the threshold that moral reflection adds to conceptuality. For Weil, understanding is the organization and consideration of multiple reasonable concrete possibilities against the background of violence.

Weil would agree with all that Brandom says about the two different types of rationality. He would agree that Kant's emphasis on the boundedness to rules is critical to understanding the philosophical project. He would also agree that the dynamic conceptual nature of *Vernunft* is more fecund and fundamental than the static representational nature of *Verstand*. He would agree that the type of normative appraisal that goes along with the rational is essential. However, what he would disagree with is that we can focus almost essentially on the rational at the expense of the reasonable. In fact, the way he characterizes violence turns on the way he distinguishes between the rational and the reasonable. The reasonable is nothing other than a meta-commitment to situate difference and doubt and to settle conflict through reasoned argumentative practices. This meta-commitment is also present in Brandom, since he notes that:

> [c]ritical thinkers, or merely fastidious ones, must examine their idioms to be sure that they are prepared to endorse and so defend the appropriateness of the material inferential transitions implicit in the concepts they employ. In Reason's fight against thought debased by prejudice and propaganda, the first rule is that material inferential commitments that are potentially controversial should be made explicit in claims, exposing them both as vulnerable to reasoned challenged and as in need of reasoned defense.[12]

Brandom recognizes this meta-commitment and thinks that making problematic inferences explicit is enough to bind people to good inferences. Precisely what Weil's critique of the rational tradition shows is that this is not the case.

It is this focus on the rational that allows us to better understand Quill Kukla (writing as Rebecca Kukla) and Mark Lance's critique of Brandom. According to this critique, Brandom's articulation of commitments and entitlements has a tendency to reduce the space of reasons to a *Platonic space* built around "some abstract normative structure."[13] Despite providing us with a robust structure in which to understand normative behavior, Brandom nonetheless passes over in silence the fact that "[w]e cannot engage in normative practices at all unless we are the sorts of beings who can recognize the claims of norms, but this is not possible unless we can transgress or fail to live up to these claims, because the binding force of norms makes sense only in the face of a possible gap between what we do and what we ought to do."[14] Everything turns on the interpretation of this gap. *Either* it is exclusively because of error, in which case human beings would not be able to participate in the game of giving and asking for reasons, *or* it is born in a knowing refusal. In other words, even though beings capable of sapience are the only ones that understand the meaning of the normative, they are also the only ones that can knowingly reject normativity. This gap is thus the key to understanding why Weil prioritizes the reasonable over the rational and why his critique of the rational tradition is so forceful.

Brandom's characterization of sapience focuses on human beings as discursive beings, as the kinds of beings that deploy reasons and are sensitive to reasons. He notes that sapient things are "rational agents in the sense that their behavior can be made intelligible, at least sometimes, by attributing to them the capacity to make practical inferences concerning how to get what they want, and theoretical inferences concerning what follows from what."[15] This means they must be *able* to do more things than just respond to their environment.[16] Weil is in full agreement with this. He agrees that this has been what has mattered most for the philosophical tradition's explanation of the human being as an animal gifted with reasonable language. However this is not necessarily the definition that matters most for the concrete

---

[12] Brandom (1994), 126.

[13] Kukla and Lance (2008), 217.

[14] Kukla and Lance (2008), 285.

[15] Brandom (2001), 157.

[16] Brandom (1994), 87.

individual, and if philosophy wants to understand itself it must understand the concrete individual's resistance to philosophy. With this in mind, we can now say that Weil's disagreement turns on the notion of possibility. Brandom says that sapient things have the *capacity* to make their behavior explicit through discursive practices, that they *can* do so if they want to make their activity reasonable. Weil's critique highlights that this capacity does not mean that they in fact do so. The concrete individual can refuse to do so and can refuse to do so knowingly instead of through ignorance or weakness of will. There thus seems to be an underlying tendency in Brandom's claim. For Brandom, because sapient things can make their behavior intelligible through inferences, and because they actually do do so part of the time, they *are bound* to do so (in both senses of the term). Brandom's notes that he is only focusing on paradigmatic cases of conceptual behavior in order to make explicit the framework in which this behavior in general makes sense. The problem however is that, precisely by focusing only on paradigmatic cases, his normative claims may be too strong. Weil claims that reason (coherent discourse in situation) is one of the human being's possibilities. The interest of Weil's project however lies in the way that this possibility interlocks with the human being's other main possibility (the refusal to be bound by any norms) and the effect that this other possibility has on discursive practices.

When defining reason as a human possibility, Weil notes that possibility designates "what the human being *is able* to do, and the human being is certainly able to be reasonable, or at least they are able to want to be reasonable. But it is only a possibility and not a necessity, and it is the possibility of a being that has at least one other possibility. We know that this other possibility is violence" (LP, 57). This does not mean that Weil abandons the normative character of reason. He notes that while it is merely a possibility and that, for there to be one possibility, there must be at least one other one, he also insists that, as an animal that is endowed with reasonable language, the individual must exercise that reasonable language in order to fully be a human being (LP, 5). The status of a human being[17] is thus for Weil a normative status that defines (and is defined by) the full exercise of reasonable discourse. This is a regulative status, which means that we *should* apply it universally to anyone who has this capacity, even when they do not exercise it.[18] In this way, the status of a human being has a similar place in Weil's work as sapience does in Brandom's. The main difference is the way that the scope of these two positions are defined.

---

[17] Weil uses the term *L'Homme* or "Man." However, given his arguments, it is clear that he is not making a gendered distinction, rather he is working in a tradition that we have moved past, one that uses Man to refer indifferently to all of humankind. Because of the consequences of Weil's argument, this term is translated systematically as "human being."

[18] This status is precisely what the Greeks refused to give to non-Greeks, since they considered them to be barbarians, that is, different from "genuine human beings." For the Greeks, the normative status of a human being was reserved uniquely for those who participated in *Greek* reason. Similar refusals to attribute this status of course exist and are often motivated by the desire to see only one single specific content as making up reason, as being reasonable. There are abundant examples of this throughout history as attested by racism, sexism, classism, imperialism, colonialism, etc.

Weil always contrasts the status of *human being* to the concrete action of concrete individuals. Thus, reasonable discourse is the dividing line between human animals and non-human animals for Weil just as it is for Brandom. The difference is that, for Weil, the full exercise of reasonable discourse is not something that the whole species does just because it has been acquired by the species. To be reasonable, each individual must, for themself, choose to be so in conflictual situations. This is a (a-reasonable) choice and an ever-receding normative horizon. It is a simple distinction, but the surprising thing about Weil's critique is the way that this simplicity belies its radicality. It causes him to reformulate the entire philosophical tradition in terms of violence while still insisting that violence is only meaningful to this tradition, which he characterizes as "the refusal of violence" (LP, 58). Weil notes that this refusal of violence, this non-violence, "is philosophy's starting point and its final goal to such an extent that philosophers often forget that they are dealing with violence" (LP, 59). This is the heart of Weil's critique: philosophy places violence outside the framework of reasonable discourse in order to ensure its coherence. Philosophers can therefore forget about it and try to reduce the world to a world without violence. The problem is that philosophy is only coherent in relation to violence. What philosophy forgets is that reasonable behavior only makes sense against a background of violence. It is reasonable behavior appearing amidst violence that allows violence to become visible, but it is the irreducibility of violence that allows action to be reasonable. This is because *reasonable* action is predicated on the refusal of violence while *rational* behavior is not. One can always rationally exercise violence.

Weil focuses on reasonability because of the way that the violent individual can be unmoved by their sensitivity to reasonability. Worse than being unmoved, the violent individual can even knowingly use this sensitivity, and the recognition of this sensitivity in others, to their advantage. The violent individual can deploy their instrumental rationality, can calculate means and ends, in order to destroy the normative force of reasonability itself, thanks to the sensitivity of others to rational and reasonable behavior. This is the lesson that Nazi Germany taught Weil, but this is also a lesson that is being taught to us right now with the rise of radical forms of nationalism and xenophobia. The political leaders that foment the discontent of social groups—social groups that feel threatened or marginalized by changes in the social makeup of the political landscape—are making great use of their instrumental rationality while at the same time refusing to hold themselves to the meta-commitment to reasonable (non-violent) behavior. In this case, technical rationality is the condition of their success and they use this rationality as they see fit without taking others into account as real dialogue partners.

The simplicity of Weil's critique does nothing other than remind us that reasonable discourse is a choice. Its radicality is that it forces a reevaluation of the entire philosophical tradition. By focusing on rational discourse, the philosophical tradition has constantly reduced both violence and the world to discourse, to life understood and not life lived. Weil's critique shows that violence is an aspect of human freedom that is irreducible to discourse, and that this irreducibility can break discourse in its refusal. To transpose Weil's critique into Brandom's language, Weil

6.2 Sentience and Sapience

recognizes sapience as the discontinuity that is essential to understanding what we do as concept users, he affirms the place of *Vernunft* over *Verstand*, and he recognizes rationality as being one of the necessary conditions for binding oneself to normative behavior. Nonetheless, he asks if this condition is sufficient. Weil's critique highlights that reasonable discourse being a choice is what is special about it. Because of this, any account of this choice must see the other possibility as also being real. This is why sapience is a normative status and not a natural one. As Brandom notes, there "were no commitments before people started treating each other as committed; they are not part of the natural furniture of the world."[19] Weil would agree with him, but also highlights that it is not a natural status. Choosing to be reasonable is itself an a-reasonable (unjustified and unjustifiable) choice that only makes sense if the choice to not be reasonable exists.

As a normative status, sapience has conditions of success and failure. Within sapience, there are different types of norms, ones that fall under rational behavior and ones that fall under reasonable behavior. Both types of norms can be refused, but the consequences are radically different. According to Weil's use of the distinction between the rational and the reasonable, when rational behavior is refused, the individual is refusing instrumental norms of success, for example all consequential reasoning that involves means and ends. Such reasoning is present in the fact that the individual can choose to die of hunger, of cold, or can choose to engage in dangerous behavior knowingly. People can refuse rational norms for reasonable ones, they can risk their life to save somebody else's. They can also prioritize reasonable norms in a way that overrides and modifies rational ones. When an individual goes on a hunger strike as a form of moral resistance, they abandon the rational norms necessary for their individual survival as a *rational* strategy meant to bend the resolve of their opponent in the name of a *reasonable* principle. This is different from choosing violence. To choose violence is to abandon the norms of reasonable behavior in order to no longer feel responsible to them. Weil's critique reminds us that any individual can refuse any normative status. This may seem slight. When it is stated in the terms of continuities and discontinuities however it is an essential difference. It implies two things. First, it implies that there is meta-commitment to reasonable behavior that is implicit in Brandom's theory and in the game of giving and asking for reasons in general. If the goal is to make what is implicit explicit, this must be brought out. Second, it implies that the individual is *always* in a relationship with the world and with the spontaneous creative production of meaning (understood as *poiesis*).

For Brandom, the goodness of normative statuses pragmatically depends on the practice of undertaking and acknowledging commitments and entitlements. Semantically, this goodness depends on the content of those commitments, on the inferences that are seen as following from those commitments, as well as the inferences that are taken to be incompatible based on the contents of one's other commitments. Pragmatically however one can refuse to acknowledge all commitments and

---

[19] Brandom (1994), 161.

entitlements. The individual who does this is indifferent to the semantic goodness of inferences and incompatibilities. Brandom acknowledges this *pragmatic* possibility without seeing the radicality that it implies. He states that:

> It is not that one *can*not undertake incompatible commitments, make incompatible assertions. Finding that one has done so is an all-too-common occurrence. But the effect of doing so alters one's normative status: to undercut any entitlement one might otherwise have had to either of the incompatible commitments, for each commitment counts as a decisive reason against the entitlement of the other, incompatible one.[20]

Brandom rightly notes that what is changed when an individual ignores discursive rules is their normative status, he misses however that the violent person not only has no worry about their own normative status, they fly in the face of normative statuses in general. This individual can thus knowingly undertake commitments that are incompatible with any other position. Because they willfully ignore what their normative status *ought* to bind them to, they are able to ignore the norms of conditional reasoning, while nonetheless still engaging in that conditional reasoning itself. Worse, this is not something they are passively ignoring, it is something they are actively refusing. This again shows the distinction between the rational and the reasonable. In the place of reasonability, they are choosing violence. This does not mean that they refuse rationality and language, they may still speak. They may even use language as an instrument to rouse others. What they are refusing is to be bound by what their language says. And they refuse this knowingly.

The possibility of refusing all normative constraints is the heart of Weil's critique put into inferentialist terms, and the language of inferentialism is particularly vulnerable to this critique. This is clear if we look at Jaroslav Peregrin's insightful reflection on normative constraints as it is expressed in rule-following behavior. Peregrin claims that the (post-Kripkean) tradition has focused too much on what it means to follow a rule. He thinks that this is a mistake and that this is not the best way to understand normative constraints. Indeed, for Peregrin, this fundamental confusion implies both unsavory metaphysical conundrums (what is a rule?) and a regress that demands a rule for following a rule for following a rule for following a rule, *ad infinitum*. Peregrin suggests that, instead of speaking about rule-following, we speak about "bouncing off rules."[21] Peregrin's point is that if we look at rules not in their prescriptive sense, as of telling us what to do, but rather in their restrictive sense, as guiding us not to do certain things, a lot of the dead-ends of "rule-following" disappears.[22] By starting from rule-following there is the idea that rules are fully articulated, and of course some are. Fully articulated rules even help to provide a model for understanding normative practices in general. Nonetheless, the notion of bouncing off rules reminds us that the force of fully articulated rules is derivative of the kinds of normative constraints we only implicitly grasp in our practical behavior. This does not mean that rule-following should only be understood as

---

[20] Brandom (2010), 120.
[21] Peregrin (2014), 72.
[22] Peregrin (2014), 72.

6.2 Sentience and Sapience

restrictive. Rather, it means that looking at rules in their restrictive sense adds something philosophically illuminating to their prescriptive sense. Weil makes a similar distinction. Instead of looking at the two sides of rules however, he looks at the restrictive and the prescriptive dimensions as articulating the tension between social constraint and the individual in their self-determining reasonable reflection. The constraints present in the normative practices of a given community are restrictive because they define the specificity of the concrete situation in which the individual will determine their own rules for action. This self-determination is prescriptive because the individual is telling themselves what they *ought* to do. It also aims at a universal scope because a good rule for action should apply to everyone who finds themselves in an analogous situation. However, if it does become a widely applied normative practice, it becomes part of the social constraints that make up another individual's concrete situation. This new individual in turn must go through the work of determining themselves and their own rules of action in order to see themself as a genuinely autonomous being. These social constraints—the rules off which we bounce—have a productive character because they allow the individual to exercise their self-determination. Weil notes that the "transition from one form of life and of labor to another does not take place without the intervention of constraint" and that it is "constraint that introduces rationality, this initial universal, by colliding into the reasonable but particular universal of historic morality" (PP, 204). Following the argument that has been sketched, the normative dimension that individuals collide into or bounce off of can be characterized as the sedimentation of the human production of meaning. It is a constraint for the individual precisely because it defines the world in which they are unsatisfied. This sedimentation, as a constraint, as constituting the world that does not satisfy them, is also a necessary condition. It allows *their* activity to become meaningful through their own self-determination.

Peregrin argues that looking at rules in this sense "allows us to see that through limiting us in what we may do they also *delimit* some new space for our actions."[23] This new space is a "space of meaningfulness."[24] This space of meaningfulness is adapted from Sellars's space of reasons. It is the space where we transform limits and barriers into the normative borders that meaningfully govern our behavior. The space of meaningfulness is opened through the restrictive character of rules. Delimiting a concept is defining it. This does not mean that meaningfulness is only brought about by bouncing off of rules. Peregrin's notion of bouncing off of rules helps us better understand how we become sensitive to limits and barriers. If we look at the way that children test boundaries, we can see them learning what they are and are not allowed to do. Testing rules teaches children the normative consequences of following a rule or disregarding it. Peregrin notes that "thinking, speaking, and acting [...] is spontaneous, creative, and unpredictable."[25] Thus, in addition to delimiting a space, lots of other things matter, such as creativity, talent, and

---

[23] Peregrin (2014), 73.
[24] Peregrin (2014), 73.
[25] Peregrin (2014), 71.

circumstances, for instance. But even creativity, talent, and circumstances become meaningful because they are applied within a delimited space.[26] An exceptional basketball player for instance depends on the conditions and rules of basketball for their talent and creativity to be realized, just as an exceptional violinist depends on musical rules to realize their own talent and creativity. Were there no basketball and only music, the person whose talent and creativity would be maximized by the practice of basketball might never come to see themself as talented and creative. The meaningfulness of a concept is thus defined and refined by the way its field of possibilities is delimited. This is the way bouncing off rules plays a constitutive role in meaning. The limit (rule) that we bounce off of restricts and thus guides us in the way we give meaning to our actions and our utterances. For Brandom these constraints are expressed in the normative force of incompatibilities and conditionals. Becoming a great basketball player or violin player requires conforming to specific norms both by recognizing what is incompatible with that activity and by understanding the if/then reasoning that maximizes it. To be a great athlete or musician, talent and creativity is necessary, but they do not suffice. One must reason according to what kind of activities are incompatible with being great and what kind of activities are necessary to become great. According to Weil's insistence on the role of specific refusals of specific determined contents, we can postulate that pragmatic refusals are transformed into the incompatibilities (abstract negations) that guide conditional reasoning. Someone who does not go out late in order to get up early to practice can explain that by such conditional reasoning: I will not stay out late because staying out late is incompatible with getting up early to practice and if I want to become great then I must practice regularly. This is a role-functional use of the human possibility of refusing any determined content. But it is, for Weil, born out of a much more radical possibility, that of refusing all normative constraint.

Keeping with the metaphor, if we see violence as the refusal of all normative constraints, we can understand it as the refusal to bounce off rules in order to break through them. This is a fundamentally ambivalent process. It is ambivalent precisely because, while others find themselves constrained to respond to the violent individual, violence opens a space of meaningfulness. Violence creates the specific conditions that the individual seeking to be reasonable is trying to grasp. The fight against this violence produces positive meaning, whether through the creation of new criteria for refusing violence conceptually, through the political organizing that stands up to violence, through the artistic expression that makes others aware of how violence is lived, or just through violence itself. The difference in the meaning produced is how universal it claims to be. New criteria for understanding racial, gender, or class realities look to grasp a certain reality universally. Marches or voting for specific rights look to make universal changes to a political reality. This is different from the pure use of violence. While this may produce meaning, this meaning rarely seeks to be universal. What is important about the idea of bouncing off rules and breaking through rules is that it allows normative constraints and

---

[26] Oulipo and Brian Eno's *Oblique Strategies* are good examples of this.

violence to be understood role-functionally. It presents them as specific types of activity and, in doing so, allows us to understand the progressive creation of meaning as being non-mysterious. The ambivalence of this process though also shows why the creation of meaning is so underdetermined. Pure violence does not allow for refined solutions. Refined solutions follow the refinement of conceptual content. The pragmatic refusals of pure violence must first be subsumed in language as abstract negations in order to be conceptualized. Once this happens, what is implicit in this violence can be brought out. Violence can then be seen as expressing something, as being a consequence of something. Individuals though can then deploy this newly conceptualized, intra-discursive violence, itself. This then leads to new refusals that require further refinement, which allows types of violence to become progressively articulated. The ambivalence is found in the fact that once the mechanisms of violence are brought out, this conceptualization can be used *either* to further universalize discourse *or* to limit this very universalization through more sophisticated uses of violence. Since concepts here are seen as rules of application, better defined concepts are seen as fuller sets of rules. The fuller the set of rules, the easier it is to see activities that inscribe themselves within these rules as meaningful. It also means that the applications are more diverse. For better or for worse.

Looking at rules in their restrictive function brings us back to the placement problem. A space of meaningfulness is defined by its boundaries. Outside these boundaries, our activity risks becoming unintelligible because these boundaries define our conceptuality itself. Limits therefore delimit meaningfulness. This is analogous to what Weil calls the *essential* inessential. When an individual acts and speaks from a specific category, they live in this category's attitude. Within the attitude, meaningfulness is defined by the scope of permissible inferences that follow from the category's incompatibilities. This is their positive discursive content. The essential inessential is the set of incompatibilities that *must* be ruled out in order to preserve coherence of the category. This does not mean however that all of a discourse's inessential can be reduced to incompatibilities. To give an example, the causally structured discourse of experimental science is inessential to the pure category of the moral consciousness. Nonetheless, *Consciousness* recognizes the importance of this discourse and builds itself off of it, by recognizing its constraints and looking for new ways to articulate them. The essential inessential is not just those things that don't matter to a discourse, it is those things that *must* be characterized as being secondary in order for the discourse to be considered coherent. Thus, following our example, in *The Condition*, values are an essential inessential, they must be considered as secondary for the discourse to remain coherent. This is what gives rise to the form that the placement problem takes for this discourse and, as we have shown, to Humean expressivism. Weil defends the existence of multiple irreducible discursive centers and different discursive positions yield different responses to the placement problem. This means that different limits open different spaces of reasons. Remember, Weil presents a two-stage conception of negation. First there is the pragmatic negation that is present in the capacity to refuse any discourse or any normative constraint and then there is the abstract negation that treats these refusals as incompatibilities within discourse. Both of these negations are of a piece with the radical refusal of discourse, which is not just the capacity to refuse any determined discourse, but is the concrete refusal of all reasonable discourse. The first negation is constitutive of discourse in the way that it opens up possibilities through the *negativity* of the *act*. It presents a *human* force that limits and guides possibilities. It is only once this new space of meaningfulness is opened with its new determined possibilities that the *linguistic* abstract negation takes hold. The abstract negation is guided by pragmatic considerations that are expressions of an implicit essential and its essential inessential.

Discourse does not invent meaning. It organizes the meaning that is expressed in and as an attitude—in the fact of living one's life as oriented and meaningful. This is why the pragmatic negation is so important, it is the first move that allows meaning to take shape. It defines what discourse will transform into claims of incompatibility. A content that threatens the solidity of our implicit central commitments is seen as incompatible to these commitments. Such incompatibilities, as abstract negations, further delimit the shape of the space of reasons and ground its unity and coherence. Any individual can live in contradiction, but it is the philosophical gesture of understanding that seeks an absolutely coherent discourse. The philosophical gesture deploys incompatibilities to organize coherent discourse to grasp an attitude and the world. It is the philosophical gesture that worries about how different moral, scientific, esthetic facts fit together into a discursive whole. It is this gesture that creates the placement problem and that looks to resolve it by *defining* incompatibilities. Weil's main insight transposed in the language of the placement problem is that anyone can refuse coherent discourse at any moment, and thus can refuse to worry about how different kinds of facts fit together. The radicality of Weil's critique also hides another, subtler, problem. The absolute refusal of all discourse is a grounding problem for philosophy, but it is not the form of refusal that most of us encounter in our daily lives, except in indifference, its banal form. The more common form is the specific refusal of specific discourses. Being able to refuse specific content is essential for the development of coherent discourse but it does not *have* to be used in the service of coherent discourse. It *can* be used progressively and positively for coherent discourse by purifying discourse. When it is, it allows us to see the limits of our discourse and hopefully to recognize when one discourse takes precedence over another. It can however also be used to shield one's central commitment from all critique.

The placement problem is an attempt to explain recalcitrant phenomena by finding where to place them in relation to central discursive commitments. Our central commitment—what is essential to our attitude—is often invisible to us. The only way of making it clear is through a meta-commitment to reasonable argumentative practices. Weil's elaboration of the philosophical categories shows that the response will be different based on different central discursive commitments. What I have called the subtler problem asks how to resolve conflict within discourse when it is precisely this plurality of spaces of reasons and its plurality of responses to the placement problem that create conflicts. There would be no conceptual conflict without incompatible claims, and there would be no incompatible claims if people could not commit to things come hell or high water. And *this* is what Weil's critique shows. There is no necessary reduction of difference into unity, discourse cannot on its own bind us to overcome conflicts, the only thing that can is our own meta-commitment to reasonability. I would like to combine Weil, Brandom, and Peregrin's insights here to develop the second argument of the chapter, which seeks to show how the language of commitments and entitlements allows us to clarify the possibility of conflict and violence precisely because it runs into it headlong.

6.3 *De Dicto* and *De Re* Ascription in a Platonic Space

Brandom tacitly recognizes the possibility of violence when he speaks about the problematic inferences in "[h]ighly charged words like 'nigger', 'whore', 'Republican', and 'Christian.'"[27] While he argues that these "inferences have seemed a special case to some because they couple 'descriptive' circumstances of application to 'evaluative' consequences,"[28] he is quick to add that these problematic inferences are in no way unique because "*any* concept or expression involves commitment to an inference from its grounds to its consequences of application."[29] Rather, what is at play in these concepts is the way that they have a substantive content that we are not ready to accept. One of the major roles of Brandom's game of giving and asking for reasons is that it "permits the formulation, as explicit claims, of the inferential commitments that otherwise remain implicit and unexamined in the contents of material concepts."[30] What is problematic about highly charged words is the way that "non-logical concepts can incorporate materially bad inferences."[31] As already noted, the notion of material inferences is of central importance to Brandom. Material inferences do not depend on their logical form but rather on their content. This is because the "*formal* goodness of inferences derives from and is explained in terms of the *material* goodness of inferences."[32] Thus paradigmatic material inferences such as that from "'Pittsburgh is to the West of Philadelphia' to 'Philadelphia is to the East of Pittsburgh'"[33] help us to make explicit what is involved in the concept of EAST for example, that is, the way it contains the concept of WEST within it. This clarifies what the content of the claim is.

In the concept of EAST, the vocabulary that is important is that *of* geographic directionality. New concepts are constantly being deployed in order to enrich existing vocabularies, whether they be esthetic, theological, zoological, or any other. With problematic concepts, this newness is not what Brandom takes issue with. He

---

[27] Brandom (1994), 126.
[28] Brandom (1994), 126.
[29] Brandom (1994), 126.
[30] Brandom (1994), 126.
[31] Brandom (1994), 125.
[32] Brandom (2001), 55.
[33] Brandom (1994), 98.

takes issue with the goodness of the content that is to be found in the application of pejorative terms such as "Boche" or "nigger." What is one implicitly committing themself to by applying these terms to Germans or to African Americans? Whatever the content, the problem is that it can then come to be seen as defining characteristics of *all* Germans and African Americans. As he says himself, "[t]he problem with 'Boche' or 'nigger' is not that once we explicitly confront the material inferential commitment that gives them their content, it turns out to be *novel*, but that it can then be seen as indefensible or inappropriate."[34] Brandom seems to think that once the inappropriate character of applying this content is understood by making it explicit, people will stop using such terms. While this certainly can happen, there is no necessary reason that it in fact does.

In order to see the lack of necessity in a reasoned use of reason, the space of reasons cannot be seen as a *Platonic* space of idealized commitments but must instead be seen as a conflictual space of concrete commitments. There has to be an articulation of different substantive contents in order to understand *why* people hold commitments that are seen as inappropriate or indefensible from another point of view. Without this possibility, a normative position that describes what we should believe and how we should act gets no traction. Weil's theory, by articulating the different types of content that follow from different conceptual grounds, provides an articulation of different substantive contents. It thus rehearses what one is held to by holding specific *concrete* commitments. Brandom recognizes this need because he asserts that differences in points of view matter and recognizes that philosophy's goal is to resolve these differences. He also recognizes that it is these differences that are important to the representational dimension of speech. By insisting on the social context of the game of giving and asking for reasons, he recognizes that this context is both irreducible and necessary because this game "from which inferential relations are abstracted, involves both inter*content* and inter*personal* dimensions."[35] However, what will be argued here is that because he articulates these different dimensions in a Platonic space of idealized commitments (at least in *Making it Explicit*), he flattens the conflict that Weil thinks is so important to understanding the philosophical project. For Brandom, the representational dimension of speech is to be understood according to *de re* and *de dicto* ascriptions. What is argued here is that there is still something missing.

Brandom notes that these ascriptions are used to help us to distinguish the *aboutness* of propositional content. He notes that traditionally these ascriptions are used to distinguish what is being said about something from the thing itself. Thus in this way "[a]scriptions *de dicto* attribute belief in a *dictum* or saying, while ascriptions *de re* attribute belief about some *res* or thing."[36] To use his example, Brandom shows that there is an ambiguity in the claim "The president of the United States will be

---

[34] Brandom (1994), 127.
[35] Brandom (1994), 496–497.
[36] Brandom (2001), 170.

6.3 De Dicto and De Re Ascription in a Platonic Space

black by the year 2025."[37] Is the person who is currently the president of the United States (at the moment this is being written, Joe Biden) supposed to become black in the year 2025? This clearly is impossible. To give a *de re* reading of this proposition it is necessary to modify the phrase (or as Brandom says, to regiment it) in order to bring out what is being spoken about. Thus a correct *de re* reading requires us to add *of* and *that* to bring out the meaning of the phrase. Being the president is holding an office, and the holder of that office can change every four or eight years. To take these changes into account it would be necessary to say, "I believe *of* the person that holds the office of president in 2025 *that* he (or she) will be black." In the first proposition the belief being attributed is about Joe Biden, whereas in the second proposition the belief being attributed is about the person that will hold the office of president and will thus be about his successor. We are ascribing two different beliefs if we read the first statement as a *de dicto* ascription or as a *de re* ascription. Brandom notes that the regimentation of natural language—which in itself is often frustratingly ambiguous—allows us to clear up this difficulty. He states that according to this change:

the *de dicto* form
S believes that $\varphi(t)$
Becomes the *de re*
S believes of t that $\varphi(it)$.[38]

What this regimentation of the two different types of ascription forms shows us, for Brandom, is that "it is the *de re* propositional-attitude-ascribing locutions that we use in everyday life to express what we are talking and thinking *of* or *about*."[39] In a *de dicto* ascription, we are no longer talking *about* the thing, rather we are trying to see "*how* things are represented by the one to whom the belief is ascribed."[40] This line of thought will be followed, but in order to do so, an ambiguity in the term attitude must be cleared up.

When Brandom speaks about attitudes he speaks about normative attitudes, propositional attitudes, deontic attitudes, alethic attitudes, etc. These are different from Weil's use of attitudes (although all of the attitudes in the Brandomian sense can be thought of as being constitutive of attitudes in the Weilian sense). Propositional attitudes, for example, describe the relation that an individual has towards the content of a proposition, thus the propositional attitude that is being ascribed in the first example is that of belief. But other propositional attitudes are found when we doubt a proposition, hope the proposition is true, etc. To take another example, deontic attitudes focus on the way that we hold commitments or ascribe them, and not on the content of the proposition. They focus on the fact that beliefs (understood as doxastic commitments) are attributed and undertaken. The *attributing* and

---

[37] Brandom (2001), 170. Brandom uses 2020 and Bill Clinton in his example. I have changed the year and the president since 2020 has already come and gone.
[38] Brandom (1994), 502.
[39] Brandom (1994), 502.
[40] Brandom (1994), 503.

undertaking of doxastic commitments with their concomitant statuses are the two principal deontic attitudes that Brandom tackles. All of these attitudes are linked to our normative attitudes, that is, to "what we practically *take* or *treat* ourselves or others as responsible for or committed to."[41] Again, these should be considered as different from Weil's use of attitudes. To understand why this is, we can look at the distinction that Weil makes between metaphysical categories and philosophical categories. Philosophical categories are part of Weil's metavocabulary. They structure an individual's discourse and thus govern the use of metaphysical categories such as cause and effect or representation. Here, we can make a conservative extension of this distinction. Philosophical categories grasp a pure attitude, or expressed differently, they grasp a coherent way of being in the world. Pure attitudes (in Weil's specific sense) are therefore seen as structural. If this is the case, then pure attitudes govern the local attitudes about which Brandom speaks. Thus someone in one Weilian attitude will deploy their propositional attitudes differently from someone in another Weilian attitude. In other words they will be willing to believe some things that are presented in discourse but not others, hope some things presented in discourse are true, but not others, fear some things presented in discourse, but not others. Following Weil's distinction between philosophical and metaphysical categories but *applied* to attitudes, we can say that propositional, deontic, alethic attitudes can be considered metaphysical attitudes whose functional roles are analogous to the metaphysical categories like causality and representation. They are important insofar as they are used in actual communication and insofar as they allow us to grasp attitudes in the sense of the *Logic of Philosophy*. It should be noted however that, if we follow Weil's argument concerning categories, this specific Weilian use of attitudes takes precedence over their metaphysical use.

To return to *de re* and *de dicto* ascriptions, Brandom notes that they are an essential part of communication and of interpretation. We grant him that. However, it is specifically in his treatment of more problematic ascriptions that the Platonic character of his usage of the space of reasons becomes clear. Again, Brandom affirms the "essentially perspectival character of conceptual contents."[42] In affirming this, Brandom is worried about establishing the possibility of communication, despite the essentially perspectival character of conceptual content. However, its possibility notwithstanding, it remains unclear how communication actually takes place, or why someone that recognizes statuses and commitments should see *themselves* as being held to them. This is the gap that Quill Kukla (writing as Rebecca Kukla) and Mark Lance speak about between the recognition of the binding force of norms and the actual adoption of that binding force for oneself. This can be shown through Brandom's example of the "seventh god." Brandom imagines a case of an interaction with a shaman. The shaman says "the seventh god graces us with his presence"[43] and Brandom notes that in this situation a person with different cultural baggage

---

[41] Brandom (2019), 13.
[42] Brandom (1994), 586.
[43] Brandom (1994), 514.

6.3 *De Dicto* and *De Re* Ascription in a Platonic Space

would be at a loss to understand what the shaman is trying to say. This person has to interpret what the shaman means in order to understand what the shaman is committed to and whether or not they can endorse the shaman's statement. By making the distinction between *de re* and *de dicto* ascriptions, we are able to understand that what the shaman is speaking *of* is the sun and that when he speaks *of* the seventh god's grace, he is speaking about the fact that the sun is shining.[44] Thanks to a *de re* ascription we can make the content of the shaman's claim explicit. We can note that the shaman "claims *of* the sun that it is shining."[45] However, just because we can interpret what the shaman says does not mean that we would endorse what follows from this claim. In order to see whether this is the case, *we* have to understand what the shaman takes to follow from that commitment. Imagine that our shaman knows full well what he is committed to by speaking of the seventh god and that, by holding the belief that the sun *is* the seventh god, he is committed to killing all those that blaspheme by claiming that the sun is anything other than the seventh god. It may be that we communicate with our shaman and we communicate that the sun is shining. Imagine that we explain to the shaman that, for us, the sun is not a god, it is the impersonal, luminous, gaseous, astronomical object that our planet turns around. Imagine now that the shaman has this knowledge of astronomy and understands what we are saying and what we ourselves are committing to. The problem that Brandom obscures is that there may be no problem of communication between us, the shaman may have all the concepts needed to understand what we are telling him, but he may nonetheless hold fast to his philosophical attitude that to talk of the gods as concrete objects is to blaspheme and that all blasphemers merit a painful death.

In this way, ascriptions *de re* and *de dicto* help us to understand what other individuals are speaking about, but they do not necessarily help us to understand what they are committed to by speaking that way. Rather what is needed is a similar mechanism in order to understand the *material* inferences that are being employed. This is exactly what Weil's use of the reprise is conceived to do. Remember, in its simplest form, the reprise is the grasp of the pure attitude under the language of another category. If we accept the characterization of categories as an inferential concept, then each category is the grasp of the material inferences and the substantive concepts that go along with its specific philosophical attitude. Following this, the reprise is what allows for the introduction of new inferences within the concept that is being modified (especially in justificatory reprises) because it takes into account changes in the conditions of application for specific conceptual content. It is also what allows for the evaluation and justification of these new inferences. The reprise allows us to understand the changes to the conditions of application and to the practical consequences of the content of inferences by providing us with the different sets of valid material inferences according to different grounding concepts. These different sets of valid inferences allow us to pick a path through what others say in order to understand what the consequences of their commitments are. *De re*

---

[44] Brandom (1994), 514.
[45] Brandom (1994), 514.

and *de dicto* ascriptions are therefore contained in the reprise because part of what the reprise looks to explain is how communication is possible. It is also seeking to explain however the changes that content itself undergoes. In Brandom's use, it is unclear how *de re* and *de dicto* ascriptions change commitments. They make them explicit yes, but part of what Weil hopes to explain with the concept of the reprise is the way that making commitments explicit modifies them. When categories are reprised, the interplay of reprises allows us to evaluate or justify commitments. But this does not happen in a Platonic space, it happens thanks to the content of concrete conceptual commitments. This is why grasping reprises modifies which commitments *should* be accepted and which *should* not.

It is to be noted that Brandom himself goes a long way towards correcting the perceived Platonism concerning spaces of reasons in his book, *Tales of the Mighty Dead*, specifically in the chapter entitled "Pretexts."[46] Therein, he is explicit about the fact that the *de re* ascriptions that he is presenting in his work are his own commitments, that they are up for debate, and that they should even be debated. What is interesting to note is that in this text, when he presents his commitments about interpreting and reading the tradition, what he calls *de traditione* ascriptions, he comes to a position that is very similar to Weil's. He notes that material inferences "that articulate the conceptual contents expressed by ordinary, nonlogical sentences are in general *multipremise* inferences" and that meaning emerges from a dialogical process that entails a type of pluralism whereby the "semantic interpretation one undertakes in specifying the content of a commitment one ascribes to another" must remain *open-ended*.[47] In this case, especially when reading texts from the philosophical tradition, he claims that the way to advance is by trying to interpret which claims are central to other positions in order to reconstruct all the permissible and incompatible inferences.[48] This allows for primary texts and secondary interpretive texts to be understood together because they can be understood separately. For Brandom, the goal of "getting clear, crisp versions of the concepts and claims that have, by an exercise in differential emphasis, been picked out as central, is to see how many of the more specific doctrines can then be *translated* into this spare but controlled idiom."[49] As I read Weil, this is exactly what he is proposing by presenting categories and reprises. I agree with Kukla and Lance's critique that there is an underlying impression of Platonism in *Making It Explicit*, but I also think that this was important for what Brandom was trying to accomplish. His historical writing is far more sensitive to this problem and he even shows how to overcome it. In doing so however, I see him as coming to a position that lines up with Weil's.

Categories are structured in such a way as to bring out all of the inferences that define (or express) a central concept. They thus help us to understand what individuals are committed to *and* what substantive claims they will be willing to make. It is

---

[46] Brandom (2002).
[47] Brandom (2002), 93–95.
[48] Brandom (2002), 112.
[49] Brandom (2002), 113.

in this sense that I claimed that the categories from the *Object* to the *Absolute* were semantic concepts. They describe the substantive content that goes along with different grounds by showing the commitments that are endorsed by each ground, the commitments that one is entitled to, and what is incompatible with them. Thus, if someone's discourse is structured by *The Condition* they will see facts as being under the purview of quantifiable causal conditions, and thus will only be able to endorse values if they are expressed as some type of quantifiable condition—whether psychological, sociological, historical, etc. Values on their own are not seen as contentful. They are thus not seen as something the individual is entitled to, or as something endorsable on their own, precisely because the articulation of values is incompatible with the category's central commitment. As long as this is the case, the fact/value opposition in *The Condition* will be seen as insurmountable. The problem, for Weil, is not the perspectival character of communication. Weil accepts this, this is why he argues that there are multiple coherent discourses. The problem is that without a meta-commitment to the reasonable resolution of conflict through argumentative practices, these multiple positions are not merely conflictual, but are incommensurable, and thus insurmountable.

6.4 Discursive Commitments and Conflict

The language of commitments and entitlements does not dodge the problem of violence. In fact, the language of commitments and entitlements is particularly vulnerable to this problem precisely because of the way that commitments and entitlements are present in conflict. They make the differences of content explicit. Brandom claims that commitments and entitlements are coordinate concepts, that is, they function together. One is needed in order to make sense of the other. In fact, for Brandom, "[d]oing what one is committed to do is appropriate in one sense, while doing what one is entitled to is appropriate in another."[50] These concepts are thus excellent tools for understanding the normative force of language games. What is important about the language of commitments and entitlements is that it allows us to capture the intersubjective social articulation of normative *deontic* statuses. It allows us to see ourselves as players in the game of giving and asking for reasons, to keep score of our deontic statuses and the statuses of those around us. Thus, in theory, once we commit to a content, if we are entitled to it, others should recognize our status. However, scorekeeping itself is not an abstract structure, it is articulated in concrete commitments. Nonetheless, the radicality of Weil's critique can be transposed into a Brandomian idiom. Brandom's presentation of the game of giving and asking for reasons focuses on cooperative games. What Weil's critique shows is that conflictual games also exist and that these conflictual games cannot be ignored.

---

[50] Brandom (1994), 159.

In order to fully understand cooperative games, conflictual games must be taken into account.

Given the differences between Weil's and Brandom's theories, we can look at conflictual games at two different levels, one at the level of language, and the other at the level of discourse. Conflict is present at the level of non-philosophical language precisely because of the ways that individuals misattribute commitments and entitlements. In philosophical discourse, on the other hand, conflict is present, not necessarily because of misattribution, but rather because of the recognition of different grounds. It is present in the disagreement between the different types of conceptual language that individuals speak when they develop a discourse, in the language in which they give their reasons and the language that they want others to speak when these others give their own. Committing is thus an essential feature of recognizing the commitments of others. However, by committing, individuals take on some commitments that they accept as being incompatible with others, and unless an incompatible commitment is shown to be reducible to another compatible one, these incompatible commitments are a source of conflict. Using this vocabulary, we can thus look at a whole assortment of ways that conflicts are present when we ascribe commitments and the way we conceive our entitlements in discourse. Conflicts are present in a different way than pure violence is. In order to clarify what I mean I am going to make a distinction between latency and implicitness.[51] Violence is latent in all discourse because violence and language are fundamentally entangled. In other words, they are both present in the particular creation of meaning. Conflict, on the other hand, is implicit in concrete discourses based on what is incompatible with its central discursive commitment. That is, conflict is implicit in the content of discourse and in the different contents of different types of discourse. Brandom notes that his goal is to make explicit in discourse—in the language of rules—what is implicit in practices. From this goal, we can note that implicitness plays an *active* but underdefined role in our behavior. This is different from latency. The notion of latency that I will be using is that of a present potentiality. What is latent in discourse may never be activated but it can be at any moment by any individual. What is latent in discourse is human spontaneity and violence. This latency only becomes clear in the opposition between philosophical discourses, precisely because the choice of the ground is free.

In its purest form, the conflict that is born of discourse reveals the latency of violence because two people hold incompatible substantive commitments and they correctly attribute the incompatible commitment to the other person and then go on to acknowledge that incompatibility. This leads to conflict precisely because the two individuals are at an impasse. Unless they find a way to reformulate their

---

[51] Weil notes that it is the insecurity of our situation that always exists "in a latent state: potentially" (PM, 23). Given that this insecurity exists as the possibility of violence it seems correct to apply the notion of latency to violence in general. Weil himself seems to confirm this when he notes that "politics always deals with the human being insofar as they are always potentially violent" (EC.I.416). In both of these cases, potentially is a translation of *en puissance* which in French refers to the pair potentiality/actuality in the Aristotelean sense.

6.4 Discursive Commitments and Conflict

commitments in order to dissolve the incompatibility, or unless they take on another commitment that is more important (such as a commitment to non-violence), this conflict translates into violence. Here we can think of the way that Eric Weil characterizes the contents of *Certainty*. In this category:

> it does not follow that discussion exists between the different contents; rather, the human being of certainty only knows one way of behaving towards anyone who does not share their truth: if the sermon does not force the adhesion of their fellow human beings (the content of course still needs to allow conversion), all that remains is the destruction of the infidel who, through their stubbornness itself, has shown that they are a human being in appearance alone and that, in reality, they are the most dangerous of animals (LP, 113).

There are two things that need to be drawn out of this passage. The first is the way that Weil's articulation of certainty allows us to better understand his position concerning the discontinuity between merely sensing creatures, such as animals, and creatures that deploy reasons, such as humans. The second is what is implied by an individual's commitment to the content of their certainty. These two aspects are linked insofar as an individual can refuse to see other human individuals as *fully* human because of their commitment to a certain discourse. In other words, individuals can consider an individual, or the members of a group, to be an animal, precisely because this other individual does not adhere to the *true* discourse, that is, the discourse that allows that person to be seen as a full-fledged member of the human community.[52] In other words, the aptitude for rational language is not *prima facie*, a sufficient criterion. In this case, the individual demands that those that have this aptitude participate in the practice of a concretely determined form of rational language—their own. As long as the content of an individual's certainty matters more than discussion, or more than the resolution of a problem, the person anchored in their certainty (in their discursive commitment) seems to have two options. Either they must bring their adversary to see the truth of their content or they must eliminate them precisely because their very existence poses a continual menace. This is the pure case. There are however myriad mixed cases. People can believe that they are being reasonable or acting in good faith and yet the way that they attribute and understand commitments and entitlements can bring out the conflict implicit in commitments. This possibility shows the way that Weil's critique touches the entire rational tradition of characterizing the human being as a rational animal, even in its modern iteration that focuses on the role of sapience in our human conceptual capabilities.

I will look at three examples of discursive exchanges in order to bring home the point that conflict is implicit in discourse. The goal of these examples is to show how exploiting Brandom's technical language can help us understand the way commitments and entitlements bring out the implicit conflict in language and how this implicit conflict can activate even the most latent human violence. This is a purely

---

[52] It may also be that when people renounce reasonable behavior they are relying more on their sentient capacities than their sapient ones. That is, they are allowing the things they have come to recognize as filling non-inferential roles to excite their irritability and arousal without demanding if they have reasons to react in the ways that they do.

logical analysis of the way that the language of commitments and entitlements hold the notion of conflict within them. This means that the logical steps must be charted. I am of the opinion however that this kind of analysis is woefully underdeveloped in our real-life practices. Because of this, moving from implicit conflict to violence is actually a much smaller step than this analysis would suggest, specifically given the hold substantive normative commitments have on us. The three examples will be imagined scenarios, but imagined scenarios that have enough verisimilitude to show how Weil's critique comes to bear on the language of commitments and entitlements. The first imagined discursive exchange will characterize the misattribution of commitments. The second will characterize the correct attribution of a commitment coupled with a disregard for this specific commitment based on other commitments. The third will be the disregard of a commitment because of a misattributed entitlement. Following this, I will give a fourth example that has a different form than the one found in the imagined exchanges. This example will draw from actual conflicts in philosophy. This form is different because it is a "virtual dialogue," that is, it happens across texts. This virtual dialogue however will show how philosophical opposition allows us to understand the latency of violence.

The primary goal of the imagined scenarios is to show that the possibility of conflict is present any time commitments are taken on, so any theory that seeks to understand what humans do in language must face this possibility. The secondary goal is to provide some concrete material to the reader so that their own imagination can get traction and can create, compare, or contrast these examples with their own. Nonetheless, these examples will not yet contain the full radicality of Weil's critique because they take for granted that individuals are seeking to be reasonable, which means they maintain the central commitment to non-violence. The commitment to non-violence that Weil develops in his presentation of *Discussion* is, for him, the central commitment to reasonable behavior. But this is exactly what Weil's critique highlights, reasonable behavior is a commitment, and like other commitments it can be abandoned. By framing reasonable behavior in the terms of a (implicit) commitment to non-violence, Weil highlights that there is nothing mysterious about it, but he also shows that individuals can always give it up.

Reasonable behavior is a commitment to non-violence and seems to be a relatively simple commitment. This does not mean however that what reasonable behavior is will always be clear to individuals. Because of the variety of commitments individuals have and the way that commitments interlock, there are many times in our own lives where we think we are presenting perfectly reasonable positions, or acting for good reasons, and then, because of conflict, we come to see that we were not. Conflict thus plays a key role in the relativization of belief that allows us to refine our reasons. This ties in with the role difference and doubt play when we abandon our naïve certainty in order to work towards mature certainty. In this way, the conflict of commitments, like doubt and difference, is not a problem. In fact, it plays a central role in the universalization of our concepts. The problem is when these conflicting commitments (which allow us to have reasonable doubt because of reasonable differences, and which can inspire the kind of sapient behavior that is paradigmatic of discussion) are the reason that discussion ends. Conflicting

6.4 Discursive Commitments and Conflict

commitments in discussion play a central role in the universalization of concepts, however that is only as long as people discuss. The conflict that can awaken the latency of violence is precisely the conflict that ends or frustrates discussion. One of the simplest ways the conflict of commitments ends discussion and has violent effects is through the misattribution of a commitment. When one misattributes a commitment to someone, they are thus misattributing a specific normative status and the kinds of things that follow from this discursive commitment. When commitments are misattributed, individuals have a hard time being able to see the person to whom they misattributed the commitment as a genuine dialogue partner. This is because they may not even acknowledge the other person's capacity to offer dialogical controls. This happens quite frequently in interpersonal relationships, we misattribute a desire or a project to somebody and don't want to bring up the subject to avoid conflict. By trying to avoid a conflict based on a misattributed commitment, this can lead the two individuals to the conflict that they were hoping to avoid. There is also the violence that goes along with the way that a misattributed commitment can limit one's autonomy. This is the violence of somebody telling us what we think or what we want and thus taking away our ability in this interpersonal relationship to define our own commitments and goals.

For this scenario, imagine a romantic couple. In this couple one person has decided that they do not want to have children. Let's call this individual Hortense. Hortense has decided for a number of reasons that she doesn't want to have kids. She is however convinced that her partner Colleen wants to have them. This could be because of indications in conversations or because of a real commitment that Colleen has previously stated. Whatever the case, imagine that Hortense is not the best when it comes to communication in a couple and so avoids bringing up the topic because she wants to avoid the conflict with Colleen. Because she is convinced that Colleen wants children, Hortense is also convinced that the disparity in the way they want to organize their lives will lead to a conflict and in the worst case, to the end of their relationship. As long as this relationship is going well, neither partner wants to bring up potential differences and so let this misunderstanding fester. Hortense can begrudge Colleen a commitment that she herself has misattributed to Colleen. Imagine now that, still without ever having spoken about whether Colleen wants kids or not, Hortense uses it as one of her justifications when she decides to leave Colleen. Imagine that, years later, after all of the interpersonal differences that the two had have been overcome, they succeed in talking about this commitment and Colleen reveals that her commitment was never as strong as Hortense had believed. Maybe she was lukewarm on the idea of children, or that she wanted them, but that they were secondary to her commitment to Hortense, or that she had never wanted them and that the hints that came out in discussion were merely the hypothetical musings that can go on between two people who talk intimately at length. In any of these possible scenarios, Hortense would have hurt Colleen based on a misattributed commitment. This example is telling because here it is assumed that these two people, precisely because they are in such an intimate relationship, share similar commitments, and a similar center of discourse with shared values, thus the first place that implicit conflict appears is in the disagreements that happen within the same category. This conflict however is much less serious than that between different discursive centers.

The second example characterizes the type of conflict that arises when individuals come to understand that their discourse has different central commitments than that of their interlocutor. In this case, the problem is that the individual disregards a correctly attributed commitment. In this scenario, one correctly attributes a commitment to someone else, but disregards that commitment because they see this commitment as not being of the same worth as other commitments or as of being of no worth at all. This type of scenario happens frequently in deeply partisan political debates. It is similar to the pure case that I have mentioned but is nonetheless subtly different. In the pure case, individuals are seen as adversaries from the get go, because they recognize the incompatibility of two different commitments. They do not enter into discussion because their conflict is clearly defined. In our example, when a correctly attributed commitment is disregarded, this commitment is not merely seen as incompatible with the other one, it is also seen as not being a commitment that a reasonable person could actually hold. In the pure case, there is a conflict of two ways of seeing the world, of two ways of life. This is in some ways an extra-discursive or pre-discursive conflict. The incompatibility of commitments is recognized and the threat precludes the individuals from entering into discussion. With a disregarded commitment, the individuals or group are either actually considered dialogue partners or *should* be considered so, as members of the same community, for example, or as partners in a shared project. In this case, the disregard for a correctly attributed commitment takes away the other person's *ability* to be an equal dialogue partner.

In the United States of America certain commitments are correctly seen as incompatible with others, this is normal for all discourse. But instead of seeing opposing commitments concerning a topic as being a valid point of discussion, one side refuses to take the other commitment seriously. In this way, with hot-button issues, we can see how the attribution of the commitment can be correct, but how the very correctness of the commitment causes it to be overlooked entirely. Take the examples of gun-control and climate change. On both sides, because the partisans of a commitment correctly attribute certain commitments to their opponents, they disregard their opponents as dialogue partners.[53] The reason that this is different from the pure case is that in the pure case adversaries are seen as adversaries from the get go. Here, they are seen as dialogue partners as long as they don't have *this or that* untenable commitment. Thus, the individual in the discussion about gun control or climate change says, "we can come to a reasonable agreement as long as you don't hold this specific unreasonable commitment (where unreasonable is taken to be coherent but unacceptable), and if you do, you are clearly someone who I can't speak with reasonably." A correctly attributed but disregarded commitment transforms the person from a dialogue partner into someone that can't be reasoned with.

---

[53] I am by no means saying that this is an all-encompassing problem and that the whole political spectrum can be reduced to this type of behavior, rather what I am saying is that one can rather easily find cases of this kind of behavior throughout the political spectrum.

6.4 Discursive Commitments and Conflict

In such cases, it is the disregard for the other person's position that opens the door to conflict and violence. Individuals dig their heels into their own commitment and when they do so, they refuse to acknowledge the possibility of error on their part, or the possibility of modification to their position. To take our examples, people on both sides of the gun debate and the climate-change debate progressively see their position as more and more non-negotiable. In fact, they don't even see it as a debate, they see it as obvious, and thus it is inconsequential if someone isn't on board because "them's the facts." This is where Weil's analysis of the paradox of certainty comes in handy. We must take a position; however, we also run the risk of anchoring this position so deeply into the fabric of our cognitive experience that it is impossible to unravel it. This scenario slides most easily into the pure position of incompatible commitments that lead to conflict. The progressive hardening of positions leads people who hold certain commitments to be grouped together as enemies and thus as something to be eliminated.

The third scenario that shows how conflict can be adequately described in the language of commitments and entitlements is linked to the second. In the second scenario, a correctly attributed commitment is disregarded because of another commitment. When this happens, the individual sees themself as correctly entitled to their position, and disregards the opposing position based on this entitlement. In the third scenario, the conflict is not born because an individual disregards a commitment but because of an incorrectly attributed entitlement. Having an entitlement allows us to act on a commitment. We see ourselves as having a legitimate latitude of action because we know what our commitment entitles us to. In this way, entitlement can be described both according to the notion of rights and that of desert. In fact, this concept is important to make sense of the positive aspects of rights and desert, but it also helps us to understand the degeneration of these concepts. According to our entitlement, we have the right to certain things and thus we also deserve to get those things or be treated in a certain way. What misattributed entitlements do is distort the correct scope of these rights and desert. An example is the vandalism or violence that people engage in because they feel that others ignore the entitlements they take to be natural. For instance, people have stumped and protested for protected bike lanes. They see this as a good way to fight climate change, to encourage healthy activity, and to make cities more agreeable. In cities where bike lanes are protected, but where the infrastructure has not changed to also support these rights, motorists park or stop in bike lanes. This raises the ire of cyclists, and they feel that they are entitled to not follow the laws that are put in place for cyclists because there is an underenforcement of laws for motorists and this underenforcement puts cyclists at risk. In fact, certain cyclists have gone further than just disregarding the laws that apply to cyclists, they start to disregard other laws and have taken to vandalizing cars that park in bike lanes, because according to these cyclists, motorists *need* to learn that this is not done. In this case, there is a core entitlement that is correct, the right to a protected bike space. What is different is that because of the validity of the core entitlement, cyclists attribute themselves an additional entitlement to teach others how to act. The importance of this case is that people go from a correct entitlement to attributing themselves an incorrect one.

Cyclists have earned the entitlement to a protected space through legitimate legal means, however the fact that this entitlement is not recognized by others leads cyclists to attribute themselves an additional entitlement that they do not have. In these cases, an entitlement can lead an individual to feel that they have the right, or more importantly, the obligation, the necessity, to defend the commitment that they feel allows the misattributed entitlement.

What these different cases show is the way that conflict is present in commitments and that, without the effort to universalize our concepts, this conflict allows the degeneration of commitments and entitlements. In fact, what is important in all these cases is that the continual poor attribution of commitments or entitlements transforms commitments and entitlements themselves. This can happen when a commitment is continually misattributed and an individual's autonomy is limited by another. It can also happen when a commitment is continually disregarded and a person is not seen as a legitimate dialogue partner. It can happen when an entitlement is misattributed and people either disrespect the entitlements of others or overstep their own entitlement by seeing themselves as entitled to something to which they are not. Continual misattributions lead individuals to see commitments and entitlements as incommensurably incompatible. In such cases, dialogue partners—or those that should be dialogue partners—become adversaries that present an existential threat to one's commitments and entitlements. The reasonable conflict that is necessary for the universalization of discourse can become the pure conflict that can only be resolved by violence. There is also another more pernicious possibility found in the reprise of the move from *Truth* to *Meaninglessness*.

The attitude of *Meaninglessness* is born when the individual refuses to see the world as meaningful, when they no longer see the world and their life in it as a meaningful whole. What this means in a theory of discourse is that there is a depreciation of all the meaning that was immediately and thus non-critically grasped in the attitude of *Truth*. If we analyze this same possibility in the language of commitments and entitlements, we can analyze the person who slips into *Meaninglessness* as the individual who sees the commitments that are present in the world as having lost all value. When *Meaninglessness* is reprised because someone is continually confronted by a dominant discourse that disregards their commitments and entitlements, the individual may reject *all* the commitments and entitlements of that dominant discourse and seek to destroy or subvert it. They see their entitlements ignored and they see themselves as subject to the overreach of the misattributed entitlements of others. This continual misattribution, disregard, and overreach undermines their faith in the normative goodness of commitments and entitlements in general. The language of commitments and entitlements becomes meaningless to them and they have no need to see themselves as bound by normative constraints because this language has failed them. What is important to add is that this is the logical analysis of how the language of commitments and entitlements explains this specific reprise of *Meaninglessness*. It is not how the individual living the experience understands it. In fact, it is precisely because the individual has entered the attitude of *Meaninglessness* that they cannot see this. This analysis is for them just one more barrage of empty words.

6.4 Discursive Commitments and Conflict

It may be that reprises depend on misattributions—especially evaluative ones—and conflicts in order to make different philosophical discourses explicit. In this way, we can look at the reprise as the method by which misattribution is transformed into understanding. By constantly reprising discourse in order to make commitments explicit, individuals see what follows from the content of these commitments. This is how individuals are able to see their content and commitments as applicable to their action. Philosophers are always individuals before being philosophers, and it is as individuals facing their dissatisfaction with a determined discourse that they become philosophers, by raising themselves up against the dominant discourse in order to create a new one. One difference between philosophers and non-philosophers is that philosophers self-consciously speak from discourse. This however does not eliminate conflict. The history of philosophy provides keen examples of this that Weil's categorial progression takes into account. Kant for example, understands the discourse of modern empirical science that is present in *The Condition*, but is unsatisfied with it. He chooses to ground his discourse in something that the philosophical discourse of scientific positivism misses. Fichte's modification of this position provides further clarification.

Gilbert Kirscher insists on the importance of Fichte for understanding Weil's position in general,[54] and Patrice Canivez notes that one of the most illuminating ways of tackling Weil's characterization of the conflict between different discourses is found in "the Fichtean reconstruction of transcendental philosophy."[55] Canivez points to what Fichte says in the *Introduction* to the first *Wissenschaftslehre* concerning the conflict between idealism and dogmatism. Fichte presents this conflict as unresolvable precisely because there is no agreement about grounding principles. In fact, for Fichte, the "object of philosophy" is different according to idealism and dogmatism.[56] For idealism, it is the independence of the "I in itself"[57] and for dogmatism it is "the independence of the thing."[58] Both positions defend the independence of their object and thus "[n]either of these two systems can directly refute the opposing one: for the dispute between them is a dispute concerning the first principle."[59] A refutation of idealism from a dogmatist viewpoint falls on deaf ears just as the refutation of dogmatism by idealism does. Idealism only convinces someone who has adopted the grounding principles of the freedom of thought and the self-positing subject. Fichte accepts this gap even though he is convinced of idealism's rectitude. However, he can also show that idealism surpasses dogmatism, precisely in the way that idealism can grasp dogmatism comprehensively, while dogmatism cannot grasp idealism in the same way. Thus for Fichte (and for us), the idealist arguments are better, that is, more convincing and more comprehensive, but

---

[54] Kirscher (1989).
[55] Canivez (2007), 171.
[56] Fichte (1992), 12.
[57] Fichte (1992), 13.
[58] Canivez (2007), 171.
[59] Fichte (1992), 15.

that does nothing to eliminate the problem. For either side to come to an agreement they would first and foremost need to agree on grounding principles, and this is exactly what dogmatism refuses to do. Idealism does not have to abandon its principles because it is able to grasp dogmatism, but for dogmatism to grasp idealism it would have to abandon or modify its principles. There is thus an asymmetry in this conflict which, for Weil, is also present every time a new category surpasses an older one. There is the paradox however. The dogmatist can stick to their principles because they are free, and so are acting from a freedom that they do not see. Even though Fichte notes that if "the first principle of either system is conceded, then it is able to refute the first principle of the other" nothing requires this to happen. If it does not happen, neither side is refuted through argument, rather both sides refuse the other's position. Because of this, as Canivez notes, we are faced with "two systems between which there is no possible dialogue."[60] However, because both correspond to a fundamental philosophical attitude, the individual can stand in either coherently.

In terms of Brandom's theory, this is to be understood as two self-consciously-chosen positions that imply different commitments and entitlements. Clearly, Weil situates himself on the side of Fichte. For Weil, the structure of human freedom allows individuals to refuse to recognize any and all normative deontic statuses. The individual can pragmatically refuse any meaning just as they can refuse meaninglessness and seek to form a coherent discourse. These, for Weil, are the fundamental human possibilities, the violent choice of violence and the a-reasonable choice of reason. But the example of Fichte shows something more. Here, Fichte is not claiming that all discourse must be refused, but rather the specific claims and commitments of a specific determined discourse. Thus, there is a conflict between these two positions. What the example of Fichte shows is that even on this side of the radical refusal of all discourse and of all normative constraints, even on the side of the choice of reason, the language of commitments and entitlements holds the structure of conflict within it. This free choice is what uncovers the latency of violence. Because the choice of a ground, the choice of a coherent discourse, under reflection, reveals itself to be a choice, it shows that there is another choice that is present that the individual can always take up. Violence is always present as a choice for the individual, even if this present potentiality is never taken up by the individual themself.

Together, the language of commitments and entitlements and the shapes of content present in the categories allow us to understand something new, namely how violence, taken as the concrete grasp of particularity as particular, enters into discourse. The conflict that is implicit in language is revealed by making commitments and entitlements explicit. However, once these commitments are made explicit, individuals may hold on to them *despite* their potential for conflict. This puts the individual face to face with their own capacity for violence. When individuals dig down to the bottom of their commitments they get to the ground of their discourse.

---

[60] Canivez (2007), 171.

As long as the individual holds this ground to be certain without taking on the meta-commitment to the reasonable, non-violent action found in argumentative practices, different discourses are seen to be incommensurable. One of the ways that individuals deploy their discourse while maintaining its incommensurability with other discourses is to reprise their concrete particularity under universal forms. In this way, they can deploy the entire history of discourse in order to defend their particular position. Individuals can reprise *The Condition*, for instance, to justify a racist discourse. They can present race as one of the conditions that define an individual's intelligence and trustworthiness. Here, instead of trying to find a way to overcome the contradictions in this position in order to find a discourse that allows the value of the individual to be described more universally, they can double down on their already-held particular belief and use it as a justification. They can claim universality while nonetheless refusing to see others as real dialogue partners. The universality they are presenting is defective however because it is used in the defense of particularity. It is used by the individual to justify not just their belief but their action. Here we can see different forms of racism, sexism, and nationalism as all operating under this reprise. People build a discourse that claims to be universal in order to deny universality to individuals who under other conditions would be granted it. These defective uses of universality are problematic not just because they lead to conflictual discourses, but because they themselves can push people to deploy violence.

6.5 The Use of Violence

One of the claims of this chapter is that violence plays an essential role in determining conceptual content by providing the particularity of the situation that will be grasped in discourse. It is important to note however that despite violence's essential importance, there is also an essential asymmetry between violence and discourse. The role of violence is ambivalent and underdetermined *because* nothing guarantees that the violence present in any situation will be grasped. It may always just be lived as violence, in other words, it may be just painfully endured as one of the myriad conditions that make it impossible to see one's life as a meaningfully-oriented whole, or to see oneself as capable of acting meaningfully in the world. Discourse is thus the privileged path of overcoming this violence. As the preceding analyses show, identifying the conflict that is present in language and discourse also shows how the progressive undermining of commitments and entitlements can lead to violence. Violence can be seen as bookending discourse: it provides what moves us to enter discourse and it is the thing that can end discourse. It can also be seen as running through the whole history of discourse. This is exactly what is shown by characterizing language and violence as fundamentally entangled. The work of providing a discourse that grasps the world, the individual, and discourse itself, the work that is normally called philosophical inquiry, is extremely difficult. And the type of critical examination that goes along with philosophy is often rightly seen as a danger. People that enter into this kind of exercise often abandon a great many of their own essential beliefs and commitments as being historically, culturally, or socially contingent. Any such examination may thus entail a radical reconceptualization of one's place in the world. There are so many material difficulties to philosophical inquiry and to reasonable discussion that it is often seen as far easier to forego this examination itself and merely disregard any overture that leads to it than actually engage in it. Discussion is a vast field with large subjects. It is long, and there are lots of things for individuals to put into perspective in order to see their opponent's position. There is nothing that guarantees that discussion will come to an end, much less to a satisfying one. Couple this with good old-fashioned stubbornness, suspicion, indifference, fear, and a variety of other things that block the passage of reasonable discourse and the problem of violence starts to become clearer.

There is no necessity in the pragmatic relationship one takes towards discourse, Weil ironizes that this is clear in the fact that every time that someone is willing to die for an idea they are also willing to kill for it (PR.I.280). Taking a stand is of a piece with having conceptual content, but what Weil's critique highlights is the way that this same stand or commitment opens the door to violence. Weil is trying to provide the tools to grasp this and also to open the path to reasonable discourse. However, it is important to note here that Weil does not proscribe the use of violence. He himself joined the French army under a fake name in order to fight his own former countrymen because he was committed to stand against Nazism. Rather, what Weil does is note that *if* one wants to be reasonable, *then* one must do so within the realm of reasonability, which is traced by the refusal of violence. The choice of violence means leaving the realm of reasonability, even when it is a choice made reasonably. However sometimes it is the violent individual that imposes the choice of violent means on others. There is a moment where all the means of discussion *are* exhausted and where even the most ardent supporter of non-violence must judge and commit, and stand up violently. There are also numerous examples in history where a commitment to non-violence produces violence. A pacifist may find themselves in a situation where their refusal to take up arms allows communities and peoples to be placed under the yoke of those who have made a radical commitment to violence. In this case, the pacifist must accept the consequences as one they are partially responsible for. This is one of the reasons that the goal of coherent discourse is to allow us to grasp our situation. Knowing the conditions that we live in allows us to identify what to do. And as Patrice Canivez notes, "with someone who refuses even the idea of a coherent discourse, there is no discussion possible. With Gandhi's means one can defeat the English, not the Nazis."[61]

Taking position means that there are fundamental commitments that will lead individuals to quit reasonable behavior from within reasonable behavior. This can be to defend or further a position or to destroy or damage some threat to that position. If they do so, they are faced with the problem of legitimacy. Once the dust

---

[61] Canivez (1999), 77.

settles and the violence is over, every action is subject to justification if this individual wants to reestablish the realm of non-violence that defines discourse. This becomes a question of the individual's, or the community's, or the State's reasons for acting. It is a question of whether these reasons can be seen as legitimate and whether these actors are able to renounce violence after the choice to leave discussion has run its course. In his essay "L'état et la violence," Weil notes that:

> the government resulting from revolution will also itself be obliged to work towards the elimination of violence, and in particular, its own, unless it wants to renounce the modern form of labor: rationality, the distinguishing feature of any modern society, presupposes everybody's collaboration, a collaboration that is only obtained when everyone finds interest and satisfaction therein (EC.II.384).

Despite characterizing this problem here in terms of the State, Weil's analysis is also applicable to interactions at the level of individuals and groups. Even a revolutionary government has to know how life is to get back to normal after the revolution is over, it has to help people return to the everyday business of living. Its legitimacy will be based on this. It has to show that a former form of life was untenable and that this new form of life allows people to live in peace. At the level of individuals then, violence is only legitimate when it is defensive, measured, and a last resort. In other words, if violence is deployed to defend something, there also has to be a reasonable reflection on the cost of the use of this violence. When it is used at all cost, violence undermines the legitimacy of any resolution that is to come out of its use. The less this violence is defensive and measured, the more it will be seen as arbitrary.

For Weil, language and violence are entangled at their deepest articulation. This is part of the latency of violence. It can crop up at any moment, but this is not a problem for the average person. The average person recognizes violence in the world and recognizes its "naturalness." It is a problem for the philosopher, for the individual who has devoted their life to reasonable discourse, to the individual who believes in reason. It poses a problem not only because this individual must try to overcome violence, to understand violence, but also because the violence that is always present is their own. Each philosopher's position is built out of a commitment. Commitments and entitlements however hold the grain of conflict within them. It is implicit at the level of everyday non-philosophical language and it is explicit in the articulation of the different ground-level concepts born of philosophical discourses. What distinguishes philosophical discourse is the meta-commitment to reasonability. When conflict is explicit in discourse without this meta-commitment, it is always a step away from becoming violent. What this means is that even the most reasonable person can abandon reason. We feel responsible to our commitments and thus we feel entitled to act because of and for our commitments, but what to do when our commitments are unjustified, indefensible, or more simply, just wrong? In Chap. 5, it was argued that the possibility of error is an essential *semantic* feature of the development of meaning. It was also suggested that this possibility *epistemologically* implies a certain fallibilism about the content itself. In other words, to understand how the evolution of semantic content is possible, what counts as legitimate knowledge claims must also be seen as being in constant evolution. We must give up the commitment of finding any single foundational certainty that can ground our knowledge and start seeing all our doxastic commitments as modifiable. This is what allows us to constantly reaffirm our commitment to reasonable discourse. We can be mistaken and we can be dissatisfied. We can make bad inferences that follow from good commitments. We can make good inferences that follow from bad commitments. We can be faced with a decision that is not resolvable in its actual state. In this sense, fallibilism (particularly if we assimilate it to the Weilian articulation of systematic openness) is built into the meta-commitment to reasonable behavior. Maintaining this meta-commitment means constantly evaluating and adjusting our other commitments. The importance of Weil's philosophical system is in large part to be found in the way that it allows this meta-commitment to be seen and articulated. This is only possible however through the articulation of the meta-commitment's diametric opposite, its other. In other words, it is only found in the attitude of *The Work*.

The attitude of *The Work* has been characterized as the refusal of discourse. From inside of the discourse that seeks to be reasonable, this can be understood as a commitment to a *purely* pragmatic relationship to discourse. Concepts act on normative beings and as the heir to reasonable discourse *The Work* understands this. But the individual in *The Work* refuses to see themselves as a being subject to norms. This is part of what is essential to the category. The individual in *The Work* deploys the resources developed by discourse while nonetheless seeing these resources as having no hold over them. In other words, they ignore their own commitment because their relationship to discourse is purely pragmatic. This commitment is visible from within reasonable discourse however. It is visible as the commitment to refuse all discursive norms (while nonetheless using discourse's other resources). For reasonable discourse, this individual commits to a world without discourse, to a world where discourse has no bearing on them as an individual or on their world. It is a commitment that dissolves all necessity and normativity because it commits to violent struggle. From within discourse, there is a "natural" rebuttal to this position: the individual committing to violence still commits and thus is still under the sway of normativity and necessity, not to mention the necessity of eating, of breathing, the necessity of nature, and the normativity that violence can impose upon us. Weil faces this objection when he writes:

> it is not the violent human being who speaks this way; for the violent human being, speaking about the essential would leave them open to the philosophers' critiques: if the violent human being made distinctions, if they recognized that certain things mattered and that others can, and must, be neglected, they would end up renouncing violence, because they would be too busy separating the essential from the accessory. It's our way of seeing that makes of the violent human being into a human being that has their own reflexive consciousness, that asks what the violent human being *wants deep down*. The violent human being does not themself want *deep down*, they do not want anything: there are things that that they do not want. Nothing keeps us from interpreting their acts and their actions and noting that, in fact, they accept *this* and refuse *that*, that, in their action, an essential and an inessential can be distinguished; but if we transformed this difference into a distinction that they consciously made, if we made their negating, and (for them) purely negative, action into an ontological discourse, we would be preventing ourselves from understanding them.

6.5 The Use of Violence

> For the violent human being, whatever we see as being essential to their existence is impossible to state and it is precisely in silence that it makes itself known, not in an absolute silence, but in the silence of the reason that claims to be coherent, not by renouncing whatever are called theories in everyday life, but by renouncing all *theoria*, by renouncing every view and every attempt at a single unified view of the whole. Violence is a problem for philosophy, philosophy is not one for violence. Violence laughs at the philosopher and dismisses them when it finds them bothersome and when it senses that they are an obstacle on the uncharted path that it sees as being reality (LP, 58).

The radical commitment to violence is thus a real possibility. Brandom's theory helps us to better understand this possibility within the structure of language. Weil's theory helps us to understand this possibility at the level of content, at the level of discourse. Together, these two theories allow us to show violence's relationship to meaning and the violence in the individual's relationship to discourse. Violence is present in the pragmatic negation that opens up spaces of meaningfulness, because they are spaces that instantiate and recognize the normative weight of better reasons. Such spaces therefore have a structural role and an application role. At the structural level, they are spaces that allow us to understand how we bind ourselves to this normative weight itself. At the level of application, they are the spaces within which all the modal claims of necessity and possibility are made.

I have sought to show that the language of commitments and entitlements is felicitous to understanding Weil's position because of the way that it allows us to make sense of the full force of Weil's critique. I have also sought to show that the articulation of philosophical categories and of the reprise help us to enrich Brandom's position by allowing us to add the concrete content that it seems to be missing. Commitments and entitlements can be interpreted as key functional concepts within categories. Within a category, an individual commits to certain contents and the permissible and incompatible inferences that accompany these commitments. They deploy these commitments within the structure of their communication with others, in order to get to the bottom of things. This shows the radicality of *The Work*. The key commitment for the person in *The Work*, from our point of view, is a commitment to refuse all normative commitment. Thus from this individual's point of view, they aren't committed to anything except perhaps to a faithfulness to themselves, to the effectiveness of their instrumental use of language on others in service of their own wants and desires. They understand what argument is. They know the difference between good and bad arguments. This is what allows them to instrumentalize argumentation itself. What is different is that for this individual this recognition does not *bind* them, it doesn't commit them to any specific content or behavior.

By framing the discussion in these terms and showing how they do not preclude violence, commitments and entitlements help us to better understand the mechanics of certain forms of violence. Conflict is implicit in the language of commitments and entitlements, and the *Logic of Philosophy* helps to understand how different irreducible discursive centers lead to different types of commitments, and entitlements. Because of this, it allows us to make that conflict explicit as material incompatibilities. This implies however a multitude of spaces of reasons. The question then is how do these spaces of reasons fit together and are they reducible to a single space? The first part of the answer, as already given, is through a meta-commitment to reasonable discourse, understood as the refusal of violence and the use of argumentative practices to settle conflict. The second part, as I will argue through the rest of this work is that they are only reducible to a formal unity. Brandom's presentation of the idea of the space of reasons places all of these discursive centers on the same level. Weil's suite of categories highlights the irreducibility of certain spaces. This brings me to my final point about what Weil's philosophical project can add to inferential pragmatism. The space of reasons, despite its usefulness as a metaphor, lacks a structure that a logic of philosophy adds.

6.6 Violence and Spaces of Reasons

The metaphor of the space of reasons allows us to understand the shape that an individual's commitments gives to their conceptuality. By formulating Weil's critique of the philosophical tradition in the language of commitments and entitlements, we can see how conflict is already implicit in our workaday language. What I would like to suggest is that, for the metaphor of a space of reasons to continue to be useful in the face of Weil's critique, there needs to be further definition of what theses spaces imply and how they interact. In other words, in order for the metaphor of the space of reasons to continue to be not just operable, but fecund, the types of *contents* found in different spaces of reasons need to be articulated. This is exactly what Weil's theory provides. By reading categories as the inferential structures that make commitments explicit according to different grounding concepts, the categories allow us to see what someone is committing themselves to if they are arguing from this or that specific central commitment, including Brandom himself. By focusing on a *Platonic* space in which scorekeeping happens, Brandom has been able to explain certain essential mechanisms of *language*, and in doing so, he explicitly calls on the resources of the philosophical tradition. He is even clear about why he calls on certain resources such as Hegel, Kant, and pragmatism and not others.[62] However, all that this means from a Weilian point of view is that in developing his philosophy he stands in an attitude (in the specific sense of the *Logic of Philosophy*) that has a certain constellation of reprises (which may be the *Absolute* reprised under *The Condition* and mediated by *Consciousness*), precisely because of what he is trying to explain (the totality of discourse as it fits into the natural world starting from judgment). This also means that he has a concrete determined discourse that will not be accepted by people who are standing in other attitudes with different clusters of reprises. Weil's goal is not to explain this kind of possibility. It is to understand the possibility of different contents as they appear in the world and as peoples grasp and live them, to understand what kind of commitments lead to this or that kind

---

[62] There are others of course, but these others are reprised by the way that Brandom reads them as mediated by certain central commitments. This is clear in the way in which he reads Frege through the lens of Kant, for example.

6.6 Violence and Spaces of Reasons

of problem or conflict. Thus Brandom and Weil's theories in a way complete each other. Brandom's theory allows us to refine the analysis of language and to fill a need in Weil's theory, whereas Weil's allows us to understand the articulation of concrete discourses that actually are deployed in real conflicts. This opens up a framework for a theory of argumentation that allows individuals to face conflict and violence reasonably. Given the possibility of violence, it becomes evident that there is tension in the idea of the space of reasons. If multiple spaces of reasons exist and if these spaces carve out different conceptual landscapes, how is this multiplicity to be grasped?

I started this chapter by saying that I would argue that three major advantages can be picked up out of Weil's position that can help an inferentialist position. The first looks at the notion of sapience and how Weil's critique of human reasonability applies to it. Weil thinks that individuals *can* be reasonable, but nothing requires them to be except their own choice to bind themselves to the normative structure of discursivity. Here I claimed that although Brandom has the resources to treat this problem, he does not deal with it head on. The second major advantage is that Weil's way of framing the question of reasonability leads him to account for human violence. By putting Weil's theory and inferentialism together we see how these positions are mutually beneficial. They allow us to finetune our understanding of conflict and violence and our understanding of human reasonability. Reprising Weil's position in a Brandomian language clarifies certain aspects of Weil's theory and Weil's conceptualization of violence allows us to see the blind spot of concrete conflictual commitments in inferentialism. The third advantage is that Weil's position helps us clarify an ambiguity in the metaphor of the space of reasons. A logic of philosophy does this thanks to the reprise. The reprise shows us how different categories interact and what the consequences of different orders of explanations are.

As already mentioned, Brandom takes up the notion of the space of reasons from Wilfrid Sellars, and while Brandom tends to imply that there is only one space of reasons, this is not true throughout the post-Sellarsian tradition. Remember, Sellars claims that "in characterizing an episode or a state as that of *knowing*, we are not giving an empirical description of that episode or state; we are placing it in the logical space of reasons, of justifying and being able to justify what one says."[63] What is at stake here is the epistemic force of discursive conceptuality. The space of reasons is a space where the achievement of discursive knowledge takes place. According to Willem deVries and Timm Triplett:

> We can think of the logical space as determined by the categorial structure that we use to carve up the world conceptually. There are categorial distinctions among objects, events, and properties; and within those categories, there are physical objects and abstract objects, and first-order properties (properties of objects) and higher-order properties (properties of properties). Sellars does not assume that there is only one possible logical space: Different logical spaces are, at least as far as we can tell, perfectly possible, and each will have a slightly different categorial structure.[64]

---

[63] Sellars (1997), §36.
[64] deVries et al. (2000), 60.

This passage uncovers an ambiguity in the scope of the concept of a space of reasons. By speaking about the strucure of conceptuality in general, there is a sense in which the reading of deVries and Triplett tends towards Weil's use of the philosophical category, however, by focusing on objects, events, and properties, there is another sense where they seem to be using it along the lines of Weil's use of metaphysical categories. All categorial structures seem to be governed by inference, however, the distinction between philosophical and metaphysical categories allows us to clarify the ambuiguity between the categorial structures that give form to human conceptuality and those that do not. It also helps us to understand how within a single formal space of reasons, there can be multiple different concrete ones. This is because within the philosophical categories, the scope is defined by the ground that governs the different inferences, whereas with metaphysical categories the scope is defined by their application. DeVries and Triplett recognize the different spaces but they investigate neither the tension that this implies nor how these spaces fit together. What Weil proposes in the *Logic of Philosophy* is an analysis of the categorial structure of different forms of discursive commitments and the conceptual tools to see how they interact. This seems to be the next analysis needed to bring out all the strength of the metaphor.

If we focus on the structural aspect of spaces of reasons that follows from different grounds we can see how spaces of reasons are to structure human conceptuality. The individual defines all of their inferences in terms of their central commitment. If we link this idea with Peregrin's idea that the social normative space is constituted not by following rules but rather by bouncing off them (understood here also in the Weilian sense of the conflict between society and the individual in their self-determining reasonable reflection), we have all the elements necessary to see why Weil's analysis is so important. Starting from a mix of Peregrin's analysis and deVries and Triplett's analysis, we find ourselves with the metaphor of a space that defines what meaningfulness is, but that also implies a fracturing of differences. Meaning happens within this space, and bouncing off of rules is one of the things that can lead to the individual's dissatisfaction that will provoke them to develop a new discourse. This however also implies that there are as many starting points as there are individuals and that we grope forward haltingly while constituting a social space that takes the normative limits that others propose into account. DeVries and Triplett's analysis is that these categorial structures can be different and that they depend on how we organize them. If we recognize that this is a public social process, then we have the notion that our social space creates a realm within which reasons take a central importance. We therefore see reasons as defining the social space itself and thus as defining our capacity to be reasonable.

What Weil's analysis shows is that there is nothing that requires people to place their activity into the space of reasons. People justify because they have a commitment to being reasonable, a commitment that is upheld and developed through social argumentative practices and through the limits and constraints that people take on or present in such practices. Weil's critique is constantly reminding us that individuals can refuse this commitment. They can always seek to destroy the efficacy of social argumentative practices because they do not want to submit themselves to the normative weight that spaces of reasons imply. This is the violence that is latent is all discourse. In its most radical form it is seen as a rejection of the modern rationality which obscures or suppresses the individual.[65] Because this violence can be activated by the conflict that is implicit in different commitments and because different commitments give different shapes to spaces of reasons, there has to be a fine-grained analysis of how these different spaces interact.

Once we recognize what different spaces see as essential, this allows us to recognize which types of inferences they will see as permissible, which they will see as necessary, which they will see as satisfactory. This will allow us to compare, judge and hierarchize these different spaces. This brings us to what we could call a *logic* of these different spaces of reasons, or, in other words, a *logic of philosophy*. Without a similar analysis, the metaphor of a space of reasons or spaces of reasons can be seen as ambiguous. Quill Kukla (writing as Rebecca Kukla) and Mark Lance, in their book *'Yo' and 'Lo': The Pragmatic Topography of the Space of Reasons*,[66] go a long way to correcting this lack, as does Huw Price, in his discussion of pluralism.[67] The first by giving a detailed analysis of how individuals make normative demands on others in order to bring them into the space of reasons and the second by showing how different discursive centers interact. I will come back to Price's position at length later in my discussion of pluralism, therefore I do not need to treat it here. In Kukla and Lance's position what I want to highlight is the way that they see "membership in a discursive community [...] [as] a precondition for normative agency."[68] This is important because this means that it is only concrete normative relations that can bring us into a discursive community. These discursive communities thus have *conceptual* borders, some of which can even keep these communities separate. Kukla and Lance are sensitive to the plurality of spaces and this is one of the reasons that they critique Brandom's reduction of these different concrete communities. Nonetheless, they also have to ask whether there is a single *conceptual* space that defines the discursive community as a whole. This is the main ambiguity in the concept of a space of reasons that Weil can help us answer. In Kukla and Lance's answer to whether there is a single space of reasons or multiple ones, they focus on the pragmatics of the space of reasons and give us many useful tools. Nonetheless, they miss exactly what Weil's critique points out: pragmatic borders can *knowingly* be put in place by individuals or by societies in order to separate communities. That is, the possibility of refusing to recognize the pragmatic, discursive and normative stances of any interlocutor always exist. This is important because it can go a long way to answering their dilemma of how to conceive of the conceptual space. In asking about the conceptual space, they wonder whether there

---

[65] Weil notes that "a partial discourse only produces partial negation and partial silence: pure violence is only opposed to absolutely coherent discourse. Thought needs to be fairly advanced for someone to be able to declare that they reach for their revolver as soon as they hear the word "civilization"" (LP, 60).
[66] Kukla and Lance (2008).
[67] Price (1992).
[68] Kukla and Lance (2008), 190.

is "a single public world" that everyone can enter into and where reasons are given the same consideration, or whether there is "one, fundamental, discursive community" that nonetheless has "provisional and derivative discursive communities" within it.[69] Weil's critique shows that the first option has trouble getting off the ground, precisely because individuals can refuse to enter into discursive relations with others. However, Weil's characterization of the formal category of *Meaning* can be understood in terms similar to the second option.[70] There is a single *formal* discursive community that allows the possibility of discussion and explains the reality of different meanings, however this does not guarantee discussion and understanding. This is the difference between comprehensiveness and completeness. Completeness would imply a *concrete* discursive community where every conflict was able to be resolved through exclusively discursive means. Comprehensiveness implies a *formal* community that is in constant evolution and that has to be open to progressive and sudden changes of meaning. By presenting that possibility, Weil's critique reminds us what exactly is at stake in these differences. What is at stake is the possibility of reasonable discourse itself, and the stakes are high, because he sees the other possibility as a world where reasonable discourse has little or no hold, where people choose or are forced to live in their violence. He sees these discursive spaces as being carved out by individuals who have sought to grasp their world coherently as an organized whole, who have sought to make explicit all the implicit inferences that are opened in a normative space through the pragmatic and then abstract negations. He offers us criteria—coherence and universalizability—that allow us to understand the comprehensiveness of the inferential scope of these different discursive spaces. This is an important step in order for the emphasis on difference not to fold into relativism. Weil thus recognizes the plurality of spaces in the form of different categories, and he insists that these spaces are irreducible to one another. He nonetheless claims that these spaces are commensurable, that this plurality can be judged, organized, and hierarchized. This is an important result. Both because it allows developing a theory of argumentation from Weil's work, and because without it, the space of reasons risks disintegrating into a frenetic melee of differences.

6.7 Conclusion

This work hopes to show what Weil's project and the type of thought born of inferential pragmatism have in common. It also hopes to show how these two projects can mutually inform each other and create a new field of analysis and discussion. What I have hoped to show in the last chapters is how Weil's project can absorb

---

[69] Kukla and Lance (2008), 196.

[70] In reality they propose three options, the first of which is philosophical relativism. They do not see this as a serious threat to their position, and I will not treat it here because I do so elsewhere.

6.7 Conclusion

Brandom's insights and in particular his pragmatic metavocabulary. These insights will hopefully allow researchers that are working in a different idiom from Weil see the pertinence and the importance of his project, specifically in philosophy of language, argumentation theory, epistemology. But this work hopefully has more widespread consequences, specifically because of the way that Weil's project allows us to conceptualize the social space as a space of conflicts. Thanks to this conceptualization we can analyze and recognize the logical structure of different forms of conflict and their material consequences. Maybe even those that specifically lead to violence. This has wide-ranging effects in moral and political philosophy. Indeed, one of the next steps for an inferentialist program is to show how its insights range over a wider domain of topics. This is an essential step for any philosophy that claims to be systematic, it must show how it brings together different branches of philosophy. By showing how Weil's project fits together with an inferentialist program, the hope is to add resources for such extensions.

In this chapter, I have tried to show that that relationship is not merely unidirectional. Weil's project helps us to better understand what is at stake in the game of giving and asking for reasons and why taking it seriously matters. As long as individuals want to live together and be able to settle debates without recourse to violence they must submit themselves to the normative weight of better reasons. Weil's analysis indicates however that this desire is not necessary. Nothing binds individuals to settle conflict reasonably, outside of their own commitment to reasonability. To show this, key differences were highlighted in the way Weil and Brandom conceive reasonability and rationality. For Weil, reasonability is a possibility that the individual has to choose, specifically because its full exercise is only found in moments of crisis. The individual only realizes that it is a choice once made and once they start to seek to understand the conditions of this choice totally. For Brandom, because he glosses over the distinction between rationality and reasonability, he reduces them both to sapience as a human faculty. This difference has deep consequences. Most importantly, it changes the way we look at commitments and at the space of reasons. By looking at reasonability as a choice, it allows us to explain the real consequences of conflicts and violence. It also reminds us to keep the possibility of conflict and violence in mind. If reasonability is obscured in favor of rationality the risk is that their essential difference (the meta-commitment to nonviolent argumentative practices) will be flattened. Commitments are thus seen as implicitly conflictual, and this indeed plays a functional role. The problem is how commitments, and the conflicts they imply in their incompatibilities with other discourses, can lead to violence.

Weil gives us the means to understand what people hold to be essential, and how that commitment leads them to see other positions as incompatible. Weil's notion of the reprise allows us to see how these different categories can and do interact, and thus how, through argumentative practices, we can bring individuals to see the validity of different reasons and see these reasons as conflictual. Despite the importance of the reprise, Weil clearly indicates that argument itself cannot force an individual to change their categorial position. Rather, the individual has to commit themselves to argumentative practices, all the while knowing that this commitment may change their attitude, and thus change their relationship to the world. In other words, for argument to take hold, individuals must have a continued commitment to the possibility of overcoming difference and conflict through argumentative means. We are taught the importance of this throughout our lives and Weil's theory implies both a theory of argumentation and a theory of education.[71] It will unfortunately be outside of the scope of this work to look at Weil's theory of education or the literature on this subject.[72] This is because one of the goals of this work is to look at and develop Weil's theory of argumentation. To that end, in the next chapter I will look at the elements that Weil puts in place in order to justify his position that reasonable action is the action that seeks to bring people to reason through argumentation.

References

Assis, A. 2016. *Educação e moral: Uma análise crítica da filosofia de Éric Weil*. Editora CRV.
Bernardo, L.M. 2011. Moral, educação e sentido: Uma leitura da philosophie morale de Eric Weil. *Itinerarium* LVII: 2–40.
Brandom, R. 1994. *Making it explicit – Reasoning, representing & discursive commitment*. Cambridge, MA: Harvard University Press.
———. 2001. *Articulating reasons – An introduction to inferentialism*. Cambridge, MA: Harvard University Press.
———. 2002. *Tales of the mighty dead*. Cambridge, MA: Harvard University Press.
———. 2009. *Reason in philosophy: Animating ideas*. Cambridge, MA: Belknap Press.
———. 2010. *Between saying and doing: Towards an analytic pragmatism*. Oxford: Oxford University Press.
———. 2019. *A spirit of trust*. Cambridge, MA: Harvard University Press.
Buée, J.-M. 1989. Éducation, cosmos et histoire chez Éric Weil. In *Cahiers Éric Weil II*, ed. C.É. Weil, 81–90. Villeneuve-d'Ascq: Presses Universitaires de Lille.
Canivez, P. 1985. Éducation et instruction d'après Éric Weil. *Archives de Philosophie* 48 (4): 529–562.
———. (1999). Weil. Les Belles Lettres.
———. 2007. Le kantisme d'Éric Weil. In *Kant et les kantismes dans la philosophie contemporaine*, ed. C. Berner and F. Capeillères, 171–190. Presses Universitaires du Septentrion.
Castelo Branco, J. 2018. Éric Weil e o papel da educação humanística no contexto da cultura técnico-científica. *Educação e Filosofia* 32 (66): 991.
deVries, W.A., T. Triplett, and W. Sellars. 2000. *Knowledge, mind, and the given: Reading Wilfrid Sellars's empiricism and the philosophy of mind, including the complete text of Sellars's essay*. Indianapolis, IN: Hackett Publishing Co, Inc.
Fichte, J.G. 1992. *Introductions to the Wissenschaftslehre and other writings*. Trans. D. Breazeale. Indianapolis: Hackett Publishing Company.
Kirscher, G. 1989. *La philosophie d'Éric Weil*. Paris: Presses Universitaires de France.

---

[71] Weil elaborates his theory of education across his work, most clearly in *Philosophie politique*, as well as in various articles such as "Education as a Problem for Our Time" (1957), "Humanistic Studies, Their Object, Methods and Meaning" (1970a, b), as well as those collected in *Valuing the Humanities* (1989) and *Cahiers Éric Weil IV* (1993)

[72] See Soetard (1984); Canivez (1985); Buée (1989); Perine (1990); Nguyen-Dinh (1996); Bernardo (2011); Perine and Costeski (2016); de Assis (2016); Castelo Branco (2018).

References

Kukla, Q., and M. Lance. 2008. *"Yo" and "lo": The pragmatic topography of the space of reasons*. Cambridge, MA: Harvard University Press.

Nguyen-Dinh, L. 1996. Éducation ou violence selon Éric Weil. In *Cahiers Éric Weil V*, ed. G. Kirscher, J.-P. Larthomas, and J. Quillien, 79–86. Villeneuve-d'Ascq: Presses Universitaires du Septentrion.

Peregrin, J. 2014. *Inferentialism: Why rules matter*. New York: Palgrave Macmillan.

Perine, M. 1990. Éducation, violence et raison: De la discussion socratique à la sagesse weilienne. In *Discours, violence et langage: Un socratisme d'Éric Weil*, 109–158. Paris: Éditions Osiris.

Perine, M., and E. Costeski. 2016. *Violência, educação e globalização: Compreender o nosso tempo com Eric Weil*. Edições Loyala.

Price, H. 1992. Metaphysical pluralism. *The Journal of Philosophy* 89 (8): 387–409.

Sellars, W. 1997. *Empiricism & the philosophy of mind*. Cambridge MA: Harvard University Press.

Soetard, M. 1984. Éric Weil: Philosophie et éducation. In *Actualité d'Éric Weil*, ed. C.É. Weil. Paris: Beauchesne.

Weil, E. 1950. *Logique de la philosophie*. Paris: Librairie Philosophique Vrin.

———. 1956. *Philosophie politique*. Paris: Librairie Philosophique Vrin.

———. 1957. Education as a problem for our time. *Confluence* 6 (1): 40–50.

———. 1961. *Philosophie morale*. Paris: Librairie Philosophique Vrin.

———. 1970a. *Essais et conférences: Tome 1*. Paris: Librarie Plon.

———. 1970b. Humanistic studies, their object, methods and meaning. *Daedalus* 99 (2): 237–255.

———. 1989. In *Valuing the humanities*, ed. W. Kluback. Paris: Historians Press.

———. 1993. *Cahiers Éric Weil IV: Essais sur la philosophie, démocratie et éducation*. Paris: Presses Universitaires de Lille.

———. 2003. *Philosophie et réalité: Tome 1*. Paris: Beauchesne.

Chapter 7
The *Logic of Philosophy* as a Theory of Argumentation

7.1 Introduction

In the preceding chapters, I presented how Eric Weil theorizes violence, what violence means to his theory, and how his manner of theorizing violence throws down a challenge which philosophy must answer if it wants to be comprehensive and reasonable. He shows how violence bookends reason, understood as coherent discourse in situation, and how violence is fundamentally entangled with language since both are the concrete expressions of human spontaneity. This, I argue, forces us to re-examine the rational tradition that characterizes the human individual as a reasonable animal. For Weil, the individual *can* be reasonable, but only because they can *also* be unreasonable, because they can refuse the normative weight that reasonable discourse places upon individuals. In other words, this normative weight holds only as long as individuals see themselves as submitted to it. This leads us to read the *Logic of Philosophy* as a theory of argumentation. What is meant by this?

The last three quarters of a century have seen an explosion of argumentation theory. The early isolated and independent efforts of Stephen Toulmin's *The Use of Argument*,[1] Chaïm Perelman and Lucie Olbrechts-Tyteca's *Traité de argumentation*,[2] and Charles Hamblin's *Fallacies*,[3] as well as the collective efforts of the German "schools" in Erlangen (centered around the work of Paul Lorenzen, Wilhelm Kamlah, and Kuno Lorenz) and in Frankfurt (centered around Jürgen Habermas and Karl-Otto Apel) have inspired a teeming field of research both inside and outside of

---
[1] Toulmin (2003).
[2] Perelman and Olbrechts-Tyteca (1958).
[3] Hamblin (1970).

© The Author(s), under exclusive license to Springer Nature
Switzerland AG 2023
S. Yiaueki, *Action, Meaning, and Argument in Eric Weil's Logic of Philosophy*,
Logic, Argumentation & Reasoning 32,
https://doi.org/10.1007/978-3-031-24082-9_7

philosophy.[4] These early developments are important because they sought to reinsert the *practical* aspect of argumentation into reasoning, notably by looking at the way that arguments imply a dialogue between different people. This lines up with one of Eric Weil's constant affirmations: philosophy is a dialogical process.[5] In fact, Paul Ricœur has noted that, for Weil, philosophy is merely an ideal case of dialogical processes, and that, in fact, all "speaking is entering into a relationship of argumentation" with an interlocutor where violence is ruled out.[6] This assessment is accepted by Perelman and Olbrechts-Tyteca, for example. They even use their reading of Eric Weil and his insistence on the refusal of violence as a prerequisite for the possibility of argumentation. This constitutes the starting point of their own theory. In line with their reading of Weil, they note that "argumentation is an action that is always aiming to modify a state of preexisting things."[7] This is one of the key elements to understanding the *Logic of Philosophy* as a theory of argumentation. According to this reading, Weil presents philosophy as a fundamentally dialogical enterprise that looks to transform the world through reasonable action—even if it does not in itself exclude the possible recourse to counter-violence. This reading also holds another key to understanding Weil's work as a theory of argumentation, namely its horizon of action. The horizon that this dialogical enterprise aims at is "the advent of a world where both individuals and communities will be able to assert and exercise their rights by exclusively non-violent means, of a world where action through the exchange of arguments alone will be effective."[8]

Reasonable action, for Weil, takes the form of a certain type of philosophical practice. It is to be understood as the deployment of arguments, not just in order to understand the natural world but in order to shape the social and political one, in order to act on humanity and on human discourse, as the means of understanding reality as a whole. In this way, Weil's theory of argumentation has much in common with the Frankfurt School, most notably with Jürgen Habermas's "theory of

---

[4] For an excellent discussion on the development of the different currents of argument theory and the way that they started to constitute a more or less unified field of study, see Wohlrapp (2014), xxxii–lviii. Nonetheless, to my knowledge, the history remains to be written detailing why Germany, in the wake of the Second World War, produced so many thinkers who dealt with argument head on. The fractures within German society brought on by the Second World War almost certainly play a constitutive role, but this cannot be the only reason. The seeds are probably also to be found in the intellectual climate before the war. The question concerning the developments that led so many people to ask the question of argumentation thus remains open. Because Weil was trained as a philosopher in Germany during the interwar period, and because his results seem so much of a piece with these developments, I think he should be placed in the same intellectual context of the Erlangen School and the second generation of the Frankfurt School.

[5] Weil has a clear position concerning the importance of dialogue, but much of *my* thinking on the subject has also been informed by the dialogical community at the University of Lille. For the most mature statement of the "Lille School" of dialogical logic, see Rahman et al. (2018).

[6] Ricœur (1991).

[7] Perelman and Olbrechts-Tyteca (1958), § 13.

[8] Canivez (2013b), 55.

7.1 Introduction

communicative action."[9] This has even led to the proposal of reading Weil's political philosophy as a *Diskursethik*,[10] and has led multiple studies that investigate this possibility.[11] While the relationship between Habermas and Apel's philosophical projects and Weil's is interesting and philosophically important, I will not be dealing with it here. Instead, in this chapter, I will sketch the place of non-violence in establishing the domain of argumentation and how, within that domain, Weil makes a difference between two registers of argumentation, namely discussion and dialogue. These differences will lead me to discuss what Weil sees as the goals and as the horizon of argumentative practices: the advent of a world where reasonable action is not only possible but effective. This horizon however can only be understood by developing certain concepts that Weil puts into place to flesh out his theory of argumentation, notably the concept of orientation and its neighboring concepts of satisfaction and contentment. Once these concepts are adequately presented I will argue that as a theory of discursive commitment, the *Logic of Philosophy* transitions into a theory of *political* action. In other words, the reasonable action that philosophy describes becomes the actual action of the individual that has moved through the circle of understanding found in the *Logic of Philosophy*. This implies acting on a world that holds the teeming multiplicity of all the "irreparable fragments"[12] of discourses that aim at meaning.

It is the admission of multiple discursive centers in Weil's work that brings him to elaborate the notion of the reprise. This concept must play a key role in any development of a theory of argumentation that can be drawn out of Weil's work. With that in mind, I will then look at the importance of the hermeneutical role of this concept in the *Logic of Philosophy* and present the analysis, by way of example, of the way that Weil presents the concept GOD through the interplay of various reprises. This will help demonstrate the hermeneutical importance of reading the *Logic of Philosophy* as a theory of argumentation and will lead me to look at Weil's notion of discursive openness that reprises help us to grasp. By focusing on the openness to possible discourses, Eric Weil's philosophy allows us to formulate a strategic hypothesis about how to use different reprises in order to bring others into argumentative practices. In fact, reading the *Logic of Philosophy* in this way will allow us to tie together everything that we have seen so far and will place us on a path towards understanding the way that the logic of philosophy can help us tackle contemporary philosophical problems. This, I argue, is the originality of the reading presented here.

---

[9] Habermas (1984, 1985). However, there is also a main difference, namely that Habermas inscribes his theory in an immanent rationality of discursive exchanges, whereas Weil shows the way that language can be used to reject the rational and above all the reasonable.

[10] Bizeul (2006), 147–151.

[11] Deligne (1998); Ganty (1997); Bobongaud (2011).

[12] Paul Ricœur uses this turn of phrase to describe the state of discourse in Weil's work while attributing it to Pierre-Jean Labarrière. See Ricœur (1984).

7.2 Serious Conversation, Dialogue, and Discussion

The theory of argumentation that we can draw out of Weil's work is tightly linked to his critique of the rational tradition. The emphasis that Weil places on the *possibility* of reasonable behavior—a possibility that only exists side by side with the possibility of violence—allows us to complete Weil's own order of explanation. This possibility is grounded by a choice to be reasonable and by a decision to stay reasonable facing the irrationality or a-reasonability of others. This is Weil's central discursive commitment. It is also a decision, an act, that grounds all other discursive commitments. It is an entry into discourse and to being reasonable. Thus, Weil's order of explanation starts from a free act to enter discourse that is counter-balanced inside of discourse by the development of semantic content, and, more importantly here, by that development's implied fallibilism (understood as systematic openness). Fallibilism is not a visible starting point. It is a result that people come to and that Weil sees as an essential component of an individual's capacity to remain reasonable. Fallibilism is the expression of the choice to be reasonable at the interior of discourse facing multiple conflicting contents. This is why it is not visible. Reasonable behavior is a slow and long historical process that is still unfinished. It is therefore only reflexive analysis that allows the individual to grasp the choice and thus to continue to labor towards reasonability.

Individuals are domesticated into reasonable behavior through their families, their education, their community, their surroundings, and so forth. This is what allows reasonable behavior, because families, education, communities transmit the sedimentation of the history of other reasonable behavior. But this is also what slows the development of reasonable behavior. Families, education, communities all also hold the structural presence of violence. This double presence of reasonability and violence is what allows individuals to refuse any given and any behavior that claims to have a monopoly on reasonability. Something they will do all the more forcefully when their education, their family situation, or their place in a social strata has excluded them from full participation in society or when their own experience is grounded in violence. Thus, bringing people to see the value of reasonability is always a pressing matter. It is only once the individual has become aware of the possibility of reasonability and once they have committed to that possibility that doubt and difference have any weight. This lines up with Weil's definition of the "task of philosophy" which is to create a dialogue between diverse opinions, points of view, and commitments (PR.I.17). Weil notes that, "philosophy can only begin its undertaking if such an undertaking is needed, if the situation is such that contradictory 'wisdoms' exist in reality, and if these 'wisdoms,' these absolute convictions, are such that a conflict between them becomes possible" (PR.I.17). This implies that a plurality of discourses not only exist, but have good reason for existing, because these discourses organize a plurality of ways of life and of human existence. In this case, philosophy cannot disregard any of these *attitudes*, but rather must see what is true and good in these diverse positions and see whether they can be organized together.

7.2 Serious Conversation, Dialogue, and Discussion

The reality of the plurality of discourses and attitudes leads Weil to refuse to see discourse as primarily establishing a relationship between the world and a mind. This is because there are always already multiple implicit understandings of the world and they reveal themselves to us through the plurality of discourses and through the plurality of oppositions that we use to make them explicit. Instead, Weil sees discourse as the means by which individuals orient their action. This practical orientation in the world is inseparable from our understanding of the world and of what is meaningful in it. This is why no relationship to the world needs to be established, it is always already there. Here, what reading Weil's position as a theory of argumentation adds is that any explanation of discourse must start from discourse itself. What we act upon when we act reasonably is our discourse and that of others. Making claims of truth or of objectivity, justifying points of view, all of the bread and butter of philosophy, implies that there are multiple claims about truth, that objectivity is not yet secured, that points of view need justification, and all this starts and progresses through argument. In other words, "the plurality of theses is essential for philosophy, a plurality that, if it is not overcome in dialogue and in reasonable discourse, makes violence an authority, of course not of judgment, but nonetheless of decision" (PR.I.12). As the category of *Discussion* shows, it is only when dialogue and reasonable discourse fail that individuals look outside of discourse to ground it, in order to hold back the violence that lies in wait. In fact, the path through the logic of philosophy teaches us that all attempts to ground discourse start in argumentative practices whether the proposed ground is an object in the world, the individual's sentiment, God, the empirical observation of the quantifiable sciences, moral consciousness, the free activity of the human intelligence, the uniqueness of the individual in their struggle with others, or even absolutely coherent discourse itself. They start in argumentative practices that are witness to the capacity of individuals to ignore arguments. It is this capacity, recognized in others, that leads individuals to become aware of the social nature and the social importance of argumentation. The refusal of coherent discourse makes us become painfully aware that this refusal itself is latent in even the most reasonable discourse as the exercise of human freedom, which can oppose itself to the truth that argumentation is working to establish by enclosing itself in a single form of coherence. This refusal shows that discourse *is* grounded in argumentative practices, practices wherein the individual is aware of the finitude of their own position and their own life, but wherein they embrace that finitude instead of forgetting it, ignoring it, or fearing it. It starts in argumentative practices that see argument as the reasonable action that can inscribe *legitimate* changes in the world and in reality.

This reading thus presents the *Logic of Philosophy* as an interactive and dynamic model of argumentation by showing how the different categories present different aspects of our human life as irreducible. This irreducibility allows individuals to create a multitude of coherent discourses from any of these aspects. However, because Weil understands each aspect as irreducible aspects of *human* experience, they all exist together in the same individual. Weil claims that:

> all the categories of reflection meet in action, as in their completion, with those of the Absolute and the absolute revolt. The *personality* that grasps itself as a feeling facing the *Absolute* that is *God*, but a God that is absolutely revealed as the coherence to be realized, has found its *work* in its *finiteness*: it is the *free consciousness* that imposes itself on the *condition* in order to transform this condition according to its own *interest* that it now knows to be singular and essential, and in virtue of which it can *interpret* what is (LP, 413).

In other words, these are the reprises that Eric Weil proposes to create a holistic image of the individual embedded in the natural world, interacting with their fellow humanity. It shows an image of the individual as the junction between Reason, Freedom, and Being, as a potentially reasonable individual with a discourse that can act spontaneously according to their feeling in the world in order to change their feeling, the world, or both. This is only possible because of the social articulation of reason. It is because reason is dialogical and not monological. Speaking itself is participating in this "dialogue that is human language: monologue and silence are born of dialogue" (PR.I.280). But because this dialogue is itself a consequence of legitimate conflicts and differences individuals must overcome, and overcome reasonably if they want to remain reasonable, they must find a reasonable way to settle them.

Reading the *Logic of Philosophy* this way focuses on the hermeneutical as well as the strategic aspects of the text, because these aspects allow individuals to grasp other forms of coherence than their own, both in order to understand them and in order to act upon them. These aspects are already present in the passage just cited. The individual in their feeling aims at a unity that allows their action, defined by their interest, to be meaningful and to be interpreted as meaningful. Here, the criteria for meaningfulness is a unity not just of thought, but of thought and action, of a life seen as a whole, as an individual embedded in a *cosmos*, embedded in a meaningful reality filled with others. This, for Weil, is the criteria for meaningful action, seeing one's action (both in the political sense and in the inter-individual sense) as having an effect and as being meaningful. When this does not happen, one is again led to degenerate forms of discursive commitment such as cynicism, skepticism, nihilism, and so forth. These forms are degenerate not because they do not exist, or because they cannot be held concretely, but because they are not autonomous. They only exist in opposition, and their coherence is found in the refusal of the positions that they attack. They only exist in relation to another substantive discursive position, and they are derivative forms of commitments. This again is why every coherent discourse has its cynics, skeptics, and nihilists. They refuse, doubt, and despair in the face of the possibility of a coherent and universal meaning. They are dissatisfied with the discourses laid out before them that claim to be coherent and universal without proposing any autonomous coherent universal alternative. Rather, they capitulate before the contradictions and difficulties of elaborating a coherent discourse that grasps itself. This leads to the degeneration of the content of other discursive commitments. The irony is that in their refusal of meaning, they nonetheless create enough of a unity of meaning to allow the individual—the cynic, skeptic, or nihilist—to orient their thought and action. Even though this unity contains an internal contradiction which creates a structural incoherence in their position, it *is*

7.2 Serious Conversation, Dialogue, and Discussion

nonetheless sufficient to orient their activity. In this way, these forms of incoherent coherence have real pragmatic effects: people act because of them. In order to understand how this happens, and to understand what Weil sees as the structure of argumentation and reasonable action, we must develop three technical concepts that will make up a Weilian theory of argumentation. These are serious conversation, discussion, and dialogue.

The distinction between discussion and dialogue is present in the *Logic of Philosophy* but it is most clearly developed in a text called "Vertu du dialogue."[13] Serious conversation, on the other hand, is only used once in the *Logic of Philosophy*. Nonetheless, based on the way that he uses the adjective "serious" throughout his work, there is good reason to think that he uses it in a specific technical sense. Seriousness (and thus serious conversation) is used to characterize a specific aspect of language use. In the *Logic of Philosophy*, Weil speaks of the dialogue that concerns serious problems (LP, 24), the weight of serious questions that we are unable to grasp and formulate (LP, 38), the serious claims that are opposed to poetic irony (LP, 250), the serious activity and the serious game that the intelligence finds in human interest (LP, 275), the constitutive act of the personality that takes itself seriously (LP, 303). It quickly becomes clear that all these examples of seriousness fall in line with serious conversation, which for Weil is, "all conversation that, in principle, is supposed to lead to agreement" (LP, 23). Serious conversation is a specific assertoric form of language use that aims at agreement. It is the term Weil uses to define general argumentative practices. In this way, both discussion and dialogue are subspecies of serious conversation. If we accept the hypothesis that "serious conversation" is the term Weil uses to characterize general argumentative practices, it becomes clear that it is dialogue and not discussion that fills the ideal of serious conversation. Weil notes that "dialogue will only last if it is serious, if it takes place in the face of a possible action, in view of a result" (PR.I.289). This lines up with Patrice Canivez's interpretation of the place of discussion and dialogue in Eric Weil's work whereby dialogue represents an "ideal of communication with interlocutors aiming at consensus based on the force of the best argument."[14] This differs from discussion, which is, for Weil, a political concept.[15] In fact, the difference between dialogue and discussion is a difference of goals. For Weil, "dialogue always ultimately bears on how we ought to live" (LP, 24). It thus governs the substantive

---

[13] This text is posterior to the *Logic of Philosophy*, nonetheless Gilbert Kirscher makes a convincing case that the distinction is already present in the *Logic of Philosophy*, in Kirscher (1990). Kirscher argues that what Weil presents as discussion in the *Logic of Philosophy* corresponds to what he will later call "*dialogue antique*," which is best translated somewhere between "ancient dialogue" and "the dialogue of antiquity," and which corresponds to the public resolution of differences through argumentative practices in order to assure the social cohesion of the city-state.

[14] Canivez (2020b).

[15] This lines up with Weil's analysis of the category of *Discussion*, which looks at arguments at the level of their form and not of their content. This is also why the goal of *Discussion* is to reground the community and not to ground our concepts. The individual in *Discussion* is only derivatively looking to grasp the world as it is in itself. We can therefore say that instead of looking to *get* things right, they are looking to *be* right.

normative content that makes up the background of our decisions and our lives. It looks to get to the bottom of our values and our beliefs in order to correct and modify them. Discussion on the other hand is at the same time both the defense of one's interest by discursive means and the debate on the meaning of values (which in its fully articulated political form is not the discussion between individuals but is between institutions and states through representatives). However, because discussion also includes the defense of one's interests, it can always devolve into a form of bargaining or haggling in order for one's interests to prevail. This leads to a situation where "decisions are made based on a sometimes laboriously concluded compromise, rarely under the form of a consensus."[16] With this distinction in mind, we can look at what Weil sees as the regulatory and constitutive laws of dialogue (PR.I.282) in order to understand what the ideal of serious conversation is and to better understand Weil's conception of argumentation. These laws are not exhaustive, rather they are the minima needed for serious conversation to take place. These laws are:

1. the ruling-out of violence,
2. the acceptance of the *method* of discussion itself,
3. grounding principles
   (a) a criterion of truth
   (b) the agreement of what constitutes a fact
4. facts

These laws are the minima, but even these minima have, throughout history, been difficult to establish. Part of the reason is that the object of dialogue can change and can turn into a discussion about the goodness of the grounding principles, such as what truth is, or what facts are. Even when these minima are met, they do not guarantee what the content of dialogue will be. This is because content inscribes itself in human history and, in this way, is part of its dynamic movement of that same history. The notion of truth that people start from and the facts that people accept are therefore, at this point, inconsequential. Dialogue has to get off the ground before it can settle anything. If this does not happen, dialogue does not exist. As Weil notes:

> no dialogue exists between human beings that are convinced of having truths that are both absolute and concrete: it is only so long as their truths are not absolute but formal, or so long as their truths are concrete, but not absolute, that they can come to an agreement or at least understand why they do not understand each other. To summarize in a single sentence: no dialogue exists unless each participant admits that the other participants are as reasonable as they are. (PR.I.282–283)

Weil sees these laws of dialogue as both constitutive and regulative precisely because they depend on, constitute, and govern dialogue's major presupposition, namely the existence of a community. However, there is an ambiguity between the

---

[16] Canivez (2020b).

notion of a *discursive* community and other forms of community.[17] In terms of a theory of argumentation, it is the discursive community that matters. This minimal criterion for agreement happens inside of a *discursive* community, which is to be understood as one where violence has already been ruled out as a way of settling conflicts. Different forms of communities exist together and in order to distinguish them we need a variety of criteria. It is nonetheless important to note that, for Weil, all communities are born in a pre-political form of organization. In this way, all communities initially start as discursive communities built around shared values, a shared criterion of truth, and a shared conception of facts. This pre-political characteristic is what distinguished the community from the State, which, for Weil, is the political form historical communities take as they continue to organize themselves in order to make conscious decisions with the aim of assuring their "long-term existence."[18] From our contemporary point of view, political communities are themselves internally differentiated into different social strata, and these strata may themselves be in conflict. In principle however, they all remain in the discursive community to the extent that (again in principle) violence is ruled out in their interactions. Modern political communities are also to be distinguished from modern society, which Weil sees as the globalizing (though not fully globalized) organization and rationalization of different laboring communities into an interconnected whole (PP, 61–92). Modern society is not a single discursive community precisely because violence is not, as a principle, ruled out in the interactions between the different communities that make up society. By giving these criteria, we are able to distinguish pre-political communities from global society and from different states, and to see how discursive communities are interwoven into these different forms of association. This also allows us to identify the discursive community as the space of serious conversation because it is therein that the object of serious conversation is decided. The State, for example, is the discursive community where the discussion between different parties, different social strata, and different unions of interest takes place (PP, 209). This discussion allows this community (both political and discursive) to collectively become aware of its conflicts and problems. It is the awareness of the collective and shared nature of these problems that acts to ground the community.

This requires however that we distinguish between different levels of language use. Reading the *Logic of Philosophy* as a theory of argumentation requires specifying what kind of language use is implied by Weil. As I have said, serious conversation, because it seeks to create an agreement that matters, can be seen as the assertoric language use that makes truth-claims. It is a specific type of language use with a specific type of goal. For Weil, it is born out of contradiction and is "destined, in principle, to lead to an agreement" (LP, 23) by confronting "the convictions that

---

[17] This may be another reason for the ambiguity in the concept of the space of reasons that was highlighted last chapter in Kukla and Lance's analysis. Materially, it is clear that no single concrete discursive community presently exists. Nonetheless, one of the goals of argumentative practices is to create one.

[18] Canivez (1993), 174–175.

are present in the historic world" (PR.I.292). What does it mean that it is born out of contradiction? When we discuss with others we are made aware of the partiality or the fallibility of our theses because other people say other things. Argument is born out of a "natural" plurality of claims about the world. If philosophy wants to resolve this problem it must take this into account. However, for Weil, this fact is obscured because, as social creatures, our situation always presents itself as the constitution of the community itself. This initial social reality is taken to be natural and so the scope of contradictions is actually already relatively limited. This is why the initial role of logic in its *Socratic* form, understood as the science of dialogue, is to eliminate remaining contradictions.

This initial *Socratic* form of logic is found in the public exchange of reasons in the discursive community. As already show, this is not the only logic that Weil identifies. Weil develops different logics according to the different fundamental oppositions that have appeared in the history of philosophy. These are: (1) the formal (but not formalized) logic of the Socratic dialogue, which opposes commitments and their accompanying incompatibilities and consequences at the level of their form; (2) the logic of classical ontology, which opposes reason and nature; (3) Kantian transcendental logic, which opposes nature and freedom; and finally, (4) Hegelian dialectic logic, which opposes determined conceptual contents as a means of unfolding the semantic consequences of material inferences. This development allows Weil to present a final opposition, the opposition between truth and freedom. As was shown in the last chapter, Weil's own opposition implies a two-stage conception of logic, the pragmatic negation, as a moment of freedom, and the abstract negation, as a moment in the determination of semantic content and truth. However, just because Weil sees this as the fundamental opposition, it does not mean that these other logical forms disappear. Because one of the goals of a Weilian theory of argumentation is to create or reground the discursive community, this Socratic form of contradiction plays a key role. As different forms of opposition, Weil's elaboration of the different logical moments reveals the order of logical reflection. The pragmatic negation comes first, but we conceptualize it last. This is why serious conversation starts from a willingness to discuss and why such reflection on the structure of argumentative practices is a later development. There is no *content* that unconditionally compels us to discuss. It is only after opponents see themselves as partners in dialogue (even when this happens implicitly) that the abstract negation has any hold on interlocutors. The first level of discussion then is always Socratic. It assumes a shared principle, and thus progresses as though the only contradictions to be eliminated were the *remaining* ones. Different breakdowns in discussion lead to the need for different discursive resources. As the logic of philosophy progresses, it becomes clear that it can no longer be a matter of eliminating remaining contradictions, but is a matter of facing the fundamental contradictions that arise because people are situated in different categories, and thus have different grounding principles. This is why, when Socratic discussion fails, individuals develop the grounding concepts of their discourses. Their disagreement is seen as going deeper than the superficial level of the form. If discussion still fails, but individuals refuse to give up their meta-commitment to reasonable argumentative practices, and if they are committed to getting to the bottom of things, other logical tools are available. By presenting the different logical oppositions the way it does, the *Logic of Philosophy* provides these tools as the steps that allow individuals to maintain their meta-commitment to reasonable discourse and to orient their goal of getting to the bottom of things. This will pass through the Kantian reflection of the role that the self-determining subject plays in determining content and through the Hegelian reflection on the role that opposition plays in allowing concrete content itself to be determined. And finally it will pass through a reflection of the kinds of relationships that individuals can have to discourse, and the kind of metavocabularies that are needed to make all of this explicit. This is one way of looking at the structure of the theory of argumentation that can be drawn out of the *Logic of Philosophy*. Coming to an agreement happens through the exchange of arguments in order to identify where disagreement lies and what each side's grounding principle is. It implies developing the consequences of these grounding principles and the individual's realization that they have a hand in determining their content, but only because the opposition with other principles and with other concrete individuals allows them to do so. The continual exchange of arguments then shows them that they must also decide *knowingly* what they want their relationship to discourse to be. Knowingly, because they understand that this will change their commitments and the discursive score, that is, the normative status attributed to them. This is, for Weil, the most reasonable way to work to modify substantive beliefs and concrete attitudes. This is action in the fullest sense.

Argumentation thus starts from the minimal agreement that is necessary for serious conversation—assertoric, truth-conditional language use—to take place. Because there are different concrete grounding principles, there is in some sense always a minimum disagreement as well, or at least, a minimum confusion. In other words, if there were not a minimum disagreement born from the natural plurality of points of view, we would have no need for serious conversation. This minimal agreement and its accompanying minimal disagreement are what allows us to go from a descriptive language to a normative language. We go from saying what *is* to what *should be*. In other words, we start by taking for granted that our grasp of the world is the way the world is. Our disagreement shows us that this is not naturally the case and we start trying to work out what one *should* take to be true, how the community *should* be organized, how one *should* act, what one *should* do, etc. Because the minimal agreement and the minimal disagreement are so closely intertwined, philosophy, serious conversation, is not always clear to itself. This is also because people flit in and out of serious conversation. This is why, for Weil, reasonability is an exceptional state. Philosophy depends on serious conversation, or what Brandom calls language's "downtown,"[19] but Weil is interested in understanding how people can, in some sense, live in the suburbs without ever going into town. If this is the case, then the majority of our language use may be further away from the serious conversation than we would like to think. It may in fact be closer to a discursive form of social grooming (something that allows us to maintain and reinforce

---

[19] Brandom (1994).

our relationships to each other), than to any ideal of dialogue.[20] So, Weil agrees with the rational tradition and the pride of place it gives to assertoric language use, because he admits that it is central to the organization of meaning (though not to its production), however he critiques this same tradition by warning us about an underlying risk. This risk is the smugness that philosophers can get caught up in when they take assertoric language use to be of greater *dignity* than all other forms because of its importance. For Weil, language in its spontaneity is the depository of *all* uses and of *all* discourses. Weil notes that "[a]ll discourse is meaningful and so participates in meaning" (LP, 54). What we can add here is that all language use participates in it as well. This does nothing to change the fact though that Weil is attacking this question as a philosopher and thus is principally interested in serious conversation.

The line of demarcation between types of language use is at best fuzzy, and at worst, not even fuzzy, but only clear in critical moments. Indeed, the fact that individuals flit in and out of serious conversation actually shows the depth of agreement that actually exists. Within the discursive community, we only need it by moment in order to correct a ship that is for the most part cutting straight through the water.[21] In other words, our attitudes are shot through with every register of language, with all types of prosodic effects, all sorts of pragmatic considerations, and the goal that serious conversation gives to itself is to reduce the conceptual fuzziness. This is important. It opens up a perspective which will be a practical result of Weil's model of argumentation. Namely, multiple strategies are needed to bring people to discourse. These strategies aim at showing people what the consequences of their commitments are and then asking them whether they are willing to face these consequences or not. Certain commitments have unsavory consequences, but nothing can keep people from accepting those consequences. Nonetheless, by making these consequences explicit, and then by presenting other reasoned options, a Weilian theory of argumentation aims at showing people what they have to gain from being reasonable while recognizing their human spontaneity, their resistance, their questions, their doubts, etc., as expression of their freedom. Bringing people to see this is bringing them to see their freedom *as* reasonable.[22] The kinds of strategies

---

[20] When language use does not make genuine claims, it is what Weil calls *speaking without saying anything*. I will come back to this later in the chapter.

[21] The corollary to this is that our level of disagreement is also for the most part well defined. Every individual has someone, whether a group or individual, with whom serious conversation is not even worth the time, because they feel that they would get nothing from the effort. This is a consequent of the material incompatibilities revealed in discursive commitments and the free decision to take on commitments.

[22] Weil analyzes this development at length in *Philosophie politique*, notably in the relationship between the individual and society (PP, 93–128). In these pages, he shows how the modern individual, who is fundamentally dissatisfied, grasps their dissatisfaction and their freedom under the form of the ethical life (in French, Weil uses the term *morale vivante*, which is his way of formulating *Sittlickheit*) that they judge in order to modify. Their judgment is "universal and reasonable" because "it aims at the positive freedom of individuality both in its universality and in its historical situation" (PP, 105).

that are needed look to bring people to see this even when they do not initially see any interest in it, or when they refuse the interest because they think that no agreement can be reached, or more seriously, when they refuse the interest knowingly and explicitly because they want to remain in their particularity. But when they seek to be reasonable, when they do seek to give expression to their doubts, questions, and interests, it is because they are oriented.

7.3 Orientation, Satisfaction, Contentment, and Action

The individual always finds themself in a community. This is what makes dialogue possible. The state of this community's institutions, of its science, of its art, are the things that give the individual a naïve sense of orientation. The individual knows what they are *supposed* to want based on their pre-reflexive grasp of the structures that surround them and that form them as individuals.[23] However, one of the characteristic developments of modern society is that it untethers individuals from the force that traditional claims place on them. This, for Weil, has been the long slow work of human negativity. The movement of the *Logic of Philosophy* is defined by the individual's dissatisfaction. Here, what we can add is that by giving their activity an orientation, the individual postulates the kind of satisfaction that they can hope to find in the world. In this way, orientation is another key aspect of Weil's theory of argumentation. He is not the sole thinker to see this. In *The Concept of Argument*, Harald Wohlrapp links the notion of theory with that of orientation and notes that together they play a central role in argument. Wohlrapp makes this move because, for him, theory is "not a representation of reality, but orientation within it."[24] Eric Weil does something very similar. For him, the role of discourse is "to allow the human being to orient themself in the world" in order to act (LP, 335). Here, Weil modifies the notion of *theoria*, the total view, the "pure sight of the eternal in its positive being" (LP, 49). It is no longer *theoria* that allows us to act, but rather, *theoria* is grounded on the reasonable action that aims at the organic unity of life and discourse, attitude and category. In other words, this is the way that Weil takes back up and reformulates the Greek notion of a *cosmos*, but as a kingdom of ends where the individual sees their life as a meaningful unity and lives it as such.[25] Weil's reading of Kant hinges on the idea that the third *Critique* discovers the

---

[23] I would argue that this pre-reflexive grasp of possible orientations is shaped by bouncing of the normative constraints that are present in any given social setting. In this way, it opens a space of meaningfulness whereby the individual knows what orientations are available to them and what their *uncritical* horizon of meaningful action is. This uncritical horizon is exactly what the free choice to understand bucks against. See the previous chapter for the discussion of how bouncing off rules works.

[24] Wohlrapp (2014), 18.

[25] In the *Logic of Philosophy* Weil explicitly calls the kingdom of ends the "true cosmos" (LP, 49) in his presentation of the way that Kant's transcendental logic subsumes violence under the logical

existence of meaningful facts, or said different, of the fact of meaning, where the world, nature, the *cosmos*, appear as a well-ordered whole to the moral subject. This is because it is in this world that the individual orients their moral action, which is meaningful because it is theirs. The individual however is forced to recognize that they live in a fractured *cosmos* because this kingdom of ends is only ever but a project. This opens a problem between philosophy and theory that Weil develops in the text "Philosophie politique, théorie politique" (EC.II.387–420), between the multiplicity of the points of view of action. For Weil "theories are true and they are at the same time particular, that is, they don't provide all the truth" (EC.II.412).

For Weil, philosophy, because it deals with the possibility of understanding, is formal insofar as it must account for the multiplicity of points of view that exist in the world, and insofar as it must provide a formal description of the possibility of this multiplicity. However, as he notes in the *Logic of Philosophy*, for the individual, in their finitude, philosophy also plays an essential historical role in helping them to decide, take a stance, and orient themself. It makes itself concrete in the individual's action. This is because in order to have an orientation one must know, if not what they want, at least what they don't what and what they won't stand for (LP, 8). This assessment has far-reaching consequences for Weil's theory of argumentation. Weil notes that:

> [a]ny global theory has always consisted in developing the contradiction between the traditional way of doing things and the necessities of the situation, the requirements of that reality in which desires must be satisfied, but which are only satisfied at the price that reality requires: if you want this, you must accept that; if you don't want to accept that, you must submit yourself to the consequences of your refusal, consequences however that you do not desire. (EC.II.402)

There are several key distinctions to unpack in this passage. First, in theory there is a tension between the particular points of view of individual people in individual situations that require individual solutions, and the naïve claims of universality and objectivity that the tradition holds. This is because the tradition is the culmination and residue of previous successful attempts of finding a way of orienting life in the world. This success however is only ever partial because it is adapted to a situation that has now disappeared. This creates a tension in the present, but only for the individual who makes *claims* of universality or of objectivity. Only a partial view can aim at a total view. It is what Weil calls "the necessities of the situation" that puts to the test the naïve orientations that are available to individuals. This is exactly what theory does, it aims at leaving particularity, with its singular situation and its necessities, to provide a global orientation that can be applied by everyone. It looks to describe the state of things in such a way that all can act in and on that state and use the already-elaborated orientation to inform their own. What is interesting here

---

role of contradiction. In his article, "Sens et fait" (PK, 55–107). Weil credits Kant with rediscovering the notion of a *cosmos* (understood as the way that modern subjectivity grasps the unity of life and discourse) in the third *Critique*, but also accuses him of obscuring this fact by expressing the problem and reality of meaning in the language of being (PK, 105). For a clear reading of Weil's interpretation of the third *Critique*, see Canivez (2020a, b).

7.3 Orientation, Satisfaction, Contentment, and Action

is that Weil links the notion of orientation and theory with that of discursive commitment. In order to orient oneself, one elaborates a theory by committing oneself. This however implies that there is already an implicit orientation or attraction towards a position, because as Weil notes, "[t]heories in themselves develop the consequences of different premises, they do not say, if they understand their own limits, whether one must accept these premises or refuse these consequences" (EC.I.405). Theory says nothing about the choice of commitments and about the form of coherence that they imply, nor whether the individual is ready to accept the consequences. The only thing that affirms this choice is the *act* of choosing. This act comes down to the free choice to understand that any individual can make, that is both conditioned and a-reasonable and arbitrary. In fact, the orientation that individuals have is, for Weil, based on the retrospective goal of justifying the choice they didn't previously understand they made. This is what Weil calls the "the hidden and unconscious stance" (EC.I.407) that individuals take. This also allows us to clarify Weil's conception of choice.

By insisting on the *retrospective* element of explaining one's action, Weil's conception of choice seems to be missing the *prospective* element of choice, whereby one projects themself into the future by deciding and planning what they will do. Of course, most choice in Weil's philosophy involves this prospective element, because the individual is always situated in a concrete situation that at least partially allows for positive orientation. The most fundamental choice, the choice between reason and violence, appears to be missing this prospective element. What is one prospectively choosing when they choose reason? While this critique is partially legitimate it misses the main point. The choice against pure violence is the choice of anything but that violence. It is in a sense negative, because the individual does not yet prospectively imagine the form this new life will take. However, the pressure of real violence can be enough to say, "I would rather die than live another day of this." If the individual makes this choice and they carry it through, a new realm of possibilities opens to them where they may then prospectively, positively, and progressively choose what their life will concretely look like. Every refusal of violence gives greater latitude to action. This choice is also revealed in conflict, where individuals either look to overcome, or look to end the conflict, with only the vaguest idea of what the world after could look like. This is also a necessary first step, a step that we must keep taking, in order for the prospective character of choosing to even become visible. This is why Weil's theory starts from concrete dissatisfactions instead of from possible satisfactions. The dissatisfaction that moves the *Logic of Philosophy* forward is however counterbalanced by the satisfaction that is posited as a second step in theory and that orients the individual's research and activity.

In other words, the concept of orientation is given in the formal concept of universality, but as a formal concept, it is without content. In order to see how orientation is deployed (how it acquires content) in the theory of argumentation that we can draw out of Weil's work, we must develop the neighboring concepts of satisfaction and contentment. This is because, as we have noted, argumentation looks to alter a state of things. For Weil, this state of things that theory (above all political theory) aims at is one where, "violence, even when legitimate, is superfluous because everyone finds themself satisfied in their deep and true aspirations" (EC.I.404). This means that it is a vague dissatisfaction that orients the individual to elaborate a notion of satisfaction that (implicitly) only makes sense within a global theory that unites discourse and life into a reasonable whole.

According to Weil, for behavior to be reasonable, that is, for it to be action, it must be directed by an individual that is able to hierarchize their goals and understand the means of realizing these goals in order for these goals to give them direction. In this way, goals and orientation depend on discursive commitments, and reasonable action is the mobilization of these discursive commitments to act upon other discursive commitments. This means the starting point of all action (understood as reasonable activity) is discursive and the goal of action is a stable agreement built out of discourse. When this action is effective it modifies individuals' naïve orientation. Naïve orientations are presented to individuals in the residue of reasonable behavior that has been deposited in the tradition and that makes up the social human second nature. However, it is through argumentative practices that individuals break away from this naïve orientation in order to formulate a new mature orientation. While the concept of orientation runs like a bright thread through the entire *Logic of Philosophy*, it is important that Weil's first substantive presentation of the concept is in the category of *Certainty*. This is because, as I have said in my inferentialist reading of the initial categories, *Certainty* is the category that develops discursive commitment. In this way, whenever anyone takes on a discursive commitment and orients their activity, they reprise *Certainty*. The individual always lives in a world. Each world fixes the goals of those that live in it. Each individual must therefore navigate the goals that are presented to them as given. The way they do this is by evaluating whether these goals, against the background of other possible goals and discursive commitments, will provide satisfaction. In this way, the notion of orientation is inseparable from the notion of satisfaction and dissatisfaction. The individual identifies what is unsatisfying in the orientations and descriptions to which, thanks to the tradition, they are heir. This identification allows them to elaborate new satisfactions, which through argumentation they can claim apply to the whole world. The problem however, according to Weil, is that this process is interminable. New satisfactions constantly unearth new dissatisfactions. This is what pushes Weil to elaborate a reflection on the idea of contentment. Contentment, for Weil, is the satisfaction of living in a meaningful world, a satisfaction that gives meaning to the diversity of one's action in this world. This form of satisfaction fills the individual's desire for the freedom to live a life in a meaningful world and a meaningful community. Contentment is thus a kind of "meta-satisfaction." It cannot be filled like individual satisfactions can because it is the satisfaction of understanding the mechanisms of the world and one's place within it.

Given the place that Weil gives to negativity in his theory, to the pragmatic negativity that opens semantic possibility, to the capacity to negate any and every given, it should not be a surprise that here again negativity rears its head. Taken as a positive result, satisfaction must pass through the dialogical controls that argument provides to be considered valid. Valid satisfaction, if achieved in the concrete existence of an actual life, is a result. In theory, it is merely a hypothesis. Thus, for Weil, we

7.3 Orientation, Satisfaction, Contentment, and Action

orient ourselves through our dissatisfaction and from that dissatisfaction we propose possible satisfactions to orient our activity. The orientation that a *possible* satisfaction provides, while necessary, is for Weil, insufficient. This is because a satisfaction (as opposed to contentment) of a specific object or thing does nothing to exhaust dissatisfaction, all it does is leave the place open to a new determined desire that creates a new determined dissatisfaction that needs to itself be filled. A sudden desire for Hawaiian pizza is only satisfied by a Hawaiian pizza. This will both satisfy my hunger and my specific desire, but my hunger will return and may create a desire for madras curry. We can understand this movement of dissatisfaction and satisfaction in Weil's theory by comparing it to the Hegelian model of bad, or spurious, infinity. According to this model, spurious infinity is "the negation of the finite."[26] In other words, in a series of finite determinations, an individual can always posit the said determination's negation of "one more" in order to continue the series. For instance, no number, no matter how great, can be said to be the last number in a series because it is always possible to add one more. Instead of calling this series infinite, it would perhaps be better to call it unfinishable, because the series is determined by the possibility of continuing. It is spurious because it has not yet proved to be or not to be infinite (this is why it is unfinishable) and because it cannot guarantee that this continuation itself is infinite. It could in fact stop at any moment, although, up until now, it never has. This is why it presents itself as infinite. Hegel notes that there are infinite new determinations but with each one "we are back at the previous determination, which has been sublated in vain."[27]

According to this comparison, satisfactions are the negation of dissatisfactions, but following the model of spurious infinity, all this does is reveal a new dissatisfaction that requires to be sated anew. For Hegel, spurious infinity is born out of the Dialectic of the Understanding (*Verstand*) which separates and determines. This is opposed to the Dialectic of Reason (*Vernunft*) that creates true or good infinity which comprehends (in both senses of the word) all determinations. If we interpret Weil's notion of satisfaction along the lines of Hegel's spurious infinity, each satisfaction is merely followed by the existence of another satisfaction, and so there is never any satisfaction of satisfaction, so to speak. This requires a different concept, a concept of freedom from dissatisfaction understood as all-encompassing, and as being stable in the face of the continual resurgence of satisfaction and its accompanying dissatisfaction. Weil formulates this notion of freedom from satisfaction according to two terms, contentment and presence, which he understands as fundamentally being the same.[28] Contentment unites satisfaction and dissatisfaction the way that true infinity unites the finite and the infinite in a dialectic that encompasses them both. Here, reason as contentment and presence is the final and absolute formulation of the goal of the *Logic of Philosophy*. It is what orients Weil's discourse

---

[26] Hegel (2015), 109/GW 21.124.
[27] Hegel (2015), 112/GW 21.129.
[28] He calls contentment "the silence filled with presence" (LP, 13) and presence "contentment in freedom" (LP, 419).

and is his claim of what the orientation of discourse is. This falls in line with the temporal analysis that we gave to Weil's position, that philosophy is future-facing. The future is not fixed. If we were just the playthings of necessity we would have no need for argumentation, but it is because we see our action as having real effects on our lives that we act. We see ourselves before a variety of different choices that will have a variety of different outcomes, and so we seek to be the agents of those outcomes. But we face the resistance of the world and of others and we need to understand that resistance in discourse if we are to overcome it thanks to discourse.

Turning, in the present, towards the past in order to turn towards the future and understand *how* to act, is the reasonable activity of philosophy. Contentment would be the achievement of this. However, there is also a modification of this notion. Because Weil presents philosophical possibilities after Hegel, contentment for him is no longer the infinity of reason that finds itself in the world through its own conceptualization of itself. It is no longer contentment full-stop that thinks, it is the individual as an individual, and not as a philosopher. In contentment, the individual would no longer need discourse because, having passed through it, they know how to act, they know how to understand the world and their place in it, a world where there is no more exteriority. It would be the fullness of reasonability and sapience, where every action can be said to be done for reasons, and where all behavior has become action. In contentment, the individual is the plaything of nothing: instinct, history, necessity are all understood as making up the individual just as the individual is seen as having a hand in making them. While this is the orientation of the *Logic of Philosophy*, Weil is very clear about two things. One, most individuals' orientations seek satisfaction and not contentment because most individuals don't need to seek anything for their lives to be united whole in the united whole of nature. They already find it in their life lived, in their mixed attitudes that are partially implicit (as the tradition that is not questioned and that is not facing any crisis) and partially explicit (in the social and political institutions that structure their lives, in this social context's literature, religion, philosophy, art, and culture). Two, contentment is the formal horizon of reasonable action, because there is a plurality of ways that life can be lived as a united whole and because there is no guarantee that this will happen. This sense of a life lived as a united whole in a well-ordered and meaningful world can also be more or less contradictory, precisely because contradiction does not prevent anyone from living. In fact, most people are even happy in their contradictions. This is because it saves them the work and worry of entering choice, in the robust sense used here, which is first the choice between reason and violence and then as the choice between different possible lives. For the individual that wants to make choices, who, in good conscience, wants to understand themselves as free, they can only find contentment in a fully developed discourse, precisely because contentment is what such discourse aims at.

Because a fully developed discourse aims at contentment, it may seem counterintuitive to place so much emphasis on the individual's satisfaction, but in fact, it reveals how the orientation of Weil's reasonable action is supposed to work towards a world where reasonable action is effective. The *Logic of Philosophy* aims at showing the reader how to think their own situation as a situation, but all historical concrete philosophy, all religion, all ideology, all historical and social sciences also do as much. They all allow the individual to think their situation or to contribute to its modification. What is specific about Weil's position is that it aims to do so by making explicit all of the resources of discourse including those that allow characterizing discourse itself. Thus, the only positive result of the *Logic of Philosophy* would be found in the discourse of the individual who factually leaves it behind to think their own experience and by doing so makes it more coherent and comprehensive. But the coherence and the comprehensiveness have to be real and effective. This is only done faced with other individuals by bringing these other individuals to see the *value* of shouldering the same effort for themselves.

Now that the elements of theory, philosophy, action, orientation, etc. are all in place we can see why Weil never calls his position a theory. Like Georges Santayana, Weil "stands in philosophy exactly where [...] [he] stands in daily life."[29] In other words, for Weil, the *Logic of Philosophy* is not a theory, it is a description of the meaningful unity he found in his practice, it shows that he is oriented and that he is acting reasonably by trying to create a world where violence is superfluous. In other words, Weil claims that philosophy must not only understand itself as a theory of free reasonable action in order to understand itself, it must *be* the exercise of that reasonable action. This point has led multiple interpreters to emphasize the transition from "first" philosophy to political philosophy that is opened by the category of the *Action*.[30] According to such readings, Weil's project is the "philosophical justification of political engagement"[31] and its orientation aims at the "real unification of humanity, [...] the inauguration of a global society where the individual will be immediate and where they will enjoy an effective recognition of their rights."[32] Thus for Weil (and after him, for Perelman and Olbrechts-Tyteca), the state of things that is transformed is historical human reality, and the means of transforming that reality is argumentation. This means two things: one, that Weil sees his work as participating in the progress of free reasonable action and two, that a key to understanding free reasonable action is in his work. In order to justify this, we have to see the way that Weil's own position is present in the category of *Action*. This is also where the reprise enters back into the story. For Weil, transforming the world into one where every individual can see their action as reasonable, and where they can see violence as superfluous, requires that the actual discourse of others be taken into account. This is what Patrice Canivez means when he notes that the *Logic of Philosophy* grounds a practice of philosophy as well as a theory of the *reception* of discourse.[33] He notes that for Weil "[t]o understand is to analyze the reprises,"[34] which implies analyzing the organization and structure of one's own discourse (and hierarchy of

---

[29] Santayana (1955), vi.
[30] Sanou (2008).
[31] Savadogo (2003), 15.
[32] Canivez (1993), 251.
[33] Canivez (2013a).
[34] Canivez (2013a).

commitments) as well as that of one's interlocutor. It is through this analysis that argumentation can be effective. It is in this way that a state of things is changed, and the reality to be changed is a *political* reality.

In the domain of non-violence, where violence also exists, but where the individual can turn away from violence in order to try to overcome it, the individual binds themself to an orientation and to specific satisfactions. This orientation and these satisfactions are the coherence they are seeking for themself. However, they also come to understand that their satisfactions are understood only in relation to their embeddedness in a social context. Thus they realize that the only way to be content is by opening the path of contentment to others, through education and argument, all the while being aware that this path can be refused, that the individual can refuse contentment such as it is proposed. This is where the importance of the sequence of categories and the concept of the reprise become all important. For the individual that has adopted the orientation of the logic of philosophy, that is, for the individual who has adopted the goal of working towards a world of contentment through discourse, and who wants to bring people to this contentment by reasonable means, it is essential to be able to identify the central discursive commitments of the person they are facing. Thus the different categories presented by Weil, with the type of permissible inferences that each category allows, provide a framework for understanding the kinds of arguments that may work to bring the interlocutor from one category to the next if they have the meta-commitment to reasonable behavior (understood as choosing to act through reasonable non-violent argumentative practices). This is where the hermeneutical and the strategic aspects of reading the logic of philosophy as a theory of argumentation start to come out.

The categories can thus be understood as a catalogue of arguments that have successfully made claims of coherence, and that, at their level and for the person that lives within them, can make a claim of comprehensiveness, of good infinity. I have already stated that for Weil, the categories are to be seen as governing the kinds of permissible inferences that, starting from a specific essential discursive commitment, structure discourse. Here, we can now add, that in the context of a theory of argumentation, the categories can also be seen as framing devices that provide orientation. That is, they provide a structure of valid claims. In this way, each category will provide a collection of valid orientations that allow the individual to see their life as meaningful. We have already underlined how the categories are ideal-types. Weil goes on to note that it is only through the reprise that they are applied to reality. The reprise is thus another key concept to understanding Weil's position as a theory of argumentation. Throughout this work, I have insisted on the importance of orders of explanation. Here, this importance becomes salient for understanding the categories as fundamental orientations and for understanding the interplay of reprises (that is, the orders of explanation that present themselves as different hierarchies of commitments) as hermeneutical and strategic tools in argumentation. In short, it allows us to understand the types of arguments our interlocutors deploy and how to make argumentative choices ourselves.

7.4 The Conceptual Analysis of the Reprise of *God*

In order to bring out the hermeneutical tools found in the *Logic of Philosophy* I will give, by way of example, an analysis of the different reprises of the attitude/category of *God*. Any attitude/category could have been chosen, nonetheless *God* seems a fitting choice for multiple reasons. It is a category that marks the transition between Antiquity and Modernity and so the outlines of the concept remain easily visible in the categories of both Antiquity and Modernity. Also, the presence of the reprises of *God* have had an enormous influence on the western philosophical tradition and on western civilization in general. This reprise makes the *Logic of Philosophy's* hermeneutical importance particularly revealing. This importance has long been recognized. Outside of the deep influence that Weil had on Paul Ricœur,[35] one of the principal hermeneutists of the twentieth century, the hermeneutical aspect has been underlined by multiple interpreters, whether comparing Weil's work to a single hermeneutist like Gadamer[36] or to multiple.[37] Luis Manuel Bernardo also provides us with an important investigation of the hermeneutical role of Weil's distinction between language and discourse.[38] In its hermeneutical role, the logic of philosophy deploys the categories and different orders of explanation to show how specific discursive positions are organized and understood. It develops the notion of individual orientation and allows us to recognize different discursive positions as real human attitudes. These human attitudes are the result of taking a discursive position that affirms an orientation in the world. Because their central discursive commitment determines an individual's interest and orientation, they see (or feel, or hope: the language here is inconsequential) it to be fundamental. This, in turn, defines both the kinds of inferences that are seen to be permissible as well as those that are seen to be incompatible. This commitment allows the individual the possibility of seeing their life and the world as a *cosmos*, that is, as a meaningful whole (there are nonetheless categories that refuse the possibility of contentment and thus also refuse the grasp of the world as a *cosmos*, these are notably *Meaninglessness, The Condition, The Work,* and *The Finite*). As an individual looks to enter different concepts into this meaningful whole (which can be interpreted here as a space of reasons), they must make these concepts fit with their central discursive commitment. This organization and constant reorganization—these reprises—determine the shape of individual concepts by determining the scope of permissible inferences and incompatibilities. Reprises thus allow us both to understand different possible positions (our own and those of our interlocutors) and to see what kind of arguments

---

[35] Not only did Ricœur come back to Weil's work over and over in order to enrich his own, in an interview in the journal *Alternatives Non-violentes* Ricœur notes "how much he loved Eric Weil" and how important Weil's influence was to his work, see Ricœur (1991). See also Roman (1988); Marcelo (2013); Valdério (2014) for investigations of Weil's influence on Ricœur.

[36] Breuvart (1987); Buée (1987).

[37] Stanguennec (1992).

[38] Bernardo (2003).

can be used in such cases. Understanding our own positions and those of others is a matter of excavating which discursive commitments are present both in our language use and in our acts. This allows us to give reasons for what we do and what we say.

One central aspect of the *Logic of Philosophy* is the claim that certain kinds of discursive positions are irreducible and that people can anchor themselves into these positions and refuse to leave. As a hermeneutical tool, the logic of philosophy allows us to see what is essential to different positions, and gives us an order in which to interpret these different positions. What this means is that even if certain positions are irreducible, there is nonetheless a certain "natural" proximity and distance between them. It is the identification of this "natural" proximity that allows Weil, for instance, to take *Consciousness* by the hand and lead it to action, by passing from an ethic of conviction to one of responsibility (which is one of the goals of the *Logic of Philosophy*). But of course, this only happens for the moral consciousnesses that allow themselves to be so led. It should therefore be easier to bring someone to see another discursive position as reasonable when that natural proximity is respected. In other words, getting somebody to see the importance of the free interplay of the intelligence should be easier if that person already accepts the freedom of the moral consciousness than it would be if that person sees the world exclusively as a causally determined realm known only through empirical experience, or if that person sees the world as the union of reason and feeling in God. Seeing the logic of philosophy as a hermeneutical tool thus allows us to interpret the kind of orientation that goes along with different concepts. It also allows us to make sense of Weil's own position. If we go back to the understanding of the individual that Weil advocates we can see how this takes place. Remember, he states that the reasonable individual is a:

> *personality* that grasps itself as a feeling facing the *Absolute* that is *God*, but a God that is absolutely revealed as the coherence to be realized, has found its *work* in its *finiteness*: it is the *free consciousness* that imposes itself on the *condition* in order to transform this condition according to its own *interest* that it now knows to be singular and essential, and in virtue of which it can *interpret* what is (LP, 413).

This shows that for Weil, in order to see the individual as a meaningful whole, multiple categories need to be reprised. It can thus be argued that these are the reprises that Weil himself uses to build a normative position about how the human individual in their concrete human experience *should* understand themself. However, this normative position defended by Weil does not undermine the different ways that the human individual *can* understand themself and their own concepts. All the concepts in this normative presentation can therefore undergo signification transformation based on categories under which they are being reprised and the order of explanation that is being used to understand the concept. Coming to our example of GOD, this concept and its place in Weil's theory has elicited enormous interest from the commentators,[39] most often investigating the status of the category in the book, or

---

[39] Just to name a few, see Vancourt (1970); Bouillard (1977); Guibal (2013).

7.4 The Conceptual Analysis of the Reprise of *God*

the status of religion in Eric Weil's philosophy. While these questions are interesting, they are not the ones I will be asking. Instead, I will look at the way that the place of this concept in different categories presents different reprises and thus different ways of understanding God. This will help to understand the hermeneutical role the categories and reprises play when we read the *Logic of Philosophy* as a theory of argumentation.

In the passage from the category of *Meaning* cited above, Weil creates an identity between *God* and the *Absolute*, but this is a very specific God, not one that is the realization of ontology thanks to the idea of totality, but rather one that realizes totality through discursive coherence. This is part of the anthropological shift that Henri Bouillard recognizes in Weil's work and notably in his interpretation of God.[40] This helps to explain why the union of reason and feeling in *God* can be lived as a human attitude. In *Meaning*, Weil presents it as the unity of the subject and the object that presents itself as the totality of reality, a reality that has not yet been completed, but that is to be brought into existence. It is brought into existence by the individual who comes to understand and defend their interest in the world and then works to make reality adequate to their interest. The individual only does so facing their own finiteness, and realizes that their interest can only be realized as the interest of humanity. So, Weil's understanding of the meaning of GOD is as a concept that individuals use in order to have a coherent grasp on their life in the world thanks to the way that the idea of totality is mobilized. This is not however the same way that other categories understand the same concept. This version of God is a far cry from the dominant Abrahamic God of the western world. This is also a far cry from the different ways that God is understood according to different categories and different orders of explanation. GOD's hermeneutical usefulness in the *Logic of Philosophy* thus rests on it being a general concept that has a long and deep history, a history that Weil treats repeatedly in his presentation of the different reprises. In this way, we can look at the development of the concept in different categories. This will help us see how the concrete content of this formal concept changes according to the central categorical commitment that an individual takes on. This will also change the way they hierarchize their commitments through reprises. This is why I called the version of the concept treated here formal. The concrete content changes according to the way that the hierarchization of commitments changes which inferences are permissible and which are incompatible.

In the category of *Truth* for example, GOD is a concept that could potentially provide an "understanding in line with universality and the absolute" (LP, 93), but because of this, it loses its singularity. BEING and TRUTH provide the same service. However, like BEING, GOD leads to possible confusion precisely because of how historically charged the reprises of the concepts GOD and BEING are. This is also important, because in tracing the different reprises of GOD we will better see what Weil's choice to start the logic of philosophy from TRUTH implies. In the early categories, before GOD is understood in its categorial purity, TRUTH, GOD, and BEING

---

[40] Bouillard (1977).

are tangled in a confusing semantic, ontological, and metaphysical bundle. It is only as these different concepts are separated that the full force of a logic of philosophy becomes clear. In its own development, GOD culminates in the category that bears its name as a unity of reason and feeling, however BEING and TRUTH are still interpreted as part of this unity. After this category, GOD is reinterpreted according to human concepts while BEING and TRUTH continue to mingle. When BEING culminates in the category of *The Absolute*, where the subject and the object meet in a rational identity, TRUTH pulls away and allows additional coherent categories to form. This is why Weil starts from TRUTH. It is more comprehensive. The culmination of the concept TRUTH surpasses the felt identity in GOD and the thought identity of BEING. TRUTH culminates in an understanding of the reality of meaning that is found in the possibility that presents itself as the meaningful unity of a discourse and a life.

The *Logic of Philosophy* recognizes this reality because every new category, as Gilbert Kirscher notes, "deals with the meaning of what the preceding category recognized as truth: it detaches meaning from the truth."[41] Thus, the intermingling of TRUTH, GOD, and BEING becomes clear in the fact that before the presentation of the category of *God*, Weil makes scant mention of the concept. He notes in the category of *Meaninglessness* that we "are dominated by a theory of history" that has its origins in Christianity and that this "history, as the order of human becoming, has a beginning and an end, and every event has its place" and so the "historical order and the logical order" coincide in God (LP, 99). Weil however is only derivatively interested in the historical order, because history, like God, logically has no beginning and end. Historically, no beginning and end can be precisely nailed down, because the recognition of this possibility implies that it has already always been there, and for it to be recognized, it must still be. He notes in the category of *The True and the False* that GOD is explained according to "an ordinary bit [...] of monist ontology" as being one and eternal (LP, 103) but precisely because of that, it is still tied up in BEING. The concept is therefore (like BEING) inapplicable because we cannot capture it in language. Rather, in reference to these concepts, only "the impossibility of speaking can be spoken about" (LP, 104). In other words, we have nothing meaningful to say about a concept there where "every predicate must be rejected, because every attribute, since it is only an attribute, is false." (LP, 104). This difficulty is further illustrated by the fact that before the category of *God* the concept GOD continues to be caught up with similar ontological and metaphysical concepts like BEING. For instance, even though the God of *Certainty* "always is and is always present in everything" (LP, 114), the way this being is bound up in the constitution of reality changes depending on the culture and the school of thought in ancient or traditional certainty. This God/Being is water or fire or spirit, or whatever other ontological totality is postulated. The struggle to define the role of God (or of the gods) is present and is brought closer to the fore in the category of *The Discussion*. In this category, whether God is present in everything or not becomes inconsequential,

---

[41] Kirscher (1989), 387.

7.4 The Conceptual Analysis of the Reprise of *God*

precisely because this is no longer a sufficient ground for decision. Reason (the formal agreement of convictions) becomes the only arbiter of action and of the tradition. In this way, the tension in the concept GOD that will later characterize the category *God* (between the existence of God as the ground of reality and God's absence in human life that is only mediated through faith), can already be felt.

Because of the way the problem is announced in *Discussion* we can skip over the cursory remarks that Weil makes concerning the concept GOD in the categories of the *Object* and the *Self* and go directly to the category of *God*, where the concept is defined as the unity of reason and feeling in a perfect transcendent being. We have already stated how Weil takes the category of *God* to be a decisive step in the development of our own historical situation. This is not just because the development of western philosophy passed through the Abrahamic concept of God, but because of *how* it passed through this concept. For Weil this category is the "origin of total reflection" (LP, 186). That is, "it is under the category of *God* that the human being sees themself and interprets themself in the totality of their life for the first time" (LP, 186–187). This total aspect is clear in the way that other categories are reprised under that of *God*. The category of *God* claims to range over all other concepts. Thus, when concepts that are born under other categories are reprised under that of *God*, we can clearly see the way these concepts are modified by different hierarchies of commitments. We can see this both in non-categorial concepts (in the sense of philosophical categories) such as ORIENTATION and in categorical concepts such as THE OBJECT. ORIENTATION becomes clear for the first time under the category of *Certainty*, even though this concept is to be found in every category. The individual's orientation will be different in different categories. This is because the kinds of goals that are available to an individual are drawn out of the category itself. In the category of *God* ORIENTATION takes on a specific dimension. The category of *God* allows for the conceptualization of totality specifically because of how it subsumes everything else under itself. Orientation is not thought of here as a choice that the individual makes, but rather as being something that is given to the individual by God, showing the individual that they have a place in God's plan and that their life is understood as being part of God's will. Weil notes that according to this modification of ORIENTATION, "if the human being wants to guide themself in their life, they must then grasp this world insofar as it is God's expression" (LP, 192). The individual understands thanks to God, but what they understand is their faith. This is evident in the way that the category of *God* reprises *The Object* so that God can be seen as a "subject" and as "the human being's only object. The world, life, the human being themself are understood in Him" (LP, 200). This plays a key role in the transformation of the Greek ontological science. In *The Object*, the individual has a place in an organized whole and the aim of their science is to reach the placid observation of that whole as the participation in reason. According to this new conception the human being is separated from the whole because:

> Science must find the infinite in the finite: God is in His creation, nature in its totality is God's total expression. By scrutinizing the work, the human being finds the Creator within it. They find Him because this Creator is absolutely reasonable, because each of His acts refer to the whole and, though this, to the Good. (LP, 200).

The individual is separated from God, but reality is nonetheless a knowable totality that is organized by rational rules because it is in this reality that the imprint of God is visible. God "guarantees natural laws" (ENHP, 16) while uprooting the individual from the natural place that the Greek *cosmos* was also supposed to guarantee. The individual is freed, but free, they are abandoned.

The hermeneutical role of the logic of philosophy allows us to understand different discursive positions by allowing us to identify different hierarchies of commitments. This becomes even more clear as we continue to follow the concept of GOD as it moves into the more "modern" categories. Indeed, Weil has called the category of *God* a philosophical turning point and "the most modern of the ancient categories, the most ancient modern one" (LP, 188). Weil defines this transition into the modern categories as a loss of faith. This does not mean that faith disappears (indeed, the reprises of *God* show that the category itself is irreducible) rather it is that "God no longer signifies anything as far as life is concerned" (LP, 203). What this means is that the concept of GOD has been surpassed by more coherent discourses that allow it to be reprised. This shift is clear in the transformation of how the individual grasps God in the category of the *Condition*. Weil notes that for the individual of the *Condition*, who has left the category of *God*, the belief in the existence of God does not pose a problem. He states that:

> [the human being's belief in] the existence of a God, guarantor of the social order, is useful, even indispensable. But they should stop relying on God's intervention: the prayers, the rites, the offerings do not exempt them from the effort, they must themself take care of their own fate, they must themself acquire knowledge about nature, for neither revelation nor miracles exist. Between the human being and God, the only relationship that exists is the relationship of morality, and the human being's piety amounts to their respect for the omniscient and absolutely just being. Defending God's "interests" is not the law's role: God has no interests, and those who attribute interests to Him are thinking of their own and disturb peaceful labor. Perhaps God will judge human beings' acts after their death; Even if the belief is highly unlikely, or, in fact, false (because science does not imagine any soul separate from body), it is of great service, provided that the following precaution be taken: religion has to be limited to social utility in pursuit of humanity's progress in light of science. (LP, 217).

In this way God is seen as a strictly social phenomenon that helps to keep the masses in place. It is no longer seen as a confusing analogue to Being, nor as the ground of human reality. This social role is highlighted even further when the concept of GOD is reprised under the category of the *Condition*. This reprise creates "progressive theology, explaining and understanding progress as continuous revelation of the divine plan for the education of humankind, or, using the additional reprise of the *self*, theologies of human unhappiness in a heartless atheist world, etc." (LP, 230). This shows not only that there are simple reprises (one category under another), but also that reprises can be stacked one upon another in order to continually modify the concept. This stacking is exactly where orders of explanation come into play. As Weil shows, different reprises in different orders give different conceptual contents. The hierarchization of commitments provided in reprises imply different permissible and incompatible inferences.

7.4 The Conceptual Analysis of the Reprise of *God*

The category of *Consciousness*, for instance, refuses the exclusively societal role that *The Condition* gives to the concept GOD and transforms it into a transcendental idea that guarantees the moral order. This is because *Consciousness*'s categorial purity, one of Kant's great discoveries, is centered on the *human* individual's moral vocation. Weil notes that:

> Within the idea of a just God, the moral law exists for the human being that is free but unaware of their freedom, in the same way that the idea of the science governing conditions represents—but only represents for consciousness—reason's spontaneity, and the way that the idea of the universal kingdom of law prefigures free determination by suppressing individual interest, and the idea of wisdom announces the total reflection of the *self* in the *I* (LP, 255).

Here:

> the human being can have a science because both they and nature have been created by God. Between cognition's general conditions and reality exists a harmony that allows the human being to pass from the general idea of an object of cognition to the particular interlinking and interlocking laws that form a system: nature cannot only be cognized in principle, but also in fact (LP, 258).

This change is important. Before *The Condition*, God is taken to have a fundamental relationship to the world. As a concept, GOD is mixed up with the foundation of reality in some way. *The Condition* changes this. It is why God's role is merely transcendental in *Consciousness* and this separation started in *The Condition* continues as the logic does. The category of *Intelligence*, for instance, presents the various articulations of conceptual contents as so many way of articulating human interest. GOD is no different, and this is why this category makes no claims concerning God, but rather becomes the first category that tries to ground its discourse on tolerance facing the variety of worldviews. Here, the hermeneutical aspect of the logic of philosophy comes out for the first time. This is normal, the *Intelligence* is the category that brings the need for and the structure of interpretation out in all its clarity. Nonetheless—and this is critical—the concept of the reprise, as a concept, is not itself born out of the category of the intelligence. The concept of the reprise is born from the logic of philosophy. It is born out of the attempt to understand philosophy philosophically and to use that understanding to act upon the world. *Intelligence* seeks to understand the plurality of worlds that present themselves as concrete human interests, as the cultural differences, and as the worldviews in which individuals articulate their lives. Thus it can (correctly) interpret how *The Condition* reduces the *belief* in God to a superstition that either gets in the way of progress or that serves as a regulatory social mechanism. It can also interpret how the moral consciousness "proves" the existence of GOD and guarantees the effectiveness of moral action. However, *Intelligence* interprets GOD (or belief, or concrete religions with their dogma, their rites, and their texts) and its reprises as making up these worlds or cultures in which individuals live. And these are human creations. This shift from the metaphysical underpinning of the universe (from a first principle outside of human reality that nonetheless grounds human reality) to a human attitude is essential. It is what allows us to understand the transformation that the concept GOD undergoes in the category of the *Personality*.

Weil himself highlights the particularity and the historical importance of the reprise of the category of *God* under that of the *Personality*. The category of the *Personality* is the category of self-creation, of conflict, of the overflow of human expression in the choice of how the individual lives their life. The reprise of *God* takes up these elements but presents God as being the source of creation and expression. Weil claims that under this reprise: "The personality is God [...] because God is the absolute consciousness: the human being is a conscious personality because God is and because the human being is God's image" and that "God has stopped being the absolute ground of a Being that would need to be accessible to reason and that is only felt by the human being; He is the present future that has swallowed the past" (LP, 314). This shift in the conception of GOD is also a shift in the notion of God's will. It is no longer what grounds the human projects that are to be brought into the world, it is the source of the individual's conflict in their struggle to realize themself. In fact, for Weil, within the development of Christianity, there is "a dialectic of God and the human being" (LP, 316) where nothing is outside of Christianity, and the whole world has to be understood through the concepts presented in Christianity. Even though we are focusing on reprises of *God* in this analysis, it is important to note here the way that the development of Christianity operates an unconscious reprise of the *Personality* under *God*.

In Christianity, Jesus Christ becomes the divine personality whose conflicts are paradoxically always present and definitively resolved. The conflicts of life and death, past and future, are present in the figure of Christ but he transcends them and thus provides a model for the rest of humanity. This conflict, where the human individual finds their salvation that is "won in suffering" (LP, 178), is defined as the resolution of a conflict that never goes away, but which is understood *in* the figure of Jesus Christ himself. Because it is in Christ that "God has truly come down to earth, he has truly made himself into a human being" (LP, 315). The human individual thus "no longer has any personal conflict, which has taken place in God" (LP, 316). Nonetheless, Weil also notes that this reprise does not "constitute Christianity (which, after the fact, *can* be understood as the religion of the personality-God): it [the reprise] enters it [Christianity] entirely, but does not exhaust Christianity or its dogmatic system" (LP, 315). Thus, despite the importance of this reprise, Weil notes that "[a]n analysis of the historical phenomenon of Christianity would have to take into account the importance that the mythical élement of the tradition reprises from prophetism, that is, the importance of the reprise of *certainty*" (LP, 314, n. 11). For a theory of argumentation, it is important to note the way that the conflict presents itself in Jesus Christ. Not only was it essential to the development of Christianity and to the western tradition, it also shows that individuals can live in or with contradictory meta-commitments. In the case of Christianity, this is the internal struggle (represented in the figure of Jesus Christ) between two different central concepts that both make claims of coherence and that both play the role of organizing discursive concepts. This is why Weil also notes that this dialectic, and thus the development of the individual as source of their own creation and source of their own

7.4 The Conceptual Analysis of the Reprise of *God*

values, "draws to a close and is fulfilled in the personality" (LP, 316). It draws to a close because, as Weil notes, "the human being *is* a personality at the core, that is, they always have been: their history is the path that leads them to discover this core." (LP, 316). This analysis of the reprise is important and, in fact, we can lean on it to further understand the life of concepts within discourse.

The different ways of conceiving of a concept are a consequence of how different hierarchies of commitments organize permissible inferences. Each different essential concept dominates how this hierarchy is articulated, but additional reprises will continue to modify the permissible inferences and incompatibilities of the concept. A concept is irreducible when it can be used as a central discursive commitment that can make claims of coherence and can govern what inferences are seen as permissible or prohibited. Coming to this irreducible character is what Weil means when he claims that the history of a concept draws to a close. For the category of *God*, the dialectic of feeling and reason unite with Being to draw to a close in the concept GOD, which individuals in the category do not see as a concept but as the ground of reality. However, the concept PERSONALITY shows that this dialectic can give way to another history. The individual who is seeking to explain and understand their experience in the world through their own self-creation and as a source of their own values refuses to see God as the ground for all reality. They therefore only see the dialectic of feeling and reason as drawing to a close in the human attitude that necessarily leads to the things that, for them, *actually* ground reality. In other words, they see reality as being grounded by the individual personality, in the choices that this personality makes in its personal conflict within the world. When this grounding concept reprises the category of *God* it gives way to the particular type of struggle that is exemplified by the figure of Christ, but *Personality* does not need to reprise *God* directly. It can reprise it under *The Condition* and see the historical figure of Christ as a personality that is used to maintain the social order through the normative constraints put in place by faith. *Personality*'s struggle for self-understanding in the creation of values is seen as valid for both the believer and the atheist. This is one of the ways that the concept shows itself to be more comprehensive than the category of *God*. But for the believer, they see the personality as the conclusion of the dialectic of God and the human being, whereas for the atheist (and the agnostic), they see this development as being constituted by different reprises according to their own personal intellectual history. In fact, it is this personal intellectual history that allows them to understand their individual struggle and to understand the choice that they make in the world to affirm their values and their goals. This position lays the groundwork for the place of the reprise of the concept GOD in Weil's normative view of the human individual, where God is seen as the Absolute. This is because in the category of the *Absolute*:

> reasoning and feeling, object and subject have disappeared, and there is no longer any *other*: science and freedom are no longer opposed because in this science Being knows that it is Reason, and Reason knows that it is Being. Reflection's circle has been traveled, and the human being in the totality of their being has recognized themselves as Being in its totality, as the un-folding of God (LP, 334).

God is understood in coherent discourse as the *absolute* coherence of this discourse, as an onto-theology, where the relationship to philosophy and religion is reversed. Philosophy is no longer the servant of religion (what allows thinking religion), rather religion is merely one of the forms under which the *Absolute* thinks itself in philosophy. One specific way that Weil differs from Hegel is that he keeps the idea of absolute coherence while evacuating the idea of the self-interpreting system as an onto-theology.

The Absolute should be understood as the terminal point of what we can call, following Jean Quillien, "the logical evolution of the discourse on being."[42] This discourse is characterized by the first-level assertoric language use that tries to fix conceptual content to things in the world, as being the actual reality of the things that are being spoken about. *The Absolute* is seen as the terminal point because, in *The Absolute*, individuals are unable to conceptualize life outside of discourse, to see discourse as an option instead of just as the armature of meaning in the world. This, as I have argued, presents the problem of the individual's relationship to discourse. It is an important development, not only in order to understand arguments as having a pragmatic function, that is, moving people to act (by moving people to see the world according to their discourse), but also because it allows us to better understand the hermeneutical function of the logic of philosophy. We can now see discourse as trying to capture all phenomena and all discourse in order to make the world intelligible. Even the recalcitrant phenomena that had previously remained problematic are grasped here, because, thanks to the development of discourse (and outside of the discursive commitments to nihilism, cynicism, and skepticism), the world is seen to already be intelligible. It is however the development of the category of *The Work* that brings out the pragmatic function of discourse the most clearly. This category presents itself in the individual who, in their individual feeling, refuses the coherence of *The Absolute*. It is the revolt of the individual who does not want to understand but who wants to feel and who wants to grip tightly to the feeling that gives their lives meaning.

Weil explicitly states that different categories have tried to capture this notion of feeling. According to the structuring role that different philosophical categories play, we can see that they do so by deploying a variety of different concepts. He states:

> So far, for us, feeling has signified the human being in the world's relationship to the *world's* essential, be it *God*, or *freedom*, or *conflict*. It was the silence in language, it was what was *indicated* amid what *appeared*, it was particularity's *for-itself* in its indomitable stubbornness, and as such, it was understood in the absolutely coherent discourse. Yet, after this discourse, all these forms are revealed to be *mediated* by what they are opposed to. This feeling was not the act of feeling, it was speaking about feeling: if it had been any different, the human being would not have wasted their time justifying themself, they would have created; they would not have sought satisfaction, and even less, the possibility of his satisfaction, they would be satisfied (LP, 354).

---

[42] Quillien (1982), 183.

7.4 The Conceptual Analysis of the Reprise of *God*

By characterizing the individual's relationship to discourse, Weil will be able to show that discourse plays a transformational role in how individuals understand the world. He will also be able to show that this transformational role is structural: it is discourse that defines the kind of content individuals have, because action is understood through discourse. The category of *The Work*, however does not yet provide this. In the category of *The Work*, the project, the work itself, is merely personal. It does not yet make any claims to universality. In fact, it does not seek to convince anyone as an equal partner in dialogue: *The Work* resists the notion of dialogical controls. If it involves others by material necessity, it does so through ruse or force, but only so that the individual can further their own personal project. The category of *The Work* thus reprises the category of *God* under the notion of a sacred mission that has to be carried out. This mission can remain personal or can be politicized, as is shown in *The Work* by the totalitarian leader. When it is politicized, the individual must create followers by acting on the feeling of dissatisfaction of others in order to bring them to help achieve this individual's goal. Whatever the case, when the individual applies the category to themselves, they see themself as the only competent person that can correctly carry out the mission that they have given to themselves, a mission that they see as necessary in order for the world to be meaningful. According to Weil, this person sees themself as:

> a *genius* that realizes freedom, they are the *historic figure* of their era that sets the way-stops on the path to progress, the *personality* that ends conflict by writing a new tablet of values, etc. In short, they are the chosen one, and herein resides the importance of the category of God: the other categories, before being able to be used for justification, must be reprised under this category, so that the relationship can be established between a level of the world (as a formal and empty idea, since revelation has disappeared) and the human being's work, in this way, and in this way only, the human being takes on the double role of a creator and of a source of revelation (LP, 366).

In its personal articulation, *The Work* is the category of egocentric solipsism, of the confidence artist, of someone who is willing to do anything to get what they want while taking others into account. In its political articulation, it is the category of the unbridled megalomaniac and the tyrant. There will always be individuals ready to see the world and themself in either of these roles, but this is unimportant for the development of the concept of GOD that is presented here. What matters is that because of this, *The Work* adds something specific and necessary to discourse. It adds the idea of a personal *project* that looks to transform the world in order for the world to be meaningful in terms of this project. When this project is taken up by the subsequent categories, it will be reprised as modified in important ways. When it is reprised under the category of *The Finite* it is seen as being a personal mission, but a personal mission among other personal missions, and one that is bound to fail. And when it is reprised by *Action*, it is seen, on the one hand, as a constant project to transform one's own discourse to make it more universal by confronting it to other projects. And on the other, it is seen as a project to use that discourse to transform the discourse of others in such a way that the world actually becomes more universal, where reason is effective and acts. It is thus the way that *The Work* is reprised by other later categories that plays a role in Weil's own normative position concerning the human being and human action.

The Work's reprise of the concept GOD provides the category with the idea of a God-given mission. But in the larger context of the development of Weil's own philosophical position it provides something different. The category of the *Absolute* gives birth to the notion of categories as the centers of a discursive commitment that organizes the totality of permissible inferences and incompatibilities. *The Work*, on the other hand, clarifies the concept of attitudes (which first appeared in *Intelligence*) as the stance that an individual takes in the concrete existence of their actual life. These two concepts are seen as irreducible, but also as coordinate. That is, attitudes are only understood thanks to categories and categories are only understood thanks to attitudes. By using the notion of discursive commitment, we can show how this happens. The individual takes a stance in their life, they inhabit a specific attitude because they are able to express their dissatisfaction with the world. At the most primitive level, this is through the resistance that they offer with a pragmatic negation. However, this stance only makes sense because it is a stance that accepts or resists conceptual *content*. This content is itself described by the kind of material inferences that the central categorial concept allows precisely because this concept allows the individual to understand themself thanks to these inferences. In other words these two positions form the dialectic of the particular and the universal. In this way, a discursive commitment is both pragmatic and conceptual.

The reprise of GOD in *The Work* is the last substantive change that this concept undergoes in the *Logic of Philosophy*. While this concept may not disappear for the individual who has passed through these categories, it has in a certain sense been exhausted. All the things that this concept is trying to capture have been doled out to other concepts. Revelation, morality, totality, meaning are no longer the exclusive domain of God. In this way, the concept GOD, under any of the other categories, is seen as a reprise, as a specific discursive commitment that helps the individual to organize their world in a coherent manner while still leaving a place for their belief. It is used to guide and organize their action on the world, but it is not what is essential to their world. According to the *Logic of Philosophy*, God is real insofar as people act from the concept, but it is as real as any other discursive commitment is. Here the hermeneutical aspect of the *Logic of Philosophy* anchors itself firmly in a theory of argumentation. Anyone that is defending God is doing so with other things in mind. *God* is being reprised under other categories and other categories are being reprised under *God* so that the individual can have, for themselves, a coherent stance in the world. Reading the *Logic of Philosophy* as a theory of argumentation helps us to see the kinds of arguments that individuals (and communities) advance, and it makes them explicit. All discursive commitments are seen as real human possibilities. However, to see if they are discursive possibilities that *we* ourselves as individuals can take up and use, we must interpret how they fit in with our other beliefs, how they fit in with our understanding of the structure of the real and of our experience. We must try to tease out our own reprises and understand our own order of explanation.

7.4 The Conceptual Analysis of the Reprise of *God*

The *Logic of Philosophy*, with its conceptual distinction between categories and attitudes—and thanks to its conceptual innovation of the reprise—aids us in this interpretative act. It allows us to create a hierarchy of discursive commitments and it shows how commitments, once held, can fall into the world with real and sometimes violent consequences. The *Logic of Philosophy* provides an important hermeneutical resource. It allows us to see the discursive centers that people argue from and it also allows us to see how their order of explanations fit together. However, the logic of philosophy should not merely be seen as a type of philosophical enigma machine that takes an input of arguments, places the permutations of the different reprises they present into the different attitude and categories, and produces an output of a central discursive commitment, a hierarchy of commitments, and an order of explanation. Yes, it allows us to interpret and understand the goals of others, and what their orientations are, but these things are not always clear. Rather it is a slow dialogical process whereby we say things, correct them, learn from them, take them back, modify them and, if and when we are lucky, in real dialogue, come to see what the actual commitments actual people have are. This is also not always clear, because people are rarely in dialogue. They are rarely engaged in serious conversation.

The *Logic of Philosophy* is part of a model that allows us to understand how this works, but it also allows us to understand the difficulties that exist in real human attitudes. Individuals learn to handle and understand conceptual content only because they are embedded in a social context in which they learn how to interpret and understand others before they learn to understand and interpret themselves. According to this model, the hermeneutical aspect of the *Logic of Philosophy* is doubly important. First, it allows us to interpret what others say, and see if their reasons fit in with our own. Second, it allows us to understand the internal monologue that individuals have with themselves as a possibility that is born in dialogical practices. In other words, argumentative practices are learned with and thanks to others. So the hermeneutical mission of the *Logic of Philosophy* in a certain sense replaces introspection. We interpret others *and* ourselves, and when we reason, we are internalizing the reasons of others in order to help us to interpret ourselves. The internal monologue should thus be seen as a dialogue with a virtual interlocutor with whom we stage a plurality of positions and possibilities. Thus this model sees the reflexive nature of the self as being tied up in inferential relations that only become clear by making different reprises explicit. That being said, it would be reductive to read it only according to its hermeneutical aspect. Reading the *Logic of Philosophy* as a theory of argument also insists on the logic of philosophy's strategic aspect, otherwise it merely would be a theory of interpretation.

Let us look back again at the normative position that Weil presents of the individual. He states that the individual is a:

> *personality* that grasps itself as a feeling facing the *Absolute* that is *God*, but a God that is absolutely revealed as the coherence to be realized, has found its *work* in its *finiteness*: it is the *free consciousness* that imposes itself on the *condition* in order to transform this condition according to its own *interest* that it now knows to be singular and essential, and in virtue of which it can *interpret* what is (LP, 413).

Even though it is possible to read the *Logic of Philosophy* as a catalogue of arguments with a primarily hermeneutical mission, this would be to miss part of Weil's point. He notes that the individual is a personality, that is, a source of values and of creation, who is filled with their feeling, something that is non-discursive but that is shaped by discourse, facing the notion of universality as a mission to be brought about, and that also shapes discourse by being the source of human dissatisfaction. Here this personality, this individual, has to make a decision concerning the kind of project they want to bring into the world, which they understand can fail, either because of the shortness of their individual life, or because they, as an individual, fail to universalize it. Nonetheless, this individual, when they seek to universalize their project, does so by making it into one that others can take up as well, which thus can change the second nature that defines the human condition. In other words, they can advance reasons that others can use as their own. This is how the individual comes to interpret and judge other projects, other claims of universality, other arguments. They oppose them to their own by fitting it in with their own, by making it a project for humanity.

Following this interpretation, we see that the individual's action that changes the world also changes their second nature, that is, the social structure in which they find themself. However, here we are faced with the definitive problem of the *Logic of Philosophy*, namely the initial agreement that governs the domain of argumentation. Community is based on a permanent agreement. Just because that is logically true does not mean that individuals see this, nor does it mean that what is considered to be a community actually includes those that ought to be full-fledged members. It becomes a question of how to bring an individual to see the importance of their continued participation in the community. What is to be done facing people who are not convinced of the value of being reasonable instead of violent? This brings out a paradox in the strategic aspect of reading *Logic of Philosophy* as a theory of argumentation. We cannot convince someone of this unless they are already convinced. All we can do is present something *as* valuable. Every individual must however take the step to enter into reasonable practices for themself. In other words, sometimes non-argumentative means, such as defensive counter-violence, are necessary. Weil himself notes that "violence exists, and there is no *argument* against violence, if the violence is consistent. The only means of fighting violence—but this means is strictly non-philosophical—is simply to fight it" (PR.I.22). The root of the paradox of any theory of argumentation is that there is no single preferred argumentative strategy, because philosophy, or reason, or argumentation—at this moment they are all identical—can start from anywhere. There is no privileged start to philosophy, and any claim to a privileged start has the inconvenience of automatically ruling out those that struggle to understand from another point of view. It also shows that although philosophy aims at unity, there are a plurality of irreducible positions. The only way to achieve any level of unity is to bring others to recognize the normative weight of better reasons.

7.5 Argumentative Strategy in the *Logic of Philosophy*

The strategic paradox of the *Logic of Philosophy* is that any argumentative strategy can only be painted in broad strokes. Any answer to the question of how to start argumentation must in fact resist all attempts to give overly precise mechanisms. This is because precise mechanisms only function when discursive centers already have great overlap of agreement. What the *Logic of Philosophy* provides us with is a theory of how to bring distant discursive centers closer. Weil shows this in multiple points in his own work. In the *Philosophie politique* he shows the way that the pure, formal, moral point of view comes to surpass itself in order to adopt that of political action (PP, 25–57). In the terms of the *Logic of Philosophy* this shows how the moral philosophy found in the category of *Consciousness* can step over the other intervening categories to land squarely in the category of *Action*. This is because *Consciousness* is already a reflection on action, but at the level of grounding the moral law. Weil also shows how to bring distant positions together in the organization of the *Logic of Philosophy* itself. He does this by inversing the historical order of the appearance of discourse in favor of a logical order of progressive comprehensiveness. In this way, he shows how *Consciousness*, exemplified in part by Kant and in part by Fichte, develops essential elements needed for a full understanding of *Intelligence*, exemplified by Michel de Montaigne and Pierre Bayle. Similarly *Personality*, exemplified by Nietzsche, helps us to understand *The Absolute*, exemplified by Hegel. The *Logic of Philosophy* develops the criteria of coherence and universality that allows us to decide the extent to which different philosophical discourses satisfy the requirement of a comprehensive grasp of meaning. Because its goal is to develop these criteria and to show the shapes of comprehensiveness, any strategic role that the logic of philosophy has will at most be pragmatic and heuristic. In this way, when a good strategy works, it does not work once and for all, but rather for that specific situation, and at most, can serve as a model for future strategies. The strategic role is thus linked to a type of *phronesis*, or practical wisdom in situation. The strategic role piggybacks on the the logic of philosophy's interpretative role. It is only once the discursive commitments and the order of explanation of an argument are understood that a strategy can look to the logic of philosophy as a catalogue of arguments that leads to greater forms of comprehensiveness. This catalogue of arguments can then be deployed strategically to pinpoint the closest arguments to the interlocutor's discursive center, arguments which can navigate their hierarchy of commitments. This is the best the strategic role can do. The choice to take up reasons as one's own remains a free choice for every individual.

Using the metaphor of the space of reasons to understand this, the best that we can do in argument is bring an individual to the edge of their own space of reasons by drawing out all the permissible inferences and incompatibilities in order to show that their position remains problematic. Argumentation in this sense aims at leading one's interlocutor to clarify their position in such a manner that they find themselves between an explicit choice where *either* they must renounce some (or all) of their premises *or* they must accept the consequences of their position (including the violent conflict that may follow).[43] Once we bring them to the edge of their space of reasons though, we cannot bring them to jump into another one. This is only done by an individual who is ready to modify their central discursive commitment and order of explanation. Because of this, the choice to enter into argument often depends on non-discursive means and thus also on a plurality of different strategies. Paul Ricœur reminds us that, "it is not certain that the problem of violence is resolved only through discourse."[44] Weil himself notes that in order to bring people to dialogue, it may be necessary to return to older techniques, to "the guarded expressions, the allusions, the seemingly banal theses that the audience must combine in order to see their scope" (PR.I.290). This is one of the strategic roles of the reprise, it allows each discursive center to act on others by expressing themselves in their language. At this level, a variety of means are needed to bring someone into dialogue, into the argumentative practices that aim at agreement. As already noted, dialogue is the gold standard of communication, but it also best describes individuals that already make up the same community. Argument is not present everywhere. Most cases are far too conflictual. Weil recognizes this. He insists on the fact that discussion is born when an opponent can neither be destroyed nor ignored, but must be reasoned with. At the individual level, there may in fact be no exhaustive list that can be presented to explain *how* individuals come to discuss, as there may be no exhaustive list of how discussion passes to dialogue. It can be interest, curiosity, desire, frustration, boredom, a dare, and so on. This is different from Plato's position where philosophy necessarily starts in wonder or perplexity, just as it is different from Descartes' position where philosophy necessarily starts in doubt. Philosophy can start anywhere. It can also stop anywhere for any reason. This is the particularity of Weil's position and one of the most difficult aspects to understand.

He insists over and over on the two forms of serious conversation—discussion and dialogue. He also recognizes that ordinarily the individual *speaks without saying anything* (LP, 91). Just as Weil uses seriousness in a technical sense, he also uses the idea of *speaking without saying anything* in a technical sense. Weil settles on this expression most likely because it allows him to translate the Greek phrase *oudén légei*[45] found, for instance, in the play *Wasps*,[46] and to exploit the common French expression *parler sans rien dire*. For Weil, the most basic aspect of speaking without saying anything is found when the individual admits that they are speaking without paying attention to the rules of logic or demonstration. In this case, they must be brought to admit that while their language use hasn't "demonstrated anything" (LP, 22), they nonetheless speak. This brings two distinctions to the forefront. First, it means that, implicitly, philosophy looks to language use to say something

---

[43] An example of this choice presents itself in the formal abstract reflection of the pure moral conscience which refuse all strategic rationality. The consequences of refusing all strategic rationality can include leaving the field of action open to the pure technicians of power and to the violent subjugation of the community.

[44] Ricœur (1991).

[45] For a good overview of the use and development of this term across Antiquity, see Chiarini (2019).

[46] Aristophanes (1996).

7.5 Argumentative Strategy in the *Logic of Philosophy*

substantive, and two, that this is not the only type of language use possible. It is meaningful that outside of the presentation in the *Introduction* of the conflict that speaking without saying anything has with logically structured argumentative practices, Weil uses this expression in four categories: *Truth, The Object, The Condition,* and *Action*. In *Truth* Weil uses the expression to contrast discourse, or serious conversation, with all other language uses. Here he notes that the individual "ordinarily speaks without saying anything [...] and whatever matters in their life happens outside discourse, and for the individual's consciousness, discourse is superfluous" (LP, 91). In *The Object*, the expression is used to contrast this new category with *Certainty*. In other words, to contrast the new ontological science with the pre-philosophical language of the tradition. In the other two categories, which each also rely heavily on a reprise of *The Object* in the elaboration of their discourse, he uses it to situate the presence of this attitude in the reprises. Each of these categories characterizes a progressively richer level of "concrete" understanding.

In these categories there is thus an evolution of what speaking without saying anything means. Because of this, it also shows the ways in which individuals are not *necessarily* bound by serious conversation. Each category gives criteria of what counts as serious conversation and thus also what counts as speaking without saying anything. In other words, these are the technical analyses that Weil uses in order to understand the placement problem in terms of argumentative practices. In *The Object*, Weil notes that speaking without saying anything is a real possibility that we face because of the failure of the ancient content of *Certainty*. What *The Object* learns from this failure is that error is a possibility. It is this possibility that transforms the individual into an *individual*, because they learn that "their speaking does not separate them from their world, where they remain and act. It is only transformed into an individual, separated from the world, knowing that language is not a natural force, that they can speak 'without saying anything'" (LP, 139). This starts to show why the strategic role of the *Logic of Philosophy* takes the form that it does. In *Certainty* the individual takes their language for a statement of fact and so they commit, but are unaware of the commitment *as* a commitment. In *Discussion* they become aware of difference and doubt, and they thus understand that any statement of fact must be grounded. They only realize this because they can speak empty words. They can have conversations that are not serious. They can say anything and everything. But they also realize that they are committed to what they say. This realization is felt in full force in *The Object*, the first category that consciously tries to ground its discourse. It is the category that discovers the possibility of speaking without saying anything and discovers why this is problematic. It is necessary to characterize anything that is not serious conversation as error in order to keep the discourse coherent.

This problematic aspect continues in *The Condition* where the *ideal* that guided *The Object* is seen to be to be absurd. Weil notes that:

> if science is defined this way [that of *The Object*], the human being will never know what grounds things—because this so-called ground doesn't exist. If we want to speak about an object (and the expression is convenient), it is necessary to speak about an object of cognition, and not of reason or of a subject: it is its own ground, and speaking of some other thing

that would be located who knows where, behind the phenomena marked out and measured by science, is speaking without saying anything. There are sense data, qualities, there is the "object" of science, to which this science reduces these data and qualities, in other words, the functions connecting and constituting measurable factors, and that's all (LP, 222).

Here, speaking without saying anything is again modified. It becomes a way of formulating the placement problem. It is ridiculous to speak of anything besides facts, everything else is empty filler (a droll contradiction). This is exemplified in the fact/value divide we have already seen, and that I have said the emotivist strains of moral expressivism is trying to grasp. Moral language is empty, people can speak it, but it doesn't actually characterize anything unless it is reformulated in a language that is sensitive to phenomenal facts, as expressions of desire or disgust for instance, expressions that can be characterized in a psychological, or better, a physiological language. We speak of moral facts, but it is merely a way of speaking. In *The Condition* all serious conversation bears on scientific matters, because this is the only "concrete" content. People can still employ language in other ways but this use remains secondary. However, as we have shown, this is exactly what the next category, *Consciousness*, will refuse. Interpreting speaking without saying anything along the lines of the placement problem allows us to understand how different categories interpret the discursive commitments of language use that falls under another category. The reason that Weil restricts this expression to the "scientific" categories is precisely because these categories speak of the world and demand concrete results. In this way, the language of these discourses is supposed to unite everybody, because the world and its laws are supposed to apply to everybody. Nowhere is this clearer than in the category of *Action*.

Action is interpreted thanks to a reprise of *The Condition* because *Action*'s "categorial consciousness belongs to the acting minority, and this minority, because it is conscious, acts on the masses by translating what it thinks into the language of the world of the condition. For it is this language that binds human beings, being common to all" (LP, 405). In this way, for Weil *Action* is materialist in its activity and:

> idealist with regard to the "role" of reason: for action, nothing is outside of reason, nothing is inaccessible to cognition, and speaking of substances that do not exist *for* reason is, for action, speaking without saying anything. But the question itself is poorly asked; the theoretical philosophy of action is that of the *Absolute* (what distinguishes the two is not a theoretical difference, but a difference between theory and realization) (LP, 407).

Here, *Action* has excised the troublesome aspect of *The Condition* in that it is post-Kantian and post-Hegelian and thus not positivist, but it is also resolutely non-metaphysical. It accepts the reflection on the conditions of possibility and on the role of an absolutely coherent discourse. For *Action*, any discourse that ignores such things speaks without saying anything. It aspires to articulate its discourse and to act thanks to a "science of action" (LP, 405), which can be both correctly and falsely carried out. This science though is best thought of as anthropological. It is the action that aims at acting on the world, but on a social world, and therefore on human discourse. This is where the analysis of speaking without saying anything plays a strategic role in argumentative practices. Weil's interest is serious conversation. He

7.5 Argumentative Strategy in the *Logic of Philosophy*

wants to understand how to act on human discourse. However, in order to do so, one must recognize that so much of our language use is not philosophical. It is not certain that serious conversation will lead to serious conversation. As part of an argumentative strategy, the analysis of speaking without saying anything underlines the way that people mostly speak non-philosophically. It also highlights the fact that when people do want to enter into serious conversation, they must face a plurality of discourses. The problem is that because of their own discursive commitments, they may not be capable of seeing these other discourses as participating in serious conversation. Along the lines of our analysis of the placement problem, each discursive center can always see another as speaking without saying anything. This is why multiple strategies are needed. On the one side, people need to be shown the importance of serious conversation. On the other, they have to be willing to see even the farthest discursive commitments as holding something reasonable within them. Even if this is only the meaning that it gives to someone's life. Weil clearly understands this because he notes that the science of action:

> must be addressed to those that do not understand it and must struggle against those who partially understand it. To the extent that it spreads through the masses, that it educates the masses, it is therefore impoverished from a philosophical point of view (reprises of the *Absolute* and, more often, of the *personality*, of the *intelligence*, of the *consciousness*, etc.): an impoverishment that is an enrichment of poor reality (LP, 405).

Strategically, *Action* must address different people using different means to get them to see the value of argument. It is only once this initial minimal agreement is met that other more precise mechanisms can be put in place. Philosophy can start anywhere, but goals only make sense in a situation, and Weil insists that this situation is structured. However, he is also sensitive to the diversity of situations that have actually appeared in human history. Instead of trying to reduce them to any single contemporary understanding, he takes them as freestanding but permeable. They are freestanding because individuals can live in them and find their goals meaningful thanks to them. They are permeable because people can be brought to see their limits and advantages *as if* from the outside thanks to other discursive positions. Here it is important to be careful. It will always be possible that some aspect of our experience is not captured in discourse, however, what we understand reflexively about our experience we understand *in* discourse and so we see the trace of this understanding all over the human enterprise that is history. In other words, the history of discourse is the repository of human action.

The corollary to this argument is that we must take the way discursive commitments structure coherent discursive positions seriously. The reason for this is banal, but it is nonetheless a reason that has defeated many a great enterprise. If we didn't take discourse seriously why should we care otherwise? Why should we so doggedly put so much effort into overcoming skepticism, relativism, nihilism, if we did not see the effects they have on human action? If they were not real possibilities? We would not need to argue against a position if it did not have real consequences. Imagine monism to be true. Imagine that we can have a direct non-inferential and immediately grounding access to some sort of supersensory. Were this the case, even the Platonic doctrine of reminiscence whereby philosophy is a corrective that slowly brings individuals to find the reason they already have would be excessive. The intellectual intuition of the whole of a reasonable reality would already be present as given to us and would suffice. A total and complete knowledge of the universe and of humanity's place in it would be known. However, if the real can be grasped in numerous ways because phenomena can be diversely grasped in discourse and because there are a variety of real goals that individuals can adopt—as history itself has shown—then the way these grasps of phenomena and history can be understood matter *to us* far more than to explain what the extra-human foundation of reality is. These grasps define the kind of action we will have on the world and define how the world itself is to be described and understood. Here we can requote a passage already cited in Chap. 2:

> [The individual's] action (as well as their discourse, to the extent that this discourse forms an integral part of their action) reveals, to the observer, what they pursue *deep down*, reveals the center they use to orient themself in their world. But this center does not appear to be the center in their own eyes, it does not even appear, just like the spot under their feet does not appear to the human being standing there. They are speaking about it constantly (for the interpreter) without ever formulating it: as soon as it were formulated, this principle could be doubted and would already be off-center in a world whose center would have changed by this discovery's very fact, in the same way that the ground that I see is not the ground that holds me up (LP, 82).

This poses the main problem of a theory of argumentation for Weil. All action is acting for reasons. This means that it is oriented. This does not mean that all reasons lead to action. This is not the case. Reasons give individuals the disposition towards action. Nothing guarantees that this disposition will be activated. Nothing guarantees that when the moment comes, what one thought their reasons to be won't prove false, or insufficient, or modified. This means that our reasons for action are not necessarily visible to ourselves. They can become visible. When they do, we interpret who we were, who we have become, and what we have to do to become who we want to be. In order to do this we must universalize our reason, but we can only universalize our reason by seeing others as legitimate partners in dialogue, as people that have something to add. The hope in doing this is that we will be moved by the best reasons. Inside of reasonable argumentative practices, reasons are transitive. They can move others because others can take on these reasons as their own. This requires opening ourselves to others but also understanding what our own reasons are.

The problem that Weil's argumentative theory reveals is that we rarely dig deep enough in discussion and argument to reach the reserve that holds our actual position—the one that governs all the other inferences that are in place. So, while argumentation must account for the transitivity of reasons, it must also account for the fact that most arguments treat epiphenomenal claims as opposed to treating core commitments. This implies that local arguments have a hard time touching the global structure of conceptual commitments. Because of this, there is more resistance to the transitivity of reasons than openness to them. Weil's goal is to open people to the openness that is required for the transitivity of reasons to hold. The strategic goal then is to help individuals to come to see what their own core commitments are and those of others. The hope is that once this is done, these same individuals will be led to make the continual reasonable choice to overcome difference reasonably through argument. *This* is what Weil means when he says that philosophy has to understand itself philosophically. This is what the person with a coherent discourse in a concrete situation works towards. This is how they understand the choice they have made to be reasonable in the face of all that is unreasonable or differently reasonable. The concrete individual understands that this choice is itself a-reasonable when they understand themselves and their choice retrospectively. Serious conversation—discussion and dialogue—is only possible based on some common ground. It can be as minimal as two interlocutors that have agreed to search for a substantive common ground without recourse to violence. In real disagreement even a meta-ground that lacks any ground-level determined content is enough because it is the concrete starting point.

The more entrenched disagreements are, the harder it will be to bring people to this minimal agreement. Because of this, a variety of means will need to be deployed. Once that has been done, individuals can pass to discussion, to the defense of their interests and beliefs, without necessarily looking for any deeper agreement, without looking to understand and to reform what their source of conflict is. When this happens though, when two (or more) interlocutors seek to get to the bottom of things, to understand how things really are, dialogue starts. In this way, we also transform the way we represent our adversary. In deep conflict we are faced with someone who is not understandable despite the fact that they "have human features" (LP, 24). We see them as only minimally being similar to us. They are adversaries, hostile enemies. If we only see them as limitedly rational, then they are people we can only have limited tense relations with. This is different from those with whom we can dialogue. We see them as equals, as making up our community. For Weil, the goal is to bring ourselves to see more people as making up part of our human discursive community. To shift to a Sellarsian idiom, we can say that the goal of argumentation is to build what are called *we-intentions*. These constitute a type of collective agency that not only allows us to act in groups, but also allows us to understand the intentions of others as being identical to our own. Sellars notes that "it is a conceptual fact that people constitute a community, a *we*, by virtue of thinking of each other as *one of us*, and by willing the common good *not* under the species of benevolence – but willing it as one of us, or from a moral point of view."[47] The goal of a Weilian theory of argumentation is the transition from a minimal agreement, through discussion, into dialogue in order to constantly enlarge and enrich our notion of who belongs in the discursive community, who makes up part of *us*.[48]

---

[47] Sellars (1992), § 132.

[48] Richard Rorty shares this goal, and this deployment of *we-intentions* is built off of his analysis of solidarity. Solidarity in this sense is not an appeal to trans-historical absolute values but is rather an insistence on a constant re-description of the notion of *us*, who we, in a given community, consider to be participants with an equal place at the table. This amounts to "reminding ourselves to

This is a modest and very human goal, but it is one of the utmost importance, because it modifies our top to bottom understanding not just of philosophy but of ourselves. In other words, reading the *Logic of Philosophy* as a theory of argumentation means that one must abandon the a-temporal target that philosophy has so long aimed at in exchange for what Gilbert Kirscher calls "the openness of philosophy."[49] This is the final commitment that is found in the *Logic of Philosophy*, it is the formal possibility that characterizes the category of *Wisdom*. For Weil, this openness is present when the individual "knows that discourse grasps all meaning and that all concrete meanings constitute discourse, because they are open to the world in Truth, as the world is open to them in the action that is the human being's creation of the meaning of the human being in the concrete achievement of meaning" (LP, 439). This openness is thus an openness to the fundamentally problematic nature of philosophy. Philosophy reveals few truths and it provides few solutions. Rather, it reveals problems and conflicts in the form of different ways of grasping the world, which are nonetheless all present in reality. This, for Weil, is the consequence of what he calls "discourse's deepest duality" (LP, 442), the duality between freedom and truth. To quote Gilbert Kirscher:

> The interplay introduced by freedom into reality and into discourse—negativity—always prevents philosophizing from merging with truth; it creates the distance that makes truth visible. By discovering the radical function of freedom, the category of *wisdom* thus returns to the category of *truth*, but by characterizing, for itself, what separates it from truth. The philosopher and finally the sage have always dealt with truth. Truth escapes the grasp that wants to nail it down and that forgets itself; it is never present without freedom, even when freedom is forgotten. The entire path of the *Logic of Philosophy* appears to us as a progressive grasp of a self-awareness of freedom. In the beginning, in the category of *truth*, the free decision of discourse is completely obscured by the meaningful content that it assumes is there. At the end, in the category of *wisdom*, this free decision is self-aware, self-thinking, self-living, self-reflecting in the sage's discourse, a discourse that is itself lived and self-aware as discourse and as life in truth.[50]

This is what allows the possibility of the reasonability of action (LP, 442), but a possibility that only exists in the face of the multiplicity of discourses that make up reality and that express human freedom. For this reason, the possibility of discourse must take all concrete discourses into account. This is also why the last two categories are formal, they must account for this possibility. All concrete discourses are normatively structured. The most that any discourse that wants to give a non-normative description can do is give a *formal* transcendental description of the possibility of meaning and of the possibility of meaningful action in a life that is lived in a holistic unity. In fact, this is what should be understood when we talk about transcendental arguments. They are attempts to give formal descriptions that account for all the concrete normative possibilities. These descriptions can be challenged and should be, but their goal is to allow individuals to understand their own

---

keep trying to expand our sense of 'us' as far as we can" so that we can "extend our sense of 'we' to people we previously thought as 'they'" Rorty (1989), 196.

[49] Kirscher (1989).

[50] Kirscher (1989), 389–390.

meaningful reasonable activity. They succeed as long as they help individuals understand why they choose to be reasonable and show how that commitment is possible.

7.6 Conclusion

The hermeneutical role of the logic of philosophy allows individuals to understand their own discursive commitments and those of their dialogue partners. This hermeneutical role helps individuals to use this understanding to judge the discursive commitments and orders of explanation in front of them to line up previous argumentative strategies with their current situation. Through argument, the individual can test different orders of explanation and different hypothetical central commitments in order to judge the inferences that their dialogue partners see as going without saying. This in turn gives way to the strategic role of the logic of philosophy. It allows us to line up an order of explanation and give a description of our central discursive commitment so that our dialogue partner sees its full weight, so that they can see it as a real human possibility—as being reasons that they can make their own. It is important to insist that there are no knockdown arguments. There is no single strategy that will convince everyone. Rather, reading the *Logic of Philosophy* as a theory of argumentation reminds us that being reasonable is a continual choice. It claims that this is the best choice we have to put aside violence. This reminder, in a way, radicalizes the notion of commitment, because it places the meta-commitment to reasonable discourse in the foreground. Reasonable discourse is a meta-commitment towards the universal understood as the form of coherence. It is only once someone makes this choice that they are entitled to be considered someone that has *something to say*, that has a substantive content. It is only inside of this choice—and for the duration of this choice—that the individual considers themself responsible to their other commitments. These other commitments, including the commitment to the content of their discourse, are subordinate to this meta-commitment. Without it, they no longer see themselves as responsible for what their other commitments hold them to. The consequence of this type of theory of argumentation is that it modifies how other philosophical programs and other philosophical commitments are seen and understood. In the next chapter I will show two paradigmatic cases of how reading Weil as a theory of argumentation changes the way we approach philosophical positions. The first is justificatory, and the second involves the debate between relativism and pluralism.

References

Aristophanes. 1996. *Wasps*, vol. 4. Trans. A. Sommerstein. Warminster: Aris & Phillips LTD.
Bernardo, L.M. 2003. *Linguagem e discurso: Uma hipótese hermenêutica sobre a filosofia de Eric Weil*. Lisbon: Imrensa Nacional – Casa da Moeda.

Bizeul, Y. 2006. Moral und Politik bei Eric Weil. In *Gewalt, Moral und Politik Bei Eric Weil*, 131–157. Hamburg: Lit Verlag.
Bobongaud, S.G. 2011. *La dimension politique du langage*. Rome: Gregorian & Biblical Press.
Bouillard, H. 1977. Philosophie et religion dans l'œuvre d'Éric Weil. *Archives de Philosophie 404* (4): 543–621.
Brandom, R. 1994. *Making it explicit – Reasoning, representing & discursive commitment*. Cambridge, MA: Harvard University Press.
Breuvart, J.-M. 1987. Tradition, effectivité et théorie chez E. Weil et H.G. Gadamer. In *Cahiers Éric Weil Tome I*, ed. J. Quillien. Villeneuve-d'Ascq: Presses Universitaires du Septentrion.
Buée, J.-M. 1987. *La logique de la philosophie* et l'herméneutique de Gadamer. In *Cahier Éric Weil Tome I*, ed. J. Quillien. Lille: Presses Universitaires du Septentrion.
Canivez, P. 1993. *Le politique et sa logique dans l'œuvre d'Éric Weil*. Paris: Éditions Kimé.
———. 2013a. La notion de reprise et ses applications. *Cultura: Revista de História e Teoria Das Ideias 31* (II): 15–29.
———. 2013b. *Qu'est-ce que l'action politique?* Paris: Librairie Philosophique J. Vrin.
———. 2020a. Eric Weil's reading of the critique of the power of judgment. In *Kant's third Critique in the twentieth century*, ed. S. Marino and P. Terzi. Berlin: De Gruyter.
———. 2020b. La philosophie comme profession et la participation démocratique dans la pensée politique d'Éric Weil. *Eco-Ethica 8*.
Chiarini, S. 2019. οὐδεν λέγειν/nihil dicere: A Lexical and semantic survey. *Mnemosyne 72*: 114–149.
Deligne, A. 1998. *Éric Weil: Ein zeitgenössischer Philosoph*. Bonn: Romanistischer Verlag.
Ganty, É. 1997. *Penser la modernité*. Namur: Presses Universitaires de Namur.
Guibal, F. 2013. L'idée de Dieu dans la *Logique de la philosophie*. *Cultura: Revista de História e Teoria Das Ideias 31*: 163–175.
Habermas, J. 1984. *Theory of communicative action Volume 1*. Boston: Beacon Press.
———. 1985. *Theory of communicative action Volume 2*. Boston: Beacon Press.
Hamblin, C. 1970. *Fallacies*. London: Methuen & Co Ltd.
Hegel, G.W.F. 2015. *Georg Wilhelm Friedrich Hegel: The science of logic*. Trans. G. Di Giovanni, rev. ed. Cambridge, UK: Cambridge University Press.
Kirscher, G. 1989. *La philosophie d'Éric Weil*. Paris: Presses Universitaires de France.
———. 1990. Éric Weil et Socrate: Discussion et dialogue. In *Discours, violence et langage: Un socratisme d'Éric Weil*, ed. P. Canivez and P.-J. Labarrière, 235–257. Paris: Éditions Osiris.
Marcelo, G. 2013. Paul Ricœur et Eric Weil. Histoire, vérité et conflit des interprétations. *Cultura. Revista de História e Teoria das Ideias 31*: 247–266. https://doi.org/10.4000/cultura.1881.
Perelman, C., and L. Olbrechts-Tyteca. 1958. *Traité de l'argumentation*. 5th ed. Bruxelles: Éditions de l'Université de Bruxelles.
Quillien, J. 1982. La cohérence et la négation: Essai d'interprétation des premières catégories de la *Logique de la Philosophie*. In *Sept études sur Éric Weil*, ed. G. Kirscher and J. Quillien, 145–185. Villeneuve-d'Ascq: Presses Universitaires de Lille.
Rahman, S., Z. McConaughey, A. Klev, and N. Clerbout. 2018. *Immanent reasoning or equality in action: A plaidoyer for the play level*. Cham: Springer.
Ricœur, P. 1984. De l'absolu à la sagesse par l'action. In *Actualité d'Éric Weil*, ed. C.É. Weil. Paris: Beauchesne.
———. 1991. Pour une éthique du compromis: Interview avec Paul Ricœur. *Alternatives Non Violentes 80*: 2–7.
Roman, J. 1988. Entre Hannah Arendt et Éric Weil. *Esprit (1940) 140/141* (7/8): 38–49.
Rorty, R. 1989. *Contingency, irony, and solidarity*. Cambridge UK: Cambridge University Press.
Sanou, J.B. 2008. *Violence et sagesse dans la philosophie d'Éric Weil*. Rome: Edetrice Pontificia Università Gregoriana.
Santayana, G. 1955. *Scepticism and animal faith*. New York: Dover Publications.
Savadogo, M. 2003. *Éric Weil et l'achèvement de la philosophie dans l'action*. Namur: Presses Universitaires de Namur.

References

Sellars, W. 1992. *Science and metaphysics: Variations on Kantian themes*. Atascadero: Ridgeview Publishing Company.

Stanguennec, A. 1992. *Être, soi, sens: Les antécédences herméneutiques de la dialectique réflexive*. Villeneuve-d'Ascq: Presses Universitaires du Septentrion.

Toulmin, S. 2003. *The use of argument (Updated)*. Cambridge UK: Cambridge University Press.

Valdério, F. 2014. Linguagem, violência e sentido: A propósito de um debate entre Éric Weil e Paul Ricœur. *Argumentos: Revista de. Filosofia 6* (11): 159–171.

Vancourt, R. 1970. Quelques remarques sur le problème de Dieu dans la philosophie d'Éric Weil. *Archives de Philosophie 33* (4): 471–490.

Weil, E. 1950. *Logique de la philosophie*. Paris: Librairie Philosophique Vrin.

———. 1956. *Philosophie politique*. Paris: Librairie Philosophique Vrin.

———. 1970. *Essais et conférences: Tome 1*. Paris: Librarie Plon.

———. 1971. *Essais et conférences: Tome 2*. Paris: Librarie Plon.

———. 1999. *Essais sur la nature, l'histoire et la politique*. Villeneuve-d'Ascq: Presses Universitaires du Septentrion.

———. 2003. *Philosophie et réalité: Tome 1*. Paris: Beauchesne.

Wohlrapp, H.R. 2014. *The concept of argument: A philosophical foundation*. Dordrecht: Springer Netherlands.

Chapter 8
Justification and Pluralism in the *Logic of Philosophy*

8.1 Introduction

Reading the *Logic of Philosophy* as opening up the possibility of an interactive and dynamic theory of argumentation implies a reflection on the practice of philosophy as the junction between contrasting and conflictual theses about reality, about the Good, the Just, the Beautiful, about what makes a life worth living as a meaningful whole. These different theses all aim at being taken seriously, as establishing some sort of consensus and authority that ranges over communities, that act upon the individual. What the logic of philosophy shows however is that there are multiple positions that make claims to certainty and that provide an orientation. This certainty and orientation are naïve when they are inherited from the tradition by the fact that an individual belongs to a community. As soon as the individual is faced with the diversity of positions and theses that may exist in the beating heart of their own community, the individual must, if they want to establish mature certainty and a mature orientation, seek ways to establish the authority that leads to consensus.

In argumentative practices this is done by creating an order of explanation that justifies one's position and one's theses. This implies creating a philosophical system that allows the individual to understand their life and their action and their beliefs as a unified and meaningful whole. In the *Logic of Philosophy*, this is done by making explicit the way that semantic content is determined and developed through opposition. As already noted, this way of seeing the development of semantic content implies a kind of fallibilism (understood as openness). This fallibilism is important to establishing discursive authority because mature certainty and mature orientation are *always* in the process of making readjustments, corrections, and modifications to their commitments. The kind of intellectual maturity implied by mature certainty and mature orientation is fallibilist because it is always situated in a meaningful natural and social reality that contains natural and social novelty. Bringing people to see and understand this, so that they shoulder this effort to become intellectually mature themselves is, for Weil, part of the horizon of argumentative practices. The diversity that presents itself to the individual in their lives implies that there are different types of argumentative strategies. This also means that there are different levels of justificatory strategies needed to bring people into the horizon of argumentation, which is the coordinated reasonable action between people with different theses and different positions. Just because this *can* happen however, nothing implies that argument moves inexorably towards this finality. According to Weil's understanding of human freedom, individuals can always turn away from reasonable action and argument. This possibility places an enormous amount of strain on the classic characterization of justificatory practices. According to this characterization, justificatory practices aim to establish knockdown arguments about what grounds our beliefs and what guarantees the authority that certain beliefs—understood as doxastic claims—are supposed to have. Because of the strain that the diversity of different theses places on justificatory practices, it is a legitimate question to ask if this diversity can be brought together under a unity. If it cannot, does that mean that there are no good doxastic claims at all? Or, if we accept that each person can make good doxastic claims and that each person does in fact make some good ones, does that mean that each of these claims are restricted to a tight circle that is traced around each individual and their subjective experience? Does Weil's position leave us open to skepticism and relativism? In order to correctly answer that question one must look at the kinds of justificatory practices that are present in Weil's work, and look at what seeing philosophy as a reasonably practiced activity implies.

This chapter will thus aim at showing the fecundity of reading the *Logic of Philosophy* along pragmatist, expressivist, and inferentialist lines by showing how the tools developed can be used to tackle two of recurrent philosophical problems—skepticism and relativism. In order to do so, I will be presenting stripped-down versions of the skeptical and the relativist positions. As stripped-down versions, it could seem that I am presenting strawmen versions of them (as well as of certain major justificatory live options) in order to more easily knock them over. However, my intention is different. By presenting stripped-down versions, I am looking to operate a critical reduction of appearances in order to get at what is essential about these positions. The strawman critique would be fair if I were not presenting the most stripped-down versions of these positions. What Weil has taught us is that only the barest-bones positions are irreducible. Any position that looks to answer specific critiques involves multiple reprises because it operates in real discussion and dialogue. To respond to legitimate critiques we combine multiple conflicting commitments to keep our position coherent. The most articulate, most sophisticated versions of these stances therefore depend on multiple reprises. So, even while sticking to their basic premise—their irreducible central claim—they are in fact defending a mixed form of justificatory practices.

The chapter will thus start by establishing the kind of justificatory practices that accompany reading the *Logic of Philosophy* as a theory of argumentation along pragmatist, expressivist, and inferentialist lines. Fully developing Weil's theory would require us to extend the analyses found herein to his moral and political philosophy. This is outside of the scope of this work, nonetheless the direction that such an analysis should take can be sketched by giving a single example that *is* in the purview of Weil's moral and political philosophy. This example is the tension between relativism and pluralism. This chapter will apply the type of justificatory practices that go along with reading the *Logic of Philosophy* as a theory of argumentation to the specific relationship between relativism and pluralism. While this case will not exhaust Weil's practical philosophy, it will hopefully show how this practical philosophy is deployed in a concrete case.

8.2 Eric Weil's Three-Tier Notion of Justification

8.2.1 Foundations, Coherence, and Contexts

The *Logic of Philosophy* as a whole does not elaborate any overt theory of knowledge or of justification. Eric Weil however does provide numerous elements that allow us to understand the structure of justification in his work. Theories of knowledge *are* found in specific categories, such as *The Object* and *The Condition*. Nonetheless, these theories of knowledge cannot be said to be *completely* representative of Weil's own position. They are of course in a sense locally valid because each category is built around an irreducible form of coherence. At a global level however any category-specific theory of knowledge is surpassed by the logic of philosophy as a whole. The theory of knowledge presented in *The Condition*, for example, is of critical importance for our grasp of physical causal phenomena, but it cannot be applied to the human sciences, which are grasped thanks to the discourse that is developed in *Intelligence*. When it is surpassed, other categories reduce *The Condition* to a reflection on a certain type of knowledge. Because of this, it is no longer seen to ground the comprehensive grasp of the world *and* human life seen as a unity in this world. This fracture was already present in the category itself, as the fact/value divide has shown. One reason that Weil does not present a theory of knowledge may be that he sees *knowledge* as implying the relationship between the subject and the object, and he sees Hegel as resolving this question. This is why every category after *The Absolute* deals with the individual's relationship to discourse and not their relationship to the world. *The Absolute* remains the category that grasps ground-level content completely. Weil sees his project as surpassing the Hegelian one however. It is not directly interested in cognition, understood as the grasp of the external world by the thinking subject. It is interested in comprehension, understood as how the world and discourse are grasped and made intelligible in discourse. Thinking the real in a coherent discourse is therefore different from establishing a relationship between a thinking subject and an object. So while there is no "theory of knowledge" in the logic of philosophy, the different resources developed throughout the history of discourse, including epistemological resources, are present within it. How these resources are organized will allow us to understand Weil's position concerning justification.

We can say that Weil separates the question of justification on two levels. The first level deals with the object-level discourse that is interested in what is traditionally called knowledge and cognition. The second level deals with the meta-discourse that is interested in comprehension. This two-level distinction explains why the fallibilism implied by Weil's theory of semantic content is not merely to be found in the recognition of error. It is also to be found in the openness to the possibility that each person has of transforming their dissatisfaction with a determined discourse into a new discourse that grasps the object of the previous discourse *as* error. Error is not the correction of some predetermined truth. It is structured by discourse itself. Despite this modification, the goal of the argument will be to show that in both cases epistemological concerns turn around a notion of authority. Both the pragmatist tradition that I have presented,[1] and Eric Weil highlight the way that epistemic authority is born out of discursive practices. The main difference is that, for Weil, these discursive practices are articulated into multiple meaningful coherent centers that are conflictual. Because of this, it is only in shared social and discursively articulated practices that individuals can make claims to objectivity at the first level and to comprehensiveness at the second. In the spirit of a theory that defends sapient argumentative practices as the best way to clarify and overcome the kinds of conflict that can lead to violence, I will show how the goal of justification is to settle conflicts by establishing the epistemic authority to which individuals bind themselves.

Here it will be useful to give an overview of the way in which I read the main competing justificatory structures—foundationalism, coherentism, and contextualism.[2] After, I will situate Weil's thoughts on justification. This will help me to deploy these terms in a homogenous way and thus show what exactly the structure of justification defended here is trying to do. This is also important because, normally, these different structures are presented as having some amount of mutual exclusion. Because this overall work is not a work of epistemology, I cannot go into all the different varieties of these positions. Indeed, contemporary philosophy is replete with sophisticated versions of all these different structures. They are positions that respond to critiques by continually qualifying and tweaking their claims. And they are right to do so. I hope to even show why they are right to do so. I am only presenting broad stroke versions of these positions.[3] As I have said, they, like strawmen,

---

[1] Wilfrid Sellars is the figure to reformulate the epistemological question in pragmatist terms as a question of authority. For analyses of the role that epistemic authority plays in Sellars's philosophy, see Kukla (2000) and Kalpokas (2017).

[2] It is inessential to my argument to look at reliabilism and other naturalized forms of justification, or virtue epistemologies, etc. While a work on Weil and contemporary epistemology would be of great interest, this is not that work.

[3] In order to paint these positions in broad strokes and to get to their irreducible core, I have drawn from numerous works, notably from Annis (1978, 1982); Davidson (1983); BonJour (1985, 2009); Chisholm (1989); Haack (1993); Williams (1995, 1999, 2001); Koppelberg (1998); deVries et al. (2000). Nonetheless, the exact formulation of these problems is my own.

8.2 Eric Weil's Three-Tier Notion of Justification

could easily be knocked down. My goal however is not to defend any of these positions in themselves, but rather to situate what I see as Weil's argument-motivated form of justification.

Starting from the first form of justification, foundationalism, we can say that, at its core, there is the idea that there is at least one basic belief. This belief is basic because it is both atomic (that is discrete), and because it is primitive (which means we can go no further down). In a sense, with such beliefs we hit bottom. There have been numerous candidates for basic beliefs across the history of philosophy such as Being, the One, God, the *cogito*, sense-data, etc. What is important in foundationalism is the way this belief is used to ground other beliefs. Because it is used to ground other beliefs, it is basic in a second sense, it is seen as the minimal unity. It is a building block of other beliefs. Because of its basicness and its primitiveness, and because it is supposed to be immediately and non-inferentially known, this basic belief is seen to have a special status called epistemic authority. Epistemic authority does two things. First, it establishes the well-foundedness of a claim, and second, it confers that well-foundedness onto claims that follow from it. Thus in foundationalism it is supposed to be the discrete, primitive, immediate qualities of the candidate of basicness that is supposed to establish its status as epistemically authoritative. This is what allows individuals to infer their other beliefs from this basic one. This is what Wilfrid Sellars calls the given. According to his critique of the given, whatever the candidate, it is supposed to be immediately available to the subject and thus immediately authoritative. The very existence of this belief is supposed to ground and guarantee knowledge. In these terms, the mere recognition or presence of the candidate of a basic belief is supposed to be sufficient to ground all the beliefs to be inferred from it. Thus we can say that the broad strokes version of foundationalism is as follows:

1. A belief is basic if and only if it is used to ground other beliefs but requires no ground itself.
2. A basic belief is grounded and needs no ground if and only if the mere appearance of the candidate for grounding is sufficient for the ground to hold.

This is markedly different from the classic broad stroke positions of coherentism and contextualism.

Foundationalism is traditionally based on a single candidate that is sufficient to ground *all* other claims, and thus the classic critique is that foundationalism holds an infinite regress. The infinite regress, simply put, highlights that we can always ask "why" one more time. In other words, in a linear model of justification, the end point seems arbitrary, any ground, no matter how secure it intuitively seems, needs another ground in order to establish its authority *as* a ground. The classic charge against foundationalism demands that foundationalists explain why grounding stops where it does, with their candidate. What is the special character of this thing that is supposed to bring an end to the regress of why? In fact, the perceived insufficiency of providing any sufficient ground, and the apparent arbitrariness of candidate beliefs are what brought about the search for a second candidate. This second candidate, coherentism, abandons the idea that some ground has any special nature that separates it from the other knowledge claims. Instead, it claims that justification rests on a set of beliefs that are reinforced by their own internal coherence. This, in theory, allows epistemologists to overcome the search for some special characteristic, because no single belief is special. Rather, it is the strength of the whole that secures the well-foundedness of justification. The only thing that defines specific certain beliefs is how deeply embedded they are in the set of beliefs, that is, how many inferences depend on them to justify their place in the set. And indeed, early inferentialists who rejected the foundational picture of knowledge often flocked to the coherentist camp, Sellars included. In this way we can define coherentism as follows:

1. A belief is justified if an only if it fits into a coherent set of beliefs.

However, just as the coherentist is often disappointed with the foundationalist's claim that some belief must have a special status that is sufficient to ground other beliefs, the foundationalist is often disappointed with the coherentist structure as well. There is also a sense in which this structure seems arbitrary. This form of justification is attacked as lacking empirical grounding and thus leading to the danger of philosophical relativism. If the only criteria for coherent justification is that a knowledge claim p fit in with other beliefs, there is nothing to guarantee that this set of beliefs is true, nor is there anything that puts a set of beliefs *necessarily* in contact with the world of everyday experience. Thus, not only can a set of beliefs not be true, there is no way to decide between different sets of beliefs. This lack of decidability is thus seen as opening the door to relativism.

Relativism is not however the only major problem with coherentism. There is an underlying suspicion that it folds into foundationalism despite its claims that it avoids the foundationalist pitfalls. This critique goes as follows: according to coherentism, beliefs are justified by the way they fit into a coherent set of beliefs, thus beliefs acquire derivative authority thanks to their place in the set. This however seems to give a special status to the belief that a coherent set is sufficient to pass authority onto other beliefs. In other words, according this critique, coherentism is merely second-order foundationalism or, as Michael Williams calls it, "foundationalism in disguise."[4] The battle between foundationalism and coherentism raged for much of the twentieth century in analytical epistemology, and because of this, people started looking for a *third way*. Here, I will only treat contextualism, one of the main candidates. The idea behind contextualism is that there are situational considerations that must enter into the justificatory picture precisely because justifying is a social affair. This implies that in different situations different individuals are better qualified to give justifications for knowledge claims and that in different situations different candidates have different levels of claims to well-foundedness. Thus, I am more likely to believe my friend the arborist about the classification of a live oak than I am my friend who is a medical doctor that has only ever lived in urban areas. The implication is that we see the interest in and sensitivity to trees as often being

---

[4] Williams (2001), 134.

much lower for city-dwellers than for people who live in the country. So, while somebody that is a medical doctor may have a deep knowledge of arboriculture, this nonetheless has to be established in a way that their knowledge of the human organism does not (being a medical doctor is one of the means of establishing their authority concerning the human organism). This implies, to use Susan Haack's phrase, that there are different "epistemic communities"[5] and that, within these communities, there is a contextual and situational recognition of what counts as a well-founded belief. According to this characterization:

1. A belief is contextually basic if and only if it is grounded by being asserted in the appropriate context by an appropriate epistemic community, and it is that context that grants it epistemic authority.

Contextualism supposes that we can identify epistemic authority, and that in the cases that matter, that authority will be seen to hold because of the way that we attribute epistemic authority. However, unlike foundationalism, this authority has to be established discursively, and is not in some way outside of justificatory practices. Here, we can however apply the same critique of coherentism to contextualism. Does contextualism not just fold into coherentism? Are epistemic communities not just other ways of understanding coherent sets? In this case, would contextualism not face the same problem as coherentism, caught between relativism and foundationalism? If this is true, justification and authority seem to fold into another ancient problem, just dressed up differently. This problem is the choice between foundationalism, relativism, or skepticism. We seem stuck with either (1) an ultimate coherent set that is able to be distinguished because there is *at bottom* a criterion that allows this distinction, or (2) no criterion because there are a multitude of different equally valid sets, or (3) no criterion because well-founded knowledge is a chimera. This is a difficult question to answer, so getting at it the roundabout way might be useful. Each of these positions uses different strategies to attribute epistemic authority, so perhaps instead of attacking these strategies head on it may be useful to unpack the notion of epistemic authority.

8.2.2 *Epistemic Authority*

In the last chapter I spoke about the transitivity of reasons. This expression is meant to capture the way that we humans are uniquely sensitive to reasons: reasons act on us, they affect and change us. Epistemic authority is used to explain the transitivity of reasons. It allows us to understand why claims should be shared and thus also why others should use these claims as their own. Because it explains the transitivity of reasons, epistemic authority is something that only happens in discourse. Individual representations, intuitions, ideas (of the self, of God, of the unity of

---

[5] Haack (1993), 20.

nature), such things can make up the background of claims of epistemic authority, but none of them are autonomous. In other words, no one's representation, intuition, or idea can be taken up by another unless it is shared in discourse and the person's epistemic authority is recognized (even if only tacitly). This is because in discourse people don't take your word for things, but they do take your words. Epistemic authority matters because of its role in establishing the transitivity of reasons and because of the way we see good reasons as acting upon our understanding of the world. It is thus a characteristic that is ascribed to claims, or people, or situations, etc. In the context given, it is what allows a conflict to be settled. It establishes the hold that one claim, person, or situation has over others. It establishes authority. But it also establishes that the content of the claim can be taken up by another person in their own reasoning. It authorizes an individual to use that content as being good, thus establishing the well-foundedness of a claim (person, situation, etc.). This version of epistemic authority leans heavily on the notion of achievement words as found in Gilbert Ryle's *Concept of Mind*[6] and exploited by Wilfrid Sellars in "Empiricism and the Philosophy of Mind," and on Sellars's own discussion of authority through this work. Ryle notes that there are verbs that signify achievements, that "signify not merely that performance has been gone through, but also that something has been brought off by the agent going through it."[7] For Ryle and Sellars, knowing is an achievement that engages both conceptual and sensuous capacities that allows the subject to "have the world in view," to use John McDowell's useful turn of phrase.[8]

Joining the notion of epistemic authority to the notion of an achievement shows that both the authority of our knowledge claims and the knowledge itself are achievements. We can read the classic definition of knowledge (justified true belief), as being the conjuncture between this specific type of authority (the justification) and of the achievement (connecting a belief to truth). This allows knowledge to be understood as the result of the process that brings about the achievement of epistemic authority. At first blush perceptual knowledge seems to be the most basic form of knowledge because our perceptual experiences are often taken to be in some way basic. However, the way that Sellars and, I will argue, Weil present authority reminds us that things are not so simple. First off, Sellars, insists over and over the way that attempts to link authority to bald perceptual experiences is tied to what he calls the myth of the given. For Sellars, this naïve form of epistemic authority already brings forth our conceptual capacities in order to judge how a bit of the world should be approached, taken, and absorbed into the rest of our body of information. The idea that there is some candidate that, just by its presence, counts as justifying a knowledge claim, and that an individual can non-inferentially and immediately recognize both what the thing is and the way that it should justify a knowledge claim, is for him wrongheaded. In fact, he highlights the way in which epistemic authority is a

---

[6] Ryle (1966).
[7] Ryle (1966), 130.
[8] McDowell (2013).

8.2 Eric Weil's Three-Tier Notion of Justification

second-order status. It is conferred through reflection. In this way, knowledge claims are inferentially articulated. They are mediated by other claims. One of the key claims that I have made throughout this work is that discourse affects and shapes our conceptual landscape. This is what is behind the notion of the space of reasons (understood as a categorial meta-concept), as well as Weil's notions of philosophical categories (which are meta-conceptual). In the context of epistemic authority, we can see how this plays out.

As a reminder, Sellars has called the space of reasons a space "of justifying and being able to justify what one says."[9] Following this characterizatiom, McDowell argues that in defining the space of reasons this way, Sellars was trying to point out that:

> the conceptual apparatus we employ when we place things in the logical space of reasons is irreducible to any conceptual apparatus that does not serve to place things in the logical space of reasons. So the master thought as it were draws a line; above the line are places in the logical space of reasons, and below it are characterizations that do not do that.[10]

Bald perceptual experiences are, for the empiricist, supposed to be enough to establish epistemic authority, and defended this way, they are of a piece with the foundationalist account of justification. The "Sellars line" tries to show that this is not the case. According to the myth of the given, foundationalist accounts of epistemic authority discount the socially articulated way that this status is attributed, endorsed, and shared. As I read Sellars here, knowledge is a social achievement that is brought out by an initial claim and then refined through the concomitant claims that go along with and against it. It is whittled down before being reconstructed, and thus it is not reconstructed out of already discrete units. This highlights however one of the most troubling things about epistemic authority. Because it is social, no single person is responsible for it. No single person can verify and check all of it. We depend on others to know.

By developing the notion of the inheritance of authority, Robert Brandom provides us with the tools to overcome this problem. Here, we can bring back in the role of commitments and entitlements in the game of giving and asking for reasons. Commitments and entitlements allow us, as discursive scorekeepers, to judge what content an individual is committed to when they say something. Furthermore, it allows us to judge what they are entitled to affirm, what they are obliged to affirm, and what they are prohibited from affirming, all based on an initial commitment. The structure of commitments and entitlements allows us to flesh out the shape of an interlocutor's space of reasons by helping us to see what further content it commits them to, based on their original claim. It also helps us to see what one is entitled to or prohibited from saying based on that commitment. However, by recognizing the goodness of an individual's claim, we, as their interlocutor, are embedding ourselves in a structure of authorization and acknowledgement. This allows us, by acknowledging the goodness of their assertion, to recognize our interlocutor's

---

[9] Sellars (1997), § 36.
[10] McDowell (2013), 5.

justification. In other words, when we see them as correctly navigating the space of reasons, we can adopt their claims as our own. Brandom has noted that these two structures, inferential moves from commitment to commitment, and from one individual's claim to another individual's claim, are the ways that commitments are inherited.[11] For Brandom, the notion of inheritance is built into what he calls *the default and challenge model of entitlement*. According to this model, "when a commitment is attributed to an interlocutor, entitlement is attributed as well, by default."[12] This means that Cartesian hyperbolic doubt, for instance, does not stand because it does not provide an appropriate challenge, rather it sweepingly challenges every claim. According to Cartesian doubt, we must demolish all of our beliefs until we reach some bedrock that itself cannot be put into doubt. But doubt itself must be justified. Therefore, individuals are not obliged to open themselves to all doubts, rather only to appropriately presented ones. In fact, by starting from a social model of the inheritance of entitlements, the majority of our commitments have a default status, and it is only when an appropriate and reasoned (that is, justified) challenge presents itself that the doubt ought to be entertained.

From Descartes and Hume, up through modern authors like Barry Stroud,[13] there has been the idea that there is something natural about philosophical doubt, that it is a type of abyss into which everyone falls as soon as they start asking themselves questions from a philosophical point of view. If that is true, I argue, that is because there is the naïve impression that *all* we do when we justify something is dig down to the belief that grounds it. When we get to that belief, we are supposed to find something indubitable that allows us to prove what we say. However often, we are left perplexed. We are perplexed because we find nothing but another belief. There is thus a structural correlation that seems to exist between accepting foundationalist justificatory strategies and skepticism. Michael Williams notes that Cartesian skepticism "presupposes substantive foundationalism"[14] because such skepticism also "*presupposes* the general priority of experiential knowledge and is thus no argument for it."[15] In other words, skepticism is tied to foundationalist accounts precisely because it makes demands for some immediately known ground, but is then frustrated that, in these terms, we never seem to get down to bottom. Weil highlights this problem when he notes that philosophy has traditionally failed to find any *single* non-discursive ground that can nonetheless be articulated discursively. He states that:

> no great philosopher thought that they could get rid of this reality above everything called real, or at least, none thought that they could get rid of the idea of a reality which transcends every given—and here *every* is taken in an unrestricted sense, at the level where sums and sets can be formed. The One, pure act, God as he in himself is, Substance, the archetypal intellect, Reason: philosophers have always ended up at *what is not* (if they have not started from there) because *this indescribable super-being*, this *unspeakable* (it is no accident that

---

[11] Brandom (1994), 176.
[12] Brandom (1994), 177.
[13] Stroud (1984).
[14] Williams (2001), 187.
[15] Williams (2001), 189.

these terms keep coming back over and over, and always in their etymological sense) seemed to ground all description, all discourse, and all being (LP, 6–7).[16]

For Weil, there has been a tendency throughout philosophy's history to try to dig down to this simple unique thing that is to ground our experience and our knowledge, that is to endow our claims with authority. However, when this claim is made, the thing that grants authority is seen to be itself different in some way from *discursive* authority precisely because it is unspeakable and indescribable. Nonetheless foundationalist justification *does* capture a specific aspect of our justificatory practices, the fact that any challenge is, first off, a challenge to a single claim found in real discursive practices.

We then abstract away everything that does not enter into the justification we are trying to establish, we indeed do try to dig down until we find something that grants our claim, *or* our challenge, authority. We are often however unsatisfied with our attempts. This, I argue, is because this is not *all* we do when we enter into justificatory practices. The fact that individuals can start from different discursive centers has the consequence that any discursive center can present a reasoned challenge to another. Any attempt to project all of discourse onto a single unique plane runs into this problem precisely because it runs into this plurality of reasonable discourses. The main problem though is that, because we have a structure of default entitlements, we take so much of our experience to already be justified. Here, in order to understand how that happens, we can look at the way Weil theorizes something similar to the default and challenge model of entitlement in his characterization of *what goes without saying*.

8.2.3 Naïve Authority and What Goes Without Saying

For Weil, as long as an individual is in a situation—in a natural and cultural context with a largely shared public discourse—there are a variety of things that are taken for granted, that *go without saying*. What goes without saying is thus the body of facts that are present in any given situation and that no one in the community even *sees*. This body of facts is so evident that it is invisible. It is the source of the naïve certainty and the naïve orientation that is given to the individual by the accident of their birth into a certain historic period, a certain community, a certain class, sex, gender, race, etc. It is, in other words, the stuff of each human cultural tradition, and because it has succeeded up to this point in allowing individuals to orient their lives it has a naïve inherited authority. In the context of justification, this situation, with its content that goes without saying, provides a default position into which individuals enter claims. It provides the structure of the goodness of claims. This default

---

[16] For Weil, the recognition that every assertion is ungrounded and false, precisely because it is unable to say the whole truth, is what characterizes the jump between the category of *Truth* and *Meaninglessness*.

position nonetheless can itself be questioned. For Weil, this happens when the individual does not find satisfaction in their situation. This dissatisfaction, which in an epistemological context can be called reasoned doubt, is the itch that keeps the individual from accepting the consequences of the discursive category in which they have become aware of their singularity. It is this dissatisfaction that is shown to be the source of reasonable challenges to the default structure of the goodness of claims that are ambient in the cultural context. In terms of the default and challenge model of justification, one sees their dissatisfaction as providing sufficient grounds to challenge the epistemic authority of a commitment that has been inherited by default.

Nothing requires the individual to challenge their cultural context, and they can even reinforce their central commitment and ignore any contradiction in order not to leave it. When a person does challenge it though, it is because they are seeking to make their discourse coherent.[17] The possibility of challenging discourse discursively is nowhere clearer than when a person has a strong grasp on their own discourse, and is able to identify where challenges hold. This can imply either the attempt to reinforce one's own claims in order to insulate them from any challenge, or an attempt to examine and judge the coherence of one's own claims. In the second case, this requires being willing to see how well claims and inferences fit together and being able to evaluate the global level of one's claims. People who insulate their claims remain in a foundationalist model. People who do not are pushed to move past it.

For Weil, doubt is only "natural" when individuals are faced with multiple reasonable options. We do not naturally doubt the world around us. The world is one of the things that goes without saying. When individuals have a discourse and orientation the philosophical problem may come up but it does not hold. The "naturalness" of philosophical doubt is thus linked to the way we put our discourse and our orientation in parentheses in order to evaluate multiple reasonable options. When we are in a real crisis of orientation and discourse, our doubt, for Weil, is not philosophical in the Cartesian sense. It is philosophical in a practical sense. This is because, as Weil notes, "philosophical eras are eras of crisis (*krinein* = to discern) where the questions are as ambiguous as the responses" (LP, 431). Thus, for him, true philosophical doubt is not doubting everything. It is the doubt about what to do when faced with multiple reasonable choices. Philosophical doubt, understood practically, thus requires that we discern and choose practical courses of action. Following this diagnosis, it is important to note that doubt does play a "natural" productive role in our belief formation, in the formation of our discursive commitments, but only in

---

[17] For Weil, this possibility is found in the tension between the particular and the universal. The individual becomes aware of their particularity when they try to square the formal abstract *universal* character of moral reflection with the concrete determined *particular and private* character of the meaning they find present in their ethical life (PP, 105–128). This conflict is resolved for the individual in the transformation of their moral reflection into political action through "the transition to the understanding of action from the point of view of action itself" (PP, 114). This passage reinforces the idea of reading Weil's work as a theory of argumentation. It is through reasonable argument that the reasonable individual acts on others.

8.2 Eric Weil's Three-Tier Notion of Justification

order to act. Following this diagnosis, radical doubt then becomes an overzealous misuse of the more measured doubt that plays a salubrious role in belief formation. Cartesian skepticism is thus a consequence of trying to build a coherent discourse out of the discursive commitment to doubt. The fact that, for Weil, there is no category of skepticism, and that each philosophical category has its own skeptics is proof that he views this commitment as a failure. In this way, for Weil, skepticism is a derivative position.

The best analysis of the interplay between radical doubt and the normal or non-philosophical life is to be found in Hume. By separating the philosophical and the vulgar, Hume provides different regimes in order to defend the pessimistic claim that philosophical inquiry leads to skepticism. His optimistic solution is to claim that life takes over and that we are unable to remain skeptical because we are unable to remain in a posture of philosophical analysis. Using the notions put together so far, we can provide a different analysis of the skeptical predicament. What philosophical inquiry shows us is how our beliefs are inherited. It shows us that this or that intuitively natural way of establishing a bit of knowledge through our own experience depends on knowledge's social articulation. Because of this, when we reach bottom we are shown that all we are left with is a more or less coherent system of inheritance. These inheritances, because they are inferentially articulated, allow us to doubt even the existence of the external world. However, precisely because the meaning of claims only makes sense in the larger context of the meaning of a life (a life with orientated action and satisfactions that aims at contentment), the orientation of our life for the most part overrides the problem of the inheritance of our commitments. We leave discourse to act, and in doing so, we stop worrying about skeptical claims.

Skepticism thus becomes a problem because of its practical consequences. It is a problem when it is converted into other commitments, when it becomes cynicism or nihilism, when it leads to an experience of meaninglessness. In these cases, it is a problem because skeptical conclusions can lead to the desire to undermine the discourse of others, either by sowing doubt for its own sake or by provoking violence. The skeptical conclusions, applied to philosophical argumentation, matter. But they matter within a conception of philosophy as a future-facing practice that helps individuals judge how to act against the background of contingency. We are not worried about skepticism because of its status as a belief, but because of its practical consequences. If this were not the case, epistemologists would not be worried about skeptical conclusions. Either we would accept them as true, and move on (which is Hume's position) or we would refuse them as unsatisfying (which is the lay position). The fact that epistemologists feel the need to provide a reasonable challenge highlights this practical worry. They are caught between the philosophical difficulty of grounding authority and the vulgar everyday conviction that our beliefs are well-grounded.[18] These possibilities nonetheless show how a theory of argumentation

---

[18] The paradox of certainty is another way of articulating this same problem, see Sect. 5.3. Skepticism is only a problem for those caught between naïve and mature certainty.

that is based on discursive commitment and that places an explicit emphasis on orders of explanation helps to overcome the skeptical dilemma. Skepticism is seen as a problem that can undermine the possibility of reasonable action, but also as a problem that can be overcome by good argumentative practices. Overcoming the potentially problematic practical consequences of skepticism requires a practical solution, not a theoretical one. This is why the lay position is so resistant to philosophical doubt. For the most part, individuals already have sufficient orientation in their lives. The dilemma is overcome naturally so to speak, tacitly and without further ado.

The skeptical question nonetheless remains. How does one ground epistemic authority? The answer is one of the key aspects of critiques of the given and is a key aspect of Weil's theory. Epistemic authority only makes sense and thus is only grounded *in* discourse. In fact, Weil states that one of the discoveries of the category of *Discussion* was that:

> [the] laws of language (or of thought) that have emerged over the course of this Socratic investigation are therefore valid for everybody and, since no knowledge is sheltered from examination and since there is no authority, the investigation in pursuit of the Good is revolutionary. The community that wants to cling to the tradition has no content and falls apart because everyone tugs the tradition in their own direction and pursues whatever they believe their advantage to be without any preliminary examination. The human being therefore has to understand that they can only be satisfied by reason and by language (*logos*). They cannot be satisfied in their personal being. Rather, they are satisfied as a universal element of the community, as a thinking individual (LP, 133).

By framing justification in terms of a theory of argumentation, we can see the criterion of universalizability as a way to present epistemic authority. Traditionally, universalizability has been something that hopes to provide knockdown arguments and to close the debate once and for all. Weil sees it differently however. Weil claims that the logical evolution of being (the history of discourse from Plato to Hegel) turns on the possibility of creating an identity between the subject and the object. In other words, the history of philosophy is largely concerned with creating a single discourse about the world where truth-conditions hold. What Weil tries to show is that philosophical understanding outruns this type of identity precisely because having a philosophical understanding of philosophy implies understanding the individual's relationship to discourse. Weil's characterization of the individual's relationship to discourse implies a plurality of reasonable claims. In this context, epistemic authority is seen to be the result of good argumentative practices that take this plurality into account. This is one of the gains of reading the *Logic of Philosophy* as a theory of argumentation: it allows us to see how epistemic authority is established.

For Weil, epistemic authority is established through a free a-reasonable choice to enter into discursive practices and to submit oneself to the normative weight of the authority that is already present in these practices. It is established there because it is only within these discursive practices that it becomes a problem. This definition of epistemic authority holds when, in the confrontation between two different beliefs, one of them is seen to be authoritative over another. It is thus not for all time and outside of every context, but is anchored in actual argumentative practices. Thus, what counts as epistemic authority is historically and socially articulated. This however does nothing to lessen its authority. *Everyone* who enters into these practices and who makes the continual choice to stay in these practices equally submits themselves. In fact, this highlights another key aspect of the skeptical dilemma. We become skeptics when we are shown that our knowledge should be framed as knowledge claims, which in fact would be better categorized as beliefs (doxastic commitments), and which don't immediately hold because their epistemic authority is seen to be merely discursive. Reading the skeptical dilemma this way, we can see that it is implicitly structured by another doxastic commitment, namely that epistemic authority must in some way be non-discursive (this dovetails with Williams's claim that skepticism and foundationalism are structurally linked). Skepticism is a consequence of finding no single knockdown argument once and for all. Faced with this kind of problem, philosophers provide candidates that are supposed to overcome it by providing some non-discursive ground. However, what a theory of discursive commitment shows is that this is not a viable solution as long as the goal is reasonable discourse. The shifting sands of epistemic authority is a problem internal to the structure of argumentation. Epistemic authority is only found in discourse because it is only in discourse that claims about universality and objectivity make sense.

8.2.4 *Justificatory Strategies and the Evolution of Authority*

Sellars rejected a foundationalist empiricist picture of epistemic authority. However, as I have already said, foundationalism does capture something about our epistemic experience. What I argue is that foundationalism holds at the level of the local confrontation between individual propositions that are grounded by the same central discursive commitment. When local justification doesn't hold, it signals a possible difference in the conceptual space from which individuals are working. In the context of the theory of argumentation that I presented in the last chapter, the primary problem is grounding and maintaining the initial agreement to reasonable action through discussion. I also claimed that philosophy can start and end anywhere. Following this argument, I highlighted how, in a context where individuals have spaces of reasons with only minimal overlap, non-discursive means play a greater role than discursive ones. What this also means is that a plurality of argumentative justificatory strategies needs to be deployed in order to create epistemic authority. This plurality aims at creating *durable* authority. As Weil acknowledges and as history has shown, violence can itself be used both discursively and non-discursively as a justificatory strategy. However, violence is unsatisfying. Even if it has already proven to be an effective *temporary* strategy to force agreement and to impose some (political) authority, violence does not itself provide durable and thus genuine epistemic authority. In fact, it is the strategy that is the most susceptible to the types of determinate negations that can undermine positions. Like violence, foundationalism also fails to establish durable authority because it assumes that there is a single unified discourse that is readily available and actually in effect and yet somehow at the same time non-discursive and everywhere identical.

Foundationalism thus responds to the first level at which we are confronted by the need for justificatory strategies. It is facing a single claim that our beliefs are initially tested. It is the reasonable challenge to an individual claim, or to an individual experience, that creates the first reasoned doubt, that presents possibilities that must be confronted and chosen between. For Weil, philosophical categories are born out of the attempt to bring irreducible elements of human experience into a coherent discourse. When specific concepts succeed in being coherently articulated, it is because individuals lead sufficiently coherent lives according to the concept's structure of commitments, entitlements, and incompatibilities. In order to understand the pull of the foundationalist's claim, it is important to see how our initial argumentative strategy will always be to use the immediately available inferences that belong to the dominant category in which the belief is situated. This is what is meant by a local level of justification. It is local not only because the resources needed to overcome the conflict are seen as locally available in the category, but also because any epistemic authority that is established treats propositions as discrete meaningful units. *Locally* they are, but again, this shall prove insufficient. In other words, in terms of Weil's theory, foundationalist justification works for in-category justification. This is the kind of justification that holds when interlocutors share a significant amount of overlap in their space of reasons—understood here as their dominant categories. This is also why regress arguments work against foundationalist justificatory structures. The regress argument exploits the local, propositional level of justification.

This also means that the agreement that allows for argumentative practices to hold is so well-established that only minor correction to any given claim is needed. Because all of us are not only part of linguistic and cultural communities, but also of epistemic communities with a certain amount of overlap, we tend to see what we do as justified. And often, given the overlap of these communities, it is. This overlap, for Weil, is found in the different *floors* of discourse. Remember, *Certainty* is the floor of tradition, *Discussion* is the floor of Antiquity, and *The Condition* is the floor of Modernity. This means that the discursive commitments and the discursive tools articulated in *The Condition* is available to everyone. It is our tradition and so we see it to be certain. However, because *The Condition* is not the last category, there exist reasoned refusals to this discourse. Reasoned doubt, disagreeing for reasons, the itch that irritates our belief, is grasped in these reasoned refusals. When we are speaking from commitments that hold at the same level of discourse, they can easily be resolved. Precisely because the majority of our interactions happen in shared linguistic, cultural, and epistemic communities (that all share the same discursive floor), our belief in the universality of our discursive position is constantly reinforced. Take our example of live oaks. If I am with a friend who is an arborist, and I misidentify a tree as a live oak and she corrects me, I will easily accept her correction because I recognize her authority and because the question at hand is placed in a domain where the authority that I recognize makes sense. The structure

8.2 Eric Weil's Three-Tier Notion of Justification

of justification is foundational here precisely because she is able to present specific claims that rest on her authority. There are also experiences which bring us out of this comfort. As soon as we find ourselves confronted by different philosophical categories, different domains of competence, or different spaces of reasons, the foundationalist strategy quickly becomes insufficient. As the overlap between the space of reasons diminishes, certain background assumptions, *what goes without saying*, in Weil's specific technical sense, no longer hold. This shows how important reflection is to establishing epistemic authority.

The kind of reflection that comes into play is one that allows the individual to relativize their claims and to compare them against each other. This demands that the individual put claims of truth on hold and compare different discursive centers and their permissible inferences. What this provides is the capacity to judge their own constellation of discursive commitments against that of their interlocutor. What I want to stress however is that, in the context of Weil's theory, this jump between different types of justificatory strategies—and between different claims of epistemic authority—must be freely taken. And it is not easy. The foundationalist justificatory strategy is outward facing. It takes one's position for granted and then defends it. When the position doesn't hold, reasonable argument demands that the position be changed. The snag is that this central discursive commitment can be seen as what provides the orientation and meaning in one's life. Any real seismic shift in one's central discursive commitment can thus be accompanied by doubt, anxiety, and insecurity. This is an often-ignored aspect of justificatory strategies. Philosophers hope to provide knockdown arguments when providing reasonable justificatory strategies. What they often forget is that when discursive positions are being confronted in argument, in discourse, or in our everyday conversational practices, they are the real discursive positions of concrete individuals who have a vested interest in defending these commitments. It is not enough to show the goodness of an argument, rather the interlocutor must recognize the value of acknowledging the goodness of the argument. This is precisely because these commitments fit into a space of reasons that defines an individual's action and the way they see their lives as meaningful. It takes a fair amount of intellectual maturity to be able to evaluate the totality of one's beliefs in this way. Kenneth Westphal provides the kind of intellectual maturity that we need in his analysis of "mature judgment" in Hegel's epistemology. Mature judgment is made up of "cardinal intellectual values" which include identifying problems, distinguishing the relevant elements of a problem, accommodating the competing considerations bearing on issues, all in order to make reasonable decisions.[19] While Weil's model of argumentation certainly looks to develop mature judgment, it is the way that his justificatory strategy characterizes the accommodation of competing considerations that is really important. Even though local foundationalist justification accommodates competing considerations, the role of accommodation ratchets up at the level of global justification. This is where individuals must put more and more of their commitments in parentheses in

---

[19] Westphal (2003), 48.

order to see how well they hold together. It is at the global level of epistemic justification that individuals are able to identify and judge *other* categories against their own according to the criterion of universality and of coherence that leads to greater levels of comprehensiveness.

Now, this does not mean that they will be able to see other categories as indeed being more comprehensive or as having a greater universal scope. It does however allow individuals to see the possibility of another way of organizing the world and beliefs as a human possibility, that is, as one that could actually be their own. Weil notes that this difference forces us "to acknowledge that there exists at least one other way of life and that this way, though not mine, is human in the strongest sense of the word, i.e., that it *could* be mine."[20] This is, as I have said, a second-level practice of justification. It is a level of justification that requires greater reflection, but it also only guarantees partial or instable epistemic authority. The piece of epistemic authority it does provide allows interlocutors to explain why their reasons hold given their other beliefs. For instance, when a Kantian is faced with utilitarian moral commitments, it is the strength and coherence of the utilitarian position that forces the Kantian to evaluate the totality of their own commitments in order to test their coherence. If the Kantian finds their position coherent faced with utilitarian commitments it reinforces the Kantian's commitment to defend their position. They see their position as authoritative because it is coherent, even though the utilitarian might not. This form of epistemic authority however is unstable for two reasons. One, the global level of justification is reflexive and thus only looks at its internal criteria. It therefore suffers from the relativity of its claims. Two, an individual can be moved by the internal coherence of their position. In other words, they may recognize reasonable critiques and be unmoved by them. Both problems are serious but it is only relativism that is specific to this form of justification. The problem of the individual who is unmoved by reasons cannot be overcome by epistemic authority alone and so this problem touches any attempt to ground discourse, thus rendering all forms of authority at least partially unstable.

The epistemic authority that second-tier reflexive justificatory practices provide is to the individual evaluating their own beliefs and not to the person providing a reasonable challenge. In order to bridge the gap between these two different levels, the local level of individual claims, and the global level of the coherence of sets of beliefs, individuals need a "polycentric" structure of justification that operates at an explicitly intersubjective level. At this level one puts their individual claims and the coherence of their set of claims into doubt. They also put their very claim to epistemic authority on the table. In other words, the plurality of forms of coherence must be taken into account and justificatory practices must put them into relation, starting from their overlap. These contextual practices are an outgrowth of the recognition of the limits of a given set of beliefs thanks to reflection. It is a response of the individual who sees that there are multiple possible discourses and that there may be no immediate way to settle the problem of this plurality of divergent

---

[20] Weil (1953), 107.

discourses once and for all. In this case, the polycentric structure of justification implies another jump. The first was from discussion to reflection, the new jump is from reflection to mature judgment.

At this new level of justification, it is the individual's core beliefs that are being examined. This touches our deepest, most hidden, discursive commitments, the ones that often go unknown or unrecognized. Here the individual's whole way of seeing the world must be placed on the altar of doubt and perhaps be sacrificed. Most defenses of contextualism put the emphasis on the fact that different epistemic claims hold in different contexts that are defined by epistemic communities. In other words, the context of each situation matters. However, the defense of contextualism here is not just that of recognizing the context in which different claims hold. It also looks to create a new context in which interlocutors see themselves as actual dialogue partners and thus as subject to the dialogical controls of others, even if that sometimes means abandoning some of their core commitments. This is the normative weight of better reasons. It is a kind of justification that demands multiple reprises and a fair deal of trust. A polycentric structure of justification tries to bring together different and perhaps opposing discursive centers. This is the moment where the non-discursive strategies spoken about last chapter come into play. Epistemic authority is an accomplishment, it is something that is tested and that requires being recognized by all parties concerned. What it accomplishes is the movement towards dialogue. As I have already stated, it is something that is established in and by discourse. It is only thanks to the argumentative practices in dialogue that epistemic authority is stably and durably produced. It may nonetheless be non-discursive means that bring people to see the value of establishing epistemic authority together.

The problem with foundationalism is that it presents a single candidate with some special quality that can guarantee epistemic authority. In seeking to create static certainty, foundationalism ignores the productive role of certainty. In terms of justification, the productive role of certainty is what allows us to disagree for reasons. It allows us to make reasoned challenges to default positions thanks to reasoned doubt. It is produced by the dissatisfaction with what a position does and does not allow us to grasp. Coherentism still has a problem. It is better at describing the more dynamic nature of justification, but it still presents the coherent set as a point that is supposed to hold in every condition. Weil critiques the possibility of a concrete absolutely coherent discourse. His critique of the possibility of a fully coherent concrete set of beliefs that provides epistemic authority is in fact far more radical than the traditional critique of philosophical relativism that applies to coherentism. He does not argue that certain beliefs cannot be judged because they are incommensurable, rather he is claiming that certain beliefs can be made incommensurable knowingly by the refusal of individuals to accept them into argumentative practices. They refuse them and refuse them knowingly precisely because they understand what being drawn back into argumentative practices implies. It implies seeking to establish a dialogue that aims at the universal. In other words, the individual can always choose their particularity and decide to dig their heels into it. They can always ignore reasonable discourse, or worse, destroy it. With this in mind, the type of contextualism defended here claims that a polycentric justificatory structure only holds when individuals recognize others as genuine dialogue partners, when they take on the effort to judge the coherence of other sets of beliefs, and when they see their own set of beliefs as modifiable. It is a practice. This falls into line with Michael Williams's critique of what he calls epistemological realism. According to this critique, the error of epistemological realism is to take epistemological objects for real objects, and thus static. It takes knowledge, justification, belief, etc. as things that are separated in one way or another from the act of knowing, the act of justifying, the act of believing etc., with their own metaphysical or ontological existence.[21] What Weil hopes to show is that stable epistemic authority is only established through the justificatory *activity*. The path of epistemological realism is the path of skepticism and despair. The polycentric picture of justification that we can draw out of Weil's work must be seen as a dynamic and open practice that seeks to establish epistemic authority. This authority is something that is created and is always itself partially unstable. This brings us back Weil's notion of the openness of and to discourse.

Epistemic authority is established through a dynamic and open practice that allows individuals to separate, in their discourse, what is contingent, arbitrary, doubtful, and false from what is necessary, reasonable, certain, and true. The goal of justification and of establishing epistemic authority remains bringing doubt to an end, just like in classic models of justification. However, because Weil claims that it is dissatisfaction that leads individuals to elaborate a discourse that can transform this dissatisfaction into error, it transforms the resolution of doubt as well. Doubt is resolved when someone finds a satisfactory discourse. However no discourse is satisfactory once and for all. We can place our trust in collective argumentative practices. These bring the individual to see the worth of the cardinal epistemic virtues that make up mature judgement. But unless we are open to reasonable dialogue and to seeing the person in front of us as providing genuine dialogical controls, we risk enclosing ourselves in a single form of coherence. Thus, epistemic authority cannot be set by any given, or any closed set of beliefs, and it cannot be set exclusively in the external world. It is born in discourse and must be set in discourse, in genuine discourse with others. The individual that sees this sees themselves as embedded in these practices with the rest of humanity. It is only through the kind of action that brings others to see their own activity as a free activity, as an activity that *can* participate in establishing epistemic authority, that epistemic authority can *indeed* be durably secured. This is why we do not see violence as a durable base for any type of authority (epistemic or otherwise). After the discovery of human freedom and autonomy, the individual sees themself as a legitimate source of value, therefore no external force can permanently hold. This also explains why even before the conceptual articulation of the concept of autonomy, violence could only temporarily provide some form of authority—it is unimportant if that authority be epistemic or political. Individuals could always be pushed to the point where they would rather

---

[21] Williams (1995), 108–109.

8.2 Eric Weil's Three-Tier Notion of Justification

die than submit to or suffer under what they come to see as a contingent injustice. Before and after the discovery of human freedom, individuals can always answer violence with violence. Eric Weil faces this possibility, but as we have noted, he presents philosophy as a possibility that refuses that option and that takes a stance against it.

The contextual strategy takes on a polycentric structure to face the real difficulties in establishing epistemic authority. Different categories provide an authoritative ground to those that live inside them. When faced with a different discourse, these people can look to make their discourse as strong as possible by showing the scope of its comprehensiveness. However, Weil's claim is that when individuals justify and when they evaluate different discourses responsibly, they mobilize all the discursive categories. They do not merely look at a single claim, or the coherence of a set of claims. They look at both of those things along with many others. The difficulty of establishing epistemic authority is that it demands the interplay of reprises. Some people may accept reprises of *The Condition* and of *God*, but not of the *Personality*, or of *Consciousness* and *The Absolute* and *The Finite*, but not of some other configuration. Some people may shut somebody out as soon as they have said a single phrase or word that raises their epistemic hackles and puts them on the defensive. This can be about immigration, sexual equality, the environment, or any number of other questions that at any given time, in any given group, counts as making up part of a discourse that is to be refused. In this sense, single words, phrases, or even manners of speaking, can become representative of entire spaces of reasons and can thus lead an individual to dismiss them out of hand. This is why a justificatory strategy grounded on the logic of philosophy must be polycentric and contextual. Authority is established together between people. If certain groups or positions are dismissed out of hand, the stability of authority is severely limited. This is the greatest problem in establishing of epistemic authority. Individuals can refuse any discourse because they know what it implies. Weil theorizes this possibility and reminds us that "the human being can reject discourse knowingly" (LP, 56).

Weil's use of the term "knowingly" highlights why one cannot ascribe a purely coherentist strategy to the forms of justification present in his work despite his continued insistence on the role of coherence in the elaboration of the philosophical categories. As we have noted, pure coherentist strategies base epistemic authority on a set of coherent beliefs. For Weil however, coherence is also linked to the notion of an absolutely coherent discourse that seeks to establish an identity between the subject and the object. But Weil is painfully aware of human finitude and human freedom. Pure coherentist strategies do not work because the individual can always in their finitude and freedom choose violence. The choice that the individual faces is between two radical possibilities, philosophy and violence.[22] Contextual polycentric justification focuses on entering freely into genuine dialogical practices,

---

[22] Weil acknowledges a third choice in pacific silence, but he has refused this choice from the get go because he is not interested in understanding how certain individuals can take themself out of the world, but rather in how individuals act and what they are committed to when they are committed to staying in the socially articulated second-nature that governs a shared human existence.

choosing shared principles, and working to get to the bottom of things together. Nothing forces this choice although many things can encourage it. Without it however, justification is merely a defense of one's own interests. For Weil, the individual that faces the double possibility of reason and violence "devotes themself to philosophy *knowingly* and *without a bad conscience* [...] [when] they want to understand without looking for the impossible justification of the understanding that predates understanding" (LP, 64). In this way, for Weil, philosophy, like violence, is a choice and an act. It is the choice to be open to the possibility of reasonable discourse coming from anywhere. It is a choice to be open to the possibility that our own discourse holds within it its share of arbitrariness and contingency and that this element can only be drawn out by the reasonable protest of another discourse. It is the awareness that this in no way ensures that the reasonable protest is correct in a given situation. It merely ensures that it is reasonable. Without this awareness, any claim of knockdown arguments is only knockdown because it ends not in arguments but rather in blows. Since philosophy sees itself as the choice to overcome difference and conflict through reason, through coherent discourse in situation, the only way to establish an authority that is truly epistemic does so through discourse. Thus, an individual engaged in argumentative practices must be able to sift through the different reprises and to identify them. Once identified, they must seek the right way to act upon them. This justificatory practice is contextual precisely because it must answer to different concrete situations. Because of this, different reprises are needed or make sense in different historical social contexts. Justificatory practices change according to whether the context is political, ethical, scientific, metaphysical, or otherwise. It changes depending on what our interlocutor's constellation of commitments is. But more importantly, it changes because even though philosophy can tell us what epistemic authority is and how it is established, it is only concretely established in *our* lives. These different contexts can thus not be flattened and people can never immediately *know* when and how these different contexts hold. It is something that they have to learn to identify, and when they do, it is a true accomplishment.

8.3 Relativism and Pluralism as Discursive Commitments

8.3.1 The Shape of the Problem

As we have seen, the theory of justification defended here is born out of the idea that the very thing a theory of argumentation establishes is epistemic authority. However, this same theory comes up against a problem. Epistemic authority is not a fixed state. It is based on a minimal agreement that allows serious conversation to get off the ground. In turn, it discovers that this minimal agreement is also what is needed to establish epistemic authority, and thus any stable justification. This creates a tension that any theory of argumentation must confront. Two of the major consequences

8.3 Relativism and Pluralism as Discursive Commitments

of this tension are skepticism and relativism. Skepticism and relativism are thus here seen as actual discursive commitments that can partially orient a life. They are also seen as unsatisfying in a theory that fixes the horizon of philosophy as a fully orientated life understood comprehensively in a concrete situation thanks to a coherent discourse. One of the goals of justification and of argumentative practices is thus to give voice to the dissatisfaction of individuals while also bringing them to see the value of choosing to seek a coherent discourse of their own. With that goal in mind, Weil rejects skepticism and relativism. I presented a three-tier model of justification that tries to capture the different goals of some of the major live justificatory options and to show how different justificatory structures are needed to overcome different problems. This three-tier model is supposed to compensate for different levels of shared background commitments and the scope of the agreement between divergent discourses. Because there are different levels of shared background commitments, the overlap between discursive spaces is not perfect. Rather, they initially present themselves as relative. Relativism is thus a real discursive possibility when faced with divergent discourse. When we argue against relativism we therefore do so because we recognize its pull and its potential consequences on our action. We argue against it because this action, like any action, will itself become sedimented as part of our social second nature. This social second nature is also what defines the horizon of action that other people face from the get go. With this in mind, my goal is to show that while relativism—like monism and pluralism—is a real possibility, it is unsatisfactory. Monism, relativism, and pluralism are not just real options, they are positions that overlay our justificatory forms. In other words, monism, relativism, and pluralism are here seen as the kind of commitments people take on when they stop in specific justificatory models.

Monism seems to be the initial vision that we have of our discursive practices. If this is true, it is linked to foundationalism. The formal goal of justificatory practices *is* foundationalist. Justificatory practices seek to bring people into the same discursive space where a shared order of explanation can ground epistemic authority and where people can settle dispute exclusively through discursive means. In the same way, the formal goal of discursive practices is to form a monist space of reasons, but this formal goal must itself face the historic weight of different discursive possibilities, as well as the possibility of novelty. Thus, while monism is the *formal* goal of argumentative practices, I argue that pluralism must be seen as the *concrete* goal. With this in mind, a philosophy that sees itself as a future-facing endeavor must also see one of the goals of discursive practices to be the overcoming of relativism by transforming it into pluralism. That is, it must seek to ground a position that makes the best of the historical moment (which is not monist) while nonetheless seeing individuals as being able to enter into meaningful discursive relations with others (which is anti-relativist).

Each person starts from their subjective and particular point of view, with the naïve certainty and orientation that they have established through their interpretation of their concrete historical situation. Because of this, real material and historic difficulties bar us from establishing a single monist image of the world. Any concrete form of monism depends on the *real* instauration of a universal and coherent discourse. But these material and historical difficulties are the background of contingency and failure against which we act. What I will thus argue is that concrete monist positions ignore these difficulties whereas relativism and pluralism do not. However, relativism and pluralism should not be put in the same basket. Relativism looks to the contingency and the failures of the past as informing the difficulties of the present in order to act and to understand. But in acting and in understanding, relativism ignores the possibilities of the future. It sees the failures and the differences that present themselves in the analysis of the past as being insurmountable. If however philosophy *is* future-facing, then it must look to the future. Pluralism, like relativism, looks at the failures of the past and the difficulties of the present, but instead as seeing them as insurmountable, it seeks to elaborate future possibilities and bring them about. Looking at philosophy this way allows us to establish the major normative claim of this whole work: if philosophy *ought* to concern itself with how to bring discourse together, how to resolve problems, then it must be a fallibilist (in the sense of openness), pluralist, future-facing endeavor that seeks to develop determined semantic content in order to establish reasonable agreement.

Here, it is important to show how a pluralism built out of a notion of discursive commitment plays out. In order to do that, I will have to present what is meant by monism and by relativism. Only then can pluralism be presented as the *goal* of a theory of argumentative practices based on discursive commitment. I will thus mobilize the helpful distinction made by Huw Price between horizontal pluralism and vertical pluralism. This will show how Weil's position can be understood as a species of vertical pluralism and show how Weil's distinction between language and discourse can provide a useful completion to Price's theory. Putting these two theories in contact will allow me to reinforce the value of reading Weil's philosophy along pragmatist, expressivist and inferentialist lines. It will show how Weil's theory dovetails with many of the commitments of the thinkers working in these idioms.

8.3.2 Monism and Relativism

Here, I am taking the default assumption of discursive interaction to be monist. When people talk, when they discuss, they assume that what they are saying is meaningful and that it is understood by their interlocutor because they take themselves to be saying something true about the world. The monism that structures our naïve conception of the world is at the same time ontological, metaphysical, and discursive. When somebody speaks they speak the truth about what is and about what the structure underlying it also is. As I have argued throughout this work, this naïve position is quickly complicated in our social discursive practices. Our condition is marked by the variety of different discourses that provide a variety of different ways of carving up the world and a variety of structural explanations about why the world should indeed be thus carved up. Monism is, at bottom, a reductionist position. All diversity and variety must be boiled down to a single principle that allows individuals to explain that diversity. That explanation must also perfectly and

8.3 Relativism and Pluralism as Discursive Commitments

eternally match that diversity. In doing so, that explanation will be said to have uncovered the fundamental laws and structure of what is and thus to explain all diversity as a totality. So, *either* discursive monism folds into ontological and metaphysical monism, *or* it unfolds, at least, into a minimal plurality that separates what is and what underlies what is from what we say about what is. For Weil however, ontological and metaphysical monism cannot be discursive. It is in only in discourse and in language that differences are disclosed *as* differences. In order to live in an ontological and metaphysical unity with the One, the individual must be outside of discourse and language. Weil notes that life without reason (coherent discourse in situation) takes two forms, "that of the animal and that of God" (LP, 416).[23] It is only in these two forms that we, as discursive creatures, can conceive of true monism, but only from the outside. In these two forms, there is no separation from the world. Animals are united with the world because the difference that discourse discloses does not yet trouble them (they are in-themselves). God is united with it because he exists at the Archimedean point where discourse cannot trouble him (he is for-himself). For Weil, humanity differs because humanity is "the movement of the in-itself towards the for-itself" (LP, 417). To reprise Weil's claim in Brandom's idiom, this monism is either the sentience that has no capacity for sapience, or the pure sapience that has no need for sentience. Weil highlights how we live *between* both these options, in a *meantime* (LP, 417). We are between the future that we don't know and the past that we at least partially do. We are between our sentient existence that makes no claims of epistemic authority, where we merely exist, and our sapient existence that makes the strong demands of epistemic authority that we create for ourselves to give meaning to our existence. Thus, here already, we can see the way a theory of argumentation comes into play.

By showing that our lives happen in the meantime, in this between, Weil shows how the demands that discourse make concerning epistemic authority mark the way in which we understand ourselves. Monism is marked by its foundationalism and its absolutism, and because of this, monism is in a weak defensive position. All its opponent has to do is show the goodness of any other possibility for monism to fold into relativism. The monist must show that their discourse can either absorb this other possibility, or show that their discourse is true and that the other is false. This is a tall order for the monist. Because monist claims are absolute in the sense that they must be true and that all other true claims must reduce to this fundamental monist claim, monism and relativism are structurally linked. As argued all the way back in Chap. 3, relativism is the nihilism of failed monism. It accepts the reality of other discourses yet also refuses to abandon the goodness of its own claims. In order to protect their claims, the relativist insulates them from all attack by asserting that discursive positions cannot be compared. According to the three-tier structure of justification defended here, nothing requires somebody to make the jump from one justificatory structure to another, and in the same way, nothing requires anybody to

---

[23] Weil also notes that it is not any God that is monist but a very specific one. He says that this God is "not the God of the pure category, but his reprise through the *object* and *consciousness*: the God of Greco-Christian theology"(LP, 416).

leave their naïve monism. Here we can understand those that cling to their naïve form of monism in terms in recalcitrant forms of religious fundamentalism. The meaningfulness of the world for the religious fundamentalist depends on the reality of *their* discourse. It is the objectivity that their subjective belief secures for them that holds their world together, and their faith shows that anybody who doubts this belief was either put here to test them or put here as their mission.[24] Non-believers must be converted. This explains the role of proselytization in certain fundamentalist communities. The only way to guarantee the kingdom of God is to save the non-believer, even if saving those that deserve a place in this kingdom requires building mountains from the bones from those that do not.

The threat of the failure of one's beliefs, and the refusal to pass from certainty to discussion, to relativize one's beliefs sufficiently in order to put them to the test, is an initial junction where pure violence can irrupt. The recognition of the possibility of violence can make the move to relativism seem to be a sensible one,[25] precisely if relativism is supposed to guarantee the tolerance for other discourses. This is exactly what Weil highlights in the category of *Intelligence*. This category presents Michel de Montaigne and Pierre Bayle as paradigmatic historical cases of the defense of philosophical relativism. For this category, relativism is a key aspect of the concept of human interest, but it is always relative to each individual. Because relativism is sufficient to ground a coherent discourse, it differs from skepticism as well as from cynicism and nihilism. These positions are always parasitic on *another* coherent discourse. However, as I will show, relativism does not guarantee tolerance. This is because relativism, while being a consequence of a failed global monism, nonetheless remains a local form of monism. This is evident in the way relativism posits the incommensurability of different discourses.

For relativism to develop, the monist has to be forced to recognize the existence of other discourses, however this does not mean that the relativist will be ready to give up on the absolute character of their own discourse. The relativist thus posits an infinity of absolute discourses that exist but that are in no way comparable. For the relativist, even though we may use a common language, the source of our discourse is individual and subjective. Jean-Pierre Cometti has noted that, to a certain extent, every discursive position must admit a normal level of relativism.[26] What this means is that we must necessarily relativize our claims if we want to communicate with others. This, Cometti notes, is very different from the philosophical position of

---

[24] Religious fundamentalism also clearly shows the way that Being, God, and Truth, comingle in discourse. They are all the same thing *because* the discourse of the fundamentalist cannot grasp their differences.

[25] It is historically significant that the elaboration of relativism was an essential move to diminishing some forms of violence. The critique of relativism that is presented here does not want to minimize that historical importance, rather it wants to highlight the way that relativism also gives way to *aporia*, difficulties, and new forms of violence that it can neither dissolve nor understand. Thus, relativism is seen as a historically and discursively significant but ultimately insufficient commitment.

[26] Cometti (2001).

8.3 Relativism and Pluralism as Discursive Commitments

relativism. The philosophical position takes a strong stance that does not just imply a general relativization of our discourses, but also an incommensurability between different types of discourses or between the discourses of different people. This incommensurability states that *no* criteria could be provided in order to put these discourses into relation. This is the position that is seen to be philosophically unacceptable and is what is to be kept in mind in arguments against relativism.[27] As already mentioned, Weil has argued that the move from the category of *Certainty* to that of *Discussion* creates the relativization of beliefs. In the *Logic of Philosophy*, this happens when differentiated communities are brought together (usually violently) into a single political union or into a stable political relationship. Internally, this differentiation is found when the relativization of the sacred of each community must be articulated within a single legal framework in order to establish social bonds between these different communities. In this case, the dominant tradition (the ethical life of the community) is transformed into a religious, cultural, and moral syncretism that concedes place to the different sacreds of each community. Externally, this happens when a single political community finds itself obliged to create stable relations with foreign communities that can neither be eliminated, subjugated, or ignored. These people cannot be written off as barbarians or as inferiors because the community is obliged to uphold a relationship with them. The "relativist" position develops under specific historical, social, and political conditions. From our point of view however, because of the intimacy of the interactions in a partially rationalized globally articulated modern society, differences are obliged to coexist and cooperate, whether between different states, within the multicultural divisions in these states themselves, or through the relationship between different social strata or cultural communities.

Because the modern situation has already generalized this coexistence of differences, this allows us to interpret the jump between *Certainty* and *The Discussion* as a jump that is constantly reprised at the level of the individual consciousness. The individual becomes aware of the possibility of relativism as soon as they start to present belief not as certainty, but as belief, as a second-order commitment that involves a certain level of reflection-demanding criteria. This is structurally linked to the demand for coherence. It is only facing dialogue partners providing appropriate controls that we learn to evaluate our discursive commitments. Remember, we have said that discursive spaces can be understood thanks to rules of permissible inference and incompatibility. We have also said that there are a variety of discursive positions that can be sketched thanks to their central commitment and their order of explanation.[28] To understand exactly how the awareness of the relativity of our beliefs comes about we can again look at what Jaraslov Peregrin says concerning "bouncing off rules".

---

[27] This does not mean people do not defend these positions. In the modern context, J.L. Mackie's defense of moral relativism in *Ethics: Inventing Right and Wrong* immediately comes to mind, see Mackie (1977).

[28] This can be either pure positions that define the category or mixed positions that imply numerous reprises and which are the shape that actual concrete discourses take.

For Peregrin, "[l]ooking at rules in their restrictive, rather than prescriptive, capacity allows us to see that through *limiting* us in what we may do they also *delimit* a new space of reasons [...] thus the rules of language also open up a new space: a space of meaningfulness [...]."[29] This space of meaningfulness is the space in which we place our statements and our claims as well as our orientations and our goals. This is what allows Peregrin to note that "rules have an inner and an outer face. From the outside they, and the spaces they create, can simply be *described* [...] [h]owever, from the inside the spaces are *inhabited*."[30] It is from the inside, from an inhabited space, that our statements and orientations make sense as being ours. This intimacy allows us to clarify the way that different spaces can be seen as an existential threat and thus why relativism is proposed. We have already endorsed the idea that discursive spaces are lived in and that when it is us who are in them, bouncing off incompatibilities gives sharpness and definition to our concepts. However, Peregrin makes this additional distinction between habitation and description. What this means is that just because we can describe and perhaps even understand different discursive spaces, we cannot necessarily imagine them as live options for ourselves. This is because our own conceptuality is always sketched from the inside. Meaning in this sense is downstream from goals and orientations, from the shape of our own space of reasons. This highlights the importance of argumentative practices, and the importance of a polycentric structure of contextual justification. This allows us to consider other positions *as if* from the inside and to consider our own *as if* from the outside. Real dialogical practices with others help us to see what kinds of inferences others make based on other central commitments. They provide dialogical controls by providing a real alternative. However, if we were in different spaces of reasons, our lives and our goals would be different, our orientation would change.

When we stick to description we cannot imagine these other spaces as possibilities because our goals and orientations are not at stake. When we enter into justificatory and argumentative practices with people from different spaces, the integrity of our own space is precisely what *is* at stake. This is also why it is not only pure argumentative practices that lead to the recognition of difference, it is also certain political and social situations that force us to cooperate with people that we have poorly understood. In these situations we cannot "agree to disagree" precisely because the disagreement is a deep source of conflict that keeps people in these political and social situations from cooperating. In these situations, relativism only holds when individuals have nothing to agree on, as is the case concerning private faith in secular political communities. In this case, faith can remain a private affair. However, when this faith spills over into public affairs and individuals need to agree on things, on the content of education, on family planning, etc. this relativism becomes inoperable. In these cases, we must be willing to establish the minimal agreement that leads to argumentative practices. We must imagine these spaces as

---

[29] Peregrin (2014), 71.
[30] Peregrin (2014), 89.

8.3 Relativism and Pluralism as Discursive Commitments

real spaces we could inhabit. When we do so, these practices themselves can help us to progressively take our dialogue partners more seriously and to see their way of life as a concrete possibility. Entering into argumentative practices is hard, precisely because we inhabit a meaningful space. Modern society however forces us into them again and again as a prerequisite for the success of our projects. Our projects rely on this internal and external differentiation. No person is an island, and no project that seeks recognition from others is strictly personal. This does not mean that the individual cannot refuse technical success as it is articulated in society. Individuals may even decide that their success holds only in the refusal of this society. Nothing requires us to enter into argumentative practices and the awareness of other spaces may keep many people from doing so.

Weil notes that when people do not want to abandon their way of life but want to reinforce it, they commit to what he calls *traditionalism*. This is important for the practical character we are giving to our analysis of relativism. Weil notes that finding agreement is insurmountable when traditionalism "emerges as an active conscious force."[31] For Weil, it is exactly this active force that can keep people from following the course of sound argumentative practices. He notes that:

> as traditionalists we do not evaluate our tradition through the mirror furnished by other traditions, we establish a theory of action. When we become conscious of tradition we develop a double personality, looking at ourselves from the outside so to speak. But as traditionalists, we decide not only to study ourselves in relation to other people, but we choose to maintain our tradition, to stick to it whatever the difficulties and the temptations, to be what we were, to be ourselves without any change or deviation. Only traditionalism we affirm, can save us, for we have arrived at a point where we shall lose our soul if we do not revert to that which makes us precisely ourselves.[32]

By highlighting the decision to dig our heels into a tradition that has disappeared or changed, Weil also highlights how all incompatibility implies a moment of decision. It is the choice between violence or discourse.[33] The choice of violence presents itself as the choice to ignore incompatibility by preferring to live in contradiction because it is meaningful. The choice is to refuse adopting the meta-commitment to reasonable action that may change or invalidate this meaning without any promise that a new meaning will be developed. It is at the level of the evaluation of different coherent discourses that relativism, like skepticism, rears its head. However, relativism poses the problem in different terms than skepticism. This also highlights the way that order of explanation gives shape to different spaces of reasons, and how inferential relationships can be sketched.

The difference is that skepticism claims that it is impossible to establish epistemic authority—despite making this as an authoritative claim. By contrast, relativism claims that there is a multitude of discourses that each have an equal claim to

---

[31] Weil (1953), 110.

[32] Weil (1953), 110.

[33] We ignore for the moment the variety of non-violent but silent stances that individuals can take on. It is enough to say here that that non-violent silence can be either rebellious towards or complicit in dominant or dominating discourse.

epistemic authority. I want to note in passing that relativism already puts the plurality of spaces into an evaluative relation by claiming that these multiple discourses have an equal claim to epistemic authority. It is therefore making an implicit judgment about the equality of the claim.[34] This however is not relativism's greatest shortcoming. Rather, its greatest shortcoming is that it is unsuccessful in securing the tolerance that it is trying to secure. Weil's sources of relativism, Michel de Montaigne and Pierre Bayle, both wrote during times of great political and religious turmoil. Because of this, the need to find wiggle room for those that thought differently was capital.[35] Michael P. Lynch however argues that Montaigne's main motivation for his arguments for relativism were to defend Catholicism from the rising tide of Reformation. He did this by showing that faith and not reason was the only way to secure social stability. From this point of view, the position that Montaigne was trying to protect through tolerance was his own. If this analysis is correct, Montaigne was asking for the tolerance not to modify his position facing the difference that had appeared in a world that had already changed. This also shows that from the get go, the structural relationship between relativism and tolerance is problematic. To understand how relativism comes up short, it is important to again look at the notion of incompatibility. We have noted that the incompatibilities in a discourse with shared discursive centers are generally easier to overcome. There is a background acceptance of what counts as epistemic authority, and so, in such cases *seeing* often *is* believing. It is sufficient to show or demonstrate an incompatibility for epistemic authority to be established. This, I have said, is one of the pulls of foundationalist pictures of justification. Much of our lives is passed in overlapping discursive spaces and so many of our intimate relationships are built by coming to understanding through a steady merger of discursive spaces. It may even be the case that many intimate relationships end precisely when we become aware of divergences in these spaces, because it is at this point that we see this continued merger of projects and values as impossible. The incompatibilities that appear because of differences between central discursive commitments are generally harder to overcome than those of shared commitments precisely because of what different discursive centers imply. Different discursive commitments imply different orientations and different lives. When such incompatibilities are uncovered, seeing no longer is believing, rather the long process of explanation and justification is needed. However, as long as certainty is maintained, this alternative discursive center is seen as a threat, and an existential one at that.

In line with Weil's theory, nothing forces the individual to skirt out to the edge of their space of reasons, just as nothing forces them to lean out over this edge and stare into the chasm of another space of reasons. Nothing can force the individual to see the possible relativity of their own discourse, even if there are social, political, and historical reasons that can encourage them to do so. Nothing can force the

---

[34] This will come back into play when I analyze the difference between vertical pluralism and horizontal pluralism.

[35] See Lynch (2012). The line of argument that is followed later in this section is heavily indebted to Lynch's analysis.

8.3 Relativism and Pluralism as Discursive Commitments

individual to seek to overcome relativity nor to accept another discourse as legitimate, even in its own sphere. This is because one can always seek to destroy discourse rather than change it. Weil notes that once:

> I have grasped myself with the help of discourse, nothing keeps me from trying to destroy discourse or from turning my back on it, either to modify it or to refuse all discourse *knowingly*; the fact nonetheless remains that even though I would be the one who is freeing myself in this way from discourse and, if it comes to it, from all language, I can also only make this choice from within the environment, the *medium* of language and discourse (LP, 67).

When an individual decides not to use violence but decides to admit the incompatibilities *between* different discourses, they are left with a plurality *of* different discourses. The question that must be asked is why this plurality leads to philosophical relativism, to an infinity of monist discourses existing side by side. It is because incompatibility signals conflict in discourse and this conflict can explode into violence. If the individual wants to avoid violence they have two options, they can fall silent or they can try to resolve the problem of violence by speaking.

Philosophy is the position that refuses both violence and silence. It speaks and aims to speak reasonably. Following this analysis we can better see how relativism is a practical attempt *to solve* the problem of incompatible discursive spaces. It tries to insulate incompatible discourses in order to keep them from being seen as existential threats. The consequence of this however is that each space becomes incommensurable. In other words, relativism admits the existence of these different spaces, but at the cost of saying that they cannot be compared. By extracting them from the normative weight of better reasons, the relativist assumes that tolerance follows. In this way, relativism is supposed to entail a notion of tolerance and tolerance is supposed to be seen as a solution to the problem of violence.[36] However, this notion of tolerance based on relativism shows its limitations both structurally and practically. We have already defined the problem of relativism as the incommensurability of discursive spaces, but it is not clear how tolerance is supposed to follow from this notion, especially since relativism claims that there is no measure by which to judge these different discursive spaces. Imagining that relativism is metaphysically true or admitting that there exists a multitude of discursive spaces that cannot be measured against one another because of a lack of criteria does not resolve the problem of violence. In this situation, these discursive spaces can still be intolerant. Someone with a specific set of essential beliefs can recognize that their beliefs are incommensurable with another set of beliefs. But because of this, they can seek to eliminate this other set of essential beliefs in order to protect the unicity of their own unique set. Relativism on its own does not entail tolerance.

---

[36] Weil describes the attitude of tolerance in the different reprises of the category of *Intelligence*. He describes its limits in the category of *Personality*.

8.3.3 The Insufficiency of Relativism

If relativism doesn't entail tolerance, the question becomes, what does? Are relativism and non-violence together sufficient to entail tolerance? The answer is no. More strongly, the answer is that these two things together show more clearly how relativism is a practical position, and how properly understood, it can actually lead to violence by limiting tolerance. Take the notion of freedom of religion in the United States. Here, religious tolerance and relativism taken together are often used as a defense of discriminatory action. We can refer to Indiana Senate Bill no. 101 known as the *Religious Freedom Restoration Act*. It states: "a governmental entity may not substantially burden a person's exercise of religion, even if the burden results from a rule of general applicability."[37] The *New York Times* notes however that "[t]he Indiana law opens the door for individuals or companies to refuse actions that impose a 'substantial burden' on their religious beliefs."[38] This includes most notably the hiring of or service to members of the LGBTQIA+ communities. The law enables individuals or businesses to use their religious beliefs as a reason to discriminate. It also allows individuals to insulate such practices from critique based on the aspects of said beliefs that would otherwise be open to critique in a public discourse. Relativism is thus used to demand tolerance for an absolutist position (here, a specific species of Christianity) so that it can itself be able to freely discriminate.[39] Similar moves have been made as well when relativized religious freedom is used in the heated battles concerning women's access to contraception or the place of the theory of evolution in public schools. Both these questions turn around how policy infringes on religious freedom and how religious freedom infringes on policy. It also shows however that relativism does not entail tolerance.

When the plea for tolerance is used as a bulwark to protect debatable positions (which are only debatable for another discourse's point of view), the weakness of relativism as a practical position becomes all the clearer. In this case, the essential belief that structures permissible inferences is *no longer* subject to interaction with other discursive spaces. By insulating a discursive space, the incompatibilities of that space become all-important. Normally, incompatibilities are resolved in argumentation when the conflictual claim of a commitment is renounced. Relativism refuses to do so. Any incompatibility is seen as an imposition from another relative space and thus does not touch the space in question. By considering other positions to be incompatible *and* incommensurable, arguments no longer function, because the participants *knowingly* refuse to consider other reasons as live options. In this situation, before an indifferent audience, the choice once again becomes a choice of

---

[37] Religious freedom restoration act (2015).

[38] Barbaro and Eckholm (2015).

[39] Weil analyses how individuals try to insulate their interest and their beliefs from scrutiny in the category *Personality*, most notably (LP, 283–286). Claudine Tiercelin, also following Michael P. Lynch, made a similar point recently in her inaugural *Connaissance, Vérité, Démocratie* course at Collège de France, Tiercelin (2017).

8.3 Relativism and Pluralism as Discursive Commitments

falling silent or the using of violence. Thanks to the previous development of the arguments, we now have the tools to see why Weil rejects silence as an option for the philosopher and why he rejects relativism. When one is silent they commit to non-violence, but they also commit to the incommensurability of relativism. The pluralist on the other hand chooses argumentative practices because while they accept non-violence like the relativist, but unlike the relativist, they also at least formally commit to the commensurability of discursive spaces.

However this does not answer the question of what to do while better reasons are being figured out and investigated. Following the analysis of different discursive categories as different spaces of reasons, we can understand relativism as a potentially disastrous practical position and not a metaphysical reality. However the roadblocks that give rise to relativism have not gone away. My suggestion is that in order to tackle these roadblocks, the structural political space must be understood as pluralistic. Why must the political space be pluralistic? It has been shown that relativism does not entail tolerance, and how relativism and non-violence can end up in silence. What I propose is that non-violence entails tolerance, and the normative weight of better reasons entails pluralism. This political space thus refuses to make a judgment about the substantive statuses of the claims that are being presented. Thus, although metaphysical, ontological, and epistemological commitments matter greatly for individuals, it is precisely these aspects of the commitments that are put on hold within the political space. Following this proposal, a question nonetheless remains. What kind of political space can provide both the non-violence and the structured argumentative practices that leads to pluralism? What I will briefly suggest in what follows is that it is specifically a democratic political space with a focus on education and equality that can do so. This is because a democratic political space is governed both by the refusal of the use of violence within the political community to settle disputes and by the application of the normative weight of better reasons to settle disputes within this same space. In this way, democratic culture is seen to engender a pluralistic tolerance. Still, as noted, real difficulties persist. For instance, the explicit structure of these spaces is born out of, among other things, implicit normative practices. In this way, the scope and understanding of discursive commitments is in constant evolution and thus it is not clear which essential beliefs should be counted as live options. More importantly, it is often not immediately evident what a person's center of discourse is or whether those essential beliefs go *against* the definition of a democratic political space, thus being seen as incompatible with democratic culture.

I have linked the relationship between the positions of relativism, pluralism, and epistemic authority. What I now suggest is that it is pluralism that defines a political space as democratic. However, since the use of violence, the notion of tolerance, and the emphasis on the normative weight of arguments can be different in different spaces, not every political space is democratic. In this case, the critique that we fall back into the same problem of relativism exists. There are two responses to this charge. First, we claim that each discursive space is already governed interiorly by the epistemic norm of weighing better reasons. For Weil, the evaluative criterion used to distinguish better reasons is the universalizability of the discourse itself.

This universalizability however is insufficient because we can still always find ourselves with mutually incompatible coherent discourses. Thus, the universalization of commitments must always be linked to the willingness to establish the minimal agreement needed for dialogue to take hold. In this way, all that is being asked of individuals from different epistemic communities is that they apply to others the same discursive norm that they apply to themselves. This is because epistemic deliberation is itself already seen as a suspension of a certain type of practical commitments in order to weigh options according to the criteria of universalizability and the overall coherence of the argument. Second, it is only when political actors decide that their reasons are privileged that the threat of relativism as a *political* position comes back into play. Nonetheless, as philosophical positions, each space is governed by the fact that it exists in a larger structural space that makes the possibility of agreement and disagreement possible. This is because particular discourses are elaborated on the floor-level discourse of the social space. For us, in our modern context, this is *The Condition*. Therefore the incompatibilities that are judged as incommensurable are seen to lean on real criteria that make the judgment of their incompatibility possible. However, and this is a real problem, nothing guarantees that we will be able to recognize better reasons, precisely because the debate about how to articulate dialogue's minimal agreement can rage on. Different discursive spaces, as spaces of meaningfulness, are understood as embodied and inhabited from the inside. In this way, when individuals enclose themselves in their single form of coherence they place major obstacles in front of themselves that block establishing a minimal agreement with others. Even where there is some overlapping consensus, different discursive spaces mean that different individuals can agree on things from different categories. There is therefore no single overarching agreement to be found. This also means however that nothing guarantees the reasons agreed on are good ones. What it does mean though is that the contradiction and conflict between their fundamental reasons have been subordinated to something that is seen as creating agreement. An example of mutual consensus based on bad reasons and different discursive commitments can be found, for instance, in the fact that secular individuals as well as people from different religions can all have an overlapping consensus about the immorality of homosexuality. Despite their consensus, someone who does not see homosexuality as immoral will neither see their reasons as good or grounded, but rather will see the consensus as a leftover from a more barbaric time. In order to define how people come to recognize better reasons it would be necessary to elaborate a theory of education, as well as go deeper into the political and philosophical considerations than is possible here. However, we can sketch the start of a response. In order to lay the groundwork for this response I shall mobilize Huw Price's notion of horizontal and vertical pluralism.

8.3.4 Horizontal and Vertical Pluralism

In the article "Metaphysical Pluralism" Huw Price abandons the notion of incommensurability and thus abandons the tag of relativism, instead he notes that the multiplicity and diversity of discourse can be understood using a spatial relation. What would normally be called relativism is what Price refers to as horizontal pluralism. Horizontal pluralists admit a multiplicity of different discourse but see these discourses as *"performing the same linguistic tasks*. There are many equally valid possible scientific worldviews, but all of them are scientific worldviews, and in that sense are on the same level of linguistic activity."[40] Price is quick to note that the example of a scientific world view is merely an example, but that horizontal pluralism can be found in partial discourses and in domain-specific discourses, such as in the case of moral or epistemological discourses. What matters here is that all the discourses are seen as performing the same task at the same level of validity. This is different from what he calls vertical pluralism. According to vertical pluralism, there is "an irreducible plurality of *kinds* of discourse—the moral as well as the scientific for example."[41] Price then goes on to compare the key characteristics of his position with other positions. What he notes is that the idea of vertical pluralism, which he also calls discourse pluralism, is that there are different discourses that are ontologically autonomous, that are legitimate, but that have no available unifying principle. When Price speaks of ontological autonomy, he is referring specifically to whether or not the discourse in question is to be considered "distinct from the background discourse."[42] He contrasts moral discourses and scientific discourses in order to show that one cannot be reduced to the other. The type of reality that these two discourses treat is different according to Price's discourse pluralism. He then asks whether or not the discourse is legitimate, and here we can put our gloss on it and show that for Price, he is asking whether a given discourse, against a background discourse is to be thought of as being a source of epistemic authority. In the terms of the two examples Price gives, we can conclude that, according his position, scientific discourses and moral discourses are both to be thought of as authoritative in their domains. This links up to the placement problem that we exposed in earlier chapters, as well as to the strategy proposed by Humean expressivists. According to Humean expressivists, the only legitimate discourse is causally-structured, empirically-known scientific discourse. Moral talk is seen to be outside of this scope. Someone who does not grant ontological autonomy to moral discourse is reductionist in the sense that they reduce moral talk to psychological states. Emotivism is an example of the kind of reductionism that refuses ontological autonomy to moral talk, and that claims that all discourses must reduce down to a causally-structured, empirically-known scientific discourse. Price's discourse

---

[40] Price (1992), 389.
[41] Price (1992), 390.
[42] Price (1992), 391.

pluralism grants epistemic authority to different discourses and thus moral talk and physical causal talk are seen to be equally legitimate in their spheres.

Next, Price distinguishes between positions that propose a unifying principle and those that do not. According to this taxonomy, his defense of discourse pluralism refuses that there is any unifying principle *available*, this contrasts with a position that admits a unifying principle, and that he calls additive monism. He states:

> additive monism agrees with discourse pluralism in rejecting reductionism and [...] forms of irrealism, accepting that multiple discourse may each be autonomous and yet fully legitimate. The disagreement is only about how these separate spaces are to be construed. The additive monist regards them as subdomains of a *single* universe of facts."[43]

According to this distinction, for both the discourse pluralist and the additive monist, there are moral facts and scientific facts. The difference is that for the discourse pluralist, moral facts and scientific facts make up irreducible discourses and have no overarching discourse that binds them. They share no background discourse. For the additive monist, both moral and scientific facts exist and must combine according to some principal in order to be bound together in a single unified coherent discourse. Price's main claim about what separates additive monism from discourse pluralism is that additive monism finds itself in a corner. It must make strong metaphysical and ontological claims and then show how these claims sort through factual and non-factual discourse. Without this it loses the unity it claims exists. He says that this strong claim is required because "*diversity* is obvious, being guaranteed by difference of subject matter (once reductionism is rejected). It is the monist's *unity* that calls for substantial agreement."[44] This is because the monist must not only show how ontology and metaphysics fit together but must show how these things are *also* bound together at a linguistic and semantic level. This is a tall order. Price's position however turns on whether one thinks that no unifying principle is available, or whether no unifying principle exists. This is an important distinction, because if pluralism claims that no principle is available and may in fact never be available, then it is normal to keep the distinctions that different domains of discourse make. It is then also normal to allow a large diversity of practices to exist. However, if the pluralist is claiming that no unifying principle exists, it is difficult to see how their proposition does not fold back into relativism, or as Price prefers, horizontal pluralism. This is because, by claiming that no unifying principle exists, the pluralist is making the same kind of claim as the skeptic, that is, they are affirming the truth of the non-existence of a unifying principle and thus are making a positive claim about this principle. Price unwittingly shows how this is problematic by showing that these positions all depend on a background discourse. The claim about the non-existence of a unifying principle thus would only make sense against a *background* discourse that grounds and confirms this claim. In this way, he would be seen to be folding into exactly what he argued against. Price though tries to argue against this when he claims that the pluralist is merely "asking us to acknowledge" that truth,

---

[43] Price (1992), 395.
[44] Price (1992), 398.

8.3 Relativism and Pluralism as Discursive Commitments

fact, assertion, belief, are "mere products of language, categories thrown up by language itself, and not therefore presupposed by a proper explanatory theory of language."[45]

What I would like to retain from this presentation is the notion of vertical pluralism as a pluralism that accepts a plurality of discourses that have ontological autonomy, that are legitimate and authoritative. I also argue however that while they have no unifying principal that is *available*, they do not rule out the possibility that one *may* exist. Here is where Weil's presentation of the suite of discursive categories is useful. There are certain concepts that can support a coherent discourse. *Consciousness*, for instance, supports a coherent discourse that is based on a central moral commitment. *The Condition* supports a coherent discourse that is based on a certain positive view about nature. There are other discourses however that have their autonomous and legitimate frame but do not succeed in creating a single coherent discourse and thus depend on multiple reprises. This is the case with esthetic discourse and epistemic discourse for example. This may be because the esthetic experience and the justificatory necessity that is found in our lives outstrips a single discourse. This may also be because no one has yet succeeded in describing what is essential about them, even though the *Personality* may be close to describing the esthetic dimension and *The Absolute* is not far off from describing the justificatory dimension. Weil's theory should be read as a form of vertical pluralism, one that accepts the autonomy and legitimacy of different discursive centers. In this way it refuses relativism. But, as I have mentioned, Weil's theory makes sense in terms of orientations and goals. The orientation of pluralism *is* monist. The goal is to overcome relativism and move people to pluralism. This is a pluralism that is based on the non-violence that creates an atmosphere of tolerance. It may be more prudent to say here that pluralism moves towards a formal monism. This merely means that we mobilize all the resources of discourse, and all the categories, in order to look at problems from multiple angles so as to take into account what is said on a subject and understand what means are appropriate in any given situation. I think this is a position that Price would accept if he had Weil's distinction between language and discourse available to him. To show this, we can look at two things he says concerning monism and language. First, Price states that "it is not enough for the monist that there be a unified world out there; it is also crucial that within each of the disputed parts of language, statements stand in the same relation to the relevant part of the single world. Otherwise, monism is trivial: it is easy to find a unified world to which every use of language relates *in some sense*. The monist requires that it always be *the same sense*."[46] Second, he asks whether "the notions of truth, fact, assertion, belief, and so on [are] foundational categories, inevitably central to any theoretical use of language."[47] The answer he gives to that question is to say, as I have already mentioned, that all the pluralist asks is that we accept this as a

---

[45] Price (1992), 399.
[46] Price (1992), 397.
[47] Price (1992), 399.

possibility, and that we must, because as he notes, "ordinary usage exhibits a unity between the discourses in question. The issue is whether this superficial unity is more than skin deep."[48]

The Weilian answer to this question is that there is a difference to be made between language and discourse. As a reminder, language is seen as the creative and expressive production in human spontaneity at one level, and its instrumental use at another. At these two levels, language makes no claims of epistemic authority, which falls exclusively under the domain of discourse. It is also this difference (and this tiered difference) that allows for language to hold all the pragmatic and rhetorical effects that it does. Thus, while there is no concrete background *discourse*, Weil claims that all discourses happen against the concrete background of language (creative human spontaneity with semantic rules). At the inside of these discourses, thanks to the different justificatory structures and the criteria of universalizability and coherence, we can indeed judge and compare different discourses. We can judge discourses that make claims to coherence, such as a moral or a scientific discourse, just as we can judge the language use that does not make claims to govern all aspects of an individual's life. Thanks to reprises we are able to cut up these discourses in different ways and to have different pictures of the world that come out. However, because pluralism is a discursive commitment, just as relativism, skepticism, cynicism, and nihilism are, pluralism demands a decision. The decision that the pluralist makes, according to Weil, is to accept the local relativity of discourses but to work to bring them together into a unity through their reasonable action. This unity is not one that reduces and flattens the difference in the world, but rather one that accepts and celebrates this difference and asks how this diversity fits together. It recognizes that the goal is to bring together different people from different discursive centers in order to build a single *human* community. It thus accepts that this human community is made up of differences. It accepts the limits of epistemic authority, but also recognizes that epistemic authority is something that has been established, that differences have been overcome in the history of human thought and in the history of humanity in general. Because it recognizes this, pluralism works to convince people of the reasonableness of this goal. Pluralism is a task, one that has many obstacles in its path which can dissuade the individual from advancing, but also one that accepts the possibility of unity. Weil presents this position in a long citation in his *Philosophie politique*. He states:

> Human beings thus confirm, through their life, what analysis discovers: abstraction, which proceeds by reciprocal negations, separates something that can neither exist nor be understood separately. The opposition war-peace (violence-nonviolence) does not constitute a subject of more or less intelligent moral debates, but constitutes a problem for action. It is not only a matter of realizing a world in which historical morality can coexist with violence: the difficulty is ancient, and morality has always *informed* the violence within every society, every community, every State. It is now a matter of realizing a world where morality can live with nonviolence, a world in which nonviolence is not a simple absence of meaning—this meaning that violence has sought within history without knowing what it was seeking,

---

[48] Price (1992), 399.

8.3 Relativism and Pluralism as Discursive Commitments

this meaning that it has violently created, and that it continues to seek through violent means. The task is constructing a world in which nonviolence is real, without being the elimination of both violence's meaninglessness and the positive meaning within the life of human beings.

And he continues:

> It is a question of a *task*, of an action to determine and to undertake at the political and the historical level. The preceding reflections have not changed any of this; but, leaving philosophy, these reflections allow formulating this task more clearly (and, in this way, have changed it in the eyes of the philosopher), since it can now be stated in the following way: how can living moralities, these particular universals, be preserved, in spite of society's formal and general universality, and in spite of the formal morality that universally corresponds to this? How can the formal universal of social labor be conserved in spite of the resistance of particular moralities, in spite of these struggles that are all the more easily born between them since this universal forces them into the closest of contacts? To put it another way, how can *a* meaning exist if we only ever encounter *particular* meanings? And how could these meanings be meaningful if none of them are *the* meaning and if formal universality has not only introduced the requirement of a meaning into the world, but the requirement of *the* meaning, of a meaning that would be universally, and thus absolutely, justified according to universal criteria? (PP, 234).

These obstacles to pluralism are thus real, just as the triumph of relativism, skepticism or any other discursive position would be real. A careful study of history will show that all of these different discursive positions have become dominant at one time or another, and that the stability that humans seek is fragile. Nonetheless, a careful study of history does not merely show the failures of coherent discourse, the failures of the communities that crumbled because they let nihilism or pessimism take hold. History also shows that humanity has done exceptional things, that higher levels of unity have been reached. It may prove to be a material fact that an absolute unity will never be reached. This can either be because new unities create their own particular dissatisfactions and injustices, or because there will always be individuals who, in their freedom, refuse the possibility of unity. People can also always work to create new coherent discourses. They may even succeed. Whatever the case, only time can provide the proof. In the meantime, Weil's philosophical project presents a task to help individuals see their own freedom and to elaborate their own problems in a way that these problems and these dissatisfactions *speak*, and speak loudly, but also coherently. This project hopes to overcome relativism, by aiding individuals to elaborate their own discourse, and to present these discourses into our social reality, but as responsible, reasonable agents, who also bend before the normative weight of better reasons. In this case, the individual, who knows why they struggle, why they work, why they question, can recognize this work and struggle in others. What happens next?

8.4 The Choice of Reason

Skepticism and relativism put us face to face with the decision to be reasonable. All coherent discourse, and all dialogue, is built on accepting certain minimal grounding principles. Once someone has made the choice of reason—the choice to be reasonable—they may continually refute discourse in its own terms in order to create the most coherent, the most rational, the most reasonable position. But the existence of this position does nothing to eliminate the moment of decision. It is every individual who wants to understand their discourse and themself who must accept these grounding principles, and no coherent discourse can make them see the reasonability of this position if they refuse it. What Weil proposes is a discourse that takes this choice into account, by taking violence into account. This however does nothing to reduce the struggle to understand the social and natural reality in which individuals find themselves and on which they act through their discourse. This does nothing to dissolve the fundamental duality between freedom and truth that Weil finds at the bottom of the philosophical endeavor. It also in no way suppresses the radical choice between violence and reason that is always in front of the individual. Rather, it allows the individual to understand that they have made this choice in *good conscience*. That they have understood the truth of freedom.

Weil claims that philosophy "is the search for truth and is only the search for truth" (LP, 89). What philosophy finds in the end is the freedom that grounds it. He thinks that it is only by understanding the radical nature of this freedom (which violence reveals again and again) that philosophy will recognize that it itself needs no justification. He notes that "as long as philosophy is unaware of being grounded on freedom, as long as it believes that it needs a justification, it is inevitably made of a partial discourse, even when it claims to be absolutely coherent discourse" (LP, 64). We justify ourselves, but only against partial discourse. We therefore do not need to justify the goal of understanding the world as a coherent whole, precisely because it is nothing more than something we freely choose to do. This does not eliminate the fact that the possibility of understanding is a historical possibility that has taken many shapes. So even though philosophy always acts in the present, it acts in a present that is already formed by discourse.

What Weil's formulation of the problem of the philosophical grounding of philosophy shows us is that even though philosophy is the search for truth, truth poses no problem for philosophy. The individual can always speak from truth, and when they are wrong they can *truthfully* be wrong. As Weil notes, "[t]ruth's *other* is not error, but violence. It is the refusal of truth, of meaning, of coherence, the choice of the negating act, of incoherent language, of a useful "technical" discourse whose use is never questioned. It is silence. It is the expression of a personal feeling that wants to be personal" (LP, 65). Skepticism and relativism, as partial discourses, remind us of violence's radical nature. Both are discourses that claim to have a necessary hold on us because they are, for the skeptic or the relativist, what is *truly* at the bottom of all discourse. They assign a metaphysical and ontological reality to these particular discourses and commit to them because of this reality. They ask

8.4 The Choice of Reason

reasonable discourse to justify itself to them, and in doing so, they often drag the individual into their game. Discourse seems arbitrary, philosophy seems to have no foundations, we seem doomed to fail in our naivety and our faith in the necessity of philosophy. What Weil tries to show is that both are a choice, that they are pragmatic *commitments* that individuals freely take on and that then guide or direct their action. We can only ever understand them as a choice, as a commitment, and not as a necessity imposed upon us by the *real* nature of discourse, if we face the fact that *all* discourse is a choice, even that of a reasonable, universal, coherent discourse that seeks to grasp the world comprehensively. For Weil, we can only recognize this radical choice of discourse (even in its most universal and coherent form) if we also recognize that any individual can make another choice, that of violence.

Skepticism and relativism are right. We are doomed to fail. But Weil's theory allows us to add, if we so choose. Any discourse can be subject to radical doubt. Any part of any given experience can at any given moment be relative and incommensurable. As long as this is the case, it is possible that it is this relative feature that moves us, and moves us under the cover of darkness so to speak, motivating us or defining the dissatisfaction that can lead us to act. However, and here is Weil's point, as long as that claim is said to be subjective and relative, it is insufficient to establish any epistemic authority or unity, precisely because the objective and universal are claimed to be incoherent. The activity that this skepticism, that this relativity and incommensurability, bring about does not count, in Weil's sense, as action, because it cannot know why it acts. The goal of pluralism then is to conceptualize those claims in a way that allows them to be grasped by coherent discourse, that allows them to hold place in our metaphysical systems, that allows them to be taken up by others and shared, to be the interlocking parts of discourse that leads individuals to see themselves as having full usage of their own reasonable freedom, because they indeed use these claims to enter into the game of giving and asking for reasons. Until this happens our dissatisfaction remains either a silent source of suffering or the arm of our violence.

The prize won at the end of the philosophical endeavor is nothing more than the *good conscience* of the philosopher who has stopped "looking for the impossible justification of the understanding that predates understanding" (LP, 64), because they have grasped the freedom of their choice as reasonable. Being reasonable is not necessary. Philosophy is not necessary, expect for the individual who chooses it. If the philosopher forgets this then philosophy:

> refrains from understanding itself as a human possibility and thus invites the concrete individual's protest, and because it wants to impose itself on the individual through discourse, it ends up being obliged to impose itself through violence, and treats whoever protests against it like a crazy person or a criminal (and this most applies to anyone who actually refuses discourse), that is, like a dangerous animal that needs to be removed or eliminated (LP, 65).

For Weil, philosophy must conceive of itself as "the human being who speaks and who by speaking, explains their realized possibilities to themself; it is the discourse of the human being who, having chosen to establish their own coherence for themself, understands everything by understanding all human understanding as well as themself" (LP, 65). The good conscience of the philosopher is nothing more than this. It is the person who, faced with the radical choice between reason and violence, chooses reason in a world filled with violence and chooses to face this violence head-on. It is the person who knows that the choice of reason is as a-rational and arbitrary as the choice of violence, but by choosing it chooses to understand meaning. This is why necessity, justification, unity, etc. are all downstream from discourse and not "in the world" so to speak.

This seems a meager modification to all that the philosophical tradition has created, and Weil admits that. However, he also claims that this meager modification has radical consequences. He states:

> If we look back over our shoulder, it now seems that the definition of the human being that we used as our starting point has only been modified in one way: instead of saying that the human being is a being gifted with reasonable discourse, we would now say that the human being is a being that can be reasonable if they so choose, that, in a word, the human being is freedom in view of reason (or for violence), that once the human being has decided to speak coherently, the universal becomes the beginning and end of their discourse, and that they can only radically free themself from discourse *knowingly*, that they can only free themself after having passed through discourse in its totality (LP, 68).

Because of this modification, if the individual wants to understand themself with good conscience, if they want to grasp meaning and the world, they can no longer view philosophy as it has traditionally been viewed. They must see it as their own activity to give meaning to their life by grasping the meaning in their life comprehensively. As Weil states, "*first philosophy* is not a theory of Being but the development of *logos*, of discourse, for itself and by itself, in the reality of human existence, an existence that is understood in its realizations, insofar as it *wants* to be understood. It is not ontology, it is logic, not of Being, but of concrete human discourse, of the discourses that form discourse in its unity" (LP, 69). Again, this is a slight modification, but it seems to be the difference that matters because without it, the individual is left defenseless facing their own particularity and violence.

References

Annis, D. 1978. A contextualist theory of epistemic justification. *American Philosophical Quarterly* 15 (3): 213–219.
———. 1982. The social and cultural component of epistemic justification: A reply. *Philosophia* 12: 51–55.
Barbaro, M., and E. Eckholm. 2015, March 27. Indiana law denounced as invitation to discriminate against gays. *New York Times*. https://www.nytimes.com/2015/03/28/us/politics/indiana-law-denounced-as-invitation-to-discriminate-against-gays.html.
BonJour, L. 1985. *The structure of empirical knowledge*. Cambridge, MA: Harvard University Press.
———. 2009. *Epistemology: Classic problems and contemporary responses*. 2nd ed. Lanham: Rowman & Littlefield Publishers.
Brandom, R. 1994. *Making it explicit – Reasoning, representing & discursive commitment*. Cambridge, MA: Harvard University Press.
Chisholm, R. 1989. *Theory of knowledge*. 3rd ed. Englewood Cliffs: Prentice Hall.

References

Cometti, J.-P. 2001. Le pluralisme pragmatiste et la question du relativisme. *Archives de Philosophie, Tome 64* (1): 21–39.

Davidson, D. 1983. A coherence theory of truth and knowledge. In *Kant oder Hegel*, ed. D. Henrich, 423–428. Stuttgart: Klett-Cotta.

deVries, W.A., T. Triplett, and W. Sellars. 2000. *Knowledge, mind, and the given: Reading Wilfrid Sellars's empiricism and the philosophy of mind, including the complete text of Sellars's essay*. Indianapolis: Hackett Publishing Co, Inc.

Haack, S. 1993. *Evidence and inquiry: Towards reconstruction in epistemology*. Oxford: Blackwell Publishers Ltd.

Kalpokas, D. 2017. Sellars on perceptual knowledge. *Transactions of the Charles S. Peirce Society 53* (3): 425–446.

Koppelberg, D. 1998. Foundationalism and coherentism reconsidered. *Erkenntnis 49* (3): 255–283.

Kukla, R. 2000. Myth, memory and misrecognition in Sellars "Empiricism and the philosophy of mind". *Philosophical Studies 101* (2/3): 161–211.

Lynch, M.P. 2012. Democracy as a space of reasons. In *Truth and democracy*, ed. J. Elkins and A. Norris, 114–129. Philadelphia: University of Pennsylvania Press.

Mackie, J.L. 1977. *Ethics: Inventing right and wrong*. New York: Penguin Books.

McDowell, J. 2013. *Having the world in view – Essays on Kant, Hegel, and Sellars (reprint)*. Cambridge, MA: Harvard University Press.

Peregrin, J. 2014. *Inferentialism: Why rules matter*. New York: Palgrave Macmillan.

Price, H. 1992. Metaphysical pluralism. *The Journal of Philosophy 89* (8): 387–409.

Religious freedom restoration act, Pub. L. No. 101, S.E.A. 2015. http://iga.in.gov/legislative/2015/bills/senate/101#document-92bab197.

Ryle, G. 1966. *The concept of mind*. London: Hutchinson & LTD.

Sellars, W. 1997. *Empiricism & the philosophy of mind*. Cambridge, MA: Harvard University Press.

Stroud, B. 1984. *The significance of philosophical scepticism*. Oxford: Clarendon Press.

Tiercelin, C. 2017, March 1. La démocratie ou l'espace des raisons. https://www.college-de-france.fr/site/claudine-tiercelin/course-2017-03-01-14h00.htm.

Weil, E. 1950. *Logique de la philosophie*. Paris: Librairie Philosophique Vrin.

———. 1953. Tradition and traditionalism. *Confluence 2* (4): 106–116.

———. 1956. *Philosophie politique*. Paris: Librairie Philosophique Vrin.

Westphal, K.R. 2003. *Hegel's epistemology*. Indianapolis: Hackett Publishing Company.

Williams, M. 1995. *Unnatural doubts (Revised edition)*. Princeton University Press.

———. 1999. *Groundless belief*. 2nd ed. Princeton: Princeton University Press.

———. 2001. *Problems of knowledge*. Oxford: Oxford University Press.

Chapter 9
Conclusion

In the *Logic of Philosophy* Eric Weil seeks to lead philosophy to grasp itself philosophically. In order to do this, he thinks that understanding violence and its ever-present latent possibility is essential. The question that has to be asked is whether he succeeds. The answer to that question is ambiguous. He succeeds insofar as he develops a discourse that allows him to understand himself philosophically as a philosopher. That is, he articulates a discourse that makes a claim of comprehensive universality that at the same time explains his free choice to philosophize. Thus it accomplishes his goal. To do so, he in a certain sense reconstructs the Hegelian philosophical project, but from the point of view of his present situation. But he is also required to go further than Hegel did, to grasp a reality that Hegel had a hand in shaping. A reality where pure violence has showed its face. Raymond Aron notes that Eric Weil told him "that he was going to bring philosophy to a close", and then goes on to note that he could only marvel at such a claim while at the same time ironically smiling about it.[1] If we ask the question whether Weil succeeded or not in light of Aron's remarks, the answer opens back up, but we must also be suspicious of Aron's claim. Nowhere in Weil's text does he claim to write the *final* word on philosophy, rather he affirms over and over again that philosophy is constantly in the process of starting over. This is even part of his critique of Hegel. Violence, philosophy's *other*, moves deeply within us all. Philosophy does not and cannot exhaust the reality of human experience in the world. Weil has not closed the book on philosophy because history is not over and people will constantly work to grasp their own time in thought.

There will always be rebellions against any concrete content that is deployed in philosophy (understood as a discourse that makes universal claims), just as there will always be new discourses that raise themselves up, pushed on by a shadowy dissatisfaction that individuals toil to bring to light. This even seems to be what Weil

---

[1] Aron (1983), 732.

is trying to teach us. The practice of philosophy is unending. It can stop, it can go underground, but it also starts over any time the individual asks the question of meaning for themself. There is however another question that underlies this one. This question asks whether his elaboration of the philosophical categories is complete and correct. The response, one that I think Weil would accept, is that only time will tell. However, even if the order should change, or if the suite of categories should be enriched by new categories that Weil could not see, either because they were not present in the tradition that he was working from or because they had not yet been developed in history, Weil clearly thinks he provides us with the tools to tackle this problem. This is why his development of *Meaning* and *Wisdom* are formal categories. They allow the grasp of the creation of meaning and the life lived meaningfully as a concrete unity. This is also why he claims that *Wisdom* fulfills the requirement of circularity that he gives to his project. The individual who works towards the category of *Wisdom* finds it by reinserting themself back into the attitude of *Truth*, but into a truth transformed by the path travelled, just as they are now armed with their mature certainty. This means that if we take Weil's project seriously, we have to respond to it. We have to subject it to reasoned critique. We cannot just dismiss it out of hand. I take Weil's project seriously and I am not fully satisfied by it. My own dissatisfaction with Weil's discourse is born of the historical consequence of finding myself in a different context with different concerns from a different point of view than Weil himself. Weil's discourse examines the western philosophical tradition. It was where he was working from. But the continued globalization of the world and the reasoned critiques that have been levied against the western philosophical tradition are both real and forceful. Does Indian philosophy really fit as neatly into the first categories of a logic of philosophy like Weil seems to think, or did it give rise to different human attitudes that express something that Weil's categories miss? And Chinese philosophy? And what of the other traditions of thought and culture around the world? Does reducing these things to European philosophical forms take something away from them? Does it restrict their full expression? Most likely. This is not a question that I am competent to answer at this point, but the presence of the problem seems real to me.

Weil modestly reminds us that the *Logic of Philosophy* is no more than "the end of its own history" and that "it is only possible after violence has been seen in its purity and, consequently, after the will to coherence, as a violent (free and unjustifiable) human decision against violence ("natural" up to this point), is understood as the center of the world where this decision is made" (LP, 84). In other words, Weil admits the fragility of his project, and recognizes that it will only be taken seriously by those that have already asked themselves how to grasp reality and themselves meaningfully, reasonably, and totally. He also recognizes that this desire to grasp oneself as such cannot be forced upon anyone or given to anyone fully-formed. It always starts from the free choice of a singular individual. Any attempt to show the necessity of Weil's project would invalidate it. Thus, the only way to show that Weil's project fails is to surpass it by providing another coherent and universal discourse that grasps our lives and the world in which we live our lives more comprehensively. However, because this project would surpass Weil's and would show

9 Conclusion

what Weil missed, it would also show the truth of Weil's project by building off the partial coherence that Weil elaborated and that this hypothetical system succeeds in showing is partial. Thus to come back to the question of whether Weil succeeds or not, the answer is now, partially, no. This is clear from the legitimate critiques that can be raised against Weil's own presuppositions and his own blind spots.

However, this question only touches the surface of his discourse. The real question is whether his discourse provides the tools to overcome its own blind spots and problems. Here, at least for me, the answer is yes. By articulating the question about the comprehensiveness of discourse in the way he does, and by focusing on the requirement of the openness of discourse, Weil provides critical tools to help individuals grasp themselves and their experience in the world more comprehensively, more reasonably, and less violently. This includes helping us to articulate what dissatisfies us with Weil's own discourse. I make this claim precisely because, in reading Weil, I have been able to give voice to my own effort to understand the world reasonably and comprehensively, and I understand that this was a choice, and a choice I freely made against the very real background of incoherence and violence of my concrete situation.

This presentation of Weil's philosophical project takes him seriously, but also seeks to enrich his project by taking into account posterior developments. The major development that is mobilized here is that of inferentialism. This development enriches Weil's project in two ways. First and most simply, it provides a technical apparatus that allows certain moves that Weil makes in the *Logic of Philosophy* to be made more explicit. However, it only does so because some of the major commitments of both projects are the same. These shared commitments in large part come from the German philosophical tradition around Kant and Hegel. The inferentialist program, by placing the emphasis on the act of committing and of taking others as committed in discourse helps to articulate some of the major commitments of the German tradition (the primacy of the practical, and the emphasis on expression over representation) in our own philosophical language. Weil seems to take these things for granted, having been trained as a philosopher by Ernst Cassirer, one of the most important neo-Kantians. He is someone that absorbed these important lessons from the German tradition. In our modern philosophical discourse, Robert Brandom has admirably defended shifting the emphasis of understanding meaning from words to sentences, because the sentence, according to him, is the minimal meaningful unity we can take responsibility for in judgment. Here Brandom explicitly looks to Kant.[2] Cassirer shares that commitment but attributes its fullest articulation to Humboldt.[3] Cassirer nonetheless reminds us that, for Humboldt, this claim is born of the double influence of Kant's notion of judgment and Herder's notion of expression.[4] This influence is clearly present in Weil's work.

---

[2] Brandom (2001), 159.
[3] Cassirer (1954), 105.
[4] Cassirer (1954), 99–108.

By presenting the technical apparatus that he does, and by sharing similar commitments born from the mobilization of the same tradition, Brandom helps to bring out the modern shape of these commitments. This is what motivates reading the *Logic of Philosophy* along pragmatist, expressivist, and inferentialist lines. However, as I have tried to show, Weil's project also has something to add to inferentialism. Brandom notes that philosophy should be viewed as dialogical, open-ended, and pluralist,[5] and in his method for tackling historical texts, he notes the need to "navigate between different perspectives or contexts specified by different potential interlocutors."[6] This, in my view, is exactly what Weil provides. Reading the different categories of the *Logic of Philosophy* as the inferential unfolding of different discursive positions develops an extremely important tool to help enrich this aspect of the inferentialist project. Both Weil and inferentialists see the need to understand the different types of inferences that lead to different substantive positions and to understand the interplay of these positions. By starting from the possibility of violence, Weil adds another piece to the inferentialist project that was missing. It provides a way of understanding how these different positions enter into conflict and what the *real* concrete shapes of these conflicts are.

This sketches the main results that I hope to be taken from this work. In other words, reading Weil along inferentialist lines adds something specific to our understanding of his project, just as inversely, reading inferentialism along Weilian lines does the same for the inferentialist project. This hypothesis motivates the moves made in this work. This reading seeks to bring out the *expressivist* motivations of Weil's distinction between language and discourse, which allows grasping the development of the discursive resources found in the *Logic of Philosophy* as inferential concepts. This modifies the traditional reading of these same resources by claiming that Weil starts by describing the most basic pragmatic attitudes that can be grasped by coherent discourse, namely those of *Truth* and *Meaninglessness*. This allows Weil to develop the concepts necessary for grasping semantically explicit coherent discourses. With these semantic concepts in place, Weil is able to give detailed description of the different semantic categories that, from *The Object* to *The Absolute*, develop different coherent grasps of meaning according to the permissible inferences of their different grounding concepts. This also leads us to read the categories *of* philosophy as pragmatic metavocabularies that characterize the individual's relationship to coherent discourse. By articulating the *Logic of Philosophy* this way, we are in a better position to understand why argumentative practices are so important. Real agreement is only reached when individuals take on the meta-commitment to reasonable (nonviolent) practices. The focus on the argumentative aspect of the *Logic of Philosophy* seeks to understand what the mechanisms of stable and fecund agreement are.

To extend this project, it would be necessary, as already said, to enter into Weil's theory of education, which outstrips the scope of this work. It would also be necessary to engage in another project that unfortunately also outstrips the scope of this

---

[5] Brandom (2002), 91–118.
[6] Brandom (2002), 111.

work, namely an analysis of how Weil deploys the argumentative resources of the *Logic of Philosophy* in his *Philosophie Politique*, his *Philosophie Morale*, and his numerous essays. Therein, we find a philosopher extremely careful to show how to engage in reasonable argumentative practices. One who takes the diversity of human discourse and experience non-reductively into account, and who shows how to dissolve the problems that can be dissolved while highlighting the real problems that remain. By showing how problems are in fact problems, he hopes to bring people to the awareness of their own positions concerning these problems and demonstrate how to tackle these problems reasonably. In other words, this would lead to what Weil calls an *applied logic of philosophy*, which is the different reprises of coherent discourse in the lived attitudes of concrete individuals. This is necessary because, for Weil, it is the concrete deployment of different reprises "that form human language and human discourses (which are not coherent, even though they claim to be)" (LP, 82).

By showing how concrete individuals live in different attitudes, and by trying to elaborate a comprehensive discourse that takes both these attitudes and their latent violence into account, we are in a better position to understand Weil's insistence on dialogical pluralism. The final result that this work has tried to show is that different metaphysical positions, monism, relativism, skepticism, nihilism, cynicism, reasonable pluralism, are themselves born in discursive commitments. If this is true then the commitments we make matter, because they act upon the world and the discourse of the world. They act upon us human beings, those specifically discursive creatures, that will never be entirely discursive. Both Weil and inferentialism hope to provide the tools needed for the individual to understand themself rationally and reasonably. But, as Weil would add, these tools are only useful to those that demand them for themselves. For those individuals, who do indeed search such tools, this work hopes to insist on the value of using them. This is important for the person who seeks to be reasonable with others in reasonable discourse but also (and perhaps above all) for the person who seeks to be reasonable faced with someone who does not. For those who accept the project of reasonable discourse and who already deploy it reasonably, this work hopes at least to clarify certain aspects of Weil's contribution to the overall development of reasonable discourse. If nothing else, this work sees itself as modest celebration of the diversity of human experience and a modest celebration of the monumental effort that has been expended to unify that experience reasonably while also recognizing the work that still needs to be done.

References

Aron, R. 1983. *Mémoires*. Paris: Julliard.
Brandom, R. 2001. *Articulating reasons – An introduction to inferentialism*. Cambridge, MA: Harvard University Press.
———. 2002. *Tales of the mighty dead*. Cambridge, MA: Harvard University Press.
Cassirer, E. 1954. *Philosophie der Symbolischen Formen: Die Sprache*. Oxford: Bruno Cassirer.
Weil, E. 1950. *Logique de la philosophie*. Paris: Librairie Philosophique Vrin.

Bibliography

Annis, D. 1978. A contextualist theory of epistemic justification. *American Philosophical Quarterly 15* (3): 213–219.
———. 1982. The social and cultural component of epistemic justification: A reply. *Philosophia 12*: 51–55.
Aristophanes. 1996. *Wasps*, vol. 4. Trans. A. Sommerstein. Warminster: Aris & Phillips LTD.
Aron, R. 1983. *Mémoires*. Paris: Julliard.
Assis, A. 2016. *Educação e moral: Uma análise crítica da filosofia de Éric Weil*. Editora CRV.
Astrup, A.-S. 1999. *Hannah Arendt—Heinrich Blucher, correspondance, 1936–1968*. Paris: Calmann-Lévy.
Ayer, A.J. 1949. *Language, truth and logic*. 2nd ed. London: Victor Gollancz.
Bacon, M. 2012. *Pragmatism: An introduction*. Cambridge, UK: Polity Press.
Barbaro, M., and E. Eckholm. 2015, March 27. Indiana law denounced as invitation to discriminate against gays. *New York Times*. https://www.nytimes.com/2015/03/28/us/politics/indiana-law-denounced-as-invitation-to-discriminate-against-gays.html.
Berlin, I. 1979. *Against the current: Essays in the history of ideas*. Princeton: Princeton University Press.
Bernardo, L.M. 2003. *Linguagem e discurso: Uma hipótese hermenêutica sobre a filosofia de Eric Weil*. Lisbon: Imrensa Nacional – Casa da Moeda.
———. 2011. Moral, educação e sentido: Uma leitura da philosophie morale de Eric Weil. *Itinerarium* LVII: 2–40.
———. 2013. A retomada na filosofia. *Cultura: Revista de História e Teoria Das Ideias 31* (II).
Bernstein, R. 1995. American pragmatism: The conflict of narratives. In *Rorty and pragmatism*, ed. H. Saatkamp Jr., 54–67. Nashville: Vanderbilt University Press.
———. 2010. *The pragmatic turn*. Cambridge, UK: Polity Press.
Bizeul, Y., ed. 2006a. *Gewalt, Moral und Politik bei Eric Weil*. Hamburg: Lit Verlag.
———. 2006b. Moral und Politik bei Eric Weil. In *Gewalt, Moral und Politik Bei Eric Weil*, 131–157. Hamburg: Lit Verlag.
Blackburn, S. 1984. *Spreading the word*. Oxford: Oxford University Press.
Bobongaud, S.G. 2011. *La dimension politique du langage*. Rome: Gregorian & Biblical Press.
Boethius, A. 1999. *The consolation of philosophy*. Trans. V. Watts, rev. ed. New York: Penguin Books.
BonJour, L. 1985. *The structure of empirical knowledge*. Cambridge, MA: Harvard University Press.
———. 2009. *Epistemology: Classic problems and contemporary responses*. 2nd ed. Lanham: Rowman & Littlefield Publishers.

Bouillard, H. 1977. Philosophie et religion dans l'œuvre d'Éric Weil. *Archives de Philosophie 404* (4): 543–621.
Bourdieu, P. 1987. *Choses dites*. Paris: Les Éditions de Minuit.
Brandom, R. 1988. Inference, expression, and induction. *Philosophical Studies 54* (2): 257–285.
———. 1994. *Making it explicit – Reasoning, representing & discursive commitment*. Cambridge, MA: Harvard University Press.
———. 2001. *Articulating reasons – An introduction to inferentialism*. Cambridge, MA: Harvard University Press.
———. 2002. *Tales of the mighty dead*. Cambridge, MA: Harvard University Press.
———. 2004. The pragmatist enlightenment (and its problematic semantics). *European Journal of Philosophy 12* (1): 1–16.
———. 2009. *Reason in philosophy: Animating ideas*. Cambridge, MA: Belknap Press.
———. 2010. *Between saying and doing: Towards an analytic pragmatism*. Oxford: Oxford University Press.
———. 2011. *Perspectives on pragmatism: Classic, recent, and contemporary*. Cambridge, MA: Harvard University Press.
———. 2015. *From empiricism to expressivism*. Cambridge, MA: Harvard University Press.
———. 2018. From logical expressivism to expressivist logic: Sketch of a program and some implementations. *Philosophical Issues 28* (1): 70–88. https://doi.org/10.1111/phis.12116.
———. 2019. *A spirit of trust*. Cambridge, MA: Harvard University Press.
———. 2020. Rorty on vocabularies. In *Revisiting Richard Rorty*, ed. P.G. Moreira, 1–24. Vernon Press.
Breuvart, J.M. 1987. Tradition, effectivité et théorie chez E. Weil et H.G. Gadamer. In *Cahiers Éric Weil Tome I*, ed. J. Quillien. Villeneuve-d'Ascq: Presses Universitaires du Septentrion.
Breuvart, J.-M. 2013. *Le questionnement métaphysique d'A.N. Whitehead*. Louvain-la-Neuve: Les Éditions Chomatika.
Buchwalter, A. 1994. Hegel and the doctrine of expressivism. In *Artifacts, representations and social practice: Essays for Marx Wartofsky*, ed. C.C. Gould and R.S. Cohen, 163–183. Dordrecht: Springer. https://doi.org/10.1007/978-94-011-0902-4_10.
Buée, J.-M. 1987. *La logique de la philosophie* et l'herméneutique de Gadamer. In *Cahier Éric Weil Tome I*, ed. J. Quillien. Lille: Presses Universitaires du Septentrion.
———. 1989. Éducation, cosmos et histoire chez Éric Weil. In *Cahiers Éric Weil II*, ed. C.É. Weil, 81–90. Villeneuve-d'Ascq: Presses Universitaires de Lille.
Burgio, A. 1990. Du discours à la violence: Avec Hegel, après Hegel. In *Discours, violence et langage: Un socractisme d'Éric Weil*, ed. P. Canivez and P.-J. Labarrière, 69–95. Paris: Éditions Osiris.
Caillois, R. 1953. Attitudes et catégories selon Éric Weil. *Revue de Métaphysique et de Morale 58* (3): 273–291.
Canivez, P. 1985. Éducation et instruction d'après Éric Weil. *Archives de Philosophie 48* (4): 529–562.
———. 1993. *Le politique et sa logique dans l'œuvre d'Éric Weil*. Paris: Éditions Kimé.
———. 1998. *Éric Weil ou la question du sens*. Paris: Ellipses.
———. 1999. *Weil*. Paris: Les Belles Lettres.
———. 2002. Le droit naturel chez Éric Weil. *Actes de l'Association Roumaine Des Chercheurs Francophones En Sciences Humaines 3*: 49–56.
———. 2007. Le kantisme d'Éric Weil. In *Kant et les kantismes dans la philosophie contemporaine*, ed. C. Berner and F. Capeillères, 171–190. Villeneuve-d'Ascq: Presses Universitaires du Septentrion.
———. 2013a. La notion de reprise et ses applications. *Cultura: Revista de História e Teoria Das Ideias 31* (II): 15–29.
———. 2013b. *Qu'est-ce que l'action politique ?* Paris: Librairie Philosophique J. Vrin.
———. 2020a. Eric Weil's reading of the critique of the power of judgment. In *Kant's third Critique in the twentieth century*, ed. S. Marino and P. Terzi. Berlin: De Gruyter.

———. 2020b. La philosophie comme profession et la participation démocratique dans la pensée politique d'Éric Weil. *Eco-Ethica 8*.
Canivez, P., and P.-J. Labarrière, eds. 1990. *Discours, violence et langage: Un socratisme d'Éric Weil*. Paris: Éditions Osiris.
Cassirer, E. 1954. *Philosophie der Symbolischen Formen: Die Sprache*. Oxford: Bruno Cassirer.
Castelo Branco, J. 2018. Éric Weil e o papel da educação humanística no contexto da cultura técnico-científica. *Educação e Filosofia 32* (66).
Chiarini, S. 2019. οὐδεν λέγει/nihil dicere: A Lexical and semantic survey. *Mnemosyne 72*: 114–149.
Chisholm, R. 1989. *Theory of knowledge*. 3rd ed. Englewood Cliffs: Prentice Hall.
Chomsky, N. 1957. *Syntactic structures*. The Hague: Mouton & Co.
———. 1966. *Cartesian linguistics*. New York: Harper & Row.
Cometti, J.-P. 2001. Le pluralisme pragmatiste et la question du relativisme. *Archives de Philosophie, Tome 64* (1): 21–39.
———. 2010. *Qu'est-ce que le pragmatisme?* Paris: Gallimard.
Davidson, D. 1983. A Coherence theory of truth and knowledge. In *Kant oder Hegel*, ed. D. Henrich, 423–428. Stuttgart: Klett-Cotta.
———. 1984a. *Inquiries into truth and interpretation*. Oxford: Clarendon Press.
———. 1984b. Thought and talk. In *Inquiries into truth and interpretation*, 156–170. Clarendon Press.
de Beauvoir, S. 2015. *The ethics of ambiguity*. Trans. B. Frechtman, reissue ed. New York: Philosophical Library/Open Road.
de Montaigne, M. 1958. *The complete essays of montaigne*. Trans. D. M. Frame. Stanford: Stanford University Press.
Deligne, A. 1998. *Éric Weil: Ein zeitgenössischer Philosoph*. Bonn: Romanistischer Verlag.
Delpla, I. 2001. *Quine, Davidson: Le principe de charité*. Paris: Presses Universitaires de France.
deVries, W.A., T. Triplett, and W. Sellars. 2000. *Knowledge, mind, and the given: Reading Wilfrid Sellars's Empiricism and the philosophy of mind, including the complete text of Sellars's essay*. Indianapolis: Hackett Publishing Co, Inc.
Dewey, J. 1916. *Democracy and education*. New York: Macmillan.
———. 1927. *The Public and its problems*. New York: Holt.
Dummett, M. 1994. *Origins of analytical philosophy*. Oxford: Oxford University Press.
Englander, A. 2013. Herder's 'expressivist' metaphysics and the origins of German Idealism. *British Journal for the History of Philosophy 21* (5): 902–924. https://doi.org/10.1080/0960878 8.2013.805120.
Fichte, J.G. 1992. *Introductions to the Wissenschaftslehre and other writings*. Trans. D. Breazeale. Indianapolis: Hackett Publishing Company.
Forster, M.N. 2012. *After Herder: Philosophy of language in the German tradition* (Reprint edition). Oxford: Oxford University Press.
———. 2014. *German philosophy of language: From Schlegel to Hegel and beyond* (Reprint edition). Oxford: Oxford University Press.
Gaitsch, P. 2014. *Eric Weils Logik der Philosophie: Eine phänomenologische Relektüre*. Freiburg: Verlag Karl Alber.
Ganty, É. 1997. *Penser la modernité*. Namur: Presses Universitaires de Namur.
Guibal, F. 2003. La condition historique du sens selon Éric Weil. *Revue Philosophique de Louvain 101* (4): 610–639.
———. 2009. *Le courage de la raison: La philosophie pratique d'Éric Weil*. Paris: Éditions du Félin.
———. 2011. *Le sens de la réalité: Logique et existence selon Éric Weil*. Paris: Éditions du Félin.
———. 2012. Langage, discours, réalité: Le sens de la philosophie selon Éric Weil. *Laval Théologique et Philosophique 68* (3): 593–617.
———. 2013. L'idée de Dieu dans la *Logique de la philosophie*. *Cultura: Revista de História e Teoria Das Ideias 31*: 163–175.

———. 2015. *Figures de la pensée contemporaine*. Paris: Hermann.
Haack, S. 1993. *Evidence and inquiry: towards reconstruction in epistemology*. Oxford: Blackwell Publishers Ltd.
Habermas, J. 1984. *Theory of communicative action: Volume 1*. Boston Beacon Press.
———. 1985. *Theory of communicative action: Volume 2*. Boston: Beacon Press.
Hamblin, C. 1970. *Fallacies*. London: Methuen & Co Ltd.
Hare, R.M. 1952. *The language of morals*. Oxford: Oxford University Press.
Hegel, G.W.F. 2015. *Georg Wilhelm Friedrich Hegel: The science of logic*. Trans. G. Di Giovanni, reprint ed. Cambridge, UK: Cambridge University Press.
———. 2018. *Phenomenology of spirit*. Trans. T. Pinkard. Cambridge University Press.
Herder, J.G. 2008. *Herder: Philosophical writings*. Trans. M.N. Forster. Cambridge, UK: Cambridge University Press.
Hume, D. 2000. *A treatise of human nature (Oxford Philosophical Texts)*. Oxford: Oxford University Press.
James, W. 2000. *Pragmatism and other writings* (New Edition). New York: Penguin Classics.
Jarczyk, G., and P.-J. Labarrière. 1996. *De Kojève à Hegel: 150 ans de pensée hégélienne en France*. Paris: Albin Michel.
Juszezak, J. 1977. *L'anthropologie de Hegel à travers la pensée moderne*. Paris: Éditions Anthropos.
Kalpokas, D. 2017. Sellars on perceptual knowledge. *Transactions of the Charles S. Peirce Society* 53 (3): 425–446.
Kant, I. 1998. *Religion within the boundaries of mere reason and other writings*. Trans. A. Wood and G. Di Giovanni. Cambridge, UK: Cambridge University Press.
Kirscher, G. 1970. Absolu et sens dans la "Logique de la philosophie". *Archives de Philosophie* 33 (3): 373–400.
———. 1989. *La philosophie d'Éric Weil*. Paris: Presses Universitaires de France.
———. 1990. Éric Weil et Socrate: Discussion et dialogue. In *Discours, violence et langage: Un socratisme d'Éric Weil*, ed. P. Canivez and P.-J. Labarrière, 235–257. Paris: Éditions Osiris.
———. 1992. *Figures de la violence et de la modernité*. Villeneuve-d'Ascq: Presses Universitaires de Lille.
———. 1999. *Éric Weil ou La raison de la philosophie*. Villeneuve-d'Ascq: Presses Universitaires du Septentrion.
Kirscher, G., and J. Quillien. 1982. *Sept études sur Éric Weil*. Villeneuve-d'Ascq: Presses Universitaires du Septentrion.
Kluback, W. 1987. *Eric Weil: A fresh look at philosophy*. Lanham: University Press of America.
Koppelberg, D. 1998. Foundationalism and coherentism reconsidered. *Erkenntnis* 49 (3): 255–283.
Kraut, R. 1990. Varieties of pragmatism. *Mind* 99 (394): 157–183.
Kukla, R. 2000. Myth, memory and misrecognition in Sellars' "Empiricism and the philosophy of mind". *Philosophical Studies* 101 (2/3): 161–211.
Kukla, R., and M. Lance. 2008. *"Yo" and "lo": The pragmatic topography of the space of reasons*. Cambridge, MA: Harvard University Press.
Lakoff, G. 1987. *Women, fire, and dangerous things*. Chicago: University of Chicago Press.
Lewis, C.I. 1923. A pragmatic conception of the a priori. *The Journal of Philosophy* 20 (7): 169–177. https://doi.org/10.2307/2939833.
Lewis, D. 1979. Scorekeeping in a language game. *Journal of Philosophical Logic* 8 (1): 339–359.
Livet, P. 1984. Après la fin de l'histoire. In *Actualité d'Éric Weil*, 83–91. Paris: Editions Beauchesne.
Lovejoy, A.O. 1908. The thirteen pragmatisms. I. *The Journal of Philosophy, Psychology and Scientific Methods* 5 (1): 5–12. https://doi.org/10.2307/2012277.
Lynch, M.P. 2012. Democracy as a space of reasons. In *Truth and democracy*, ed. J. Elkins and A. Norris, 114–129. Philadelphia: University of Pennsylvania Press.
Mackie, J.L. 1977. *Ethics: Inventing right and wrong*. New York: Penguin Books.
Marcelo, G. 2013. Paul Ricœur et Eric Weil. Histoire, vérité et conflit des interprétations. *Cultura Revista de História e Teoria das Ideias* 31: 247–266. https://doi.org/10.4000/cultura.1881.

McDowell, J. 1996. *Mind and world*. 2nd ed. Cambridge, MA: Harvard University Press.

———. 2013. *Having the world in view – Essays on Kant, Hegel, and Sellars (Reprint)*. Cambridge, MA: Harvard University Press.

Menand, L. 2001. *The metaphysical club*. London: Flamingo.

Misak, C. 2013. *The American pragmatists*. Oxford: Oxford University Press.

———. 2016. *Cambridge pragmatism: From Peirce and James to Ramsey and Wittgenstein*. Oxford: Oxford University Press.

Montague, M. 2007. Against propositionalism. *Noûs 41* (3): 503–518.

Morresi, R. 1979. Filosofia, politica, e violenza nella *Logica della filosofia* di E. Weil. *Annali Della Facoltà Di Lettere e Filosofia Dell'Univerrsità DiMacerata 12*: 105–134.

Nguyen-Dinh, L. 1996. Éducation ou violence selon Éric Weil. In *Cahiers Éric Weil V*, ed. G. Kirscher, J.-P. Larthomas, and J. Quillien, 79–86. Villeneuve-d'Ascq: Presses Universitaires du Septentrion.

Oehler, K. 1981. Notes on the reception of American pragmatism in Germany, 1899–1952. *Transactions of the Charles S. Peirce Society 17* (1): 25–35.

Okrent, M. 1988. *Heidegger's pragmatism: Understanding, being, and the critique of metaphysics*. Ithaca: Cornell University Press.

Peregrin, J. 2014. *Inferentialism: Why rules matter*. New York: Palgrave Macmillan.

Perelman, C., and L. Olbrechts-Tyteca. 1992. *Traité de l'argumentation*. 5th ed. Bruxelles: Éditions de l'Université de Bruxelles.

Perine, M. 1982. *Philosophie et violence: Sens et intention de la philosophie d'Éric Weil*. Trans. J.-M. Buée. Paris: Beauchesne.

———. 1987. *Filosofia e violencia*. *Sintese 49*: 55–64.

———. 1990. Éducation, violence et raison: De la discussion socratique à la sagesse weilienne. In *Discours, violence et langage: Un socratisme d'Éric Weil*, 109–158. Paris: Éditions Osiris.

Perine, M., and E. Costeski. 2016. *Violência, educação e globalização: Compreender o nosso tempo com Eric Weil*. Edições Loyala.

Piercey, R. 2007. What is a post-Hegelian Kantian? The case of Paul Ricœur. *Philosophy Today 51* (1): 26–38.

Plato. 1997a. *Gorgias*, ed. J. M. Cooper. Trans. D.J. Zeyl. Indianapolis: Hackett Publishing Company, Inc.

———. 1997b. *Protagoras*, ed. J. M. Cooper. Trans. K. Bell and S. Lombardo. Indianapolis: Hackett Publishing Company, Inc.

Price, H. 1992. Metaphysical pluralism. *The Journal of Philosophy 89* (8): 387–409.

———. 2011. Expressivism in two voices. In *Pragmatism, science and naturalism*, ed. J. Knowles and H. Rydenfelt, 87–113. Frankfurt am Main: Peter Lang GmbH, Internationaler Verlag der Wissenschaften.

———. 2013. *Expressivism, pragmatism and representationalism*. Cambridge UK: Cambridge University Press.

Quillien, J. 1982. La cohérence et la négation: Essai d'interprétation des premières catégories de la *Logique de la Philosophie*. In *Sept études sur Éric Weil*, ed. G. Kirscher and J. Quillien, 145–185. Villeneuve-d'Ascq: Presses Universitaires de Lille.

Quine, W.V.O. 1960. *Word and object*. Cambridge, MA: MIT Press.

Rahman, S., Z. McConaughey, A. Klev, and N. Clerbout. 2018. *Immanent reasoning or equality in action: A plaidoyer for the play level*. Cham: Springer.

Religious freedom restoration act, Pub. L. No. 101, S.E.A. 2015. http://iga.in.gov/legislative/2015/bills/senate/101#document-92bab197.

Renaud, M. 2013. La confrontation des trois premières catégories de la *Logique de la philosophie* d'Éric Weil avec la dialectique hégélienne. *Cultura: Revista de História e Teoria Das Ideias 31*: 63–69.

Rescher, N. 2005. *Studies in pragmatism*. Frankfurt: Ontos Verlag.

Ricœur, P. 1984. De l'absolu à la sagesse par l'action. In *Actualité d'Éric Weil*, ed. C.É. Weil. Paris: Beauchesne.

———. 1991. Pour une éthique du compromis: Interview avec Paul Ricœur. *Alternatives Non Violentes 80*: 2–7.
———. 2013. *Le conflit des interprétations: Essais d'herméneutique*. Paris: Éditions du Seuil.
Rockmore, T. 1984. Remarques sur Hegel vu par Weil. In *Actualité d'Éric Weil*, 361–368. Paris: Beauchesne.
Roman, J. 1988. Entre Hannah Arendt et Éric Weil. *Esprit (1940-) 140/141 (7/8)*: 38–49.
Rorty, R. 1982. *Consequences of pragmatism: Essays 1972–1980*. Minneapolis: University of Minnesota Press.
———. 1989. *Contingency, irony, and solidarity*. Cambridge UK: Cambridge University Press.
———. 1991. *Essays on Heidegger and others*. Cambridge UK: Cambridge University Press.
Roth, M. 1988. *Knowing and history: Appropriations of Hegel in twentieth-century France*. Ithaca Cornell University Press.
Roy, J. 1975. Philosophie et violence chez Éric Weil. *Dialogue 14* (3): 502–512.
Ryle, G. 1966. *The concept of mind*. London: Hutchinson & Co. LTD.
Sanou, J.B. 2008. *Violence et sagesse dans la philosophie d'Éric Weil*. Rome: Edetrice Pontificia Università Gregoriana.
Santayana, G. 1955. *Scepticism and animal faith*. New York: Dover Publications.
Sartre, J.P. 1992. *Being and nothingness*. Trans. H. E. Barnes. New York: Washington Square Press.
Savadogo, M. 2003. *Éric Weil et l'achèvement de la philosophie dans l'action*. Namur: Presses Universitaires de Namur.
Sellars, W. 1992. *Science and metaphysics: Variations on Kantian themes*. Atascadero: Ridgeview Publishing Company.
———. 1996. *Naturalism and ontology*. Atascadero: Ridgeview Publishing Company.
———. 1997. *Empiricism & the philosophy of mind*. Cambridge MA: Harvard University Press.
Seneca. 2004. *On the shortness of life*. Trans. C. D. N. Costa. New York: Penguin Books.
Shepherd, W. 2019. *Persian war in Herodotus and other ancient voices*. Oxford: Osprey Publishing.
Soetard, M. 1984. Éric Weil: Philosophie et éducation. In *Actualité d'Éric Weil*, ed. C.É. Weil. Paris: Beauchesne.
Stanguennec, A. 1992. *Être, soi, sens: Les antécédences herméneutiques de la dialectique réflexive*. Villeneuve-d'Ascq: Presses Universitaires du Septentrion.
Stevenson, C.L. 1944. *Ethics and language*. New Haven: Yale University Press.
Strauss, L. 1997. *De la tyrannie. Correspondance avec Alexandre Kojève, 1932–1965*. Paris: Gallimard.
Stroud, B. 1984. *The significance of philosophical scepticism*. Oxford: Clarendon Press.
Strummiello, G. 2001. *Il logos violato: La violenza nella filosofia*. Bari: Edizioni Dedalo.
———. 2013. Ripresa, a priori storico, sistemi de pensiero. *Cultura: Revista de História e Teoria Das Ideias 31*: 195–212.
Talisse, R.B., and S. Aikin. 2008. *Pragmatism: A guide for the perplexed*. London: Continuum.
Taylor, C. 1977. *Hegel*. Cambridge UK: Cambridge University Press.
———. 1985. *Human agency and language*. Cambridge MA: Cambridge University Press.
———. 1989. *The sources of self*. Harvard University Press.
Thomas-Fogiel, I. 2000. *Critique de la représentation: Étude sur Fichte*. Paris: Librairie Philosophique J. Vrin.
Tiercelin, C. 1993. *C.S. Peirce et le pragmatisme*. Paris: Presses Universitaires de France.
———. 2017, March 1. *La démocratie ou l'espace des raisons*. https://www.college-de-france.fr/site/claudine-tiercelin/course-2017-03-01-14h00.htm.
Toulmin, S. 2003. *The use of argument (Updated)*. Cambridge UK: Cambridge University Press.
Valdério, F. 2014. Linguagem, violência e sentido: A propósito de um debate entre Éric Weil e Paul Ricœur. *Argumentos: Revista de. Filosofia 6* (11): 159–171.
Vancourt, R. 1970. Quelques remarques sur le problème de Dieu dans la philosophie d'Éric Weil. *Archives de Philosophie 33* (4): 471–490.
Venditti, P. 1984. La philosophie du sens. In *Actualité d'Éric Weil*, ed. C.É. Weil. Paris: Beauchesne.

Voparil, C.J. 2011. Rorty and Brandom: Pragmatism and the ontological priority of the social. *Pragmatism Today* 2 (1): 133–143.
Weil, E. 1950. *Logique de la philosophie*. Paris: Librairie Philosophique Vrin.
———. 1953. Tradition and traditionalism. *Confluence* 2 (4): 106–116.
———. 1956. *Philosophie politique*. Paris: Librairie Philosophique Vrin.
———. 1957. Education as a problem for our time. *Confluence* 6 (1): 40–50.
———. 1961. *Philosophie morale*. Paris: Librairie Philosophique Vrin.
———. 1965. Science in modern culture, or the meaning of meaninglessness. *Daedalus* 94 (1): 171–189.
———. 1970a. *Essais et conférences: Tome 1*. Paris: Librarie Plon.
———. 1970b. Humanistic studies, their object, methods and meaning. *Daedalus* 99 (2): 237–255.
———. 1970c. *Problèmes kantiens*. 2nd ed. Paris: Librairie Philosophique Vrin.
———. 1971. *Essais et conférences: Tome 2*. Paris: Librarie Plon.
———. 1973. The Hegelian dialectic. In *The legacy of Hegel: Proceedings of the Marquette Hegel symposium 1970*, ed. J.J. O'Malley, K.W. Algozin, H.P. Kainz, and L.C. Rice. The Hague: Martinus Nijhoff.
———. 1989. In *Valuing the humanities*, ed. W. Kluback. Chico: Historians Press.
———. 1993. *Cahiers Éric Weil IV: Essais sur la philosophie, démocratie et éducation*. Villeneuve d'Ascq: Presses Universitaires de Lille.
———. 1998. *Hegel and the state*. Trans. M. A. Cohen. Baltimore: Johns Hopkins Press.
———. 1999. *Essais sur la nature, l'histoire et la politique*. Villeneuve-d'Ascq: Presses Universitaires du Septentrion.
———. 2003a. *Philosophie et réalité: Tome 1*. Paris: Beauchesne.
———. 2003b. *Philosophie et réalité: Tome 2, Inédits suivis de Le cas Heidegger*. Paris: Beauchesne.
———. 2020. Pratique et praxis. *Encyclopædia Universalis.*. Retrieved June 10, 2020, from http://www.universalis-edu.com/encyclopedie/pratique-et-praxis/.
———. Forthcoming. *Logic of Philosophy*. Trans. S. Yiaueki. University of Chicago Press.
Westphal, K.R. 2003. *Hegel's epistemology*. Indianapolis: Hackett Publishing Company.
Williams, M. 1995. *Unnatural doubts* (Revised edition). Princeton: Princeton University Press.
———. 1999. *Groundless belief*. 2nd ed. Princeton: Princeton University Press.
———. 2001. *Problems of knowledge*. Oxford: Oxford University Press.
Wohlrapp, H.R. 2014. *The concept of argument: A philosophical foundation*. Dordrecht: Springer.

Index

A
Aikin, S., 108, 109, 143
Annis, D., 282
Apel, K.-O., 110, 233, 235
Arendt, H., 2
Aristophanes, 18, 268
Aristotle, 2, 24, 26, 33, 43, 51, 69, 72, 76
Aron, R., 1, 323
Astrup, A.-S., 2
Augustine, 33, 77
Ayer, A.J., 7, 126, 127

B
Bacon, M., 143
Barbaro, M., 310
Barnes, H.E, 176
Bayle, P., 33, 34, 53, 54, 81, 267, 304, 308
Beauvoir, S. de, 90, 91
Belnap, N., 137
Berlin, I., 126
Bernardo, L.M., 5, 253
Bernstein, R., 106, 107, 143
Biden, J., 205
Bizeul, Y., 4, 16, 235
Blackburn, S., 7, 125, 126, 131
Bobongaud, S.G., 4, 235
Boethius, 90
BonJour, L., 282
Bouillard, H., 254, 255
Bourdieu, P., 2
Brandom, R., v, 3–8, 32, 33, 77, 86, 99, 101–105, 107, 109, 111, 113–115, 117–122, 124, 126, 129, 130, 135–137, 139, 143, 160, 162, 164, 166, 173, 176, 177, 183, 187–198, 200, 203–211, 218, 223–225, 227, 229, 243, 287, 288, 303, 325, 326
Breuvart, J.-M., 4, 253
Buchwalter, A., 131
Buddha, 63
Buée, J.-M., 4, 230, 253
Burgio, A., 14

C
Caillois, R., 30
Canivez, P., 5, 16, 17, 19, 26, 27, 30, 37, 39, 50, 53, 56, 63, 78, 80, 89, 92, 217, 218, 220, 230, 234, 239–241, 246, 251
Cassirer, E., 126, 325
Castelo Branco, J., 230
Charles V, 156
Chiarini, S., 268
Chisolm, R., 282
Chomsky, N., 124, 133
Clinton, B., 205
Cohen, M.A., 2
Cometti, J.-P., 143, 304
Comte, A., 34, 78
Costeski, E., 230

D
Davidson, D., 101, 111, 129, 282
de Assis, A., 230
Deligne, A., 4, 235
Delpla, I., 101

Derrida, J., 89, 111
Descartes, R., 117, 126, 268, 288
deVries, W., 225, 226, 282
Dewey, J., 103, 107, 108, 111, 143
Dummett, M., 108

E
Eckholm, E., 310
Eddington, A., 118
Englander, A., 131
Eno, B., 200

F
Fichte, J. G., 34, 42, 53, 100, 161, 217, 218, 267
Forster, M., 127, 131, 132, 166
Foucault, M., 4, 32
François I, 156
Frege, G., 131, 135, 224

G
Gadamer, H.-G., 4, 253
Gaitsch, P., 4, 30
Gandhi, M., 220
Ganty, É., 4, 17, 53, 86, 235
Guibal, F., 5, 14, 17, 30, 47, 50, 54–56, 78, 165, 254

H
Haack, S., 282, 285
Habermas, J., 4, 110, 233–235
Hamann, J.G., 132, 165
Hamblin, C., 233, 234
Hare, R.M., 7, 126
Hegel, G.W.F., 2, 6, 14, 25, 26, 33–38, 40, 42, 43, 56, 59, 60, 65, 66, 73, 84, 86, 91, 100, 108, 111, 126, 131, 132, 135, 161, 191, 224, 249, 250, 262, 267, 292, 295, 323, 325
Heidegger, M., 4, 89, 144
Herder, J.G., 7, 126–132, 134–136, 164–167, 325
Hitler, A., 41
Humboldt, W. von, 126, 131, 325
Hume, D., 126–128, 130, 153, 163, 288, 291
Hyppolite, J., 2

J
James, W., 103, 107, 111, 143, 144
Jarczyk, G., 14
Jaspers, K., 89
Jesus, 260
Juszezak, J., 14

K
Kalpokas, D., 282
Kamlah, W., 233
Kant, I., 22, 24, 26–28, 33, 34, 36, 43, 53, 54, 80, 165, 168, 191, 193, 217, 224, 245, 246, 259, 267, 325
Kirscher, G., 5, 14, 16, 17, 23, 30, 41, 42, 50, 52–56, 58, 67, 78, 86, 100, 217, 239, 256, 274
Kluback, W., 2, 30, 50, 77, 86
Kojève, A., 1, 2
Koppelberg, D., 282
Koyré, A., 1
Kraut, R., 162
Kuhn, T., 32
Kukla, Q. (writing as Rebecca Kukla), 4, 136, 137, 194, 206, 208, 227, 228, 241, 282

L
Labarrière, P.-J., 14, 16, 235
Lakoff, G., 114
Lance, M., 4, 136, 137, 194, 206, 208, 227, 228, 241
Lewis, C.I., 175
Lewis, D., 115, 173
Livet, P., 14
Lorenz, K., 233
Lorenzen, P., 233
Lotze, H., 143
Lovejoy, A., 107
Lynch, M.P., 308, 310

M
Mach, E., 144
Mackie, J.L., 305
Marcelo, G., 4, 16, 32, 253
Marx, K., 91
McDowell, J., 4, 114, 286, 287
Menand, L., 110
Merleau-Ponty, M., 2
Misak, C., 110

Montaigne, M. de, 33, 34, 53, 54, 81, 90, 267, 304, 308
Moore, G.E., 126
Morresi, R., 16

N
Nguyen-Dinh, L., 230
Nietzsche, F., 34, 53, 81, 267

O
Oehler, K., 144
Okrent, M., 144
Olbrechts-Tyteca, L., 233, 234, 251

P
Parmenides, 41, 59, 63, 64
Peirce, C.S., 96, 103, 107, 111, 143
Peregrin, J., 4, 188, 198, 199, 203, 226, 305, 306
Perelman, C., 233, 234, 251
Perine, M., 16, 87, 230
Piercey, R., 2
Pinkard, T., 37
Plato, 22, 24, 26–28, 43, 51, 72, 75, 76, 84, 91, 104, 169, 268, 292
Poincaré, H., 144
Price, H., 7, 118, 119, 123, 126, 130, 164, 165, 188, 227, 302, 312–316
Putnam, H., 108, 110

Q
Quillien, J., 5, 16, 56, 262
Quine, W.V.O, 101

R
Renaud, M., 59
Rescher, N., 143
Ricœur, P., 2, 4, 14, 88, 234, 235, 253, 268
Rockmore, T., 14
Roman, J., 4, 253
Rorty, R., 103, 108–111, 113, 143, 144, 273, 274
Roth, M., 14
Roy, J., 16
Ryle, G., 286

S
Sanou, J.B., 251
Santayana, G., 251
Sartre, J.-P., 176
Savadogo, M., 17, 30, 47, 50, 73, 80, 165, 251
Sellars, R.W., 110
Sellars, W., v, 3, 110–114, 129, 132–135, 137, 166, 167, 173–175, 188, 199, 225, 273, 282–284, 286, 287, 293
Seneca, 90
Shepherd, W., 18
Socrates, 22, 24, 26, 52, 66, 67, 71, 75, 147, 182
Soetard, M., 230
Stanguennec, A., 253
Stein, G., 114
Stevenson, C.L., 7, 126
Strauss, L., 1, 2
Stroud, B., 288
Strummiello, G., 4, 32

T
Talisse, R., 108, 109, 143
Taylor, C., 20, 125, 131, 132
Thomas-Fogiel, I., 161
Tiercelin, C., 143, 310
Toulmin, S., 233
Triplett, T., 225, 226, 282

V
Valdério, F., 4, 253
Vancourt, R., 254
Venditti, P., 53
Voltaire, 78
Voparil, C.J., 104

W
Wahl, J., 2
Weber, M., 4
West, C., 107
Westphal, K., 157, 295
Whitehead, A., 4
Williams, M., 282, 284, 288, 293, 298
Wittgenstein, L., 111, 131, 136
Wohlrapp, H., 69, 234, 245
Wundt, W., 144

Printed by Printforce, the Netherlands